Artificial Companion for Second Language Conversation

Sviatlana Höhn

Artificial Companion for Second Language Conversation

Chatbots Support Practice Using Conversation Analysis

Sviatlana Höhn
University of Luxembourg
Esch-sur-Alzette, Luxembourg

ISBN 978-3-030-15506-3 ISBN 978-3-030-15504-9 (eBook)
https://doi.org/10.1007/978-3-030-15504-9

This Springer imprint is published by the registered company Springer Nature Switzerland AG
The registered company address is: Gewerbestrasse 11, 6330 Cham, Switzerland

Preface

I started the research described in this book with the attractive and inspiring idea of Artificial Companions that will be our helpers, our little artificial friends. They will know us and our preferences and serve us in many different tasks without having a specific purpose. They will interact with us for a prolonged period of time. They will entertain us and help us to manage our duties and leisure activities. And they will do all this using natural language and have a nice personality. It was April 2011 and I was a beginner PhD student at the University of Luxembourg.

But why should a person with a normal social life be interested in engaging in longer interactions with a machine instead of talking to their relatives, friends or neighbours? It was not difficult for me to find an answer to this question. I was born in the Soviet Union, and I grew up in Belarus. I started learning German as a second language when I was seven years old and continued learning and studying it after my school graduation. All the language teachers and university lecturers were non-native speakers of German. There was no possibility to practice German with native speakers in my home town, and it was not affordable for my family to go to Germany for vacations. With this background, it was quite an intuitive decision to create a machine that helps learners of a foreign language to practice conversation and behaves like a language expert in order to help learners like me that time.

In the very first discussions of these ideas with my thesis advisory board I was confronted with questions that further challenged not only my own understanding of what is given and what needs to be discovered, but also the views of other computer science persons on the board. What is *a natural language*? What is *a personality*? Who is *a language expert*? And who is *a human*? As Gudrun, the board member who asked me all these questions, put it: *there is no such animal as a bird. There is a parrot, there is a pigeon, there is a penguin, which in turn has a bit of a bird but also a bit of an animal. And it is not much different with humans.*

These questions were the reason I started learning and digging deeper and deeper into Conversation Analysis, where researchers believe that every tiny detail in talk between people plays a role and nothing is unimportant, asking *why that now?* Conversation Analysis became one of the most important tools that I had at hand to accomplish this work. Conversation Analysis inspired and shaped my approach to dialogue research at that time, and it still plays a huge role in my view of understanding and modelling conversation.

From my perspective, a close collaboration between Conversation Analysis and Natural Language Processing would be beneficial for the two disciplines. While many books on Conversation Analysis and many books on Natural Language Processing and Dialogue Processing exist, it would be hard to find a book handling both, as they sometimes have contrasting and conflicting views on the rules of conversation and language in a broader sense. I hope that this book starts a movement bringing together researchers from the two worlds, Dialogue Processing and Conversation Analysis, in order to build better dialogue systems and, finally, better understand ourselves when we are talking.

Overview of the book

This book presents a novel approach to design of dialogue systems. Starting with the general idea of creating a machine that behaves like a language expert in conversations with non-native speakers, this book shows how Conversation Analysis can be included in the multidisciplinary research paradigm of Communicative Intelligent Computer-Assisted Language Learning (Communicative ICALL), sometimes also referred to as Dialogue-based ICALL. While many other books focus on implementation questions, this book concentrates on the detailed analysis of the specific type of dialogues that should be simulated with an artificial conversation partner. Therefore, a lot of space in this book is dedicated to intensive discussions of multiple examples, and only one chapter focuses on practical advice on a possible implementation.

This book is divided into three parts. Part I offers an introduction to the research area and provides a cross-disciplinary perspective on the research subject. Part II presents a detailed analysis of the dataset collected for this research and makes generalisations necessary for an operationalisation of the findings in a dialogue system. Part III explains how a possible implementation of the models introduced in Part II can be done. Because this research opened more new questions than it provided answers, several future research directions are outlined in Part III. Part IV contains supplementary material.

Acknowledgements

I would like to thank my scientific advisors Stephan Busemann and Gudrun Ziegler for all the inspiring and encouraging scientific discussions and mentoring, from which I learned how to do high-quality research and to be a researcher. I thank the members of my thesis advisory board Leon van der Torre and Charles Max for their advice and comments, which helped to make this work better. I would like to thank my thesis supervisor Christoph Schommer for the academic freedom and the possibility to find my own way and to develop as an independent researcher.

I thank lecturers from the Masherov University Olga Sheverinova, Marina Zuy and Ludmila Galchenko who helped me to collect my data, which formed the basis of the whole research. I also thank the anonymous chat participants from Belarus, Germany and Luxembourg who spent hours chatting and, as I came to know later, found the chat pleasant most of the time.

I enjoyed my collaboration with the DICA-lab and the MultiLEARN Institute; I thank all colleagues for the fruitful discussions of my messy data during the data sessions and in personal discussions: Natalia, Adrienne, Claudia, Martin, Nathalie, Jun, Delia, Charles, Gudrun and all the others.

I thank Nicole Recklies who helped me to annotate the data. I thank the Tech Transfer Office of the University of Luxembourg for their help in publishing the corpus.

I also thank all reviewers of all the earlier versions of the manuscript for their help in making the text more readable and correcting my non-native English: Anne, Janelle, Winfried and Adrienne. All remaining errors are my own, of course.

I thank Jean and Detlef Wotschke who helped me to discover myself as a researcher and to develop my passion to do research. I also thank Marie desJardins, my mentor at the AAAI doctoral consortium, in which I participated while I was expecting my first child. Marie gave me a few important pieces of advice about finding the right balance between my two identities – mother and researcher.

Last but not least, I thank my family: Winfried, Philipp, Sandra and Mom for their support during the time of doing this research and writing this book. I would never have even started writing this book without your encouragement and help.

October 2017 *Sviatlana Höhn*

Contents

Part I Background

Part IV Supplements

Part I

Background

1 Setting the Scene

Abstract Research and development in the field of Communicative Intelligent Computer-Assisted Language Learning (Communicative ICALL) enable people to develop communicative competence in a foreign language and to conquer their language barrier. This book shows how to improve Communicative ICALL applications by adding Conversation Analysis to the research paradigm. Following a brief introduction, this chapter describes the multidisciplinary nature of Communicative ICALL, the research aims of this book and the chosen methodology. The final section provides details on the scope and the structure of this book.

1.1 Introduction

The ability to speak foreign languages has become one of the key competences in the globalised world. People learn foreign languages for professional purposes, with the goal to study abroad or for private reasons. Distance language learning and training based on tutoring videos or online exercise books offers a convenient way to integrate language classes into a busy day. Practicing conversation with an artificial agent is seen as a good alternative if a native speaker is not available or not affordable. Computer-Assisted Language Learning (CALL) was expected to facilitate learning and teaching by providing electronic workbooks with automatic evaluation and vocabulary training. CALL technology extended with Natural Language Processing (NLP) techniques became a new research field called Intelligent Computer-Assisted Language Learning (ICALL). Language technology has been integrated into CALL applications for the purposes of automatised exercise generation (Ai et al., 2015), complex error analysis and automated feedback generation (Amaral, 2011).

Education, industry and language learners benefit from various deployed applications, for instance (Heine et al., 2007; Sagae et al., 2011; von Ahn and Hacker, 2012). A number of mobile applications in the AppStore and GooglePlay Store target conversation training and traditional task-based language instruction. Frequently cited real-life ICALL applications are E-Tutor for German learners (Heift, 2002, 2003), Robo-Sensei for Japanese learners (Nagata, 2009) and TAGARELLA for learning

S. Höhn, *Artificial Companion for Second Language Conversation*,
https://doi.org/10.1007/978-3-030-15504-9_1

Portuguese (Amaral et al., 2011). Conversational agents, chatbots and dialogue systems for foreign language training have been developed as stand-alone conversation partners (Jia, 2009; Zakos and Capper, 2008; Timpe-Laughlin et al., 2017) and as part of intelligent tutoring systems (ITS) (Petersen, 2010), serious games (Gray, 1992; Sagae et al., 2011; Wik et al., 2007; Amoia et al., 2012) and micro-worlds (DeSmedt, 1995). A new trend in technology-aided language teaching is robot-assisted language learning (RALL) (Han, 2012). Robotic language teaching assistants have been studied in a traditional language classroom (Chang et al., 2010; Kwok, 2015; Mubin et al., 2013) and for teaching autistic children to speak foreign languages (Alemi et al., 2015).

Petersen (2010) makes a distinction between Communicative ICALL and Non-Communicative ICALL. He sees Communicative ICALL as an extension of the human-computer interaction field. His understanding of Communicative ICALL is that "Communicative ICALL employs methods and techniques similar to those used in HCI research, but focuses on interaction in an L2 context" (Petersen, 2010, p. 25). As a consequence, corrective feedback in Communicative ICALL should incorporate corrections of L2 errors into dialogues with the user. Hence, an ability to provide corrections of linguistic errors in conversation is seen as one of the key features of such a dialogue system or a conversational agent. Consequently, the majority of ICALL applications see the artificial agent in the role of a tutor or a teacher who has the right to provide corrections. While students and teachers in language classrooms have been taken as "role models" for user and agent models in Communicative ICALL applications, there is a gap in computational simulation of types of interaction other than the language classroom. More specifically, conversational agents playing the role of a peer who is more knowledgeable in linguistic matters are under-represented in Communicative ICALL research. This work seeks to close this gap and to show that new data-driven user and agent models are needed for designing conversational agents that act in other roles than a teacher or a tutor. To approach this objective, Conversation Analysis is included to the multidisciplinary research paradigm of ICALL.

1.2 The multidisciplinary nature of ICALL

ICALL research labs usually employ specialists bringing expertise in Software Engineering, Natural Language Processing, Pedagogy, Computer Science and CALL (Greene et al., 2004). The multidisciplinary nature of CALL research is recognised and claimed in CALL literature. For instance, Greene et al. (2004, Sec. 3) list four research principles of the ICALL lab of Dublin City University: "(i) reuse of existing NLP resources, (ii) reuse of existing CALL research experience, (iii) user-centred design and evaluation and (iv) interdisciplinarity". CALL works at the intersection of Computer-Mediated Communication (CMC) and Second Language Acquisition (SLA) research, which in turn are also multidisciplinary fields of work employing Computer Science, Linguistics, Psychology, Foreign Language Teaching and Sociology specialists among others. Thus, an interdisciplinary or multidisciplinary perspective and involvement of the latest results in related disciplines is a must in building ICALL applications of high quality. Nonetheless, Schulze (2008, p. 513) confirms Oxford's critique of ICALL research based on "homespun notions of language learning or notions borrowed from discourses in SLA which had long been criticised severely and/or superseded by theoretical approaches with improved explanatory power" (Oxford, 1993). Schulze (2008) also emphasises the importance of multidisciplinary cooperation for ICALL research:

> Of course, ICALL cannot afford to ignore current discourses in SLA [...] but also needs to consider issues related to the computational implementation of SLA theories and approaches in language pedagogy. This makes it more important for ICALL researchers to foster links with researchers in SLA and NLP, and such links can only be established after fruitful discussions in which researchers from both communities participate (Schulze, 2008, p. 513).

However, for realistic and individualised user models and dialogue design for Communicative ICALL applications, relying only on SLA results is not sufficient. Markee (2000) criticises the rationalistic, traditional approach to SLA studies because "an experimental, quantitatively oriented methodology inevitably loses important details of individual behavior" (Markee, 2000, p. 29). He suggest developing an alternative, emic perspective to SLA studies and "a critical attitude toward quantified data" (Markee, 2000, p. 29).

Effects on learning with an ICALL system and learning when using text- voice- and video-based communication for language learning were studied earlier from the educational perspective. Modern SLA theory mainly follows the Interaction Hypothesis usually credited to Long (Long, 1996) but very similar to Krashen (1981)'s Input Hypothesis. SLA theory emphasises the role of specific dialogue routines in language learning. ICALL research from its perspective is mainly focused on opportunities (affordances) provided by the technology to elicit such dialogue routines in interaction with learners. Such routines include for instance corrective feedback (Lyster et al., 2013) and meaning negotiations (Varonis and Gass, 1985). Corrective feedback and meaning negotiations are seen as important conditions for learning. Imitation as a language acquisition strategy formulated as the Imitation Hypothesis (Aguado Padilla, 2002) has received less uptake in the ICALL community.

Corrective feedback is acknowledged as an important tool in language instruction to help the learner to notice the produced deviations and to give the learner a chance to improve. Classifications of corrective feedback in the language classroom have been obtained from classroom data (Panova and Lyster, 2002; Lyster et al., 2013) and compared to corrective feedback in computer-mediated communication (CMC) in various language-learning or language-practicing scenarios; see for instance (Sauro, 2009; Zourou, 2011). However, not every error is corrected even in a language classroom, specifically, if the focus is on fluency. In non-educational situations, corrections of linguistic errors are dispreferred, and therefore rarely occur. This observation has been taken up by the designers of conversational systems for SLA; see for instance (Wik and Hjalmarsson, 2009) where the authors make a distinction between two embodied conversational agents. One of them plays the role of a virtual language teacher, and therefore, provides corrective feedback on pronunciation and language use. The other agent is a role-play conversational training system with the goal to maintain an interesting conversation. Here, the agent "has the role of a native speaker, for example, a person with a service occupation, whom you need to communicate with using your new language" (Wik and Hjalmarsson, 2009, p. 1039) and therefore, the user cannot expect any corrective feedback from this agent.

The subject of research in Conversation Analysis (CA) is naturally occurring interaction. However, because more and more people use a foreign language for their everyday interaction in business, educational, institutional and leisure contexts, foreign language talk also came under the lens of CA. For instance, CA analyses how participants of an interaction construct together identities of language experts and language novices, and whether there are differences between conversations with learners and between learners, and native-speaker-only talk. CA-driven research showed, for instance, that language learners are able to accomplish all complex social actions even with limited linguistic resources (Markee, 2000). There are also attempts to identify the process of learning by CA methods. Kasper (2004) proposed to perform *longitudinal studies* to capture the learning process in naturally occurring data. Markee (2008) introduced a learning-behaviour-tracking system that is not easy to implement in practice. The system suggests recording *learning behaviour* and *learning objects*, again in a longitudinal perspective, to see the development of specific structures and the influence of learning behaviour on this development. González-Lloret (2011) proposes to change the definition of learning itself to make use of CA as a tool for research on learning:

> As for the methodological feasibility of CA to demonstrate learning, expanding the definition of learning may be necessary, [...] so that SLA is not limited only to linguistic features but also includes the social context and sequential development of interactions. In this sense, learning is understood as participation based, focusing on the improvement of the interactional resources used by learners for talk-in-interaction rather than just on their linguistic skills (González-Lloret, 2011, pp. 317-318) citing (Markee, 2008).

Studies applying methods of Conversation Analysis for research on Second Language Acquisition (CA-for-SLA) show that non-native speakers interacting with native speakers in non-educational settings engage in various types of talk focusing on linguistic matters, including error corrections provided by native speakers (Markee, 2000; Hosoda, 2006). Corrections of linguistic errors form a dispreferred social action both in native/native speaker and native/non-native speaker talk (Schegloff, 2007). However, the language learners whose talk is analysed in this work reported that they prefer to be corrected more often in order to learn (Danilava et al., 2013a).

Corrections of linguistic errors belong to a type of talk dealing with troubles in interaction in a broader sense. Such types of talk are referred to as *repair* in CA. Repair may deal with problems with comprehension of terminology, understanding of the purpose and pragmatical function of utterances, and problems with production of utterances or accidental mis-productions. Because repair is not always concerned with linguistic matters, we will use the term *repair with linguistic trouble source* to refer to the types of repair where the source of problems has a linguistic nature, such as difficulties in comprehension of the meaning of a word or difficulties in the production of a correct form in a foreign language.

Hosoda (2006) points out that repair sequences distinguish interaction with non-native speakers from native-speaker-only talk in the following way. Repair with linguistic trouble source is found in conversations with non-native speakers more frequently and is typical even for informal conversations between non-native speakers and their native speaker peers outside the classroom. Corrections of linguistic errors are frequently found in institutional talk (non-classroom) between native and non-native speakers (Markee, 2000), however the types of corrections differ from those in informal conversations described for instance by Hosoda (2006). Thus, types and frequency of repair with linguistic trouble source might be different for different types of discourse, or different *speech exchange systems*.

Kasper (2004) argues that there is a separate type of informal talk, which she termed a *Conversation-for-Learning*, where conversation parties come together *because* one of them has a higher level of language proficiency than the other. Examples of Conversations-for-Learning can be found in language tandems and various informal language cafes. Multiple occurrences of linguistic repair in chat dialogues produced by native speakers without being instructed to correct indicate that the context of a Conversation-for-Learning seems to modify social preferences, providing opportunities for repair and minimising face threatening (Tudini, 2010, p.64). The term Conversation-for-Learning reflects more precisely the application scenario where users engage in dialogues with an artificial agent in order to practice their language skills in an informal conversation. The learners would use such a system *because* they want or need to practice. ICALL developers need to be careful in dialogue and task modelling, because CA has shown that different types of speech exchange systems work differently, and insights from research on institutional talk, such as a teacher-fronted language classroom, are not necessarily valid for informal conversation or a Conversation-for-Learning (Schegloff, 1993; Markee, 2000).

Chat-based Conversations-for-Learning between an artificial conversational agent and a language learner can be investigated from different perspectives and incorporate first of all technological and sociolinguistic but also learning aspects. From the technological perspective, research results in both Computer-Mediated Communication (CMC) between learners and native speakers and Human-Computer Interaction (HCI) between learners and artificial agents may be relevant. CMC studies analyse how communication mediated by a technology influences the interaction. In the SLA context, these studies demonstrate how technology provides opportunities for learning. SLA theory-driven studies have shown that chat communication positively influences oral performance in terms of language quantity (Abrams, 2003). A small number of CA-informed studies of native/non-native speaker chat communication provide qualitative and quantitative analysis of different phenomena in chat interaction, such as error corrections and explanations of unknown words in Italian (Tudini, 2003, 2010) and German (Marques-Schäfer, 2013). Another study shows how Spanish learners develop the competence to interact in trouble-talk (González-Lloret, 2011). In particular, the study by González-Lloret (2011) showed that

> CA can be an appropriate tool for the study of [...] [Synchronous Computer-Mediated Communication], depending on the focus of the study. CA is better suited for discovering patterns of how the participants carry out the interaction and how they orient to the sequences developed while they construct authentic conversation, and CMC produces large quantities of authentic materials, being one of the fastest growing communicative media in the world. (pp. 317-318)

For these reasons, expertise in Conversation Analysis, and specifically CA-for-SLA, may be an additional advantage for creating Communicative ICALL applications. Looking at conversations with foreign language learners through the lens of CA-for-SLA can help to identify characteristic features of dialogues between language learners and native speakers in order to understand to what extent the native speaker may be a model for the artificial agent and which of the key features are implementable.

1.3 Participants orientation to linguistic identities

The idealised concept of a *native speaker* was for a long time accepted in applied linguistics as the object for studies of communicative competence (Canale and Swain, 1980). The native speaker was put in the role of a language expert, and the non-native speakers were automatically classified in the complementary category of *language novices*. However, as Hosoda (2006) criticises and discusses in detail, these two absolute categories were "poorly supported by the sociolinguistic evidence" because "native speaker status does not necessarily correlate with a high command of the language" (Hosoda, 2006, p. 25). For a critical discussion see also (Markee, 2000; Wagner and Gardner, 2004; Kasper, 2006; Vickers, 2010).

The concept of *expertise* is seen as better reflecting the empirical research results on interaction, specifically in the context of second language communication, because the participants of an interaction may change their roles of experts or novices during the interaction. Hosoda (2006) argues that the notion of the *differential language expertise* suggested by Kasper (2004) is attractive for CA studies because

> in CA, language expertise, like any other social category or attribute, is not primarily subject to an outside observer's judgment. Instead, analysts are licensed to invoke descriptions pertaining to the participants only when the parties orient to such matters through their talk and other interactional conduct. [...] Consequently, whether or not language expertise is relevant at any point in the interaction is determined by the participants themselves through their observable orientation to linguistic matters" (Hosoda, 2006, p. 26).

Along the same line Brandt (2011, Sec. 2.3.3) analyses how participants make differential language expertise relevant in non-native/non-native speaker conversations in which the native/non-native speaker relationship does not exist. Kurhila (2006) uses the term *the knowledgeable participant* instead of *expert* and the term *non-expert* instead of *novice*, allowing less extreme formulations of the differences in linguistic knowledge of the two.

With this motivation, in this book we will use the terms *native speaker of the language X* to refer to persons who learned a particular language X in the process of their first language acquisition, and *language expert* to refer to participants of a conversation when they make their more advanced language expertise relevant in their talk. Thus, the terms *language expert* and *native speaker* are not used as synonyms in this book. As a complementary category for the "non-experts", we will use the term *non-native speaker of language X* or *learner of language X* to refer to persons who learn a language X as a foreign language, and the term *language novice* to refer to participants in a conversation when they orient to their linguistic identity as not-yet-fully-proficient speakers of a particular language.

Although CA-for-SLA researchers clearly define language experts, it remains difficult to assign the status of a language expert to one of the participants in local sequences of talk where the differential language expertise is made relevant in conversation. We still need to keep in mind that the participants who position themselves as language experts in conversation may make mistakes even in the turns of talk where this positioning is performed.

Example 1.1. The native speaker corrects an error and provides wrong metalinguistic information ("denken" is in fact not reflexive). Orig. excerpt 61 from (Marques-Schäfer, 2013, p. 185), line numbers and translation added. M is the learner, G is the tutor and a native speaker of German.

1 11:39:25 M er denkt nur an selbst
*he thinks only of [*error: missing reflexive pronoun] self*
2 11:39:49 M verstehst du mich?
do you understand me
3 11:40:07 G Der Chef?
The boss?
4 11:40:39 M du kannst mich korrigieren wenn ich fehler schreibe
you can correct me when I write [error: lexical] mistakes*
5 11:40:53 M ja der chef Bush
yes the boss Bush
6 11:41:26 G Okay, denn es heißt richtig: Er denkt nur an sich selbst.
okay, then it is said correctly: He thinks only of himself.
7 11:41:57 G Denken ist ein reflexives Verb.
to think is a reflexive verb
8 11:41:57 M seine politik macht wennig sinn
his policy makes little [error: orthography] sense*
9 11:41:57 M danke
thanks

Example 1.1 shows a sequence from a native/non-native speaker chat interaction that took place as part of the project *JETZT Deutsch lernen* where learners of German communicated in chat with other learners and tutors (Marques-Schäfer, 2013). The excerpt in Example 1.1 is taken from a tutored session, and G is a tutor and a native speaker of German. She is explicitly asked by M, the learner and non-native speaker, to correct errors, in turn 4. In turn 6, G corrects an error that M made in turn 1, and provides metalinguistic information in addition to the correction. However, the metalinguistic information contains an error: the verb *denken* (Engl. to think) is in fact not reflexive. Nevertheless, the learner accepts the correction and the explanation in turn 9.

In Example 1.1, the native speaker G, who has in addition the tutor role, is selected by the learner M as a language expert by M's request to correct errors. G accepts this role by providing a correction; however, G also produces an error. This example demonstrates that there is a difference between *doing being a language expert* and *being a language expert*. These discrepancies may be described by the terms *epistemic stance* (expectations towards one's own and others' knowledge) and *epistemic status* (the factual state of the knowledge) (Heritage, 2012). The participants of an interaction position themselves as experts when they *think* they are more knowledgeable than their partners. They normally do not pretend to be experts while knowing that they are wrong. However, this does not mean that they objectively do not produce any errors. Moreover, even if they produce errors, they may still be more knowledgeable than their partners, which is already stated by the term *differential language expertise*. In Example 1.1, G appears to be more knowledgeable than M in constructing a correct German sentence, even if the theoretical explanation of the rule for this construction is wrong.

This is an extremely important difference for the research described in this book. A conversational agent can possess as much linguistic knowledge as we can prepare for it using all available linguistic resources, but all this knowledge is useless as long as there is no need to make it relevant in conversations with the user. Even if someone positions himself or herself as a language expert in conversation, it does not mean that he or she is no longer allowed to make mistakes. The focus of this boo is knot the actual language expertise of the conversational agent, but the *practices of orientation to differential language expertise in conversation* are under the loupe.

1.4 Research aims and objectives

This work aims to contribute to the field of Communicative ICALL by bringing Conversation Analysis as a research methodology into ICALL application design. Specifically, it seeks to address the following two research objectives:

I Find and describe interactional practices in native/non-native speaker chat-based Conversation-for-Learning where chat participants orient to their linguistic identities of language experts and language novices.

II Create computational models of those practices and analyse technical requirements and limitations to implement the resulting models in a Communicative ICALL application.

Inspired by Conversation Analysis, this research is based on the analysis of near-to-natural conversations between native and non-native speakers of German via instant messenger. Looking ahead to the results of the empirical part of this research, it makes sense to disclose early the specific research questions that were formulated after the initial research phase of "unmotivated looking" at the data:

RQ1 Which interactional resources do language learners use in a chat-based Conversation-for-Learning with native speakers to initiate repair in order to deal with troubles in comprehension and how do native speakers deal with these repair initiations?

RQ2 How can other-initiated self-repair when the machine is the trouble-speaker be handled in a chat-based Communicative ICALL system?

RQ3 Which types of other-corrections of linguistic errors exist in the dataset representing a chat-based Conversation-for-Learning?

RQ4 How can these types of other-corrections of linguistic errors be modelled in order to be implemented in a chat-based Communicative ICALL system?

RQ5 Apart from the occurrence of an error, are there other factors that are relevant for the occurrence of a correction of a linguistic error in native/non-native speaker chat-based Conversation-for-Learning?

RQ6 If such factors exist, how can they be modelled in order to be implemented in a chat-based Communicative ICALL system?

The restriction to chat-based communication in the research questions is necessary because of the specific speech exchange system and a specific communication medium, namely medially written and conceptually oral dyadic Conversation-for-Learning. Based on the observation by Hosoda (2006), it can be expected that there might be other interactional phenomena in native/non-native speaker chat that distinguish it from native/native speaker chat. Specifically, we may expect to find other types of sequences than error corrections in chat where participants orient to their linguistic identities in talk.

With regard to corrections of learner errors, we should not expect to find big numbers of occurrences of those in the data because such corrections are dispreferred even in native/non-native speaker conversations. However, from the point of view of qualitative language research, it is interesting to find what is *typical*, but not necessarily frequent (typical sequences, typical structure of such sequences). Conversation is a cultural action; therefore, chat participants formulate their turns in such a way that the action is recognisable for the partner. At the same time, they formulate their turns individually in order to be different from others. For this reason, plain prototypes of particular actions are very rarely seen in natural data, and the variants of these prototypes can be found more often. Even for a small number of occurrences of a particular type of sequence, it is possible to analyse how a *typical* sequence of this kind is organised. Therefore, generalisation based on a small number of instances is common in CA. Therefore, we can see this as a valid approach to computational modelling with the purpose to cover the variance to some extent.

1.5 Methodology

The methodological novelty of the research described in this book consists mainly of bringing Conversation Analysis into the ICALL research paradigm with the goal to discover new models for the expert and novice behaviour in a Communicative ICALL application. Specifically, methods of Conversation Analysis are used to identify typical structures in close-to-natural longitudinal chat interactions between native speakers of German and advanced learners of German as a foreign language (Heritage and Goodwin, 1990; ten Have, 2007; Schegloff, 2007; Liddicoat, 2011). The CA-informed research was performed in three phases:

1. So-called "unmotivated looking" in which researchers look at the data without any preconception of what may be found. Collections of similar structures in the data are built in this phase.
2. Micro-analysis of specific structures in which generalisations can be made in order to obtain patterns (or prototypes) from those structures,
3. Computational modelling of the identified typical structures based on the generalised structures and patterns from phase 2.

Finally, the implementability of the new models is validated by an implementation case study and an analysis of the required language technology and knowledge bases.

Only a short description of the dataset is provided here. Comprehensive documentation about the data collection process and data preparation can be found in Appendix A. The participants of the data collection were nine advanced learners of German as a foreign language and four German native speakers. All of the learners were Russian native speakers and students of German at a Belorussian university. Native speakers were (and still are) all friends and colleagues of the book author. Each native speaker was assigned to two or three non-native speakers in pairs according to the time slots that the participants specified (when they had time to chat). Only the first appointment was arranged: the researcher connected the participants in pairs according to their times of availability for the first chat. The only instruction was "just chat". The participants were expected to have a free conversation and to talk about whatever they wanted. The goal communicated to the participants was to produce eight dialogues in total and to interact twice a week for four weeks, every session lasting approximately 30 minutes.

The participants interacted using Google Talk infrastructure. A forwarding chatbot hosted on Google App Engine was used to collect the data instantly. Participants did not see each other directly; they sent the messages to the bot and the bot instantly forwarded the messages to the partner. All the chat logs were available to the researcher immediately. The participants were informed at the beginning of the data collection that their talks would be recorded. The participants agreed to publish the produced chat data prior to starting the interaction.

The participants produced 73 dialogues in total (eight dialogues by each of six pairs, nine dialogues by each of two other pairs, and seven dialogues by the ninth pair). Besides that the participants sometimes missed each other or forgot appointments. In these cases, the participants sent each other notifications and apologies, but in some cases several days passed between turns. The decision was made to include only full dialogue sessions in the final dataset. Each dialogue is between 20 and 45 minutes duration. The total size of the final dataset is 4,548 messages, which correspond to 236,302 text symbols. The message length ranges from 1 to 774 symbols with an average length of 58.5 symbols over all pairs. Table 1.1 summarises the corpus statistics.

Metrics	Pair 1	Pair 2	Pair 3	Pair 4	Pair 5	Pair 6	Pair 7	Pair 8	Pair 9
MaxTL	335	405	774	313	414	277	637	460	232
MinTL	1	1	2	1	2	2	2	2	1
AvTL	62.98	72.40	105.13	38.13	86.80	38.99	42.23	48.85	31.38
# Turns	365	410	346	650	218	421	730	694	714
# Symb.	22,989	29,683	36,374	24,784	18,923	16,413	30,825	33,903	22,408

Table 1.1: Corpus statistics: MaxTL - maximum turn length (# symbols), MinTL - minimum turn length (# symbols), AvTL - average turn length (# symbols) followed by the total number of turns and total number of symbols for each pair

The reader will see many examples of specific pieces of dialogues that illustrate the identified phenomena. All examples are formatted so that the reader can easily grasp the intention of the example. Each turn (message) contains a message number, a time stamp, a speaker code and a message body. Line breaks added by the speakers were kept as in the original message and marked by a line break tag. All other line breaks in the examples are caused by the page width and were not added explicitly to the formatting. Each message body contains the original wording and spelling of the message and an English translation in italics, if needed. Messages consisting of only an emoticon or an "OK" were not translated. A word-by-word transcription is added between the original message and the translation if it is required for the understanding of the discussed phenomena. Errors are annotated in the examples only where it is necessary for the analysis. An inline error annotation containing the error description was performed either in the transcription line or in the translation line and is inserted in square brackets [] and marked with an asterisk *.

1.6 The scientific contribution of the book

The research described in this book shows that Conversation Analysis as a research methodology can be effectively used for the purpose of computational modelling of dialogue. Specifically, this work shows that the multidisciplinary field of Communicative ICALL may greatly benefit from including Conversation Analysis. As a consequence, this research makes several contributions to the related research disciplines, such as Conversation Analysis, Second Language Acquisition, Computer-mediated Communication and Artificial Intelligence.

The study described in this book contributes to research on identities and membership categorisation, advances the state of the art on learner and expert models, roles and personalities in dialogue research, conversational agents and Communicative ICALL. The identified sub-dialogues prepare an empirically grounded basis for an informal functional specification of conversational agents in Communicative ICALL in roles other than tutors or teachers. Though the description of what the user and the agent can do outside of these sub-dialogues remains open by the intuitive concept of a free conversation, the effort that may be needed to simulate a "free conversation" with a chatbot becomes clearer.

In contrast to SLA-driven classifications of corrective feedback obtained from classroom data, which are usually used in Communicative ICALL applications, this work introduces a classification of correction formats obtained from chat-based Conversations-for-Learning. The advantage of the new classification is that the pragmatic function of different linguistic devices for corrections is taken into account for modelling, such as highlighting, repetitions, replacements, accountings and backlinks. Moreover, sequential environments for embedded corrections were analysed. Specific data-driven models of exposed and embedded corrections provide the required basis to offer the user a variety of correction formats as part of the ongoing conversation. In addition, a first step towards formulating a feature-based decision model for corrections in conversation is made. The study of other-corrections of linguistic errors contributes to research on corrective feedback (SLA, CA-for-SLA) and learner language research (error and dialogue moves annotation) and advances the state of the art in Communicative and Non-Communicative ICALL by separation of error recognition from local models of correction and decisions to correct.

Overall, this work is a further step toward mutually beneficial multidisciplinary collaboration between Conversation Analysis and Communicative ICALL as well as Artificial Intelligence as a larger research field.

1.7 Structure of the book

The book is divided into three parts. **Part I** includes the present chapter, which introduced the research field and the research objectives.

Chapter 2 discusses the relevant academic publications in the fields of Computer-Assisted Language Lning including error correction and automated feedback, Conversation Analysis and its potential for Communicative ICALL, learner language and learner corpus research, Natural Language Processing, Dialogue Modelling, the impact of Conversation Analysis on Artificial Intelligence, and last but not least, chatbots and conversational interfaces, their use for SLA and their evaluation methods. The contribution of the present work to each field is also highlighted.

Part II includes five chapters presenting the research results for each research question as stated in Chapter 1. A very brief summary of each chapter is provided below.

Chapter 3 is concerned with the analysis of the collection of examples of other-initiated self-repair and a formal model of this type of repair. These are the cases where non-native speakers do not (completely) understand what the native speaker or the chatbot may say and ask for a clarification. The empirical findings and the computational model are compared to the state of the art discussed in Chapter 2.

Chapter 4 focuses on explanations of unknown words and expressions initiated by the non-native speakers. Such sequences are referred to as *other-initiated self-repair*; and the sources of trouble in comprehension are produced by native speakers. Based on a collection of such sequences, a computational model of other-initiated self-repair when the native speaker is the trouble-speaker is introduced. The technical feasibility of the model is discussed in comparison to the related academic publications.

Chapter 5 presents a detailed analysis of explicit corrections of non-native speakers' linguistic errors. The corrections are analysed from the perspective of turn formats and turn-taking. The analysis provides the necessary basis for the computational modelling of exposed error corrections, which will be discussed in Chapter 7 together with embedded corrections.

Chapter 6 analyses another major type of corrections of linguistic errors - embedded corrections. These corrections do not become the interactional business of the talk, but they are noticed by non-native speakers. This chapter presents the empirical results with regard to turn design and the working mechanism of embedded corrections. The computational perspective and the potential for a computational reproduction are further discussed in Chapter 7.

Chapter 7 focuses of the local models of all types of corrections of linguistic errors as they were found in the dataset and analysed in Chapters 5 and 6. First, the problem of an automated error detection is discussed. Second, local correction practices are modelled for each type of the correction. Results are discussed in comparison with recent academic publications.

Chapter 8 makes the first attempt to formulate a correction decision model. Because only a small number of all occurring linguistic errors have been corrected by native speakers in chat, it is an important question for a computational model of corrections, how the machine should decide, if an error needs a correction or not. After a detailed analysis, a feature-based model is introduced. The results are compared to state of the art and discussed from the perspective of possibilities for an implementation in an ICALL system.

Chapter 9 evaluates the method of CA-informed dialogue modelling proposed in this book and applied in the context of Communicative ICALL taking native/non-native speaker chat-based Conversation-for-Learning as a specific application case. The SWOT method is applied for the evaluation. Theoretical implications are discussed. Recommendations for future Communicative ICALL are formulated.

Part III concerns the implementation case study and the validation of the models presented in Part II. Some suggestions for further research directions and the SWOT analysis of the research presented in this book are also provided in Part III.

Chapter 10 discusses a practical implementation of the models introduced in Part II of this book. The implementation builds upon an existing open-source chatbot that uses Artificial Intelligence Mark-up Language (AIML) as its main language understanding and generation engine. Besides repair questions discussed in Part II in detail, this chapter addresses other issues, such as input restriction and the chatbot's individual style.

Chapter 11 outlines multiple potential research directions as possible continuation of the research efforts started in this book. These directions include other types of repair not analysed in detail here but mentioned in Chapter 3, dialogue processing and affective computing, and long-term human-machine interaction.

Chapter Summary

This chapter introduces the research area of Communicative ICALL and explains its connection to empirical studies of chat-based native/non-native speaker communication. The arguments are presented how the multidisciplinary domain of ICALL would benefit from including Conversation Analysis into the research paradigm. Further, research objectives are presented and the research methodology is explained. A very brief summary of each chapter of this book is provided.

2 Learning from Others' Experience

Abstract This chapter explains the relationship between the work presented here and the related fields of research at the time of the research described in this book. Three large fields have impact on the presented research: ICALL, NLP and CA. Specific fields using CA for dialogue modelling are also of high relevance for this work. The current state of the art in the area of chatbots and conversational interfaces and the problems with evaluation of the dialogue quality are also discussed. The specific contributions of this research to each area are highlighted in each section.

2.1 Introduction

A large number of various CALL and ICALL projects have been described in different review articles. L'Haire (2011) provides a list of 152 CALL and ICALL systems that appeared from 1970 to 2011. This list includes three authoring software tools, 42 educational software tools, 12 micro-worlds, 36 intelligent systems and 22 writing assistance tools. Heift and Schulze (2007) found 119 ICALL applications that appeared between 1978 and 2004 and were documented in German and English.

Schulze (2008) criticises the situation with academic publications on ICALL, specifically mentioning that there is a small number of journals dedicated to CALL, and a large number of publications, but a very small number of authors. In addition, many CALL publications appear in a variety of other academic publishing resources, for instance in Computational Linguistics. Schulze, citing (Zock, 1996, p. 1002) orients to the "communication problem and a mutual lack of interest concerning the work done in the neighbouring disciplines" (Schulze, 2008, p. 511) in his critical review of ICALL literature. Addressing the multidisciplinary nature of ICALL in Section 1.2 we claimed that Communicative ICALL will benefit from including Conversation Analysis in the circle of related disciplines. However, the reader needs to pay attention to the differences in language (concepts and terminology) used by different communities as one of the obstacles in multidisciplinary collaboration. Therefore, this inclusion will imply conceptual work on terminology and (re-)definitions of commonly used notions borrowed from Second Language Acquisition, Natural

S. Höhn, *Artificial Companion for Second Language Conversation*,
https://doi.org/10.1007/978-3-030-15504-9_2

Language Processing, Human-Computer Interaction, Artificial Intelligence and Conversation Analysis.

Building on Oxford's key desiderata for ICALL (Oxford, 1993), Schulze (2008) reflects on how each of them was met in the 25-30 years before he wrote his article (Schulze, 2008, p. 512). The key desiderata discussed by Schulze (2008) are:

1. Communicative competence must be the cornerstone of ICALL.
2. ICALL must provide appropriate language assistance tailored to meet student needs.
3. ICALL must offer rich, authentic language input.
4. The ICALL student model must be based in part on a variety of learning styles.
5. ICALL material is most easily learned through associations, which are facilitated by interesting and relevant themes and meaningful language tasks.
6. ICALL tasks must involve interactions of many kinds, and these interactions need not be just student-tutor interactions.
7. ICALL must provide useful, appropriate error correction suited to the student's changing needs.
8. ICALL must involve all relevant language skills and must use each skill to support all other skills.
9. ICALL must teach students to become increasingly self-directed and self-confident language learners through explicit training in the use of learning strategies. (Oxford, 1993, p. 174)

The sociolinguistic notion of communicative competence credited to Hymes (1972) converges with the concept of interactional competence in Conversation Analysis (Markee, 2000, p. 52).

Communicative ICALL is first of all focused on development of communicative competence, interpreting the remaining eighth points of Oxford's desiderata as a condition for its development. Unfortunately, current Communicative ICALL prototypes and applications offer mostly simulations of student-tutor or student-teacher interactions in contrast to desideratum 6. However there are a few exceptions, as Section 2.2.2 will show. While points 2-6 and 8-9 reflect concerns of all ICALL applications, Communicative ICALL handles the requirement to provide error corrections (desideratum 7) in two ways:

- either simulating a language teacher in a language classroom and maximising the number of corrections
- or taking ordinary native/native speaker conversations as a model where corrections of linguistic errors are absolutely dispreferred, and therefore, not provided by Communicative ICALL systems.

Existing Communicative ICALL systems will be discussed below in detail in Section 2.2. Specifically, Section 2.2 will address issues in learner language understanding, user modelling, learner corpus research and error corrections.

To start the announced work on a common terminology required for collaboration, the basic important concepts and the relevant research results from CA and

CA-for-SLA will be explained to the readers in Section 2.3. It will be discussed how they may improve the quality of Communicative ICALL research.

There are many successful attempts to integrate CA into Human-Computer Interaction (HCI) and dialogue modelling to obtain models for human-robot communication and dialogue systems from naturally occurring interaction data and experiments with robots in the wild. Related research projects are discussed in Section 2.4.

With the recent popularisation of chatbots and conversational interfaces driven by software giants such as Facebook, Microsoft, IBM and Google, Section 2.5 describing the current chatbot landscape and their use for SLA has been added to this chapter to make the present book up to date. Issues in dialogue quality assessment are also discussed in Section 2.5.

2.2 Communicative ICALL

Many factors influence the effects of learning with a computer system, for instance learner motivation and learner self-efficacy. However, the effects of ICALL systems on learning also depend on different properties of the system itself. Is it communicative or just an electronic workbook? If it is communicative, which technology exactly is used as a communication medium? Section 2.2.1 will discuss the communication modalities chosen for Communicative ICALL in earlier academic publications. The ways chosen by researchers to approach user and activity modelling will be the focus of Section 2.2.2. Issues in learner language understanding will be addressed in Section 2.2.3.

Communicative ICALL research has shown that learners benefit in a similar way from corrective feedback provided by a human tutor as compared to an artificial agent (Petersen, 2010). Because error correction has a prominent position in language acquisition research, it received an important role in ICALL (communicative or not). Therefore, Sections 2.2.4 and 2.2.5 provide a review on recent achievements in automatic error recognition and automatic feedback generation.

Because this research chose a CA-informed approach assuming work with learner language data, Section 2.2.6 will explain the situation with respect to learner corpus research and learner corpus annotation.

2.2.1 Communication modalities

Every communication medium provides affordances and sets constraints for communication in terms of *interactional resources* that can be made available by interaction participants. Interactional resources are all sets of symbolic, verbal, non-verbal and possibly other types of signs that can be used by interaction participants to express meaning, to perform social actions and to regulate social closeness. They include written and spoken words, gestures and intonation. In chat communication emoticons, special abbreviations and orthography belong to interactional resources. In addition, every way of communication with artificial agents implies technological limitations and provides opportunities for implementation. Conversational systems of different complexity and communication modalities (text, voice, video) have been employed for helping learners to practice conversation.

Even simple chatbots not explicitly designed for communication with second language learners have been tested as conversation practice helpers with a concluding recommendation to use them for advanced or keen learners (Jia, 2004; Fryer and Carpenter, 2006). In order to make chatbots more useful for a broader language learner audience, researchers and developers introduced additional functionality such as spelling-error correction (Jia, 2009) and knowledge of the learner's native language, which should facilitate the communication for beginners. For instance a chatbot presented by Zakos and Capper (2008) targets beginner learners of English with Greek as mother tongue. Avatars, talking heads and embodied agents as well as integration of text-to-speech engines became nice-to-have extensions for chatbots because they appeared to positively influence users' engagement in chat, though a simple chatbot was still hiding behind them (Stewart and File, 2007; Zakos and Capper, 2008). Selection of an utterance from a set of possible utterances is offered by the Let's Chat conversation training system (Stewart and File, 2007). This kind of interactional resource is normally not available in human-human chat communication. Section 2.5.2 will discuss several recent chatbots for practicing foreign language conversation in more detail.

Speech recognition techniques have become more mature in recent years, so that they can be successfully used for conversations with learners, specifically for pronunciation and prosody training; see for instance (Wik and Hjalmarsson, 2009; Bonneau and Colotte, 2011; Ai and Xu, 2015). Multimodal interaction using humanoid robots in language classes in the role of a teaching assistant was investigated in (Chang et al., 2010; Mubin et al., 2013; Kwok, 2015; Alemi et al., 2015). It was found in the research field of Robot-Assisted Language Learning that robots positively influence engagement and learning.

The choice of the communication modality has influence on competences that can be improved when the communication is bound to the set of interactional resources that can be made available within this specific modality (Darhower, 2008). In particular, pronunciation cannot be improved when the communication modality is limited to only text chat. With regard to this, text chat has been found helpful for language learners to improve language accuracy and support their vocabulary acquisition (Kim, 2003; Kost, 2004). Moreover, text chat may be helpful in acquiring complex language structures, improving fluency and oral performance (Abrams, 2003; Fredriksson, 2013). These findings may be explained by the fact that chat interaction is medially written but conceptually oral (Koch, 1994; Beißwenger, 2002).

Chat interaction has advantages for language learners because the learners can re-read the chat history, they have more time for production and comprehension, and they can even use other tools to deal with troubles in production or comprehension, which is not possible in oral conversation. In addition, text chat helps to avoid implementation issues related to speech recognition in learner language, as described, for instance, in (Ivanov et al., 2015).

With this motivation, this book will focus on text-based chat dialogues between advanced learners of German as a foreign language and native speakers of German in the data analysis phase. Based on the data analysis results, we will target computational models of specific structures in text-based conversations where language learners are supposed to communicate with an artificial conversation partner.

2.2.2 User models and interaction models

In the domain of dialogue systems, to which Communicative ICALL belongs, a user model is “a knowledge source [...] which contains explicit assumptions on all aspects of the user that may be relevant for the dialog behavior of the system" (Wahlster and Kobsa, 1986, p. 50). Such aspects may include users’ beliefs, goals and plans. The attempt to grasp individual characteristics of a particular user was made y assigning specific *conversational roles* to the users and the dialogue system, for instance a hotel guest and a hotel manager, a library visitor and a librarian, or a beginner UNIX user and a UNIX consultant (see (Wahlster and Kobsa, 1986) for references to specific projects on each of them).

Many academic publications are concerned with user modelling in ICALL (Martinez, 2013; Chrysafiadi and Virvou, 2013; Read and Bárcena, 2014; Heift, 2015). Schulze (2008) and Vandewaetere and Clarebout (2014) emphasise the importance of *student* models and *expert* models in ICALL systems. This reflects the common understanding in ICALL that the role of student has to be assigned to the user and the system has to be put in the role of tutor (Yang and Zapata-Rivera, 2010; Gardent et al., 2013). This role dichotomy determines the system’s behaviour – the system is expected to mimic a teacher. Such a role distribution makes the interaction with contemporary ICALL systems similar to a language classroom. Other roles of ICALL systems have rarely been considered, but there are a few attempts to escape from the tutor-student dichotomy. For instance, Greene et al. (2004) mention an artificial German co-learner. Different roles are involved in a role-play application for culture and language training in Arabic where the user is involved in a simulation of talks with local speakers in a village (Sagae et al., 2011).

Amaral and Meurers (2011) describe the student model used in a real-life ICALL application. The model includes personal information, interaction preferences and knowledge of linguistic forms. Amaral and Meurers (2007) see the need to include a set of competences in the user model, which they call *strategic competences*:

> the student model needs to be extended to include the learner’s abilities to use language in context for specific goals, such as scanning a text for specific information, describing situations, or using appropriate vocabulary to make requests (p. 340).

This claim is supported by findings reported in CA-for-SLA literature, which we will discuss in Section 2.3, that communicative or interactional competence goes beyond knowledge of vocabulary or grammar. Learners’ ability to perform specific social actions using the foreign language is as important as grammar and fluency.

Individualised instruction and adaptive ICALL have been approached by creating learner personas (Heift, 2007). The author observed how learners interacted with E-Tutor, which is an e-learning platform for German as a foreign language (Heift, 2002,

2003). Learners choose different options to go through the material. Heift (2007) tracked which links they use and which material they are interested in (more cultural or more grammar and vocabulary notes). In addition, Heift (2007) considered learner variables such as gender or level of L2 proficiency, although gender did not give a significant difference. She found different interaction patterns for learners with different levels of L2. Nonetheless, all possible paths in the interaction with E-Tutor are determined in advance by the system's developers. User-centred design approaches to ICALL may help to create ICALL systems tailored for learning needs of different learner groups and offering more specific options for personalisation and incremental adaptation of the system to a particular user (Petrelli et al., 1999).

Data-driven methods have frequently been used to approach user-centred design and persona-based user modelling (McGinn and Kotamraju, 2008). In light of the decision to use text-based chat as a communication medium and having a free chat conversation as the only activity for the study (as motivated in the preceding Section 2.2.1), the question that needs to be answered in the user-modelling phase is "If there are different user types in a free conversation with a conversational agent, what are the important differences for user modelling?"

The research described in this book will approach the problem of user modelling in roles other than teachers or tutors by using methods of Conversation Analysis. In particular, it will focus on informal text-based instant messaging conversations to find typical structures in conversations between advanced learners of German as a second language and German native speakers with the purpose to obtain user models from the learners' behaviour. The system's behaviour will then be modelled based on patterns obtained from native speakers' talk. Because the learners' and the native speakers' behaviours in interaction are not independent, special attention will be paid to mutual dependencies in learner and native speaker social actions performed through chat talk.

2.2.3 NLP tools and learner language understanding

Learner language is described as *non-standard* and *non-canonical language* in NLP literature because "learners tend to make errors when writing in a second language and in this regard, can be seen to violate the canonical rules of a language" (Cahill, 2015). Other examples of non-canonical language are dialects, ordinary conversation and historical texts because they violate the standards of written language. Different approaches have been used to manage the contents of the conversation with the user and to deal with learner errors. Wilske (2014) mentions constraining possible input and error diagnosis as strategies used by researchers and software developers in order to deal with the complexity of learner input.

Dodigovic (2005) discusses different techniques from Human Language Technology used by ICALL systems to evaluate the language produced by language learners. The systems discussed in her book are designed to support and evaluate production of medially and conceptually written language such as essay grading. Dodigovic (2005) noticed two trends in her discussion of automated essay grading:

1. the inconsistency of automatic essay graders in scoring native speaker writing compared to non-native speaker writing;
2. the inability of parsers designed for native speaker language to deal with non-native language errors.

She compares different grammar formalisms according to a list of criteria specified in (Matthews, 1993). The criteria are computational effectiveness, linguistic perspicuity and acquisitional perspicuity. The following formalisms were compared:

1. Context Free Phrase Structure Grammar (CFPSG).
2. Augmented Phrase Structure Grammar (APSG) and Definite Clause Grammar (DCG).
3. Shift-Reduce Parser.
4. Principles and Parameters Theory (PPT), Principle-based parsing and Chunk parser.
5. Lexical Functional Grammar (LFG).
6. Head-Driven Phrase Structure Grammar (HPSG).

She concludes that HPSG appears to be the system with the most advantages, specifically because it combines semantic and syntactic information.

Meurers (2009) points out that it is not easy to determine the state of the art in automated analysis of learner language in terms of influence of error properties on their automated diagnosis, kind of learner language and task type. He emphasises the importance of learner corpus research for the automated analysis of learner language in ICALL and summarises:

> feedback and learner modelling in ICALL systems and the annotation of learner corpora for SLA and FLT [Foreign Language Teaching] research are both dependent on consistently identifiable learner language properties, their systematisation in annotation schemes, and the development of NLP tools for automating such analysis as part of ICALL systems or to make the annotation of large learner corpora feasible. (Meurers, 2009, p. 470)

Amaral and Meurers (2011) see constraining the learner input as one of the main challenges in designing an ICALL system, but a necessary step because of the need to restrict the search space for syntactic processing and meaning analysis. Constraints on input in a talk with a conversational agent can be made for instance in the form of domain restriction (Pulman et al., 2010; Gardent et al., 2013) or activity restriction (Petersen, 2010). Domain restriction in an SLA context is frequently achieved through strategies such as role-play in a serious game (Wik and Hjalmarsson, 2009; Sagae et al., 2011), task-based dialogues (Raux and Eskenazi, 2004b), micro-worlds (DeSmedt, 1995) and virtual worlds such as Second Life (Duquette, 2008) where the interaction is determined by the role of the agent or avatar. The activity chosen by Petersen (2010) was restricted to questioning. The user's task was asking questions that were then analysed and responded to by an artificial agent Sasha.

Other approaches to dealing with the limitations in learner language understanding are offering the learner only a predefined set of possible inputs and using pattern-based language understanding that allows the coverage to be kept as wide as possible and the responses as generic as possible, for instance by means of Artificial Intelligence Markup Language (AIML) (Wallace, 2003). A predefined set of phrases that can be used by the user are offered in (Stewart and File, 2007) where a chatbot helps the learner to acquire prototypes in specific communicative situations.

Similar to applications targeting mostly L1 speakers, the same general observations regarding the depths of language understanding can be made for the learner domain. Namely, there is a tradeoff between deep language understanding covering only very restricted domains, and shallow language understanding with very limited understanding capabilities, for instance pattern matching and keyword spotting. There are also techniques combining the both (Schäfer, 2008).

Typical examples of pattern-based language understanding with wide coverage and generic responses provide AIML-based chatbots. Free AIML sets for various languages can easily be found on the Internet, for instance in German (Droßmann, 2005). AIML chatbots are easy to use and to configure; therefore there are attempts to improve very limited conversational skills by incorporating ontologies (Al-Zubaide et al., 2011; Hallili, 2014), linguistic information and reasoning (Klüwer, 2009; Jia, 2009) and knowledge about repair initiations (Höhn, 2015a, 2017)[1].

Spelling-error correction has been formulated as a machine translation problem from a language $L*$ with errors to the language L without spelling errors. Hasan et al. (2015) use statistical machine translation techniques to correct spelling errors in user queries in the e-commerce domain. The open-source machine translation system Moses (Koehn et al., 2007) was used for the error correction task. Recent machine learning approaches based on Deep Neural Networks also have the potential to be successfully used for language understanding with errors. Zhou et al. (2017) suggested using Recurrent Neural Networks (RNN) for spelling-error correction for the same domain of e-commerce search. The RNN-based approach showed the best performance with word-to-word byte pair (BPE) partial encoder and decoder and with 62.5% accuracy slightly outperformed the approach suggested by Hasan et al. (2015), who reached 62.0% accuracy. These two approaches need to be tested on learner language corpora in order to see their effectiveness when applied to non-native speaker communication.

Statistical approaches to error correction as a machine translation problem need large amounts of training data to be effective. Progress in the area of automated error detection, which we discuss more intensively in the next section, is limited by the sparse availability of training data. To overcome this problem, Rei et al. (2017) suggest using machine translation approaches to enrich training data with errors according to special error models. In this case, the translation needs to transform correct language into incorrect language. In contrast to other artificial error generation approaches, Rei et al. (2017) covered all error types contained in the test corpora FCE and CoNLL 2014. The results show that error detection clearly improves when training an error detection model with artificially generated data.

This research work seeks to describe data-driven models of typical structures in interaction with language learners. Different NLP tools of different complexity may

[1] These publications are earlier versions of Chapter 4 of this book.

be required to make the desired models part of Communicative ICALL applications or integrate them into dialogue systems and conversational agents. We will discuss the required NLP tools and knowledge bases for the respective research part in Parts II and III in order to make practical applications benefit from the insights of this work.

2.2.4 Learner-error recognition

Learner-error recognition cannot be clearly separated from the task of learner language understanding discussed in the preceding Section 2.2.3. A correct interpretation of learner input (utterances or texts) is not possible without techniques to deal with linguistic errors produced by language learners (native or non-native). Therefore, a large number of academic publications focus specifically on error diagnosis in learner language. This section provides an overview of the academic literature in this area.

Meurers (2012) classifies methods for error diagnosis in learner language into two main categories:

1. *pattern-matching* approaches and
2. *language-licensing* approaches.

Pattern-matching approaches rely either on specific error patterns or on context patterns for error recognition. Licensing approaches are based on formal grammars that either provide a set of constraints that need to be satisfied or a set of rules according to which valid strings of the language can be recognised. This is usually done by a definition of explicit *mal-rules* for recognition of deviations from standard language. Such error recognition methods focus on errors of form (syntax, morphology, orthography) but cannot deal with vocabulary or pragmatics errors. Some efforts have been made towards automatic analysis of meaning in learner language; see (Meurers, 2012) and references therein.

Precision in the error diagnosis is very important for ICALL applications. This has been emphasised in multiple academic publications, for instance (Bender et al., 2004; Amaral et al., 2011). Bender et al. (2004) argue therefore that mal-rule-based error recognition techniques have advantages compared with constraint-relaxation-based techniques:

> The increased precision afforded by adding particular mal-rules rather than removing constraints on existing rules increases the utility of the grammar as a component of a dialogue-based language tutoring system (Bender et al., 2004, Sec. 4).

Amaral and Meurers (2011) criticise some research approaches for creation and evaluation of new techniques for parsing learner language because of the mismatch between the aim to recognise errors in student sentences and the application to hand-constructed examples. However, using artificially created hand-constructed examples for modelling and/or evaluation is a frequent practice in ICALL research, because datasets with the required properties are rarely available. For instance, for the work done by Petersen (2010) and discussed in the next paragraph, a dataset of learner questions with different types of annotated errors might have been helpful.

Petersen (2010) made use of various open-source English NLP tools for automated analysis of grammatical and semantic structures in written questions in a conversational system called Sasha. The agent communicated with learners of English as a second language (ESL). A standard NLP pipeline was applied to each user's input: spellchecking, tokenisation, lemmatisation, POS-tagging with the Brill-tagger and syntactic parsing. The Collins parser implementing a probabilistic context free grammar was re-trained on ill-formed questions which were artificially created from a set of examples. The author remarks that neither the Brill tagger nor the Collins parser were intended to work with non-native-like input; therefore, a set of post-parse checks were needed to analyse the integrity of the structural representation of compound nouns, prepositional phrases and embedded clauses (Petersen, 2010, p. 92). The system tried first to recognise and correct all lexical, morphological and syntactic errors in learner questions. In other words, the system had to determine the *target hypothesis*, and thus reconstruct the utterance intended by the learner. However, multiple target hypotheses may exist for the same learner input. Both agreement on a target hypothesis and correct parsing of learner data are challenging tasks even for human annotators (Reznicek et al., 2013; Ragheb and Dickinson, 2013).

The obstacles to parsing learner language are mastered by prediction-driven parsing in a micro-world for learning intermediate German (DeSmedt, 1995). The learner plays the role of a crime detective and has to solve a murder mystery by questioning five suspects. The parser tries first to identify the verb and then to extract all the other parts of the sentence with relation to the verb. Since questions are the most likely input type in this setting, the parser was probably not challenged by the whole palette of possible inputs occurring in a free conversation.

NLP problems with learner language are often known problems in general NLP. For instance, Bender et al. (2004) see the problem of error detection based on mal-rules as closely related to the problem of parse selection, because parse versions for an input with and without mal-rules will be concurring. As Meurers (2012) points out, recognition of errors in meaning is closely related to NLP tasks such as paraphrase recognition and textual entailment.

While error detection for conceptually written language (e.g. essays) is quite advanced, error recognition for conceptually oral language (e.g. free text chat) remains very challenging. One of the reasons for that is that oral language allows more freedom in expression so that some deviations from the written standard are no longer considered to be errors in oral language; see for instance the discussions in (Schlobinski, 1997). In addition to that, there are conventions in text chat allowing even more freedom in expression. All this makes a definition of an error in oral language or text chat language a conceptual problem. Because the standard norms for oral and text chat language are not easy to define, error recognition for these areas remains under-researched. This research makes an attempt to solve this problem at least partially by description of rules for "real" errors in chat, thus errors that are substantial enough to receive a correction in a chat-based Conversation-for-Learning.

2.2.5 Automated feedback generation

Dodigovic (2005) examines some theoretical views on what the origin of an L2 error is and what chances exist to correct it. She notes that different SLA theories have different views on the meaning of L2 errors produced by learners, and therefore, different views on the usefulness of error corrections. Dodigovic (2005) concludes that the error correction behaviour of an intelligent system supporting language learning will depend on the underlying SLA theory. The majority of academic ICALL publications ground their theoretical argumentation in interactionists approaches to SLA. These approaches emphasise the role of interaction, input and feedback; see for instance (Heift, 2003; Petersen, 2010; Wilske, 2014).

For both ICALL and Communicative ICALL, two conceptually different questions exist with regard to automatic feedback generation:

1. When to provide feedback?
2. Which form of feedback should be selected?

The answer to the first question is solved for the majority of ICALL systems by the selection of the expert and activity model where the occurrence of an error triggers generation of feedback. The number of corrected errors is maximised, therefore such feedback strategies can be called greedy. However, correcting too many unimportant mistakes may lead to the learner's frustration and disengagement, therefore, even greedy feedback strategies do not correct *every* error; neither do language teachers in a language classroom.

Amaral and Meurers (2011) see providing feedback based on linguistic, learner and activity information as one of the major challenges for ICALL. They list criteria for corrective feedback considered by human tutors:

> 1. Information about the learner: level, age, L1, knowledge of grammatical terminology, motivation to learn etc.
> 2. Information about the task: type of activity (reading, listening, composition writing etc.), type of question item (wh-question, fill-in-the-blanks, link the columns etc.), level of question in relation to level of student, time available, material to be consulted (dictionary, grammar book, internet) etc.
> 3. Information about the language: grammatical competence exhibited by the linguistic properties of the learner language (lexical, syntactic, semantic, pragmatic), the nature and type of deviations in ill-formed utterances (duplication of letters, agreement, wrong synonym, lack of anaphoric reference etc.), level of learner language in relation to scales of language complexity and development, as well as sociolinguistic, discourse and strategic competences. (Amaral and Meurers, 2011, p. 10)

This is in line with research on feedback in the classroom showing that there are dependencies between different learner and task variables and the feedback effectiveness (Lipowsky, 2015). Learner variables include the learner's level of competences, motivation and self-efficacy. Task variables are mainly related to the task complexity. Amaral and Meurers (2011) criticise the majority of existing ICALL systems for their selection of only the language aspect for their correction decision and focusing exclusively on the grammatical competence. However, the authors list several exceptions where the student model plays a role in the selection of the feedback form (Heift, 2003; Amaral and Meurers, 2008). Nevertheless, the occurrence of an error is still seen as the determining event which automatically triggers a correction. This is not supported by the CA research (Markee, 2000).

Sometimes researchers in ICALL take a radical perspective towards feedback types. For instance, Delmonte (2003), building on the classification of corrective feedback proposed by Lyster and Ranta (1997), makes the following statement:

> We believe that recast, clarification request, elicitation, and repetition are totally inadequate for feedback generation on a computer. As to explicit correction, perhaps it could be done for grammar drills, but it is certainly much harder in semantically based drills. We assume that only metalinguistic feedback is fully compliant with the current state of human-computer interaction (Delmonte, 2003, p. 514).

Although this decision is not supported by sociolinguistic data nor it is supported by SLA or HCI research, only one feedback type is then considered by Delmonte (2003), following this assumption.

Because the majority of Communicative ICALL applications see corrective feedback as not necessarily part of the ongoing conversation, they do not cover the richness of the types of corrective feedback described in SLA classroom research, which are classified and described for instance in (Lyster and Ranta, 1997; Lyster et al., 2013). The few attempts to build upon an existing classification of corrective feedback (Morton et al., 2008; Petersen, 2010; Wilske, 2014) argue for the need to restrict the variety of feedback types in order to obtain an acceptable feedback quality. This also shows the complexity of the problem. For the cases where feedback is implemented for a dialogue interaction with the learner, it is frequently done in the form of a pop-up window laid over the chat window which is not part of the ongoing conversation, or in the form of a retrospective summary at the end of an activity.

A pedagogical agent Dr. Brown is a representative of the systems providing feedback in the form of a retrospective summary. It was used to engage the user, who is an ESL learner, in request games (Yang and Zapata-Rivera, 2010). The learners received a problem description and were asked to negotiate with the pedagogical agent to solve the given problem. Thus, the task of the system is to provide the learner with an opportunity to practice their knowledge of pragmatics in simulated interactions in the academic context. The dialog processing is implemented as a finite-state machine (FSM) able to recognise hard-coded well-formed and ill-formed learners' utterances. The FSM was created based on a dataset from a pilot study where English native speakers had to complete the same tasks. The number of potential dialogue moves for the tasks was considered to be very limited. Therefore Yang and Zapata-Rivera (2010) chose to predict all possible learners' inputs for all dialogue situations. Keyword-based language understanding was used to evaluate the appropriateness of learners' utterances. The authors defined appropriateness as the degree of directness and politeness compared to native speakers' responses in the same situations. At the end of each situation, learners received feedback based on the appropriateness score of their utterances.

The micro-world *Herr Kommisar* represents Communicative ICALL systems providing feedback in the form of pop-ups during the conversation. It provides corrective feedback on *every* recognised error in the form of an explicit correction (DeSmedt, 1995). A small number of standard templates is used for feedback generation. The user's response to correction was encoded into buttons to close the pop-up and return to the chat window. A similar approach to corrective feedback was chosen in (Lavolette et al., 2015).

Some efforts have been made to incorporate the research results on different types of corrective feedback into ICALL systems. Petersen's work discussed in Section 2.2.4 was only focused on recasts as a type of corrective feedback. Recasts produced by human tutors were compared with recasts produced by an artificial conversation partner Sasha (Petersen, 2010). Recasts are defined in the SLA literature as "teacher's reformulation of all or part of a student's utterance, minus the error" (Lyster and Ranta, 1997). This definition covers a wide range of correction formats. The learners were asked to formulate questions about pictures presented to them, and the system provided corrective feedback in form of a recast and then produced a response to the content of the question. Only one form of recasts was allowed in (Petersen, 2010)'s work: a repetition of a complete question where all morphosyntactic errors were corrected. *Every* recognised ill-formed user question was followed by a recast. Petersen sees study with Sasha as delivering recasts in a manner comparable to recast provision in spontaneous oral interaction. However, from the perspective of CA, question elicitation cannot be seen as spontaneous naturally occurring conversation. Nevertheless, the work shows the high complexity of target hypothesis generation even when restricted to question reformulation.

Recasts in Communicative ICALL have been also handled in (Morton et al., 2008; Anderson et al., 2008; Wilske, 2014). The *SPELL* system (Spoken Electronic Language Learning) targets corrective feedback in the form of recasts (Morton et al., 2008; Anderson et al., 2008). Examples of feedback provided in the academic publications are all acknowledgement-based reactions to learners' responses delivered after the agent's questions. Wilske (2014) describes a text chat-based system that is able to produce recasts and metalinguistic feedback in a task-based dialogue with the learner. Only one type of grammatical errors was considered for experiments. The work focused on comparison of recasts and metalinguistic feedback in ICALL and classroom studies.

The task in communication with the speech-based system *Let's Go* is to plan a journey. The system produces confirmations of user's journey plans. These confirmations are preceded by corrective clarification requests in order to ensure the system's correct understanding and to deal with "linguistic mismatch" (Raux and Eskenazi, 2004a). *Let's Go* provides error corrections within the dialogue with the user, but all of them are based on a *Did you mean* followed by a correct reformulation.

In all these cases, the software was assumed to play the role of a teacher eligible to correct explicitly and as much as possible. This corresponds to an unequal-power speech exchange system as discussed in Section 2.3.1. However, the dataset collected for this research shows that corrections in a free conversation between peers are more diverse and in more than 50% of the cases implicit.

The opposite of the greedy correction strategies can be found in Communicative ICALL applications working with expert models other than a teacher or tutor. For instance, a conversational agent in a trading role play does not provide corrective feedback at all (Hjalmarsson et al., 2007). This is another extreme, which we can call *zero-correction*.

A combination of a pedagogical agent and a conversational agent in an ICALL system can be chosen to handle both accuracy and fluency as two independent tasks. For instance, Wik and Hjalmarsson (2009) describe two embodied conversational agents for L2 training. The first agent should simulate a teacher and provide feedback on phonetics, the second agent should play the role of a conversation partner and focus on fluency assuming that no feedback is given in a free conversation context. The conversation training system *DEAL* is also described in (Hjalmarsson et al., 2007) and in (Wik et al., 2007).

Conversation Analysis distinguishes between *exposed* and *embedded* corrections (Jefferson, 1987; Brouwer et al., 2004). In exposed corrections, *correcting* becomes the interactional business while embedded corrections are accomplished implicitly, without focusing on the action of correcting. Corrective feedback described in SLA the literature covers only exposed corrections. Section 2.3 gives a more detailed literature review on exposed and embedded corrections.

In the research described in this book, efforts were taken to contribute to the research on automated corrective feedback (exposed corrections) in the following way. Because there is a difference in the speech exchange system between a teacher-fronted classroom and a chat-based Conversation-for-Learning, it is first necessary to obtain a data-driven classification of error corrections from the dataset. The found types of corrections will then be compared with the classification of corrective feedback obtained from classroom data (Lyster et al., 2013). Based on these findings, we can construct computational models of error corrections for Communicative ICALL application resembling chat-based Conversations-for-Learning. This is documented in Chapters 5 to 8.

While a lot of research effort has been put into automatic feedback generation in the form of exposed corrections, none of the academic publications in ICALL reports about studies of automated embedded corrections in interaction with language learners. This is caused on one hand by the strong connections between the ICALL scene and interactionists SLA research. The *noticing hypothesis* emphasises the importance of the noticing of the error by the learner in order to produce modified output (Schmidt, 1990), and evidence of noticing after embedded corrections is extremely difficult to find. On the other hand, embedded corrections may have been out of scope in ICALL research because the empirical research did not produce any ready-to-implement model for embedded corrections. This work makes an attempt to operationalise embedded corrections with the purpose to create a computational model for embedded corrections in conversations with language learners. Chapters 6 and 7 report about the success of this research endeavour.

Conversations-for-Learning combine characteristics of both informal talk and a language classroom, as explained in Section 1.2. Therefore, a new decision model for corrections is required. The desired correction decision model should act somewhere between the greedy correction and the zero-correction models, allowing us to come closer to the correction behaviour of native speakers in a chat Conversation-for-Learning. This book seeks to make a step towards closing this gap. We will make an attempt to create an empirically grounded decision model for corrections. Chapter 8 of this book documents the findings.

2.2.6 Learner corpora and error annotation

As Meurers (2009) notes, the annotation of learner corpora is mainly focused on annotation of learner errors; however, annotation of linguistic categories in learner corpora is also of interest. To create stable models of learner language for statistical NLP tools, information on occurrences of linguistic categories and their dependencies is required. This need is met by linguistic annotation of learner corpora, similarly to how it has been done for native-speaker language. Linguistic annotation in learner corpora has been addressed by Amaral and Meurers (2009) who focused on tokenisation in Portuguese interlanguage, and Díaz-Negrillo et al. (2010) who addressed the problem of Part-of-Speech-tagging (POS-tagging) in interlanguage. Related to the annotation of conceptually oral language, the challenge of POS-annotation in chat language has been addressed by (Bartz et al., 2014).

Error annotation of a corpus assumes a non-ambiguous description of the deviations from the norm, and therefore, the norm itself. The creation of such a description may even be problematic for errors in spelling, morphology and syntax (Dickinson and Ragheb, 2015). In addition, different annotators' interpretations lead to a huge variation in annotation of errors in semantics, pragmatics, textual argumentation (Reznicek et al., 2013) and usage (Tetreault and Chodorow, 2008). Multiple annotation schemes and error taxonomies have been proposed for learner corpora, for instance (Díaz-Negrillo and Domínguez, 2006; Reznicek et al., 2012). Because error taxonomies are language-specific, we focus here only on error annotation in German (native and non-native) learner corpora.

The corpus of German emails posted to USENET users described in (Becker et al., 2003) consists of ca. 120,000 sentences. An error typology of orthographic, morphological, morpho-syntactic, syntactic and syntactic-semantic errors was taken as a basis for the error annotation; however, only 16 error types from the typology were used for the corpus annotation.

Different error-tagging systems for learner corpora have been described by (Díaz-Negrillo and Domínguez, 2006). The authors note that "[error] taxonomies should be grounded on the description of observable data and include well-defined linguistic categories to minimise subjectivity". Consequently, many different error taxonomies have been created to serve specific corpora.

There are not so many error-annotated corpora of German as a foreign language. The major conceptual work on the annotation scheme and error taxonomy was done by the FALKO team (Reznicek et al., 2012, 2013) and frequently reused or taken as a starting point for further development by followers (German part of MERLIN, EAGLE, WHiG). WHiG is part of FALKO but contains texts from native speakers of British English who are intermediate learners of German (Krummes and Ensslin, 2014). The LeKo corpus is accessible though the FALKO platform.

All of the error-annotated corpora consist of argumentative essays, and the developed error taxonomy is suitable for error-tagging in essays, but needs further elaboration to cover the needs of annotation of conceptually oral language such as chat and instant messaging exchange.

The error annotation for the mentioned corpora was approached in the following ways. The LeKo-corpus was probably a pilot project; it was created earlier than FALKO and by the same principal investigator (Lüdeling et al., 2010). The researchers elaborated an error taxonomy on a small learner corpus of 30 texts that were written manually and then re-typed to make the resources digitally available and analysable. The difficulties with error annotation that were faced by the annotators of the LeKo corpus were taken into account in the annotation definition phase for the FALKO corpus. Specifically, some of the errors can be tagged differently depending on the interpretation of the learner's intention, or *target hypothesis*. Dealing with such ambiguities became an issue for learner corpus annotation.

A multilevel annotation was introduced in the FALKO corpus in order to deal with different target hypotheses (Lüdeling et al., 2005). The first target hypothesis (originally German term *Zielhypothese*) ZH1 should only address errors in orthography, morphology and syntax, and make the sentence "understandable" for NLP tools. The second target hypothesis ZH2 should address all other types of errors, such aws semantics, lexical choice, pragmatics, style and so on (Reznicek et al., 2012).

An extension of the FALKO annotation schema has been suggested in the EAGLE corpus of beginning-learner German where error numbering was introduced to deal with overlapping errors (Boyd, 2010). Multiple target hypotheses were addressed by setting a preference for the target hypothesis that minimises the number of annotated errors.

ALeSKo is a corpus of annotated essays of advanced learners of German with Chinese as the first language (Zinsmeister and Breckle, 2012). The annotation contains manual marks of topological fields (fields and error marking), referential expressions (definiteness, specificity, target hypothesis) and vorfeld[2] use. The subject of the ALeSKo study was coherence in learner texts based on the annotation of syntactic, referential and discourse information. German-native-speaker part of the FALKO corpus was used for native/non-native speaker comparison. A specific focus of the annotation in ALeSKo lies in referential expressions (Breckle and Zinsmeister, 2010), which are also in general an important area of NLP research and relevant for this work not only from the point of view of learner language understanding, but

[2] Topological model of the German sentence structure.

Title	L1	GFL level	Data type	Size	Error-annotated	Available
ALeSKo	Chinese	Various	Written texts	43 texts	Partial	Yes
CLEG13	English	B-C	Written texts	731 texts	NA	Yes
FALKO	Many	Intermed.-advanced	Written texts	Under development	Yes	Yes
WHiG	English	B2	Written texts	279 texts	Yes	Yes
MERLIN		A1-C2	Written examinations	1,033 texts	Yes	Yes
LeKo	Many	Various	Written texts	30 texts	Yes	Yes
LeaP	Many	Various	Speech	183 records of 2-20 min	No	Yes
EAGLE		Beginners	Online work book, essays	50 work books & 81 essays	Yes	Yes
LINCS	English	Intermed.-advanced	Written texts, longitudinal	Under development	NA	No
ADS	English	Beginner-intermed.	Threaded discussion, chat, essays, longitudinal	Under development	NA	No
Telecorp	English	Various	Email, IM, essays	1.5 million words	No	No
deL1L2IM	Russian	Advanced	IM	52,000 tokens	Partial	Yes

Table 2.1: German non-native learner corpora at the end of 2015

also from the perspective of generation of embedded corrections. Models of embedded corrections will be the subject of Section 7.4.

A specific characteristic of the CLEG13 corpus is that it has a "truly longitudinal core" of texts produced by students from their first year to their final exams.

In contrast to the written resources described above, the LeaP corpus includes phonologically annotated speech recordings of German and English learners of German (Gut, 2009). The corpus includes readings of nonsense word lists, readings of a short story, retellings of the story and free speech interviews.

German as a learner language can also be seen as the standard linguistic competence acquired by German native speakers. The corpus KoKo is part of the project *Korpus Südtirol*, and focuses on German as the first language learned in the multilingual context of South Tirol by school pupils (Abel et al., 2014).

The situation with German error-annotated learner corpora is that there is a very small number of corpora, and only a small number of them are publicly available. The website "Learner Corpora around the World"[3], maintained by Amandine Dumont and Sylviane Granger (Université catholique de Louvain) lists in October 2015

[3] https://uclouvain.be/en/research-institutes/ilc/cecl/learner-corpora-around-the-world.html, retrieved on 31st January 2018

only 11 German learner corpora, 10 medially written and one medially oral (the corpus used for this research was already included). In addition, there are a few publications about German error-annotated corpora not mentioned on the web page. Table 2.1 provides an overview of German learner corpora at the end of 2015. The table includes only information about the German part for multilingual Corpora (LeaP, MERLIN).

The corpus requirements for the present study were defined as follows: it should be longitudinal text chat dialogue between language learners and native speakers of German. None of the previously existing corpora satisfy these requirements, therefore a new data collection was created. The deL1L2IM-corpus is a new linguistic resource that was created to serve the needs of this research. Table 2.1 shows how the new corpus fits into the German learner corpus landscape. The details of the data collection process and data quality can be found in Appendix A.

The research described in this book approaches the problem of error taxonomies from the perspective of the need for correction. In contrast to a writing-assistance program that has ideally to identify and correct *every* error, only a small proportion of all errors are usually corrected in a Conversation-for-Learning. Not every error is corrected even in a language classroom in a fluency context. Therefore, the artificial conversation partner will need to distinguish errors that might potentially be corrected in an instant messaging dialogue with the learner from those which should not be addressed. We will make use of the two target hypotheses in Chapter 6 to deal with errors in questions posted by the language learners in the dataset and to come up with a model of embedded corrections in answers to such questions. Because understanding of the errors is a prerequisite for any correction, Section 7.2 will deal with the problem of conceptual understanding of linguistic errors in chat.

2.3 What Communicative ICALL can learn from Conversation Analysis

While Human-Robot Interaction benefits from CA-informed research (discussed later in this Chapter in Section 2.4, page 51), Communicative ICALL mostly relies on Second Language Acquisition theory for user and expert modelling, activity design and interaction with the user. The aim of this section is therefore to outline how Communicative ICALL research would benefit from extending its multidisciplinary connections to CA or, even more specifically, CA-for-SLA as related research areas.

Huge differences in the organisation of different types of discourse have been emphasised in the CA literature (Schegloff, 1993; Markee, 2008). An interview for instance is structured differently than a teacher-fronted classroom, and a conversation with a student office specialist differs from a talk between a client and a bank clerk in its sequential organisation, preference system and identities involved. These examples of discourse represent different speech exchange systems. They also differ in the practices that are applicable to handle errors and to deal with troubles in understanding and production. In addition to the need to handle a Conversation-for-Learning as a distinct type of discourse, there is a need to model communication roles of the system other than teacher or tutor, as argued in Section 2.2.2. For these reasons, we first turn first our attention to a discussion of a chat-based Conversation-for-Learning as a specific speech exchange system in Section 2.3.1. Building on this, we will see several problems that exist with instant messaging research in SLA. These problems will be addressed in Section 2.3.2.

Several CA-driven studies of native/non-native speaker chat achieved important results in understanding of processes contributing to the construction of linguistic identities of a language expert and language novice in talk, as was already outlined in Section 1.3 of the Introduction, page 8. Section 2.3.3 will describe the most significant results. We will continue the discussion of linguistic identities in Section 2.3.4. Because various forms of repair are employed in participants' orientation to linguistic identities, and because some types of repair are seen as important for learning in SLA reseach, we will take a closer look at relevant research on repair in Section 2.3.5 and embedded corrections in Section 2.3.6.

2.3.1 Chat-based Conversation-for-Learning as a speech exchange system

CA research shows that it is extremely important to pay attention to the interactional rules of the specific interactional setting. Such sets of rules are referred to as *speech exchange systems* in the CA literature (Schegloff, 1993; Markee, 2000). Examples of speech exchange systems are ordinary conversation, interview, business meeting, news conference, therapy talk, teacher-fronted classroom, debate and ceremonial talk. They differ in terms of turn allocation and organisation of repair (Markee, 2000, pp. 72-73, 84). As Markee citing Schegloff (1993) points out,

> data collected in laboratory settings inevitably reflect a member orientation to a speech exchange system that is demonstrably different from that of ordinary conversation (Markee, 2000, p. 33).

Kasper (2004) uses the term *Conversation-for-Learning* to describe interactions where the participants use a foreign language to construct talk-in-interaction. Kasper (2004) sees Conversations-for-Learning as category-bound events because the participants of the interactions come together due to their status as a native speaker and a non-native speaker (or a language learner).

The notion of *informal learning* is further analysed in CA as a distinct speech exchange system that can be seen as very close or equivalent to Conversation-for-Learning used in an SLA context. Sawchuk (2003) analyses the "nature of informal learning as a distinct speech-exchange system" and claims that

> 'informal learning' shares qualities of 'formal classroom interaction' [...], and 'everyday conversation' [...]. More specifically, it exhibits a form of topic continuity similar to school-based (expert/novice) speech-exchange systems but which is not seen in everyday conversation. And, it exhibits shared control over turn-taking that is often associated with everyday conversation but which is not seen in school-based speech-exchange systems. (Sawchuk, 2003, p. 295)

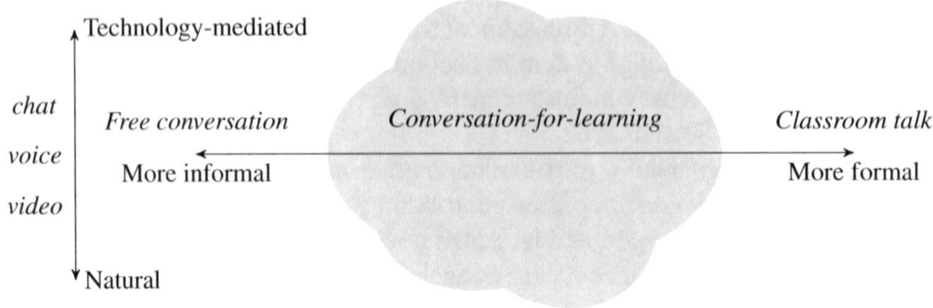

Fig. 2.1: Conversation-for-Learning combines structures of formal and informal conversation and involves interactional resources provided by the communication medium

The analysis of technology-mediated communication would not be complete if the tool itself were not taken into account. However, only a few studies of computer-mediated communication focus on the "constraints and affordances" in interaction that exist *because of* the tool, but see for instance (Brandt, 2011). Doing more formal or more informal talk in a face-to-face interaction involves different interactional resources than doing the same in text chat or in a phone conference, as illustrated in Figure 2.1.

The fact that text-based interaction in chat is different does not make text chat interaction less powerful or participants somehow handicapped. There are just *different* sets of resources that participants *can* make use of in interaction to express themselves. From the learner's perspective, text chat interaction even has many advantages because the production pace is slower than in oral synchronous communication; they have more time to think about the wording and the grammar, and even look up in dictionaries for words that are not immediately available for them, either for their own production or for the comprehension of the partner's talk. In addition, they can re-read the chat protocol for a better comprehension or learning. The nature of text chat is that everything is recorded online and is available to the participants later. However, pronunciation cannot be heard or practiced in a text chat. This is compensated by the possibility to practice writing and orthography, which is not possible in oral communication.

With regard to these issues, we will need to look at the dataset collected for this research from the perspective of a specific speech exchange system, namely *chat-based Conversation-for-Learning*. As several publications have already demonstrated (Orthmann, 2004; Tudini, 2010; Marques-Schäfer, 2013) and as we will see in Part II of this book, this speech exchange system combines properties of informal oral interaction and formal oral classroom which are put into the frame of medially written and conceptually oral interaction. However, the relation between the structures typical for informal and formal interaction may vary in different chat datasets. The proportions of them are influenced by many factors. The next section will argue that the data collection procedure is one of them, in support of the importance of gathering naturally occurring data, which is frequently emphasised in CA (Firth and Wagner, 1997; Markee, 2000; Kasper, 2004). Readers who prefer to have more details about the data collection process at this point may want to look at the description of the procedure in Appendix A.

2.3.2 The problem with instant messaging data

Previous research on the influence of CMC on language learning occurred in experimental setups where the interaction itself was treated as a black box. Researchers carried out pre-tests and post-tests, and drew conclusions on the influence of the black-box on language learning (Abrams, 2003; Loewen and Erlam, 2006). Though this approach is valid, it does not help us to understand the mechanism of the influences of CMC on SLA.

While group text and video chat allows for quite easy observation and recording by the researcher in order to collect data for further analysis of different aspects of learning (Brandt, 2011; Marques-Schäfer, 2013), private dyadic text chat between learners and native speakers remains an underexplored field. This may result from the fact that data cannot be collected as easily as in a group chat. As Marques-Schäfer (2013) puts it:

> Die Speicherung von Chat-Protokollen ist die häufigste Erhebungsmethode der Chat-Forschung in der Linguistik und in der Fremdsprachendidaktik.
>
> *The storage of the chat protocols is the most frequent data collection method in chat linguistics and foreign language didactics research.* (p. 117, Engl. translation added).

Obtaining the stored instant messaging protocols for research purposes from the instant messaging service provider is only possible when the study is organised in a way which allows the data to be obtained either directly from the server or from the users. The former is normally not possible if the researcher has no relationship to the service provider. Privacy is the next issue, even when the researcher has a relationship to the service provider. If instant messaging dialogues are in focus, then privacy is a bigger issue than for group chats and none of the public providers will just give the researcher the permission to 'listen' to other people's private talk.

Unfortunately, researchers frequently omit to provide information about how they got their data (De Marco and Leone, 2012; Fredriksson, 2012). The data capture methods reported in the literature are based mainly on experimental settings where the participants in the dialogue have to use a specific hardware-software combination for the study, for instance PC-pools at an educational institution for task-based conversation (Kost, 2004). This makes the whole interaction an experiment and restricts the communication in terms of time, place and frequently topics of discussion. The dataset described by (Sauro, 2009) is used for several other studies, for instance (Vandergriff, 2014). Though it is a valuable resource for research on different SLA issues, the way the data were obtained does not allow for analysis of natural native/non-native speaker interaction. The native speakers in the dataset collected by Sauro (2009) were made familiar

> with the target form and trained in the provision of the different types of corrective feedback as well as strategies to avoid supplying the learners with positive evidence of the target form. (Sauro, 2009, p. 100)

It is specifically problematic if the research focuses on the influence of natural interactions between learners and native speakers on SLA development or if researchers pose open questions such as: "What happens if a native speaker of a language and a non-native speaker of the same language interact in text chat?"

Another problem is that researchers usually use specific software as a web service where users have to create their own accounts and log in with the goal to improve their language skills (Blake and Delforge, 2004; Blake, 2008; Tudini, 2010; Marques-Schäfer, 2013). This makes the interaction closer to a classroom interaction, which is definitely also worth attention, but then, we still do not know anything about the naturally occurring native/non-native speaker chat interaction.

In order to avoid the experimental character of the CMC data and to obtain data from close-to-natural chat interactions, researchers usually ask the participants to store the data locally and to provide them with a copy of the data log (Lee, 2007; Jin, 2013). This, in turn, puts researchers in a subordinate position and makes the whole study dependent on the charity of the data suppliers, i.e. the participants. In such situations, researchers cannot access the data immediately, nor can they control the consistency and the completeness of the data, because the participants are free to decide what to show and what to hide. It becomes even more complicated if the study should have a longitudinal character (long-term interaction).

In addition to the described problems with the data quality, there is an issue with comparability and reuse of the datasets. Marques-Schäfer (2013) lists 40 studies related to using chat for SLA that were published between 1994 and 2010 and criticises the bad comparability of achieved results due to very individual study settings. She suggests specifying the attributes of each study, which would help to make at least the setups better comparable, even if results are still very individual. Moreover, the datasets described in the CALL and CMC literature are never available, mostly for privacy reasons. It is rarely possible to perform different studies with the same dataset, or to use the same datasets to confirm or to challenge the results presented by the researchers.

During the literature review on the description of data collection of text and video chat that was initiated at the beginning of the research presented in this book, 18 attributes have been identified in which the datasets may differ. These attributes are data collection time (date and duration), participants' demographic information (first language, other spoken languages, level of knowledge of the non-native language in focus, method of selection), target language, study description (modality of the talk, e.g. text, voice, video, instructions to participants), number of participants, size of the dataset, data selection for analysis, software used, software availability, researcher's role, ethics, privacy protection and data availability. Variance in each of these attributes is one of the reasons for insufficient result comparability. Furthermore, technology develops rapidly and ICALL research needs to follow all technological innovations in CMC in order to deliver up-to-date results. Hence, the impact of new technologies on interaction and learning is worthy of empirical investigation (Brandt, 2011).

Though instant messaging as a communication technology is already several decades old, ways of communication have changed dramatically in the last decade. Mobile devices and cloud-based services have made instant messaging highly available and popular. This, in turn, has changed user's attitude towards instant messaging services. It has become completely normal to text not only with peers of parents, but also within a professional and learning context. In 2014, messaging apps became the dominant platforms for communication and overtook social networks in terms of the number of active users per month. For these reasons, new datasets open for public research and reflecting all these developments are required.

2.3.3 Conversation analysis of native/non-native speaker chat

Marques-Schäfer (2013) lists 40 studies documented between 1994 and 2010 in the major CALL journals - *CALICO*, *ReCALL* and *Language Learning and Technology* (Marques-Schäfer, 2013, Sec. 3.2.2.). While many SLA-inspired studies of native/non-native speaker chat have been reported in CALL publications, relatively few CA-driven investigations of native/non-native speaker chat are documented in the academic literature.

Tudini (2010) describes a long-term study of communication between Australian learners of Italian and Italian native speakers in dyadic text chat. She focuses mainly on repair sequences "as this is where SLA behaviours are most evident" (Tudini, 2010, p. 6). Among other repair types, the author discusses various types of other-correction and concludes that the types of error correction build a "continuum of explicitness of exposed correction in online text chat" (Tudini, 2010, p. 101) ranging from explicit (exposed) corrections on the fly to teacher-like corrections accompanied by accountings and metalinguistic information.

Vandergriff (2013) analysed dyadic task-based interactions between previously unacquainted participants in English as a second language. Specifically, she investigated how participants of a native/non-native speaker chat make their differential linguistic expertise relevant in conversation. Her findings show that these orientations primarily occur outside of other-repair sequences and therefore, do not play a role "in mitigating and/or sanctioning a face-threatening act." (Vandergriff, 2013, p. 393)

Though the work by Marques-Schäfer (2013) is not CA-driven, the author uses qualitative methods for data analysis. Marques-Schäfer (2013) analysed a subset of chat protocols from the *JETZT Deutsch lernen* project offered by the German Goethe-Institute [4]. As part of this project, learners of German as a second language could chat with other learners and native speakers. The dataset consists of tutored and untutored group chat sessions (Marques-Schäfer, 2013, p. 180). She found that

[4] http://www.goethe.de/z/jetzt/

the number of corrections in tutored sessions was higher than in untutored sessions. Marques-Schäfer (2013) concludes that the presence of tutors in chat emphasises the didactic character of online chat. It seems natural to expect more teacher-like behaviour from the tutors in chat due to their pre-assigned role of more knowledgeable participants.

Although CA-driven and qualitative studies of native/non-native speaker chat gained important insights into specific aspects of repair, sequential organisation and participants' identities, operationalisation of the identified structures for computational modelling still needs to be performed. The research documented in this book makes a step in this direction.

2.3.4 Constructing identities of expert and novice in conversation

Participants in an interaction may *choose* to orient to their linguistic identities in talk, but they do not have to, as argued in Section 1.3 of this book (page 8). In addition, membership in the categories *novice* and *expert* is not fixed. Hosoda (2006) shows how non-native speakers of Japanese switch their roles from language novices to language experts in informal conversations with their native speaker friends. Marques-Schäfer (2013) observed that learners corrected linguistic errors produced by other learners in tutored chat sessions of the project *JETZT Deutsch lernen*:

> die Tutorin [ist] nicht die einzige Person in einer tutorierten Stunde [...], die eine Fremdkorrektur übernehmen kann. Die anderen Chat-Teilnehmer zeigen sich [...] hilfsbereit und sprachlich kompetent, um einander zu helfen und zu korrigieren.
>
> *The tutor [is] not the only person in a tutored session [...] who can perform an other-correction. The other chat participants show themselves as willing to help and linguistically competent in order to help each other and to correct* ((Marques-Schäfer, 2013, p. 186) Engl. translation added).

Thus, non-native speakers may choose to position themselves as language experts. This observation has been confirmed for instance by a study of the use of English as Lingua Franca in non-native/non-native speaker interaction (Hynninen, 2012). The author discusses how linguistic identity may appear in interaction due to the participant's status as a native speaker or a language professional, but also be negotiated in the course of non-native/non-native speaker interaction. Hynninen (2012, p. 13) shows that "even if the courses are not language courses, language sometimes becomes the topic of discussion in the form of language correcting and commentary."

Hosoda (2006) focuses in his study on informal oral communication between friends who are native speakers of Japanese and learners of Japanese as a foreign language. He points out that orientation to the roles of the language expert or novice in conversation is especially salient in "remedial" sequences such as repair or correction, but the repertoire of sequences for such orientations *is not limited to repair or correction* (Hosoda, 2006, p. 26, emphasis added). The study has demonstrated

> [...] on the occasions that participants in ordinary [native/non-native speaker] conversation orient to differences in their linguistic expertise, the structures

> of the conversation may become similar to those of language classrooms (Hosoda, 2006, p. 44).

Vandergriff (2013) analysed how institutionally structured identities of student and teacher have been integrated by the study participants in their interactional roles as a language novice and language expert. She documented with multiple examples that the interactional role of a novice is not restricted to the institutional identity of a language student. In particular, facework in the broader sense plays a major role in constructing the interactional role of a language novice, such as (re-)indexing of the social self existing in the second language, building and maintaining social rapport with the co-participant and cultivating social presence (Vandergriff, 2013, pp. 393, 404).

A one-year longitudinal study of video-recordings of native/non-native speaker interaction in Spanish is described by (Dings, 2012). Based on analysis of six conversational interactions, the author examines the interlocutors' orientation to their identities as language novice and language expert. Dings (2012) found the following forms of orientation to linguistic identities: discussion of language learning, learner-error corrections initiated by the native speaker, and learner-error corrections initiated by the non-native speaker. In addition, (Dings, 2012) found changes in patterns of correction. While repair in the beginning was more formfocused, it tended to be more meaningfocused later.

The complexity of the notion of linguistic expertise can be understood even more deeply on studies where a second language is used for work and the conversations do not have the primary purpose of language practice. Vickers (2010) examines audio-recorded team-meeting data between engineering students, one native and one non-native speaker of English, jointly working on a project. The author demonstrated that language competence may be blended with other types of competence through the use of specific interactional strategies. Linguistic and non-linguistic identities of experts are locally constituted in native/non-native speaker interaction. Vickers (2010) argues that these linguistically and non-linguistically based identities are interrelated so that the linguistic identity of a novice has a bearing on the achievement of the non-linguistic identity of an expert. This means in practice that for example students or professionals working in a context requiring communication in a second language may have difficulties positioning themselves or being accepted as experts in their profession *because* of insufficient second language knowledge.

In contrast to the work described earlier in this section focusing on how a participant of a conversation presents herself as a member of a specific category, *interaction profiles* are concerned with *individual* shapes of interaction participants (Spranz-Fogasy, 2002). The subject of the analysis is how the conversational activities of all participants of an interaction become systematic and stable with the focus of one participant, and become in this way an interaction profile. Spranz-Fogasy (2002) defines an *interaction profile* as

> die auf einen einzelnen Gesprächsteilnehmer bezogene Verlaufskonfiguration des interaktiven sprachlichen Handelns aller Teilnehmer in einer je-

weiligen Interaktion, wie sie sich aus dem Gesprächshandeln ergibt und zugleich auf dieses Handeln zurückwirkt und es anleitet
a configuration in the process of conversational behaviour of all interaction participants with respect to a single interaction participant, how such a process configuration emerges from the interaction and at the same time influences and guides the interaction (p. 47, Engl. translation added).

Spranz-Fogasy (2002) shows in a very detailed analysis of multiple interactions from various situations (public group discussions, family conflict talks and institutional arbitration talks) how specific interaction practices used by interaction participants become recognisable patterns or types of behaviour. In other words, an interaction profile is something that emerges in interaction and is influenced by *all* interaction participants and the interaction history when participants use specific language practices. The number and the kind of available practices is open.

To summarise, there are various possibilities in interaction to orient to linguistic identities. The identity of a language expert (or more knowledgeable participant) can only exist in a dichotomy paired with the identity of a language novice (or less knowledgeable participant). The individual shapes of these identities may vary and can only partially be influenced by the acting participant (the participant who initiates such orientations). The reacting participant (who responds to this initiation) may accept or reject the role assigned to her. For the purpose of a Communicative ICALL application, different local models of orientation to linguistic identities may be provided to the machine, but it is not possible and not necessary to determine in advance which of them will be activated. A notion of interactional relevance needs to be made accessible to the machine in the form of a decision model for the activation of specific actions from that pool. In this way, an *individual interaction profile of a language expert* may emerge in interaction between the machine and the language learner. This idea has been developed in (Höhn et al., 2015) and will be discussed in Section 3.5.2.

2.3.5 The power of repair

Liddicoat (2011) describes repair as "the processes available to speakers through which they can deal with the problems which arise in talk". More precisely, Hosoda (2006) describes the types of problems that can be handled by repair in native/non-native speaker interaction:

> repair in the CA sense deals with any problems in speaking, hearing, or understanding, such as clarification requests, understanding checks, repetitions, restatements, offers of candidate hearings, and the like, and it includes but is not limited to corrections of linguistic errors. (Hosoda, 2006, p. 27)

From the CA perspective, repair is not something that disturbs the interaction. Rather the opposite is true, because repair is seen as a principal resource that participants of a conversation have at their disposal to maintain intersubjectivity, thus, to construct shared meanings (Markee, 2000; Schegloff, 1992).

Following previous work on repair (Jefferson, 1974; Schegloff, 1997; Dingemanse et al., 2014) we will use here the common terminology distinguishing among practices, devices and formats. Dingemanse et al. (2014, pp. 10-11) provide the following definitions, which we adopt in this book:

Practices are generic, language-independent techniques such as 'repetition' and 'questioning'.

Devices are particular, language-specific linguistic resources, such as 'particles', 'question prosody' or 'noun-class specific interrogatives', and rules for their application.

Formats combine generic practices and language-specific devices to deliver social actions.

For the analysis of repair work, it is necessary to distinguish between several sequentially different contributions to the repair by different speakers. We need to see:

1. Who produced the repairable also known as *the trouble source*? This speaker is sometimes also called a *trouble-speaker*.
2. Who initiated the repair (produced a *repair initiation*)?
3. Who carried out the repair?

From the perspective of the trouble-speaker, CA researchers differentiate between *self-initiated* and *other-initiated* repair. Similarly, the repair can be carried out by the trouble-speaker or the recipient of the trouble-talk. These two types of repair are referred to as *self-repair* and *other-repair* respectively. Thus, we can have four types of repair *per speaker*:

1. self-initiated self-repair (or self-correction);
2. self-initiated other-repair (usually dealing with difficulties in production);
3. other-initiated self-repair (e.g. a clarification request followed by an explanation or a confirmation);
4. other-initiated other-repair (or other-correction).

Nothing in the language is a trouble source by itself, but everything can appear to be a trouble source in a conversation if it is marked as a trouble source by the conversation participants. However, there are structures in all languages that have a greater potential to become a trouble source for non-native speakers because they require a higher level of language proficiency to use or to understand them correctly. Such linguistic structures include idioms, figurative expressions and proverbs. In addition, some social actions appear more difficult to perform in a foreign language, such as responding appropriately to compliments (Golato, 2002).

Since everything can become a trouble source, repair initiations can occur after any turn at talk, even after silence (Schegloff, 1993). However, different repair *formats* might be appropriate for different speech exchange systems. For example, a German expression *Wie bitte?* (En.: *How please?*) is a practice to other-initiate self-repair. The recipient of the trouble-talk asks the trouble-speaker, for instance, to repeat an utterance. This is rather untypical for medially written communication, because the recipient normally has the possibility to re-read the messages of the interaction partner(s). Therefore, such a repair initiation would be interpreted differently if it occurs in a text chat (e.g. it may express anger or surprise).

There are specific positions dedicated to specific types of repair initiation in conversation. Due to a preference for self-repair, first-position repair initiations are dedicated to self-repair (same-turn or transition-space repair) (Schegloff et al., 1977). The first position where an other-initiation of repair can occur is the first speaker change, after the trouble source turn. This is the so-called second-position repair initiation. This position is dedicated to other-initiation of repair. Third-position repair may be relevant when the first speaker understands from the reaction of the second speaker that the previous utterance was wrongly understood. This position is dedicated to self-initiation of repair. The last position where repair initiations have been found till now is the fourth position, which is dedicated to repair other-initiation. However, this type of repair initiation is very rare and requires the biggest amount of interaction management work of all repair types (Schegloff, 1992; Schegloff et al., 1977; Schegloff, 2000; Liddicoat, 2011).

While other-initiated self-repair and other-initiated other-repair are relatively well analysed in face-to-face and chat data from CA and SLA perspectives, less is known about self-corrections in chat due to difficulties in capturing the data (Smith, 2008). From the CA perspective, this is not a big problem, because "what happens before turns are posted is not relevant to the interaction unless [...] the participants themselves orient to it during the interaction" (González-Lloret, 2011, p. 318).

There are several studies focusing on repair in specific languages. Benjamin (2013) contributes to the research on repair with the study of other-initiated repair in naturally occurring social interaction in English. Word searches and candidate understandings are the focus of the study of Russian and Finnish as lingua franca in (Pikkarainen, 2015). Egbert (2009) analyses the German repair mechanism in oral conversations and compares the findings to repair structures in different languages. She concludes that the basic structure of repair mechanism is language-independent, but there are language-specific and culture-specific features that can be embedded in repair activity.

> Es gibt eindeutige Hinweise darauf, dass der Reparatur-Apparat ein sprachübergreifender Mechanismus ist, welcher in seiner Grundstruktur unabhängig von sprachlichen oder kulturellen Unterschieden ist, jedoch Möglichkeiten beherbergt, kulturelle Merkmale, Besonderheiten im linguistischen Repertoire und spezifische Handlungen im Zusammenhang mit der Reparaturaktivität zu berücksichtigen.
> *There is unambiguous evidence that the repair apparatus is a mechanism that is valid across languages and is independent of language or culture differences in its basic structure, however, it contains the possibilities to take into account features of specific cultures, specific linguistic repertoire and specific actions related to the repair activity.* (Egbert, 2009, p. 166, Engl. translation added.)

In line with this finding, Dingemanse et al. (2014) describe formats of repair other-initiations for oral data across 10 languages not including German. They show that there is a set of interactional resources in each language that correspond to open-class repair initiations and restricted class repair initiations. Open-class repair initiations are also analysed by (Drew, 1997; Enfield et al., 2013).

Open-class repair initiations signal *that* there is a problem with the previous utterance. Examples of such repair initiations are *huh?* in English and *hä?* in German. Restricted class repair initiations allow the speaker to narrow the scope of the trouble diagnosis.

> With interjections, single question words, and formulaic or apology-based formats we have exhausted open formats. The set of restricted formats, i.e. formats that zoom in on specific items in the trouble-source, is larger and more internally varied. [...] Despite this variety, the types of linguistic resources used are relatively limited. They consist of content-question words, full and partial repetition, and various types of candidate understandings. (Dingemanse et al., 2014, p. 17)

Analysis of repair sequences in native/non-native speaker chat was performed by Tudini for a dataset of dyadic interactions between students of Italian at an Australian university and native speakers of Italian based in Italy (Tudini, 2010). This chat interaction was part of students' assessment although the students were asked to interact with native speakers in their free time outside the classroom. Topics for the interaction were provided. The participants interacted almost every time with a different person; therefore, the long-term development of the interaction is not systematically observable.

Specific types of repair are in the focus of SLA studies because they have been considered indicators of learning. These are *meaning negotiations* (Varonis and Gass, 1985) and *corrective feedback* (Lyster and Ranta, 1997). The trouble sources in corrective feedback sequences are normally deviations from the language standard and non-native-like constructions. The trouble sources in meaning negotiation sequences are normally expressions in the foreign language that are not completely clear to the learner and need an explanation. In this book, we will call such types of repair *repair with linguistic trouble source*, no matter by whom they were initiated or carried out.

Varonis and Gass (1985) proposed a sequential model of meaning negotiation that consists of a trigger (trouble source), an indicator (repair initiation), a response (repair carry-out) and a reaction to the response. Meaning negotiations can be initiated by the trouble-speaker and by the trouble-talk recipient; thus, they include two sequentially and substantially different repair types, which makes a turn-by-turn analysis very complex. Meaning negotiations initiated by the trouble-speaker may for example deal with troubles in production. Meaning initiations initiated by the trouble-talk recipient may deal with troubles in understanding. Each participant may be a native speaker or a non-native speaker. This can make a difference in the use of interactional resources for repair.

Markee (2000) criticises the sequential model of meaning negotiations as methodologically problematic, because it is only supported by data from institutional talk such as teacher-student or psychotherapist-patient. The model suggested by Varonis and Gass (1985) does not take into account the differences in speech exchange systems and is, as Markee (2000, p. 85) argues, not applicable to equal-power speech exchange systems such as ordinary conversation. Building on the work by Kasper (1985), Markee (2000) differentiates between repair during the language-centred phase of a classroom interaction, and repair during the content-centred phase. Kasper (1985) found that "participants oriented to different, and indeed more complex, patterns of repair" during the content-centred phase.

Corrective feedback corresponds to other-corrections (or other-initiated other-repair) in CA terminology. Many studies on the typology of corrective feedback in language classroom data and Computer-Mediated Communication have been published (Lyster and Ranta, 1997; Panova and Lyster, 2002; Zourou, 2011). One of the recent classifications of corrective feedback in language classrooms was presented in (Lyster et al., 2013, p. 4) and will be given here for comparison. It includes the following nine types of corrective feedback:

1. **Conversational recast** is a reformulation of a non-native speaker's utterance in order to resolve a communication problem. A frequent form is a confirmation check.
2. **Repetition** takes the form of a 1:1 repetition of a problematic expression marked with interrogative intonation in order to highlight the error.
3. **Clarification request** signals a misunderstanding or a communication problem by a phrase like "I don't understand".
4. **Explicit correction** contains a clear identification of an error with a reformulation of the learner's expression and an explicit presentation of the correct form.
5. **Explicit correction with metalinguistic information** signals an error explicitly, providing a correct form and information about, for example, grammar and pragmatics.
6. **Didactic recast** is a reformulation of the learner's utterance in the absence of a communication problem.
7. **Metalinguistic clue** is a metalinguistic statement aimed at eliciting a self-correction.
8. **Elicitation** directly enforces a self-correction, and may often take the form of a content question.
9. **Paralinguistic signal** is a non-verbal elicitation of the correct form.

Because this classification was constructed based on oral data, not every type of corrective feedback (or its CA equivalent) can be expected to be found in text-based chat communication. Moreover, some of the types of corrective feedback may appear too teacher-like to be applied in a Conversation-for-Learning. In addition, the categories in the classification proposed by Lyster et al. (2013) are not disjoint. For instance, it is not easy to make a clear distinction between confirmation checks and clarification requests, conversational and didactic recasts. In addition, clarification requests may be based on a repetition, which overlaps with recasts. The overlapping classes make computational modelling of various correction types problematic. Therefore, we will look in this book at other-corrections of linguistic errors in the dataset through the lens of computational modelling. We will try to identify patterns in other-corrections that can be taken as an operational basis for an implementation of an artificial conversation partner.

Error typologies as a base for correction are discussed in (Vicente-Rasoamalala, 2009, Sec. 4.3.3.). However, in previous CA research, no dependencies between error types and correction types were found (Schegloff, 1987b). Moreover, Schegloff (1987b, p. 216) emphasised the importance of "disengaging trouble (error and non-error) from the practices employed to deal with it". In addition, not every error is corrected in a language classroom, and not every error is corrected in a Conversation-for-Learning. Further investigation is needed of the circumstances under which an error can and should be corrected in an informal conversation with language learners. This book makes an attempt to find a solution for this problem in Chapter 8.

Corrections may be delivered immediately after the error or later. Different time points of correction delivery in a language classroom have been discussed in (Vicente-Rasoamalala, 2009, p.147). In addition to immediate corrections, delayed and postponed corrections may take place. Delayed corrections may appear at a transition point in conversation or at a subsequent point of the same lesson (or chat session). Postponed corrections may occur in another lesson (or chat session). The right point for correction delivery is an important issue for correction generation in a Communicative ICALL application. Therefore, we will look specifically at timing features in the analysis of other-corrections in this book.

While very detailed descriptions of teachers' reaction to learner errors in a language classroom already exist (see for instance (Vicente-Rasoamalala, 2009) for a detailed comparison of multiple classifications), a detailed description of sequential environments, practices and turn formats for corrections in a Conversation-for-Learning needs first to be created in order to prepare a basis for computational modelling.

Jefferson (1974) shows that error corrections are used in native speakers' talk as an interactional resource to negotiate and reformulate the current set of identities. She argues that "error correction is a systematic feature of speech, and [...] it is achieved by the application of a specific device, the Error Correction Format" (Jefferson, 1974, p. 188). For instance, she describes Contrast Class Errors including "error correction formats involving words having the same features with opposite values" (Jefferson, 1974, p. 187). Building on this idea, we will look at different error correction types. We will call them *error correction formats* following the terminology suggested at the beginning of this section.

Kurhila (2001) examines the selectivity of error correction in native/non-native speaker talk based on an analysis of a corpus of naturally occurring non-pedagogical conversations. The author suggests that native speakers' decisions to correct may be explained by environments in which errors can be corrected in general. Kurhila (2001) concludes that grammatical errors produced by language learners are most likely to be corrected by the native speakers in non-pedagogical talk when they occur in a 'repetition slot' or when they can be used to initiate repair. Nonetheless, "despite the rather frequent occurrence of other-correction in these environments, other-correction is still constrained in its occurrence in NS-NNS [native/non-native speaker] conversation, as in NS [native speaker] talk." (Kurhila, 2001, p. 1107).

To simulate repair sequences of different kinds in dialogues between an artificial conversation partner and a language learner in a Communicative ICALL application, a more detailed operationalisation of the repair components (whatever they are) is needed. Specific linguistic resources that can be used for specific types of troubles and specific types of repairs need to be described on a level that can be incorporated in a computational model of repair. For instance, a model distinguishing between repair initiations and all other utterances is of interest. After that, the trouble source needs to be extracted from the repair initiation and an appropriate repair needs to be generated.

In light of the discussion in this section, this book seeks to contribute to the analysis of repair in chat-based Conversations-for-Learning in the following way:

1. Computational modelling of other-initiated self-repair when the native speaker is the trouble-speaker requires a more detailed analysis of the interactional resources used to signal and locate troubles in comprehension.
2. An empirical base for other-corrections specific to the speech exchange system in focus needs to be created. Interactional resources used for corrections of linguistic errors need to be described and operationalised for computational modelling. The timing of corrections in chat needs to be described.
3. A Communicative ICALL application needs clear decision criteria for correction, for which we will try to find an empirically grounded base and describe it in this book.

These three issues are the major focus of the research described in this book.

2.3.6 Embedded corrections as a form of implicit feedback

The difference between exposed and embedded corrections in English native speaker talk was first described by Jefferson (1987). She distinguished between corrections where *correcting* becomes an interactional business and those that happen by the way, without focusing on the *correcting* in the interaction. Jefferson defines embedded corrections "as by-the-way occurrence in some ongoing course of talk" noticing that "the talk which constitutes embedded corrections does not permit of accountings" (Jefferson, 1987, 95). She introduces the term *accountings* to refer to all those "attendant activities" of the correctings such as instructing, complaining, forgiving, apologising and ridiculing. Kasper (2004) found that non-native speakers activate their interactional roles first of all through accountings.

The examples of embedded corrections provided by Jefferson are all recordings of native/native speaker interactions and do not contain corrections of linguistic errors. The replacements in Jefferson's examples are: police → cops, wales → threads, kilns → kils, eve → night, pretty → beautiful. Only the sequences of the initial and the new terms are provided here. The reader is welcome to have a look at all the examples described by Jefferson (1987) in the original work.

Similarly, the analysis of corrections (including embedded corrections) of self-references in conversation performed by Lerner and Kitzinger (2007) shows that despite the correctness of the un-repaired version (*I* instead of *we* or the other way round) "speakers can select a self-reference term so as to fit the referent to the kind of action (or personal state) formulated within the turn" (Lerner and Kitzinger, 2007, pp. 538-539). In other words, phenomena besides corrections of linguistic errors are subject to repair and are in focus of studies on embedded corrections.

Embedded corrections in native/non-native speaker conversations are in focus of only a few studies in face-to-face interactions (Brouwer et al., 2004; Kurhila, 2006; Kaur, 2011; Hynninen, 2013) and in chat (Tudini, 2010). Hynninen (2013) prefers the term *embedded repair* in her analysis of English as lingua franca because "repair (in CA) refers widely to any kind of modifications that do not necessarily focus on correcting" (Hynninen, 2013, p. 122). Tudini (2010) characterises embedded corrections as " ...inexplicit indirect feedback", "correction with discretion". In this book we will interchangeably use the terms *embedded correction* and *implicit correction* to refer to this phenomenon.

Kurhila (2006) discussed embedded corrections in institutional and every day conversations between native speakers of Finnish and learners of Finnish as a second language. He found out that embedded corrections are produced more frequently in an institutional setting, arguing that this is because of the need for confirmed, clear information (Kurhila, 2006).

Brouwer et al. (2004, p. 86) describe the procedure of embedded corrections in oral non-native speaker talk in the following way:

> In embedded corrections, the speaker in the ongoing turn B corrects an item in a preceding turn A while doing some possible next action to this preceding turn A. Thus, the main work of turn B is on this next action and not on the correction. It is this 'next action' which is consequential for turn C, then, and not the correction; in other words, the speaker of the trouble-source turn A does not orient to the correction in turn B. Embedded corrections therefore do not open a 'side sequence' [...] but proceed with the main business of the sequence.

The mechanism allowing corrections to be embedded into the ongoing business of the talk without focusing on the activity of correction is related to procedures for "consecutive reference to same objects" in conversation (Jefferson, 1987, p. 90). Jefferson describes three possibilities to refer to objects in conversation:

1. The next speaker uses proterms to refer to the entities named by the prior speaker;
2. A term used by a speaker is repeated by the next speaker;
3. An *alternative* term is used by the next speaker instead of the term introduced by the initial speaker. An alternative pronunciation is a variant of this for spoken interaction. An alternative writing may be an equivalent for chat interaction.

Jefferson notes, "when a next speaker produces, not a proterm or a repeat, but an alternative item, *correction* may be underway".

Academic literature documents contradictory findings with regard to occurrences of embedded corrections in native/non-native speaker interactions. Brouwer et al. (2004) identified embedded corrections of linguistic errors as typical for non-native speaker face-to-face interaction. In contrast, embedded corrections of linguistic errors were rare in the dataset used by (Tudini, 2010) for her study of native/non-native speaker chat interaction. She concludes that 'further attention is required in a separate study to determine why dyadic online intercultural chat favours exposed correction to deal with pedagogical repair". We will see later, whether the dataset used for this research confirms or challenges these findings.

With regard to places of embedded correction in interaction, the academic literature reports different situations. Kurhila (2001) describes places where different sorts of corrections often occur, regardless of the linguistic surface of the trouble turn: corrections *en passant*, repetition-based answers to questions and third turn by the native speaker after a question-answer pair. Corrections *en passant* are referred to as corrections *on the fly* and classified by other authors as exposed correction; see for instance (Tudini, 2010). However, the other two types belong to embedded corrections. As opposed to this finding, Brouwer et al. (2004, p. 85) report that all errors corrected implicitly in their collection were located in a first pair part (e.g. question), and the embedded corrections were always part of the second pair part (e.g. answer to the question). We will look at positions where embedded corrections occur in the dataset that we selected for this research.

Using the wording chosen by Brouwer et al. (2004, p. 86), a more detailed specification of the possibilities for "the speaker in the ongoing turn B" to correct "an item in a preceding turn A while doing some possible next action to this preceding turn A" is needed to generate embedded corrections for conversational agents and dialogue systems. Building the bridge between the findings of CA and CA-for-SLA in the area of embedded corrections on one hand and the needs of Communicative ICALL and AI in the broader sense on the other hand is one of the contributions of this book. The book will provide an analysis of the error types and correction formats for all pairs of turns consisting of the trouble turn and the embedded correction turn in the first part of Chapter 6 preparing a base for formal modelling of these phenomena. A formal model for embedded corrections in one sequential environment will be introduced in the second part of Chapter 7. The model operates on the level of grammar and turn-taking.

With regard to the analysis of learning, embedded corrections present a particular difficulty. As Kurhila (2006, p. 43) notes:

> Embedded correction is one reason why language learning is difficult to explore in authentic conversations between native and non-native speakers. In the laboratory data, the NNSs [non-native speakers] are being tested after they have been corrected and, thus, some claims can be made about the possible improvement or learning. In real NS-NNS [native/non-native speaker] conversations, however, correction can be introduced in a way that specifically makes it possible for the NNS [non-native speaker] not to respond to it.

Therefore, the issue of learning (or having registered the new form) remains ambiguous.

Recordings of long-term interaction such as the dataset used for this research can help us to understand how particular items are used by learners and how they develop in conversation over time. Effects of native/non-native speaker chat on learning are not the main focus of this work. However, some observations and recommendations came out during this research and will be discussed in Section 7.5.3, page 217 of the book.

2.4 Conversation Analysis in Artificial Intelligence

Conversation Analysis was taken up by several AI subfields, mainly in four ways:

1. CA concepts were adopted for a further investigation in a subfield of AI. One example of this is speech recognition and the concept of repair.
2. CA findings were operationalised for specific AI applications. For instance, laughter as a feature for topic change was described in CA (Holt, 2010) and operationalised for the estimation of the topic change in a dialogue system (Gilmartin et al., 2013).
3. CA methods were taken in research on human-machine interaction. Many examples of this are discussed below in Section 2.4.3.
4. A mixture of these.

All these four types can be termed *CA-informed research*; however, the grade of the influence of CA on the respective AI subfield is in each case different. Although CA findings open useful insights into the structure and sequential organisation of interaction, it appears to be very difficult to operationalise them for an implementation in a dialogue or robotic system.

Application of CA methods to the field of Human-Computer Interaction (HCI) is mentioned as a field of applied CA in CA textbooks (ten Have, 2007, Ch. 10). The earliest work mentioned therein comes from the late 1980's where the problem of plans and situated action was adressed (Suchman, 1985). Later on, qualitative research methods, such as CA, Interaction Analysis and Ethnography, were used to solve various design problems in Artificial Intelligence (AI), Human-Computer Interaction (Peres and Meira, 2003) and Human-Robot Interaction (HRI) (Chee et al., 2010; Plurkowski et al., 2011; Sussenbach et al., 2014). Evaluation of interaction between technical systems has been also addressed using qualitative research methods (Robins et al., 2004; Lee and Makatchev, 2009; Lee et al., 2010; Sabelli et al., 2011; Alemi et al., 2015). The technical systems in focus were first of all robots and dialogue systems, but augmented reality also caught the researchers' attention as a tool for linguistic research to study interactional modifications caused by the technology (Pitsch et al., 2013c).

Studies described in this section achieved valuable results by applying qualitative research methods in HCI and HRI. Some of the results can be transferred into

Communicative ICALL. Some of the questions that arose from the studies discussed below are also relevant for Communicative ICALL research. At the time of writing this book, all attempts to find academic publications (besides the author's own publications) about using relevant insights from CA-for-SLA for design or evaluation of a Communicative ICALL system were unsuccessful.

2.4.1 Conversation Analysis for Dialogue Processing

The relationship between CA and NLP was difficult in the beginning. This is well reflected in a review article *Does Conversation Analysis have a Role in Computational Linguistics?* (Hirst, 1991) of the book *Computers and Conversation* (Luff et al., 1990).

The difficulty of the relationship between CA and HCI was caused by several factors. First, CA always analysed naturally occurring interaction, in the beginning audio-recorded phone conversations (Sacks, 1995; Schegloff, 2007). The speech technology at that time was not mature enough, the majority of dialogue systems were text based, and CA findings from audio recordings were not directly applicable to medially written human-machine dialogues. Second, various concepts of CA were not operationalised to be directly transferable to dialogue processing; therefore, other theories have been preferred, such as Speech Act Theory (Searle, 1969b) and the Belief-Desire-Intention model (Georgeff et al., 1999). This gap between the knowledge about conversation gained by CA and its technical implementability was (and still is) huge, which is clearly visible in the review of *Computers and Conversation* (Hirst, 1991) and still remains relevant almost two decades later. Nevertheless, Hirst (1991, p. 225, original emphasis) concludes optimistically:

> There is a sense in which it is clear that CA *must* have a role in NLU [natural language understanding], because there is a sense in which ethnomethodology is just a small subfield of artificial intelligence (although that might come as a surprise to the ethnomethodologists).

Despite all difficulties in the beginning, a lot of research effort has been invested to bring various insights gained from CA into Dialogue Processing. Several attempts have been made to involve CA in dialogue-based human-machine interaction. Waterworth (1986) reports how CA methods were applied to design a speech-based database inquiry system. Laughter has been found in CA to occur at a topic change (Holt, 2010) and a speech recognition study was built on this insight to estimate the time within the topic change borders (Gilmartin et al., 2013). Special attention was paid to turn-taking and adjacency pairs in dialogue; see for instance (Thórisson, 2002; Edlund et al., 2005; Johansson and Skantze, 2015) and references therein. How people take turns at talk has been studied to improve speech segmentation and to make human-robot interaction more natural.

Unfortunately, sometimes researchers mix up terminology from different fields in their work on turn-taking for dialogue systems. For instance, Lison (2014) presents an approach for structured probabilistic modelling for dialogue management where turn-taking is one of the key questions. In his introduction he explains turn-taking from the CA perspective. The author claims that "turns are structured into basic communicative units called *dialogue acts*" (Lison, 2014, p. 10). In CA, turns consist of *turn-constructional units* (TCU), which do not correlate with speech acts. The notion of speech acts was adopted from the Speech Act Theory (Searle, 1969a) and intensively used for dialogue processing. However, as Schegloff (1988, p. 61) argues,

> what a [...] speech act theoretic analysis misses is that parties to real conversations are always talking in some sequential context. [...] formulated in terms of more or less proximately preceding and projectably ensuing talk.

This shows that even if some researchers in dialogue processing start with concepts from CA, such as turns, what they do with them later in their work is not necessarily CA conforming nor CA informed. Nevertheless, the newest dialogue act annotation schemes such as DiAML and DAMSL allow at least some of the sequential context to be captured: turn management, time management and discourse structuring (Bunt, 2011).

Another topic addressed in CA that received a lot of attention in HCI is repair. The reader is invited to look at the most relevant academic literature in Section 2.4.2.

Nowadays, HRI gets most benefit from CA methods applied to design and analysis of multimodal interaction. Section 2.4.3 will discuss these achievements and how they can be transferred to Communicative ICALL.

2.4.2 Types of repair for conversational interfaces and dialogue systems

Types of repair for conversational agents described in state-of-the-art academic publications are closely related to the application scenarios and user models. Because language learners are usually not considered as the main user group, the assumption that human users understand everything that an artificial agent or robot may say dominates the research on repair for conversational agents. This assumption is reflected in the two main problems addressed by research on repair for conversational agents:

1. Dealing with the user's self-correction, which may make speech recognition difficult;
2. Managing the system's lack of information in order to satisfy the user's request.

These two research areas may be found under the keywords *self-repairs*, sometimes *speech repairs* or *disfluencies*, and *clarification dialogues* in AI and NLP publications, for instance (Shriberg, 1994; Martin and Jurafsky, 2009; Zwarts et al., 2010). What is referred to by the term *self-repair* in the speech recognition domain corresponds to user's same-turn self-correction (self-initiated self-repair) in CA terminology. Example 2.1 illustrates this type of repair and is frequently cited in academic literature on speech recognition.

Example 2.1. Same turn self-correction (Schegloff et al., 1977, p. 363 (5)).

L: Is his one dollar all right or should he send more
$\rightarrow$ than that for the p- tuh cover the postage.

User's same-turn self-correction is the subject of research in, for instance (Purver and Hough, 2014). The application in focus is incremental recognition of self-corrections performed by users of spoken dialogue systems in real time. Only same-turn (same turn-constructional unit) repair is considered. The system is trained and tested on data from the Switchboard corpus of English phone conversations (Godfrey et al., 1992).

Skantze and Hjalmarsson (2010) differentiate between overt and covert self-corrections for incremental speech generation. This differentiation is motivated by psycholinguistic studies on speech production that found that speakers self-monitor the output by listening to their own speaking (overt monitoring) and by mental checking of the planned speech (covert monitoring) (Levelt, 1993). Following this, overt self-corrections deal with already produced trouble sources, and covert self-corrections deal with not-yet produced planned trouble sources. Skantze and Hjalmarsson (2010) distinguish in addition between a segment and a unit repair where a segment is only a part of a syntactic unit that needs to be repaired. Both segment and unit repairs can be accomplished in a overt or covert manner depending on the system's state. All these differences are required to identify automatically what should be replaced by what. Thus, the trouble source needs to be replaced by the repaired part of the turn in order to make the puzzle complete for speech recognition, language understanding and speech generation.

Speech recognition errors may lead to further problems in maintaining the dialogue with the user and task continuation. Modelling human clarification strategies (repair initiations) in response to speech recognition errors has been addressed in (Stoyanchev et al., 2013).

The majority of academic publications on same-turn self-correction for speech recognition build upon the model for such repairs proposed by (Shriberg, 1994). The model suggests that the turn containing a same-turn self-correction can be split into a sequence of units with a specific function. The units are shown in Table 2.2.

until you're	*at the le-*	||	*I mean*	*at the right-hand*	*edge*
start	reparandum	moment of interruption	editing terms	alteration	continuation

Table 2.2: A sequential pattern of a self-repair as proposed by (Shriberg, 1994)

Shriberg (1994) uses the term *reparandum* to refer to what is called a *trouble source* in CA. The sequential model shown in Table 2.2 distinguished between pauses (moment of interruption) and lexicalised means to focus on the replacement (editing terms). Both are interactional recourses used by speakers to signal trouble in production and to make a pre-announcement of a coming replacement (alteration).

The term *clarification dialogues* or *clarification sub-dialogues* is mostly used to describe repair sequences in AI to deal with insufficient information available to the system after speech recognition or language understanding (Hayes and Reddy, 1979; Allen and Small, 1982; Maier, 1997; Gabsdil, 2003; Kruijff et al., 2006, 2008; Jian et al., 2010; Buß and Schlangen, 2011).

The term *miscommunication* was introduced to distinguish between *non-understandings* and *misunderstandings* (Dzikovska et al., 2009; Meena et al., 2015). Non-understandings take place when the system cannot match the user's input to a representation. Misunderstandings happen when the system matches the user's input to a wrong representation. These repair types correspond to other-initiated self-repair when the user is the trouble-speaker (the machine initiates and the user carries out the repair).

Clarification dialogues have been studied from the point of view of managing lack of information to satisfy the user's needs in task-based dialogue systems, question-answering systems, information systems and robotics. Therefore, mainly the case of other-initiated self-repair where the system does not (fully) understand the user's input has been covered. For instance, the VERBMOBIL translation system plays only an intermediate role in communication between people, and only seldom engages in active dialogues with the user, as for instance, in clarification dialogues (Maier, 1997).

Though in AI repair initiations are frequently referred to as *clarification requests*, they should not be confused with clarification requests in SLA theory. In SLA theory this term is used to refer only to a particular form of corrective feedback (Lyster et al., 2013), but also to a dialogue move in meaning-negotiation sequences (Varonis and Gass, 1985). These two models were discussed in Section 2.3.5, page 42.

Repair initiations are usually generated from manually created templates specific to each trouble source type (Maier, 1997). In a speech-based information retrieval system SPEAK! (Grote et al., 1997), clarification sub-dialogues may be system-initiated by means of intonation to clarify the user's needs. In (Kruijff et al., 2008), robots need to negotiate what people say to them. Robots know what is unclear to them and can produce clarification requests. Clarification is seen as a continual planning process.

Rodríguez and Schlangen (2004) present a multidimensional classification scheme for form and function of clarification requests and apply it to a corpus of German task-oriented dialogues for annotation. It is an attempt to analyse the structure of repair initiations and to improve a state-of-the-art classification scheme. Clarification dialogues described in (Quintano and Rodrigues, 2008) are required to disambiguate a user's request in a question-answering system.

Dzikovska et al. (2009) focus on *non-understanding errors* (cases where the system does not find any interpretation for the user's utterance) in a chat-oriented tutorial dialogue system for tutoring the basics of electricity and electronics. The research is focused on repair initiations produced by the dialogue system. A repair initiation is generated according to a single template: an apology followed by a reference to the trouble source followed by a request to reformulate the utterance. The system tries to elicit a reformulation of the problematic utterance from the user.

The huge body of research on user's self-correction and other-initiated self-repair when the user is the trouble-speaker signals the assumption that the user always understands everything. Rarely has the opposite been the subject of research studies. However, the importance of the types of repair for artificial agents when the users display the need for clarification is acknowledged in a body of academic publications; see for instance (Purver, 2004, 2006):

> It is also very unusual for systems to be able to understand and respond when the user asks a CR [clarification requests]. Designers (very sensibly) try to avoid user CRs by making system prompts as clear and informative as possible, and sometimes training users with those prompts. However, as systems start to deal with complex tasks, wider domains and wider audiences, [...] it seems inevitable that they will have to deal with users asking CRs at some point. (Purver, 2006, p. 260)

Emphasising the importance of a correct recognition of a user's clarification requests, Purver (2004) provides an empirical, theoretical and implementation study of various types of clarification requests. We will look at Purver (2004)'s classification here in detail because it is used in many follow-up publications, for instance (Purver, 2006; Ginzburg et al., 2007; Ginzburg, 2012).

Purver (2004) uses the HPSG framework to cover the main classes of the identified classification scheme. The relationship between the form and the function of clarification requests is investigated (clarification form vs. clarification reading). The *clarification forms* identified by Purver (2004) from a corpus of phone conversations are:

1. *Non-reprise clarifications* including such repair initiations as *What did you mean?*, *What did you say?*
2. *Reprise sentences* including full repeats of the trouble source utterances. Some of the examples discussed in (Purver, 2004) to illustrate this type of clarification requests can be re-analysed as topicalisation (Purver, 2004, Ex. 48 p. 62) and doing surprise (Purver, 2004, Ex. 47 p. 62).
3. *WH-substituted reprise sentences* including full repeats of the trouble source utterance where the trouble source is replaced by a question word.
4. *Reprise sluices* consisting of a bare question word or question phrase such as *To where?* and *Who?*.
5. *Reprise fragments* consisting of a partial repeat of the trouble source utterance. The trouble source is specified more precisely; only the relevant part of the trouble source utterance is repeated.
6. *Reprise gaps* consisting of a partial repeat of the trouble source utterance which projects that the trouble source immediately follows the repeated part.
7. *Conventional* repair initiations including all open-class repair initiations based on excuses, question words and *eh?*-like expressions.
8. *Gap fillers* including repair initiations dealing with trouble in production in contrast to all other preceding types of clarification requests.

Because different functions might be expressed by a clarification request of the same form, Purver (2004) analyses the *clarification readings* to cover the correspondence between the form and the meaning of the repair initiations.

1. *Clausal* reading can be mapped to phrases like *Are you asking/asserting P?*, *Is it X about which you are asking/asserting P(X)?* or *For which X are you asking/asserting P(X)?* where *X* represents the trouble source.
2. *Constituent* reading can be mapped to one of the following template questions: *What/who is X?*, *What/who do you mean by X?* or *Is it Y that you mean by X?*.
3. *Lexical* reading targets the surface form of the trouble source utterance and requires a repetition as a response. It can be mapped to questions like *Did you utter X?* or *What did you utter?*.
4. *Correction* reading can be mapped to the question *Did you intend to/should you have uttered X (instead of Y)?*.

In light of recent academic publications on repair initiations in cross-linguistic CA studies discussed in Section 2.3.5, specifically (Dingemanse et al., 2014), several points for critiques may arise regarding this classification of clarification requests. We keep in mind that the work by Purver (2006) was published a decade earlier; however there was a body of publications on repair already available, such as (Schegloff, 1987a, 1992, 2000). For instance, some utterances may be formatted as repair initiations but have a different interactional function, such as expressing surprise and topicalisation (not listed as possible readings). In addition, repair initiations designed to deal with troubles in understanding are put together with strategies for dealing with troubles in production (e.g. *gap fillers*). From the CA perspective, *gap fillers* correspond to self-initiated other-repair, and thus are sequentially completely different from all other types. Therefore, modifications in the classification proposed by Purver (2004) may be needed in order to better comply with studies in CA, and therefore better reflect the state of the art in CA-informed dialogue research.

Nevertheless, the general idea of having a map between various forms of doing a particular action in conversation (e.g. repair initiation formats) and the basic meaning behind these forms (e.g. request for repetition to resolve troubles in hearing) is reasonable, while some inconsistencies in the classification of readings and examples provided in (Purver, 2004) can be identified. For instance, the correction reading is illustrated by three examples, one of which contains an other-correction (Purver, 2004, Example 70, p. 69) and the other two contain self-corrections (Purver, 2004, Examples 71 and 72, p. 69), therefore it may be confusing how to interpret this reading from the perspective of the classification of various forms of repair other-initiations.

Ginzburg et al. (2007) analyse similarities between same-turn self-correction and other types of repair. They motivate their study by CA research, but choose to use an existing HPSG-based formalism described for instance in (Purver, 2004) and criticised from the CA perspective earlier in this section. Nonetheless, (Ginzburg et al., 2007) succeeded in including same-turn self-corrections in an HPSG-based formalism, which previously aimed at covering only clarification requests (repair other-initiations in CA terminology). In this way they showed that there is a possibility to describe the repair system by one, complete formal model. However, the critique points regarding the relationship between repair initiations and turn-taking and various ways of dealing with troubles in understanding and production remain valid for the extended model, too.

Schlangen (2004) analyses communication problems leading to clarification requests focusing on trouble source types (what caused the communication problem). Building on the classifications by (Clark, 1996) and (Allwood, 1995), Schlangen (2004) makes clear that a more fine-grained classification of causes for requesting clarification in dialogue may be needed. Specifically, the author argues that a model distinguishing between different cases in Example 2.2 would be an advantage. To approach different sources of trouble from the computational perspective, Schlangen (2004) suggests to use the classification scheme presented here in Table 2.3 and compares it to the classifications introduced by (Clark, 1996) and (Allwood, 1995).

Example 2.2. Different types of causes for clarification used in (Schlangen, 2004, Ex. (12)) to illustrate the need for an extended classification.

a. A I ate a Pizza with chopsticks the other day
   B A Pizza with chopsticks on it?
b. A Please give me a double torx.
   B What's a torx?
c. A Please give me a double torx.
   B Which one?
d. A Every wire has to be connected to a power source.
   B Each to a different one, or can it be the same for every wire?

From the CA perspective, factors such as speakers' linguistic and professional identities and preferences play a role in speakers' selection of a specific format of a repair initiation. Speaker B in Example 2.2.b. positions herself as a novice in torx matters with her repair initiation, while speaker B in Example 2.2.c. positions herself as knowledgeable in torx matters. In addition, utterances may be designed as repair initiations, but may in fact have a different function. For instance, the repair initiation produced by B in Example 2.2.a. may be analysed as a joke not requiring an explanation.

Level	Clark, 1996	Allwood, 1995	Schlangen, 2004
1	Execution & attention	Contact	Establishing contact
2	Presentation & identification	Perception	Speech recognition
3	Meaning & understanding	Understanding	3a: parsing 3b: resolving underspecification 3c: contextual relevance, computing the rhetorical connection
4	Proposal & consideration	Reaction to main evocative function	Recognising speaker's intentions; evaluating resulting discourse structure

Table 2.3: Models of sources of troubles in conversation

Other-initiated self-repair when the machine is the trouble-speaker (the user initiates and the machine carries out the repair) is explored in (Gehle et al., 2014). Based on a corpus of video-recorded human-robot interactions in a museum, the authors analyse multimodal interactional resources used by museum visitors to signal troubles in understanding the robot's talk and dealing with the robot's misunderstandings. The authors conclude that "different types of trouble [...] lead to a similar way of dealing with trouble" (Gehle et al., 2014, p. 367).

The potential user of a Communicative ICALL system is a language learner who may have troubles in comprehension. While user-initiated repair has been the subject of research studies in human-robot interaction and dialogue systems, not much attention has been paid to text-based human-computer interaction. A chat-based Conversation-for-Learning may provide opportunities for the language learner to engage in repair sequences with linguistic trouble source. Hence, it may be expected that language learners will initiate repair in order to deal with troubles in comprehension.

This book seeks to contribute to the research on computer-mediated native/non-native speaker communication by a microanalytic study of sequences of other-initiated self-repair when the native speaker is the trouble-speaker. Specifically, repair initiation formats and practices of referencing the trouble source in the repair initiations are of interest. In addition, practices of dealing with such repair initiations deployed by native speakers may provide patterns for repair carry-out. Based on the results of the empirical study, the problem of computational modelling of a system's reaction to learner's repair initiation will be addressed. The machine will need to recognise repair initiations, to extract the trouble source and to deliver an appropriate response. The results of the study will improve language understanding for dialogue systems tailored for second language learners, and may be included in user and expert models for Communicative ICALL applications.

2.4.3 Conversation Analysis in Human-Robot Interaction

Microanalysis of recordings of human-human interaction have been used to create patterns for human-robot interactions. Methods of Conversation Analysis focusing on talk-in-interaction and Interaction Analysis focusing on use of multimodal resources have been employed for this purpose. Specifically, researchers paid attention to moments in interaction such as dialogue openings and closings (Pitsch et al., 2009; Bono et al., 2014), interactional resource coordination (Yamazaki et al., 2008), managing participation (Katagiri et al., 2004; Pitsch et al., 2013a), referential practices (Pitsch and Wrede, 2014) and engagement (Rich et al., 2010).

Sussenbach et al. (2014) use ethnographic methods in order to find an empirically grounded model for motivation in a task-based interaction setting with robots where robots play the role of a fitness companion for indoor cycling. Yamazaki et al. (2008) employed CA methods to develop a museum guide robot that moves its head at interactionally significant points during its explanation of an exhibit. Patterns of coordination of verbal and non-verbal actions obtained from human guide-visitor interactions positively influenced visitors' reaction to robot non-verbal behaviour.

These studies showed that the transfer of interaction patterns from human-to-human interaction into human-robot interaction resulted in a positive interaction experience with robot companions.

The task of creating a functional specification for an artificial companion has been addressed using ethnographic methods (Yaghoubzadeh et al., 2013; Kramer et al., 2013). The focus of the study was on acceptability of the companion by a specific group of target users, namely, elderly people and people with mental disabilities. However, it is quite a challenging task to evaluate non-existing technology, therefore, results of studies with a similar focus may be contradictiory. Nonetheless, the authors succeeded in finding out how an artificial companion can be integrated into the daily routine of potential user groups by an analysis of what the people *really do* as opposed to other projects with similar ambitions where an artificial application scenario was invented and the potential users were confronted with it.

Inspired by CA, conversation openings with a robot museum guide have been studied in (Pitsch et al., 2009). An Aibo robot dog acting as a museum guide in a Japanese museum was provided with a simple pause-and-restart strategy to ensure visitors' attention. The same strategy is frequently used by people in conversations when they notice that their conversation partners do not listen. The authors showed that, similarly to human interactions, openings have a significant effect on a user's engagement in the continuation of the interaction. However, the robot showed in only 52.9% of the cases a "contingent entry into a focused encounter" (Pitsch et al., 2009, p. 991).

A similar study was set up in a German arts museum with a humanoid Nao robot focusing on the influence of the robot's gaze on visitor participation in interactions with multiple visitors (Pitsch et al., 2013a,b). Specifically, the situations of inclusion of an additional participant into an ongoing dialogue and disengaging a participant from a group were in focus. Pitsch et al. (2013b) analysed video recordings of real-world interactions of museum visitors with a robot museum guide as compared to interactions with a human tour guide. The authors conclude that knowledge about interactional coordination, incremental processing and strategies for proactive shaping users' conduct is required for a robot museum guide in order to manage real-world interactional situations. These studies show how important every tiny detail of an interaction is and how much influence it can have on the interaction continuation. Nothing is unimportant!

Schnier et al. (2011) used CA methods to investigate the influence of an augmented-reality device on interaction using a head-mounted display. They showed that forms of interaction change as compared to face-to-face communication, but their function remains the same, and that the changed forms are the result of negotiated adaptation processes. These findings confirm results reported in studies of Computer-Mediated Communication saying that the communication medium changes the set of available interactional resources, but the new set is successfully used to execute specific interactional functions, for instance, dealing with trouble in interaction (Kitade, 2000; Kim, 2003).

All studies discussed in this section show that microanalysis of human understanding of social actions expressed through various modalities in interaction is important for the development of the interaction process and users' engagement or disengagement. Looking at every tiny detail in dialogues between language learners and native speakers may provide valuable insights into the role and the consequences of each single contribution of each participant at every moment of an interaction. Patterns obtained from microanalysis of human-human dialogues belonging to a specific speech exchange system may help to make dialogue systems and conversational agents better communicators. This book describes how we can take a step in this direction. Supported by the findings in the HRI domain, a successful application of CA methods for dialogue design in Communicative ICALL can be expected. Nevertheless, because nothing is unimportant, we need to bear in mind that every modelling assumes a simplification to some extent. The degree of simplification will play a crucial role in the model effectiveness and the later "naturalness" of the resulting dialogue system.

2.5 Conversational interfaces and chatbots

The research described in this book was initiated in April 2011 and finished by the end of 2015. At the beginning of this research, it was not so easy to implement the idea of having a machine that communicates with the users, who are language learners just via instant messenger by simply adding a new contact to the contact list. While chatbots and conversational interfaces have already existed for commercial applications more than ten years, they have normally been deployed as web chat integrated into a website of the vendor. Instant messenger providers usually explicitly prohibited integrating chatbots as chat users. Fortunately, the vision of a chatbot that is a friend from a contact list became reality by the end of this research as the big instant messenger providers such as Facebook, Telegram, Kik, WhatsApp and others announced their chatbot APIs to facilitate chatbot integration into messengers. This was in turn a reaction of businesses to the fact that the majority of internet users spend most of their time in messengers. In this way, new possibilities for research on dialogue systems and conversational interfaces were opened.

With this background, this section has two purposes. First, it provides a review of chatbot APIs for several messengers and discusses opportunities to implement a chatbot for practicing second language conversation using the respective API in Section 2.5.1. Second, several existing chatbots for foreign language conversation are discussed from the perspective of interaction management, dealing with learner language and user models in Section 2.5.2. For the review of the current state of the art in this technology for practicing conversation, we focus here mainly on two types of chatbots:

1. Duolingo and Mondly chatbots deployed on language-learning portals (web and mobile);
2. Busuu Quizbot deployed as a messenger bot.

This section will be closed with a discussion of various approaches to the evaluation of chatbots and conversational interfaces.

2.5.1 Chatbot development landscape and applications

Here we look at the huge number of tools and various tool types for rapid prototyping and production chatbot development that have emerged since 2015. Two main types of tools supporting chatbot development exist on the market today:

1. Natural Language Understanding as a Service (NLUaaS) providing pre-trained and extendable machine learning models to support understanding of the user's *intents*;
2. Instant Messenger APIs supporting deployment of the chatbots to messengers.

Each of these categories will be discussed more intensively below.

In addition to these two types of tools chatbot developers can also choose to use speech technologies (speech recognition and text-to-speech), face recognition, sentiment analysis tools and many others to improve user experience of their chatbots. Depending on the application case, different aspects of user experience may be important. The book by Shevat (2017) may be good reading as it explains various factors in interactions with users that need to be considered to make good chatbot design choices.

Natural Language Understanding as a Service

Understanding human language is a core requirement for all chatbots. However, nowadays it is no longer necessary to develop a separate, standalone language-understanding solution for each dialogue system. A new type of service emerged on this market in the last five years called Natural Language Understanding as a Service (NLUaaS). Different vendors offer libraries accessible via API to support easy development of conversational services. Representatives of this category are:

1. api.ai acquired by Google in 2016 (currently renamed to Dialogflow),
2. wit.ai acquired by Facebook in 2015,
3. RASA, an open-source platform, rasa.ai,
4. IBM Watson Conversation,
5. Amazon LEX,
6. Microsoft LUIS,
7. Recast.ai,
8. SNIPS.

Most of these APIs also support integration of the created chatbots into various messengers. All of these APIs are grounded in the Belief-Desire-Intention theory. All of them except for LEX work with so-called *intents* as a basic unit. Intents are representations of utterances with the purpose to manage the variance in human languages in expressing meanings and performing social actions through language. Intents represent the pragmatic purpose of the entire utterance and usually contain *concepts*, which may be named entities or other special important parts of an intent needed to perform a specific action in response to the user's intent.

Because each potential utterance of a potential user needs to be mapped to an intent, and the number of utterances expressing the same intent can be quite large (thousands of utterances expressing three to five intents), NLUaaS platforms offer machine learning capabilities. Developers can train NLUaaS with their own data to get better results in intent recognition and concept extraction. An example of an utterance with labelled concepts and the intent is provided in Figure 2.2.

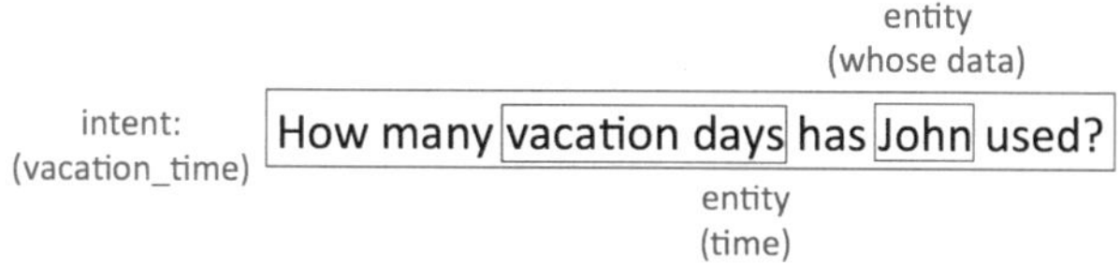

Fig. 2.2: A labelled utterance with concepts and intent

Which of the NLUaaS platforms is better depends on the application case and it is reasonable to compare the performance of several services prior to starting the development of a practical system. Because the NLUaaS systems are under continuous development, the results of such an evaluation may be very different at different points of time for the same data.

Braun et al. (2017) systematically compare the performance of six of the NLU services: LUIS, Watson Conversation, api.ai, wit.ai, Amazon LEX and RASA. Arguing that wit.ai and LEX do not support batch import of new data, Braun et al. (2017) continued the evaluation for the four remaining services: LUIS, RASA, api.ai and Watson Conversation. The authors compared their performance on two corpora: Chatbot Corpus (public transportation domain) and StackExchange (user support domain). Both corpora are available under the Creative Commons CC BY-SA 3.0 licence[5]. The study showed that on these two datasets, LUIS had the highest F-Score (0.916) and performed better than the competitors on each dataset. The lowest F-Score was achieved by api.ai (0.687) and this service also performed worse that the competitors on both datasets. RASA (0.821) and Watson Conversation (0.752) showed different labelling quality depending on the dataset. To obtain more details on the evaluation on each intent and concept per vendor, the reader is invited to go through the original publication (Braun et al., 2017).

Savenkov (2017) compares the performance of seven different NLU services: api.ai, wit.ai, Watson Conversation, LUIS, Amazon LEX, Recast.ai and SNIPS. While the first six are cloud services, SNIPS runs on a device. The SNIPS.ai dataset[6] containing seven different intents was used for the evaluation. The intents in the dataset came from the domains of search (events, books, movies etc.), weather, restaurant booking, music (play music, add to playlist) and book rating. On this mixed-domain dataset, the performance of the NLU systems was different from the

[5] https://github.com/sebischair/ NLU-Evaluation-Corpora
[6] https://github.com/snipsco/nlu-benchmark

results reported by Braun et al. (2017). The best F-Score was reached by Watson Conversation (0.997) followed by api.ai (0.996), LUIS (0.992), SNIPS (0.975) wit.ai (0.974), Recast.ai (0.97) and finally Amazon LEX (0.965). Amazon LEX was trained on a smaller dataset because of API limitations, as Savenkov (2017) notes. All of the NLU services show quite high F-Scores that differ a lot from the results reported in (Braun et al., 2017). Savenkov (2017) mentions that for some types of intents (e.g. get weather) all providers are good. However, for other intents that are hard to classify, having a good service provider is crucial. He concludes that although LUIS, api.ai and Watson Conversation have the best overall performance, wit.ai should be chosen if broad language coverage is of interest. Because the performance varies very much for different intents, it is recommended to test several providers with the specific dataset of each application. In this way the two studies comparing the performance of different NLUaaS providers come to the same conclusion, though different F-Score numbers.

A distinct type of NLUaaS platform is represented by Pandorabots[7], which does not work with the concept of intents. Pandorabots is based on the AIML (Artificial Intelligence Markup Language), which was already mentioned in Section 2.2.3, page 22. AIML, an XML dialect, is an example of pattern-based language understanding. The main building block of an AIML file representing the brain of the chatbot is a so called *category*. An example of an AIML category is shown below:

```
<category>
   <pattern>ARE YOU HUNGRY</pattern>
   <template>
     YEAH! Let's order a Pizza!
   </template>
</category>
```

Each category provides an instruction within the `<template>` tag how to respond to an utterance that matches the pattern described in the `<pattern>` tag. A detailed specification of the AIML 2.0 language is provided in Pandorabots Playground where new Pandorabots developers called *botmasters* can create an account. The older version of the AIML 1.0 standard is described in (Wallace, 2003).

MacTear et al. (2016, Chapter 7) discuss in detail how to create a chatbot using the Pandorabots API. In addition to the creation of informal conversations of question answering on a specific topic, various location-based services can be integrated into an AIML-based chatbot, as MacTear et al. (2016, Chapter 7) explain. In this sense, an AIML-based chatbot designed with the intention to provide a useful service to its users, may offer a good solution.

While the first eight NLU services provide their own language models, which can be trained on the developer-defined utterances with labelled intents and concepts (also referred to as *mentions*) to cover also unseen inputs, botmasters in Pandorabots need to define all the possible input strings manually. Although several approaches to creating AIML files automatically from text data have been described in the literature

[7] https://www.pandorabots.com

(De Gasperis et al., 2013), the majority of AIML-based chatbots have been created by manual AIML dialogue script editing.

AIML allows mapping of multiple surface strings to the same meaning (or intent) by the symbolic reduction tag `<srai>`. Following this tag, the same response/action will be produced to all utterances that are linked as synonyms using `<srai>`. Though there is no explicit notion of intents in AIML, the symbolic reduction mechanism has the same effect as the intent labelling in the intent-based NLUaaS systems such as the first eight systems mentioned at the beginning of this section.

None of the NLUaaS platforms is specialised on learner language or communication with language learners. Section 11.3.4 will discuss some ideas to make the NLU services mentioned in this section useful for a chatbot offering practicing conversation as a service.

Instant Messenger APIs

While the NLUaaS providers take care of a working back end of a chatbot, the instant messenger providers offer a front end to enable live communication between the chatbot and its users. However, it is not mandatory to use any of the NLUaaS platforms or machine learning to create a chatbot. Depending on the use case, simple rule-based conversations may already be sufficient for a specific service.

Though it is possible to deploy a chatbot from one back end to different messengers, each messenger has its own special requirements, making special connectors between the chatbot in the back end and the messenger necessary. Some of the NLUaaS providers, for instance LUIS and api.ai therefore also offer a connection service where a chatbot developed using the respective service can be connected to various messengers.

Instant messengers provide their own APIs for chatbot integration, for example Slack[8], Facebook Messenger[9], Telegram[10], Skype[11], Kik[12], Viber[13] and Twilio[14]. The examples are usually provided for node.js and Python, sometimes also for other languages such as Java and C++. Normally, chatbots use a REST API or web sockets, and therefore can be implemented in any language.

2.5.2 Chatbots for practicing foreign language conversation

Several language-learning portals offer chatbots to their customers as a new learning resource. Here we will take a closer look at two of them: the Duolingo chatbot and the Mondly chatbot. As discussed earlier in Section 2.2.3, learner language understanding may be a very difficult task depending on the proficiency level of the

[8] https://api.slack.com/bot-users
[9] https://developers.facebook.com/docs/messenger-platform
[10] https://core.telegram.org/bots/api
[11] https://dev.skype.com/bots
[12] https://dev.kik.com
[13] https://developers.viber.com/docs
[14] https://www.twilio.com/docs/api

learner. Therefore, input restriction is one of the possibilities to deal with learner language. In addition, the system's initiative helps to manage all possible turn types and also the user's input in this way. In this section, we look at the two chatbots from the perspective of input restriction and turn management.

Duolingo Chatbots

At the beginning of 2017 Duolingo announced that a new user experience is now available for language learners: they can practice conversation with bots. Duolingo chatbots were at this time only available for iPhone users in the Duolingo app. The users have to complete at least three levels in a new language in order to activate the chatbots. Those of the readers who would like to see the bots but do not have the required hardware or the required passion may be interested to look at the review videos of Duolingo bots that can be found on YouTube.

Fig. 2.3: An excerpt of the Duolingo chatbot list for French

Figure 2.3 shows the first step in the interaction management with the bots. Every chatbot in the chatbot list covers only one topic. In accordance with Duolingo didactic principles, the users can activate more advanced chatbots only after they have completed their conversations on all preceding levels.

The Duolingo bots are designed for learning. They therefore offer different kinds of help to facilitate comprehension and production in the language to be learned. Figure 2.4 shows how a conversation with the bot called *Welcome aboard!* starts.

This chatbot helps to practice simple interaction openings (greetings) and closings (good-byes). At the top of the screen the learner sees the objective of this exercise. If needed, a translation of the bot's utterance can be shown. If the learner has difficulties with production, the bot offers help with the reply. In this way, the user can deal with difficulties with comprehension and production within the chat app and without any repair initiations.

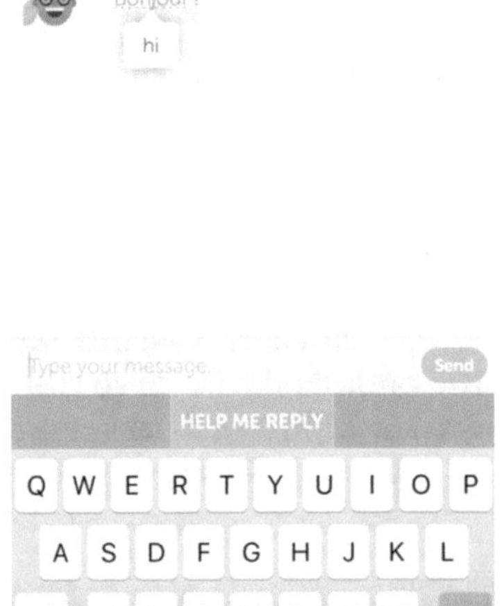

Fig. 2.4: Duolingo chatbot for French starts a new conversation

As the reader will see later in the discussion of the data in Part II of the book, non-native speakers can use similar resources (online dictionaries and machine translation) to deal with problems in comprehension and production. However, they need to leave the messenger for this. Although such little helpers make the interaction with the bot less similar to a natural native/non-native speaker interaction, they anticipate potential problems and offer an aid.

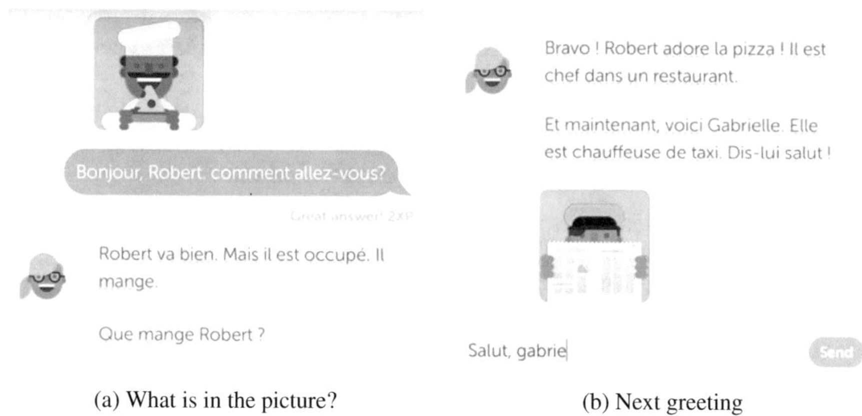

(a) What is in the picture?

(b) Next greeting

Fig. 2.5: Continuation of the interaction

After a correct production of a greeting, the user receives extra points for the performance (Figure 2.5a). In this way, the greetings-bot becomes a mixture between a conversation partner and a teacher who evaluates the performance. Then the bot continues asking questions about the first personage shown in a picture: "What does Robert eat?" (at the bottom of Figure 2.5a).

The interaction becomes even more similar to a language classroom talk, and the user is asked to describe a picture.

After the user's response about the first picture, the chatbot presents the next picture 2.5b and again asks the user to greet the personage in the picture. This allows the user to practice different forms of interaction openings. However, the chatbot does not allow the user to take the initiative. The chatbot has absolute control over turn management.

In addition to these input control mechanisms, there is one more input restriction implemented in the Duolingo bot: the user is not allowed to type as she/he wants. The user's input is controlled while the user is typing. If the user tries to type something

Fig. 2.6: Input restriction

that the bot does not expect as a valid input, the app shows a message in the keyboard area "Not an accepted word". This form of feedback is shown in Figure 2.6.

Such a word-level input restriction has the advantage for the system that there is no need to deal with learner errors for language understanding. This form of input restriction may be also an advantage for language learners, who receive indirect system feedback about their errors: they only have the information about the correctness of their production (yes/no), but no specific information about the error diagnosis is provided. In this way, a simple and robust solution is found for the problem with an automated error correction.

Unfortunately, Duolingo decided to suspend chatbots after a while. In the beginning of 2018, Duolingo forum was full of sad posts written by users who embraced this kind of technology. One os the users, for instance, puts it:

> I miss my only friends... I mean chat bots.. (yes, I got attached). I didn't even get a chance to say farewell! This feels like the last scene in Her...when all the A.I. left and everyone was sad and miserable again. I didn't even get a chance to say au revoir, adios amigos. Where did they go? Are they having a bot party I wasn't invited to?[15]

However, Duolingo promises to bring the bots and the conversations back in a "more integrated way"[16].

Mondly Chatbot

Mondly is a language-learning portal accessible as a web application[17] or a mobile application for different platforms. We will take a closer look at the chatbots working in the Mondly web application. In contrast to the Duolingo three-level restriction, Mondly's language learner only needs to complete the tutorial in order to see the chatbot on the web site; see Figure 2.7.

By clicking on the chatbot icon the learner is redirected to the window where a number of different chatbots are offered (Figure 2.8). However, the user needs a premium account to activate the chatbots other than the chatbot that helps to practice the greetings topic (or Hello-bot for short).

Figure 2.9 shows a short excerpt of a conversation with the Hello-bot on Mondly. Every chatbot's utterance is pronounced so that the learners can practice listening comprehension in addition to reading comprehension. While the Mondly chatbot provides the opportunity to practice pronunciation using speech recognition technology in addition to the written responses, it is even more restrictive than the Duolingo chatbot in terms of users' input control. The learner is explicitly asked to pick one of the phrases from a short list presented as possible responses to the chatbot question,

[15] https://forum.duolingo.com/comment/26865418/They-Removed-Chat-bots-Now-I-m-confused

[16] https://support.duolingo.com/hc/en-us/articles/360002594432-What-happened-to-the-Chatbots-

[17] https://www.mondlylanguages.com

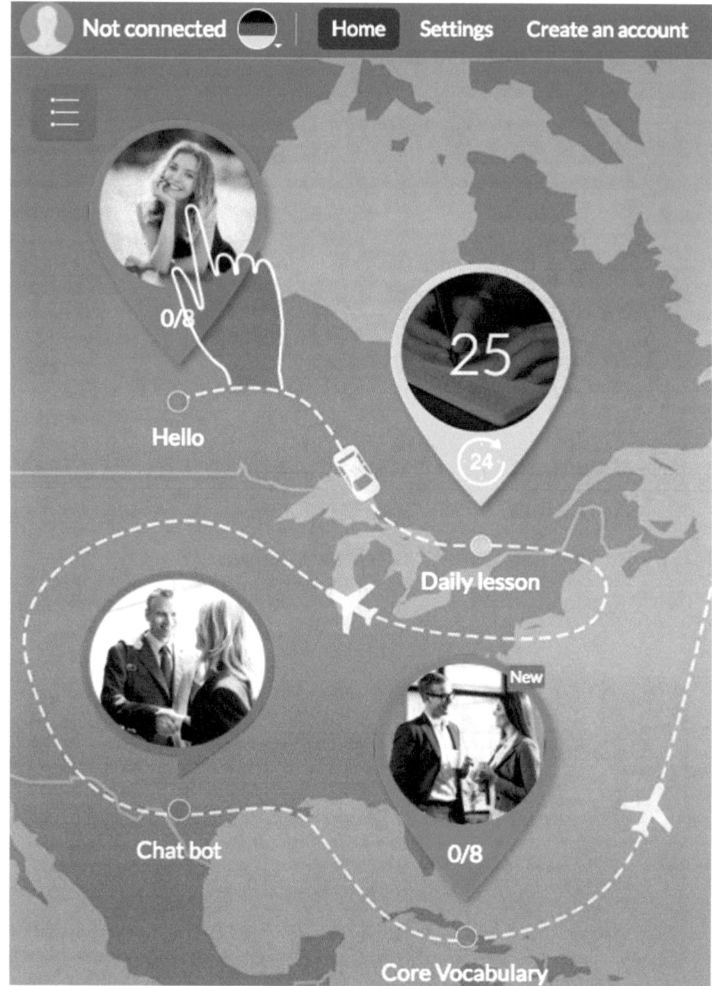

Fig. 2.7: The accessibility of the chatbot at Mondly

which is one of the techniques of input restriction discussed earlier in Section 2.2.3. Both content restriction and activity restriction are applied in the Mondly chatbot. The learner does not even have a chance to say her or his real name in response to the question "What is your name?" Nevertheless, very small pieces of learner-defined input are allowed. For instance, in response to the question "Where are you from?", the user can select one of the predefined places or even type their own place name using the template "I am from _____."

Another specific characteristic of the Mondly chatbot is that it does not support chat communication as it happens naturally in instant messengers. The user cannot re-read what has been said earlier: all the past utterances disappear from the screen and a new question is shown to the user.

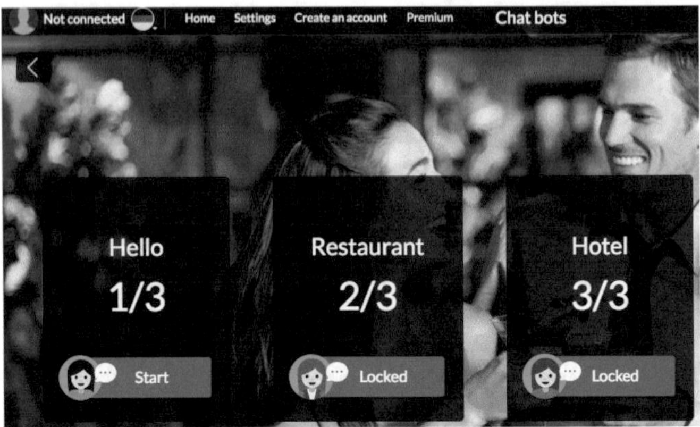

Fig. 2.8: Bots selection at Mondly

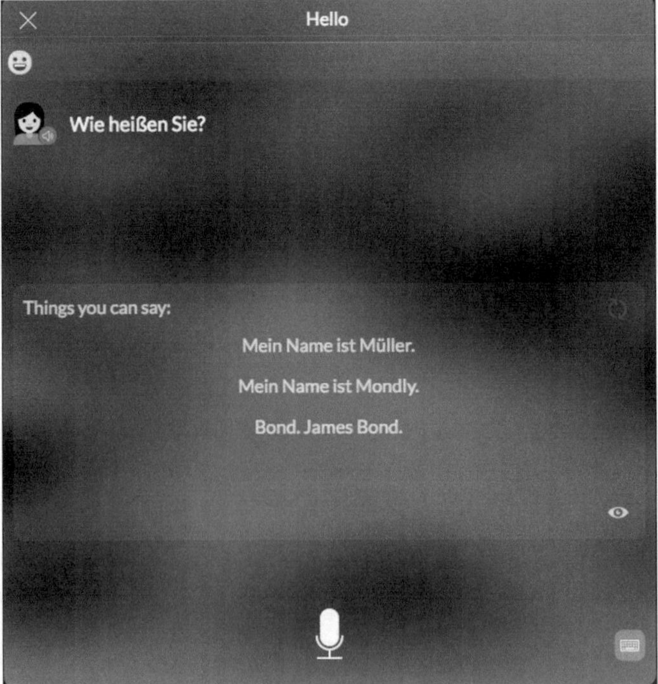

Fig. 2.9: A conversation with the Mondly chatbot

Busuu Quizbot

The Busuu Quizbot operating in Facebook Messenger was created using the Microsoft LUIS API (Rubio, 2017). The Microsoft Chatbot Builder supports deployment to a number of platforms using the same back-end functionality. In this way, the Busuu Quizbot initially created for Microsoft Teams was later deployed to Facebook Messenger.

The primary purpose of this chatbot is vocabulary training with a quiz. Thus, typical problems with learner language understanding, error correction and response generation are here related to a quiz situation, which is also a specific speech exchange system.

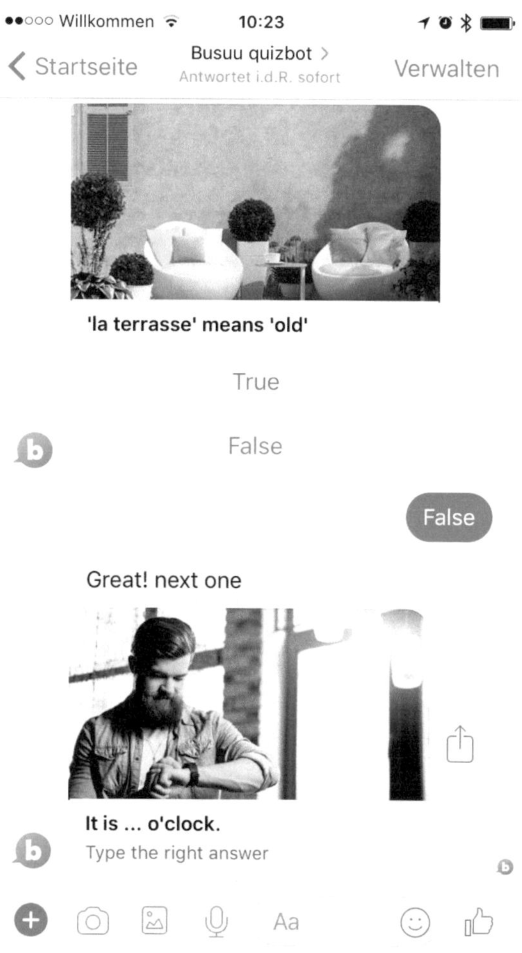

Fig. 2.10: Busuu Quizbot

Language learners will be asked at the beginning which language they want to practice. At the time of writing this review, three languages were offered: German, Spanish and French. All the questions and all the subtitles (explanations of the quiz tasks) are posted in English. After the language is set, the learners will be asked about their proficiency level: beginner, elementary or intermediate. After this step, they can make a choice on how many questions from five to 25 they prefer to have. The settings are finished after this step and the quiz starts. Figure 2.10 shows an excerpt of such a quiz.

The Quizbot employs the short response functionality of the Messenger API to capture responses from the user. Buttons for short replies such as "True" and "False" in Figure 2.10 allow dealing with the potential variance in learner input, because even for questions requiring only a yes/no answer the number of valid answers may be large. In this way, the Quizbot simply transfers a traditional multiple-choice-like quiz structure into the messenger.

Learner-error recognition is therefore quiz-specific, too. The Quizbot knows which answers are correct. It provides positive feedback after correct answers, which is usually simple feedback confirming the correctness. After incorrect answers, it either provides simple feedback giving only the information about incorrectness, or sometimes also presents the correct version. How much such types of feedback are helpful depends on many variables, including learner level of proficiency and motivation (Lipowsky, 2015). Feedback designed to support learning is also called *formative feedback*; see for instance (Shute, 2008; Narciss, 2013).

Chapter summary

This chapter provided an overview of the most important research disciplines relevant for the design and development of a novel type of conversational system for practicing conversation in a foreign language. The important design and research questions include:

- Which communication modality to choose?
- Which user models and interaction models are most helpful?
- How to deal with learner language when using NLP tools?
- How to handle learner errors?
- Should feedback be generated and if yes, in which way?
- Can error-annotated learner corpora be helpful?

Further, this chapter discussed the potential scientific relationship between Conversation Analysis and Communicative ICALL. Aspects of chat-based conversations as a specific speech exchange system have been discussed. Because Conversation Analysis usually works with naturally occurring conversations, the problem of data collection in instant messengers has been addressed. Earlier academic publications on native/non-native speaker chat data have been introduced. Different views on specific repair types from a CA and SLA perspective have been presented. Embedded corrections as a specific type of implicit feedback have been discussed.

After the intensive discussion of the relevant results in Conversation Analysis, this chapter provided a short overview of existing and ongoing cross-disciplinary publications where Conversation Analysis is used for design and evaluation of dialogue systems and robotics. Special attention has been paid to research on repair for dialogue systems.

Finally, an overview of recent technological changes in the area of chatbot design and Natural Language Understanding has been presented. Current examples of chatbots for practicing conversation have been discussed from the perspective of dealing with learner language and input restriction.

Part II

Using Conversation Analysis for Dialogue Modelling

3 Patterns for Expert-Novice Chat

Abstract This chapter documents the results of the data exploration and provides a bird's eye perspective on various ways to construct identities of language learners and language experts in instant messaging conversation. Different interaction practices how chat participants orient to their linguistic identities will be the subject of the detailed analysis in this chapter.

3.1 Introduction

Due to the way in which the participants for the data collection for the present study were acquired, it seems natural that the participants of the dialogues had particular expectations regarding their potential interaction co-participants. The native speakers knew that they would communicate with young people from Belarus who are studying German as a foreign language. The learners had been contacted through their university, and practicing conversation was one of the reasons for them to participate. Therefore, participants on both sides interacted from the very beginning through the lens of their expectations of whom they would be interacting with. For the German native speakers, it was a person who was studying their native language. For the learners, it was a person who spoke the language that they were studying as the mother tongue. Such expectations become visible in the interaction through the phenomenon known as *recipient design* and *stances* (Sacks et al., 1974; Hutchby, 1995; Pillet-Shore, 2012). The full description of the data collection process can be found in Appendix A and may be of interest for readers who plan to compile similar datasets.

Guided by the stances and recipient design, participants in the conversation construct their identities of language learners and language experts in specific sequences of talk where the participants orient to their *differential language expertise*. This can be done in different ways, and sequences of repair with linguistic trouble source are probably the most prominent of them.

Repair sequences with linguistic trouble source have been analysed in the CA and SLA literature, and the findings were discussed in Chapter 2. However, the actions

S. Höhn, *Artificial Companion for Second Language Conversation*,
https://doi.org/10.1007/978-3-030-15504-9_3

and practices used by chat participants to position themselves as novices or experts are not limited to repair sequences. In the dataset collected for this research, three main classes of such actions were identified:

1. *Face work and evaluation*: In these sequences, the learner's level of second language proficiency is the subject of the talk. It may have the form of learners' excuses for mistakes, fishing for compliments or native speakers' (always positive) evaluations and encouragements;
2. *Meta-talk and learning together*: These are sequences where language learning becomes the subject of the talk. It may take place when, for instance, native speakers offer help in language learning tasks and exam rehearsal;
3. *Repair sequences with linguistic trouble source*: Such sequences include (but are not limited to) explanations of expressions unclear to the learner, corrections of linguistic errors, word searches, vocabulary checks and definition work.

In addition to the practices of talk-in-interaction where participants' linguistic identities become relevant, the form of the chat language chosen by some of the native speakers in conversations with learners differs a lot from the form of the language used, for instance, in retrospective interviews with the researcher. In conversations with learners, a variation of German close to a German standard may be preferred. For instance, the native speaker N01 starts every turn and every noun with a capital letter in chat with learners. In contrast, the same native speaker writes everything in lower case in the retrospective interview. The reader will find a more detailed discussion of examples of both in Section 8.2 with regard to the definition of linguistic error and language standard in chat. For the purposes of this chapter it is important to keep in mind that there are specific points in conversations, where linguistic identities of participants are made relevant. Besides these specific points, native speakers may *choose* to present themselves constantly as *role models*, as persons who use the language *correctly*.

The following sections of this chapter will analyse the three types of participants' orientation to their linguistic identities. The unit of analysis will be a turn. We can see a turn as a unit corresponding to a message in chat because this is what chat participants post and receive. They cannot intervene in a message-at-production prior to receiving the entire message, even if the message is long and could potentially be delivered in shorter units. For instance, turn parts belonging to different threads or topics can be delivered in separate messages or put into one long message. However, the speakers can start talking (that is producing a message) at any point of time; they do not have to fight for their right to talk. In this sense, chat can be seen as more relaxed than face-to-face or phone interaction. Participants take a turn when they think it is relevant, and they make it as long as they think iappropriate. Putting pieces belonging to different threads or topics into one turn is an interactional resource that participants make use of in order to deal with, for instance, trouble with their network connection.

3.2 Face work and evaluation

One of the most frequent practices used by learners to position themselves as language novices found in the dataset was the excuse for making mistakes which the learners have made and have not yet made. Such excuses have also been combined with a self-assessment as a not yet fully proficient speaker. Native speakers, in turn, replied with a positive evaluation of language knowledge and encouragement, positioning themselves as language experts in talk. In fact, such excuses and self-assessments were not real excuses, because there were not necessarily any real mistakes, and they did not do any harm to the talk. The function of these excuses and evaluations was to maintain face, as will be demonstrated with several examples.

The first prototypical sequence of this kind is shown in Example 3.1. The learner L07 makes her not-yet-perfect language skills, which the native speaker N03 might notice in the future, relevant in turn 8. It takes place just after the exchange of greetings in the very first conversation when the participants have just met.

Example 3.1. Small mistakes.

8	15:30:30	L07	das macht nichts...sofort bitte um Entschulding für meine Fehlerchen...´‘=)) it does not matter... immediately ask for apologise [* error: typo] for my errors [diminishing] ... [smile] *it does not matter... I immediately apologise for my small mistakes*
9	15:30:57	N03	kein problem! *no problem!*

The learner refers to her errors as “small mistakes" using a diminishing German form that marks the potential errors as not very large or not to be taken seriously. The native speaker accepts the apology. The fact that the learner apologises for all the “small mistakes" that she might make in the future shows that she assumes that N03 would notice them. In the words of Heritage (2012), it is his “territory of knowledge". With her apology, the learner L07 positions herself as a novice and, at the same time, assigns the role of language expert to the native speaker. By accepting of the apology in turn 9, N03 also accepts the role of the language expert that just has been assigned to him by the learner. Thus, the adjacency pair of apology-acceptance is used to construct identities of experts and novices in conversation.

With the “error announcement" and apology in turn 8, L07 gets permission for all possible “small mistakes" that may happen in the future. The permission is “granted" by the acceptance of the apology. The announcement of the possible errors allows her to save face in communication using a language that she has not yet fully mastered.

In Example 3.2, the learner L06 apologises in turn 10 for all the mistakes and errors that she has produced and will produce in the future. This happens at the very beginning of the conversation, after the participants have just met and exchanged greetings. Thus, there was not too much space for any mistakes, yet. In addition, she informs the native speaker that it might take longer for her to write in a foreign language using a computer keyboard. The native speaker evaluates learner’s German writing skills in turn 12 and positions himself as an expert in German. In addition, he says that it is okay to make mistakes in order to encourage the learner to keep on trying.

The native speaker switches his role from an expert to a non-expert in the same turn pointing out that he cannot write the learner's native language at all and emphasising her area of expertise. Further, in turn 13, the native speaker negotiates spelling rules, suggesting that writing everything in lower case does not count as an error. The learner agrees in turn 14 and positions herself again as a not yet fully competent speaker. She evaluates her comprehension competence as not sufficient to understand everything. In addition, she negotiates her right to ask for explanations and negotiates the convention that it is alright to do definition talk. The native speaker agrees in turn 15.

Example 3.2. Numerous errors.

10	15:33:19	L06	ich möchte mich zuerst für meine zahlreiche Fehlern entschuldigen. und du musst geduldig sein, damit so lange Zeit auf meine Antwort warten I would like first to apologise for my numerous errors [* error: wrong plural]. and you must be patient so that [* error: wrong conjunction] such a long time for my answer wait *First, I would like to apologise for my numerous errors. And you need to be patient because you will have to wait a long time for my responses*
11	15:33:37	L06	;)
12	15:35:13	N03	also bist jetzt hast du noch (fast) keinen fehler gemacht. und das ist ueberhaupt kein problem! ich kann gar kein russisch schreiben! *well, till now you have made (almost) no errors. and this is not a problem at all! I cannot write a single bit of Russian!*
13	15:35:23	N03	ist das ok wenn ich klein schreibe? is it ok if I write small? *is it ok if I write only lower case?*
14	15:39:18	L06	Gott sei Dank! du kannst schreiben, wie du willst, hoffentlich verstehe ich alles. wenn nicht, dann musst du dich ein bißchen bemühen, damit mir das erklären Thank God! you can write whatever you want. hopefully, I understand everything. if not, then you must make an effort a little bit so that [* error: wrong conjunction] explain me everything *Thank God! you can write however you want. I hope I understand everything. if not, you will have to try a little bit more to explain those things to me*
15	15:39:40	N03	na klar! *of course!*

Example 3.3 shows that a positive evaluation of the learner's language skills is not necessary a direct response to the learner's weak self-assessment. The learner L06 tells in turn 21 about the planned exams that will take place some time after the conversation. In turn 22, the native speaker first evaluates the new information and then encourages the learner. The encouragement takes the form of an evaluation of the learner's language proficiency.

After the assessment of language skills was made relevant at the beginning, N03 provides an additional positive evaluation of L03's skills in the continuation of the talk in turn 22. This chat session consists of 55 turns in total; thus, it is approximately the middle of the first conversation. The learner thanks the native speaker for the positive evaluation in turn 23. This looks more similar to a response to a compliment than to a receipt of a "grade". Here, the native speaker did not really have the time to assess the learner's skills in German, especially for the assessment of the probability of the learner passing the exams.

Example 3.3. Your German is very good.

21	15:47:51	L06	ich habe Prüfungen in Deutsch, Englisch, Literatur und Linguistik. Also 4 Prüfungen und 4 Tests in diesen Disziplinen. Um Prüfungen abzulegen, sollen wir zuerst Tests schreiben *I have exams in German, English, Literature and Linguistics. So, 4 oral exams and 4 written tests in these disciplines. In order to take the exams, we must first take the tests*
22	15:48:55	N03	das klingt nach viel arbeit. aber deutsch schaffst du auf jeden fall, dein deutsch ist sehr gut. studierst du auf lehramt? *that sounds to be a lot of work. but you will make it in German anyway, your German is very good. Are you studying to become a teacher?*
23	15:52:42	L06	danke. ja,aber ich werde nicht nur Lehrerin, sondern auch Dolmetscherin,wie uns versprochen wurde. Aber ich kann mich in dieser Rolle nicht vorstellen *thank you. yes, but I will become not only a teacher but also a translator, as it was promised to us. But I cannot imagine myself in this role*

The learner's apologies for her errors in her second language can be also followed by a confirmation of comprehension, as Example 3.4 illustrates. The learner makes many mistakes in a long narrative turn 165. The native speaker needs time to read the long message and to reply to the content of the message. The learner therefore has a chance to re-read the just-produced message and to detect errors in it, and even to produce an apology in turn 166. The native speaker first replies to the apology in turn 167 with a confirmation of comprehension instead of an explicit expression accepting or rejecting the apology.

In her apology in turn 166, the learner positions herself as a novice because she made mistakes. At the same time, she positions herself as a person who *can* recognise the errors in the long just-produced turn. The apology is accepted indirectly with the "I understand everything" in turn 167, at the same time showing that linguistic accuracy is not that important in this chat, but the fluency and the comprehension are important. N02 returns to the topic immediately, focusing on the social trajectory of this talk.

Example 3.5 shows a different case of a native speaker's evaluation in turn 406. The learner thanks the native speaker for the evaluation in turn 407. This example presents the final closing sequence of the last conversation (farewell for ever). The learner does not make the level of language proficiency relevant in the conversation, there are neither excuses nor self-assessments; thus, this evaluation was not elicited by the need to maintain face. The participants neither exchanged contact details to continue the communication as their private business, nor did they plan to meet again in some way. The evaluation is produced after eight long dialogues, so that the native speaker had enough time to get an impression about the real language proficiency of the learner.

Example 3.4. I understand everything.

165 13:58:47 L03 ich meine, das hängt von unserer Mentalität. bei und wollte fast niemand in einem Dorf wohnen, weil dort zu wenig Arbeitsplätze und und überhaupt Angebote vorhanden sind. die Menschen auf dem Lande trinken zu viel, vielleicht hast du darüber gehört, deshald streben die Jugendlichen in die Städte umziehen. und die die Kinder auf dem Lande haben wenige Ansprüche und hiesige Ausbildung gilt als unqualifiziert, und die Kinder aus dem Lande lernen oft in der Oberschule in der Stadt. aber über solche Situation kann man nur pauschal genommen reden. es gebt natürlich viele Ausnamen. und überhaupt das Leben ist heutzutage imme mehr nach Wsten orientiert und viele wohlhabende Bürger ziehen in die Dürfer um, nach dem europäischen Beispiel, aber sie arbeiten doch in der stadt
I mean, it depends on our mood [* missing separable prefix]. at and [* error: probably typo] wanted almost no one in a village live, because there are too few jobs and in general opportunities there. the people in rural areas drink too much, maybe you have heard about that, therefore [* error: typo] aspire [* error: word choice] the teenager to move [* error: word choice] in the cities. and the the [* error: double det.] children in rural areas have few demands and local education counts as unqualified, and the children from rural areas learn [* error: word choice] often in secondary school in the city. but one can speak about such situation only in average. there are [* error: typo] of course many exceptions [* error: typo]. and in general the life is nowadays more and more [* error: typo] oriented to the West [* error: typo] and many wealthy citizen move [* error: typo] to the villages, according to the European model, but they still work in the city
I mean, it depends on our mood. here almost no one wanted to live in a village, because there are too few jobs and in general opportunities there. the people in rural areas drink too much, maybe you have heard about that, therefore the young people seek to move to the cities. and the children in rural areas have low standards and local education counts as unqualified, and the children from rural areas often go to a secondary school in the city. but one can speak about such situation only on average. there are of course many exceptions. and in general life is nowadays more and more oriented to the West and many wealthy citizens move to the villages, according to the European model, but they still work in the city

166 14:03:58 L03 Entschuldigung für zahlreiche Fehler;)
Sorry for numerous mistakes [smile]

167 14:05:26 N02 ich verstehe alles :) Das ist echt interessant [... elided]
I understand everything [smile] It is really interesting [... elided]

The evaluation as part of the final closing sequence discloses the view of the native speaker on the past conversations as "what we did here was practicing conversation, and you did your job very well". The learner shares this view, which is confirmed by her "thank you... great honour..." in the response.

The evaluations can be connected to each other with backlink tokens such as *noch mal* (En.: one more time) and *wieder* (En.: again). This "here *again* a special word of praise" in turn 406 refers to a different conversation between these two participants where they talked about reading books and the native speaker was impressed by the learner's knowledge of German literature. A simplified excerpt is provided in Example 3.6 for a better understanding of the relationship.

Example 3.5. Final evaluation.

404	22:00:10	N01	Ich wünsche dir schon einmal viel Erfolg bei deinen letzten Prüfungen! *I wish you good luck on your final exams!*
405	22:00:23	N01	Und natürlich alles Gute für die Zukunft ;-) *And of course all the best for the future [smile]*
406	22:01:01	N01	Hier noch mal ein dickes Lob: Du sprichst sehr gut deutsch !!!! Here again a thick praise: you speak very good German !!!! *Here again a special word of praise: you speak very good German !!!*
407	22:02:27	L02	Vielen Dank! Das ist für mich sehr ehrenvoll das von dir zu hören!))) *Thank you very much! This is a great honour for me to hear this from you!*
408	22:02:45	L02	Ich wünsche dir auch alles Gute! *I wish you all the best, too!*
409	22:03:52	N01	Sehr gerne! (Es ist ja auch die Wahrheit!) Vielen Dank für deine Wünsche! Tschüss !!! *You are welcome! (This is just the truth!)* *Thank you very much for your wishes!* *Bye-bye !!!*
410	22:04:27	L02	Tschüss!!! *Bye-bye!!!*

Example 3.6. The native speaker evaluates the learner's knowledge of literature.

199	20:47:15	L02	Das Buch muss interessant sein. Es brachte mir "Den kleinen Prinz" von Exurery in Erinnerung. Ein kleiner Junge lernt mit der Welt der Erwachsenen, mit ihren Charakteren, Überzeugungen und dadurch auch mit sich selbst kennen. Früher, in der Schule, verstand ich dieses Buch nicht... *The book must be interesting. It brought "The Little Prince" by Exupéry to my mind. A little boy gets acquainted with the world of adults, with their moods, beliefs, and in the same way, with himself. Earlier, in school, I did not understand this book...*
200	20:48:48	L02	[elided, turn belongs to a different thread]
201	20:49:05	N01	Ja, das ist ein sehr guter Vergleich, so ähnlich ist "Sofies Welt" vom Prinzip her. Mensch, ich muss dir mal ein dickes Lob aussprechen. Du kennst dich wirklich sehr gut aus :-) *Yes, it is a good comparison, "Sofie's World" is in principle similar. Man, I just have to express a special praise for you. You really know a lot [smile]*

In Examples 3.6 and 3.5, the native speaker does *real* teacher-like evaluation in addition to the expression of being impressed. This praise is not elicited by the learner, but is a reaction to an impressive performance, as if it was provided by a teacher or a tutor. Finally, the native speaker presents himself as someone having the right to evaluate, which is accepted by the learner already before the last closing sequence.

3.3 Learning in meta-talk and collaborative learning

The data collection took place when most of the learners were in their examination period. Preparations for the exams and the results of the exams were therefore frequently a topic of the talk. In such parts of the dialogues, the participants talked about learning, but this meta-talk did not necessarily contribute to the construction of the learners' identities as novices or native speakers' identities as experts.

Example 3.7. I have good practice.

94	18:05:59	N03	was hast du heut s gemacht? *what did you do today?*
95	18:08:06	L07	heite war ich wie immer in der Uni...die letzte Vorprüfung abgegeben.... jetzt muss ich mich auf die Prüfung vorbereiten....die habe ich am montag schon-=((today [* error: typo] was I as always in the uni... the last test submitted.... now must I to the exam prepare....it have I on Monday already [sad smiley] *today I was at the university, as usual... I had the last preliminary test.... now I have to prepare for the exam.... it is already on Monday*
96	18:08:36	N03	oh
97	18:08:46	N03	na dann musst du viel lernen,oder? *ok, then you have to learn a lot don't you?*
98	18:09:47	L07	nun schaffe ich irgedwie..... erste Prüfung ist Deutsch...so habe ich gute Praxis jetzt :) *I will manage it somehow... the first exam is German.... so, I have good practice now*
99	18:10:11	N03	haha
100	18:10:18	N03	muendlich oder schriftlich?!!! *oral or written?!!!*

However, meta-talk about the exam preparation can be taken up by the native speaker as an invitation to rehearse the exam. The meta-talk can be transformed by the participants into online exam preparation and collaborative learning.

One such sequence of meta-talk ending up with an exam rehearsal is shown in Examples 3.7 and 3.8. The meta-talk starts in turn 95 in Example 3.7 as the learner tells the native speaker about the upcoming exam and her preparation after his invitation to tell about her day. The learner explicitly declares the conversation with the native speaker as conversation practice in turn 98. The native speaker interprets it as an invitation to "practice" the exam. After the learner tells the topics of the upcoming exam, which she obviously does not like, the native speaker starts questioning her about these topics in turn 103. Later in turns 145-147 the participants explicitly claim the talk-in-progress as an exam rehearsal. Turns 106-135 contain the "exam".

The reader is invited to look at the entire sequence in Appendix C Example C.1, page 321.

Example 3.8. Continuation of the talk from Example 3.7. The participants engage in an exam role play. N03 plays the role of the examiner, L07 has the student role.

101	18:11:08	L07	leider muss ich meinem Lektor über EU, Menschenrechte oder Globalisierung erzählen... *unfortunately I have to tell my lecturer about EU, human rights or globalisation...*
102	18:11:20	L07	:'(
103	18:12:09	N03	das sind doch aber spannende themen! *but those are exciting topics!*
104	18:12:26	N03	was denkst du denn ueber die EU und ihre derzeitige situation? *what do you think about the EU and its current situation?*
105	18:13:45	L07	insbesondere EU-Gremien und so viele Daten aufeinmal viel zu viel für ein Mädchen :) especially EU-committees and so many data [* error: lexical choice] at once [* error: missing space] too much for a girl *especially EU-committees and so much information at once too much for a girl*
...	...	...	[elided: turns 106-135 native speaker tries to elicit learner's talk on these topics]
136	18:37:44	N03	aber was ist nicht gut? *but what is not good?*
137	18:37:50	N03	in der EU? *in the EU?*
138	18:37:58	N03	an der globalisierung? *with globalisation?*
139	18:38:00	N03	...
140	18:38:02	N03	;-)
141	18:39:24	L07	hahaha........ Arbeitaplatzverlagerung, Ausbeutung im Süden, Überflutung von Informationen usw....!!! :) :) :) *hahaha workplace relocation, exploitation in the South, information flood etc.....!!!*
142	18:40:33	N03	ok
143	18:40:40	N03	usw klingt gut *etc sounds good*
144	18:40:43	N03	;-)
145	18:42:24	L07	willst du jetzt meine Prüfung mal repetieren..? :) want you now my exam repeat [* error: lexical choice]..? *do you want to rehearse my exam now?*
146	18:42:42	N03	ja *yes*
147	18:42:51	N03	also ich dachte das koennte nuetzlich sein *well I thought this could be useful*
148	18:43:02	L07	:)

A variant of post-exam work found in the dataset contains a sequence where the learner asks the native speaker questions that she had in her written test. She already knew the answers and just wanted to show the native speaker what the exam was about. However, in the majority of cases when the native speaker offered help for exam preparation, it did not go beyond meta-talk. The native speakers invited the learners to ask them questions when they prepared for the examinations. However, the learners did not make use of this opportunity to get help.

The meta-talk about language learning can also lead to discussions of the grammar systems of the languages spoken by the participants, as illustrated in Example 3.9. The learner explains in turn 72 why English is so difficult for her to learn. The native speaker compares English grammar to German in turn 74, pointing to a simpler system of determiners in English. The learner makes her general difficulties with determiners relevant in turn 76. Then, the roles of expert and novice change. The native speaker positions himself as a novice in Russian and Belorussian, asking how many determiners there are in those languages. The learner, in turn, positions herself as an expert in Russian/Belorussian by telling him that these languages do not have any determiners (turns 79-80). She formulates it as a surprise source. The roles change back in turns 81-84 where the native speaker formulates his turn in a way that is not easily accessible for the learner. The learner positions herself again as a novice by the repair initiation in turn 82, which starts a repair sequence

Example 3.9. Discussion of determiners after meta-talk (simplified).

72 18:07:40 L08)nun für mich Englisch ist sehr schwer... besonders die Zeitformen..."ein dunkler Wald")))
[smile] well for me English is very difficult... especially the tenses... "a dark forest"
well, English is very difficult for me... especially the tenses... quite confusing

74 18:09:44 N04 dafür gibt's im Englischen nur einen Artikel, während es auf deutsch 3 sind :-)
on the other hand there is only one determiner in English, while there are 3 in German

76 18:11:04 L08 haa)) ja Artikel ist ein Problem))
yes, determiner is a problem

78 18:14:05 N04 wieviele Artikel gibt es im (Weiß-)Russischen?
how many determiners are there in (White-)Russian?

79 18:14:51 L08 für dich wird es eine Überraschung!!!=)))
for you will it a surprise!!! [* error: missing main verb]
it will be a surprise for you!!!

80 18:15:06 L08 wir haben KEINE Artikel))))
we have NO determiners!

81 18:16:35 N04 oh... auch gut... dann erschließt man sich das wohl aus dem Zusammenhang?
oh... good too... then one must deduce it probably from the context

82 18:17:43 L08 verstehe ich nicht
I don't understand

83 18:18:16 L08 aaa verstehe verstehe=))
aaa understand understand
oh, I see, I see
84 18:19:15 N04 ah gut... hab grad überlegt, wie ich das umformulieren soll :-)
ah good... I was thinking how I should paraphrase it
85 18:19:30 L08 wir haben Endungen des Substantivs, die Kasus zeigen
we have endings of nouns which show the case

To sum up, the meta-talk about language learning can be used by chat participants as a preparation for collaborative learning. However, collaborative learning does not necessarily emerge after such meta-talk. Collaborative learning can relate to practicing conversation on a particular topic of interest (e.g. to prepare for an exam or an interview) or focus on specific aspects of the language (e.g. grammar or lexicon). These observations are important for many design aspects of artificial agents that help to practice conversation, such as dialogue design, dialogue topics and long-term interaction with artificial companions.

Specific aspects of language become the topic of the talk also in sequences of repair with linguistic trouble source. Types of repair with linguistic trouble source are analysed in the next section.

3.4 Repair with linguistic trouble source

As the discussion of the literature in Chapter 2 showed, sequences of *repair with linguistic trouble source*, also referred to as *pedagogical repair* (Tudini, 2010), offer an excellent opportunity to study participants' orientations to their linguistic expertise in conversation. This section will analyse how differently initiated and differently carried-out repair sequences help to disclose participants' orientations to their differential language expertise in chat conversation for learning.

3.4.1 Native speaker's self-initiated self-repair

Same-turn self-initiated self-repair is normally not visible to the recipient of the repaired turn in chat, because it is completed before the turn is posted. Exceptions may occur when chat software is used that shows turns-in-production to the recipient; the text message is then transferred symbol by symbol. Such messengers are, however, rarely used nowadays. In contrast, self-initiated self-repair that is done later than the same turn, becomes visible to the turn recipient. Both learners and native speakers corrected some errors in their talk later than the same turn if they made some errors. However, there are also multiple instances of self-initiated self-repair produced by native speakers that do not deal with errors in their own talk. They rather *anticipate* problems with comprehension on the learner's side and explain some terms in their talk to the learner without request. This type of self-initiated self-repair is referred to as *proactive explanation* in an earlier work (Danilava et al., 2013a).

Example 3.10 contains in turn 60 an explanation of the word *Staatsexamen*. The learner did not mark this word as somehow unclear, but the native speaker anticipated potential difficulties in comprehension and explained the concept. In this way, the native speaker positions herself as an expert in German language (explanation of a word), in German culture (knowledge about details of teachers' education) and in her profession (teacher). When N02 provides additional information on teachers' training, which was not specifically asked about, with the assumption that the concept *Staatsexamen* might not be (fully) clear to the learner, the learner is put by the native speaker into the category of potential novices in the German language and in the German teacher's education system.

Example 3.10. The native speaker explains the concept of "state exam".

59 18:26:44 L04 und hast du dein Studium in diesem Jahr absolviert?
and did you complete your studies this year?
and did you finish your studies this year?
60 18:27:46 N02 nein, ich bin 2009 fertig geworden und habe jetzt zwei Jahre mein zweites Staatsexamen gemacht, das ist eine Lehrerausbildung direkt an den Schulen
no, I graduated in 2009 and it has now been two years since my second state exam, this is teachers' training directly at schools

A cultural note: the concept of *Staatsexamen* (госэкзамен, translit.: *gosexamen*) exists in the Russian language, too. However, it has a different meaning in the professional education system in Belarus where the learners are from.

The native speaker's assumptions about the chances for the learner to comprehend the just-produced talk can also be based on their previous interaction history. For instance, if a particular expression was not clear to the learner and was marked in a repair sequence as a trouble source, and then the same expression is used with a different sense, an explanation (self-repair) might be produced without request. Example 3.11 illustrates such a proactive explanation of an expression that caused a repair initiation in the preceding talk.

The native speaker N04 uses an expression in turn 386 in which the meaning is not completely clear to the learner. The learner L08 initiates a repair in turn 388, providing a candidate understanding. The learner positions herself as a novice in this way. N04 clarifies the meaning of the expression in turn 390, confirming the candidate understanding suggested by the learner. Later in the same conversation, the native speaker uses the same expression again in a different sense. He provides an explanation of the expression and positions himself as a language expert who also understands and anticipates potential difficulties that the learner might have with a different meaning of the same expression. The native speaker contributes to the construction of his own identity as a language expert and also as a helpful and collaborative conversation partner.

Proactive explanations in the form of self-initiated self-repair are not limited to the repeated use of a previously utilised expression. Inferences about the need to repair can be done on a higher level of abstraction, as the dataset suggests. For instance, if a learner had difficulties in comprehension of abbreviations in the past, and the native speaker uses a new abbreviation in the just-produced turn, the native speaker can choose to explain the new abbreviation without request from the learner's side.

Example 3.11. Self-initiated self-repair as a proactive explanation.

386 20:39:52 N04 alles klar?
everything clear?
everything alright?
387 20:40:05 L08 ist es nicht zu spät?
is it not too late?
388 20:40:53 L08 alles klar- alles in Ordnung?
all clear- everything fine?
389 20:41:38 N04 nein, es ist nicht zu spät, hier ist es ja 1 Stunde früher :-)
no, it is not too late, here it is 1 hour earlier
390 20:41:55 N04 und ja, alles klar = alles in Ordnung.
and yes, all clear = everything fine.
391 20:42:33 N04 gerade spielt Schweden gegen England, sehr spannend!
Sweden is playing against England, very exciting!
392 20:42:41 L08 au fsolche Weise, alles ist klar!)
in this way everything is clear!
`later in the same session`
473 22:04:47 L08 bestimmt)ok, NATIVE04_FN ich muss jetzt meine Spickzettel zur nächsten Prüfung ausschneiden)
sure, ok, NATIVE04_FN I need to cut out my cheat sheet for the next exam now
474 22:06:36 N04 alles klar. (das heißt diesmal: "verstanden"). Dann wünsche ich Dir viel Erfolg bei der Prüfung und eine gute Nacht!
all clear. (this means this time: "understood"). Then I wish you good luck for the exam and a good night!

To sum up, the need for self-initiated self-repair is not only determined by actual "errors" in the just-produced turn, but also by participants' stances and the interaction process. In addition, native speakers may assume that there might be a need for an explanation because their co-participants somehow oriented to their language expertise as not fully professional. Thus, decisions for proactive explanations can be made based on past interactions or assumptions about learners' linguistic and non-linguistic knowledge. Such observations need to be taken into account when modelling repair decisions in an artificial conversation partner that should behave "like a language expert".

3.4.2 Other-initiated self-repair with linguistic trouble source

If we ask someone a question, we normally expect that this person can answer this question, i.e. that this person has the necessary expertise or necessary knowledge to answer. If the learner asks the native speaker for an explanation of a just-produced turn or part of it, then the learner demonstrates that:

a. his/her own knowledge is not sufficient and
b. the native speaker's expertise is expected to be high enough to clarify the problem.

Example 3.12 illustrates this distribution of expertise. Here we look at this excerpt from the perspective of how the expert-novice relationship is constructed in talk-in-interaction. The native speaker is the trouble-speaker in this example. The other speaker (the learner) initiates the repair, and the native speaker repairs her previous utterance. Thus, we speak here about *other-initiated self-repair (OISR) when the native speaker is the trouble-speaker*.

Example 3.12. Ins Auge fassen.

122	13:08:39	N04	zugegeben, ich war dieses Jahr auch noch in keinem See, aber so langsam könnte man das mal ins Auge fassen :-) admitted, I was this year not in a lake, either, but slowly one could reach this into the eye *I admit I was this year not at a lake, either, but I could slowly consider it*
123	13:10:47	L09	ins auge fassen? *reach into the eye?*
124	13:11:56	N04	das heißt _hier_ etwa soviel wie "planen" oder "bald mal machen" *it means here something like "to plan" or "to do soon"*
125	13:12:16	L09	:) :)
126	13:12:22	L09	klar okay

In turn 122, the native speaker N04 uses an idiomatic expression, which is marked as problematic by the learner L09 in turn 123. The native speaker has to determine what kind of trouble the learner may have with this expression. In turn 124, the native speaker explains the meaning of the expression. This makes visible for both the learner and the researcher that the native speaker interpreted the repair initiation as the need to fill a gap in the learner's language knowledge. Turns 125-126 show that it was a correct interpretation.

In Example 3.12, the native speaker is the trouble-speaker. However, it is also possible for the learner to be the trouble-speaker and for the native speaker to other-initiate self-repair. The practice of questioning may be chosen by native speakers to initiate repair (clarification requests, repetition-based repair initiations). Such repair initiations produced by native speakers sometimes deal with real communication problems, and sometimes function as didactic corrective feedback. The goal of the questions is sometimes to clarify a communication problem caused by non-native-like expressions. The native speaker pushes the learner at the same time to correct. However, sometimes the goal is to elicit the production of a correct expression in the absence of a communication problem. In any case, such repair initiations will not be equivalent to classroom-like elicitations of the type *How do we say that in German*. Since the native speaker is the participant who has the right to judge what is correct and what is not correct, it is the native speaker who positions himself as an expert, assigning the role of a language novice to the learner.

A detailed look at Example 3.13 will help us to understand how the profiles of expert/novice are constructed in OISR sequences when the learner is the trouble-speaker. In turn 420 the learner chooses to use the word *maßstäblich*, which is a correct German word but has a different sense. It does not make much sense in the context of the talk. The native speaker initiates a repair by copying the trouble source and marking it as problematic with a question mark after the word in turn 421. Such repair initiations are called *repetition-based* or *repeat-based*. The learner is forced to describe the sense of what she was going to say with other words. In contrast to the native speaker in Example 3.12 she does not simply explain the meaning of *maßstäblich*. This is an important difference in repair production for these two types of OISR. The native speaker accepts the explanation in turn 423, signalling that the communication problem is resolved.

Example 3.13. Maßstäblich.

416	20:59:09	L08	nun...Moskau wie Stadt(im großen und ganzen) hat mir nicht beonders gefallen: sehr viel Lärm,die Leute sind "ohne Gefühl" *well... I did not like Moscow as a city [* missing space] (in general) much [*error: typo]: very much noise, [*missing space] the people are "without feelings"*
417	21:00:13	L08	aber die Architektur ist wunderbar!!man kann eine Gebäude eine Stunde lang beobachten. *but the architecture is wonderful!! [* missing space] one can observe one building [*error: wrong gender] one hour long.*
418	21:01:36	N04	ich war leider noch nie dort. Von Fotos kenne ich den Kreml. *unfortunately, I have never been there. I know the Kremlin from pictures*
420	21:02:32	L08	ja, ich war dort. es ist sehr maßstäblich *I was there. it is very full-scale [* error: lexical choice]*
421	21:03:30	N04	maßstäblich? *full-scale?*
422	21:04:02	L08	hmm...sehr sehr groß, umfangreich *hmm...very very big, wide*
423	21:07:34	N04	ah, ok!

Why do the repair initiations look similar but the repairs are different? Participants' expectations and attitudes towards their chat partners (stances) play a role in their interpretation of the trouble, and influence their choice of interactional resources for repair. First, both native and non-native speakers are expected to know what they want to say. In addition, native speakers are expected to understand what learners say in the native speakers' native language. Therefore, a different word with a *similar meaning* is delivered by native speakers to carry out a repair initiated by a learner, in an attempt to select linguistic resources accessible to the learner. In contrast, the learner tries to deliver a *different* meaning expressed by different words after repair other-initiated by the native speaker, in an attempt to find correct linguistic resources to express what they wanted to say. An artificial conversation partner needs to be able to see this difference.

3.4.3 Self-initiated other-repair: word searches and definitions

This section will discuss interactional practices used by learners to deal with difficulties with the production of a particular meaning. As reported by the participants in the retrospective interviews, they usually use the most common strategy of looking up words in a dictionary if they do not know how to say something or do not have a specific word at their disposal. However, in some cases the learners preferred to ask the more knowledgeable peer for help. Example 3.14 shows how a word search sequence may be organised.

Example 3.14. Word search in two stages.

430 21:14:17 L08 wie heißt es auf D., wenn man selbt mit dem Auto fährt?
how is it called in G., if oneself drives a car?
how do you say it in German, if you drive a car?

431 21:15:22 N04 ich fahre mit dem Auto
I drive a car

432 21:15:50 N04 hab ich Deine Frage richtig verstanden?
did I understand your question correctly?

433 21:16:01 L08 nein, und wenn man KANN mit dem Auto fahren
no, and if one CAN drive a car

434 21:16:19 L08 führen?
to lead?

435 21:18:19 N04 ich fahre, du fährst, er/sie/es fährt, wir fahren, sie fahren, ihr fahrt
I drive, you drive, he/she/it drives, we drive, they drive, you [pl.] drive

436 21:18:45 N04 Verzeihung, stehe ich gerade auf dem Schlauch?
Sorry, am I not getting it?

437 21:20:19 L08 =)auf Engl- drive
in English - drive

438 21:23:15 N04 ah, ob es heißt "mit dem Auto fahren" oder ob anstelle von "fahren" etwas anderes gesagt wird?
ah, if it is called "to drive a car" or if we use something else instead of "drive"?

439 21:23:21 N04 nein, es heißt "Auto fahren"
no, it is called "to drive a car"

440 21:23:40 N04 war das die Frage?
was this your question?

441 21:24:34 L08 ach, ja)so, ist das richtig:du kannst mit dem Auto fahren, d.h. du hast ein Fahrerschein. ich habe richtig verstanden?
ah yes so, is this correct: you can drive a car, this means you have a driver licence. did I get it right?

442 21:25:50 N04 ja, ich habe einen Führerschein und ich fahre selbst :-)
yes, I have a Führer licence and I drive myself
yes, I have a driving licence and I drive myself

443 21:26:08 N04 (kein blöder Witz: es heißt wirklich "Führerschein")
(no stupid joke: it is really called Führer licence)
(this is not just a stupid joke, we really say headman licence)

444 21:29:31 L08 klar. ich will im August in die Schule gehen um einen Führerschein bekommen. HAst du schon lange F. bekommen?
I see. I want to go to a driver's school in August and get my driving licence. Did you get your D. long ago?

445 21:30:31 N04 ja, vor mehr als 10 Jahren
yes, more than 10 years ago

The word search sequence is divided into two stages. First, the learner wants to know whether the word *fahren* (En.: *to drive*) is used in German to say that a person can drive a car. As it becomes clear later on, she wants to tell the native speaker that she is going to get her driving licence and to learn how to drive. It is not completely clear at the time point of turn 430, where this request is posted, that she might have difficulties with *production*, and that the request in turn 430 is in fact a self-initiation of other-repair. After multiple attempts to clarify the meaning of this request (turns 432-437), the native speaker finally understands the question and presents the word that the learner has been searching for.

In the second stage, the learner uses the German for drive - *fahren* - to formulate *Fahrerschein* (corresponds to En.: *driver licence**) in turn 441. However, a different base word in German is used for that. The native speaker corrects this created word by presenting the correct German word for *driving license* in turn 442, emphasising that it was not just a joke in turn 443 because the word has a semantic relation to the word *Führer* (En.: *headman, conductor*), which was used as a form of address for Hitler. In turn 444, the learner finally uses the word that she was searching for and says what she probably wanted to say, closing the repair sequence in this way.

Example 3.15. Learner displays hesitation and uncertainty in chat by symbolic means. Originally Excerpt 51 from (Marques-Schäfer, 2013, p. 171) (A - tutor A., D - learner Diego, turn numbers added).

1 09:52:11 D Gestern haben wir auf diesen Chat die Witze geerzält (?)
Yesterday have we on [*error: wrong preposition] this [*error: wrong case] chat the [*error: no det. required] jokes telled [*multiple errors: wrong use of the regular verb tense morphology, orthography] (?)
Yesterday we told the jokes in this chat
2 09:52:22 A erzählt
told
3 09:52:28 A ohne (ge)
without (ge)
4 09:52:35 D ohne ge
without ge
5 09:52:40 A ja
yes
6 09:52:59 A Wir haben gestern in diesem Chat Witze erzählt
Yesterday we told jokes in this chat

Word searches can be performed in a less prominent manner. For instance Kurhila (2006) describes “repair as response to uncertainty" in oral data. Language learners may display hesitations and uncertainty during production, and native speakers may respond to it with help to find the target (Kurhila, 2006, Sec. 3.3.1). Such close-to-oral displays of hesitation are not contained in our chat dataset; only explicit searches like “I don’t know what is the German for X" occur in our dataset.

It is possible that chat participants preferred to search the web or look in dictionaries for words that they want to say. Specific characteristics of responsiveness in chat allow the participants to take their time for production, as opposed to oral conversations. However, Marques-Schäfer presents instances of self-initiated other-repair when the learner has trouble with production and displays hesitation by symbolic means in chat (Marques-Schäfer, 2013, Excerpt 51, p. 171).

For comparison, one example from a tutored session is reproduced here to show how hesitation can be displayed in chat. In Example 3.15 the learner D produces many errors in turn 1. The native speaker A, who has the tutor role in chat, selects only one of the errors for correction in turn 2, the one trhat was marked by a hesitation in the trouble turn using *(?)* just after the unit marked by the learner as a trouble source. However, in turn 6, the tutor provides a correct version of the learner's turn correcting all the errors. It remains an open question why expressing hesitation does not occur in the main dataset collected for this research. Factors such as the less formal character of the chat, the size of the dataset and the learners' proficiency level may play a role.

3.4.4 Other-corrections of linguistic errors

Exposed corrections of linguistic errors produced by the learners are probably *the* places in conversation where native speakers position themselves as language experts. Embedded corrections, in contrast, offer a lot of space for interpretation. The differential linguistic expertise is just applied in talk, but it is not by itself the business of the talk. This is a kind of hidden, indirect way of being expert. However, the learners took up the corrected units after embedded corrections. Therefore, it can be also seen as implicit positioning. Doing things right is also a kind of being expert. In the remainder of this section these two types of corrections will be discussed from the perspective of how participants orient to their linguistic identities in other-corrections.

Exposed corrections

Exposed corrections are probably the most "teacher-like" type of positioning as language expert in conversation. The participants reported that they preferred to be corrected by the native speakers more frequently so as to improve their language learning. However, exposed corrections disrupt the conversation, therefore, the native speakers corrected learners' errors very sparingly, and some of them correct almost no errors at all.

Example 3.16 shows a prototypical sequence of an exposed correction. The learner L09 produces an expression in turn 49 which is marked as an error by the native speaker N04 in turn 51. N04 rejects the word used by the learner (sein) and replaces it with a correction (haben). This replacement is framed by accountings (left-hand side: *falls ich korrigieren darf*; right-hand side: *smile*). He labels what he was doing in turn 51 as correction. The learner thanks him for the correction and takes up the corrected expression (turns 52-53).

Besides this prototypical structure of exposed correction (trouble source – correction – uptake), correction variants come with more or without any accountings, without uptake or with delayed uptake.

Example 3.16. An exposed correction of a linguistic error.

49 19:40:59 L09 Zur Zeit bin ich frei um Diplomarbeit zu schreiben
at this time I am [* error] free in order to write [* error: 0-determiner] diploma thesis
at the moment I have free time to write my diploma thesis
50 19:41:15 L09 danke schön! :)
thank you very much [closing of a previous sequence]
51 19:41:58 N04 Falls ich das korrigieren darf: Du "hast" frei, nicht "bist". :-)
If I may correct you: you "have" free, not "are". [smile]
52 19:42:48 L09 Danke
Thank you
53 19:43:16 L09 Ich habe frei :)
I have free [smile]
I have free time

However, exposed corrections always come with a component that is explicitly marked as wrong for some reasons, and another component that would be a better alternative from the corrector's perspective. This change is described by Jefferson (1987) as a sequence of replacements in the corresponding sequence of turns: Speaker A uses term X, next speaker uses a different term Y, speaker A, in turn, may keep on using the new term Y or go back to X. Such replacements occur in talk enveloped in a particular turn format (a combination of linguistic practices and devices). Various turn formats of exposed corrections will be discussed in Chapter in detail 5.

Embedded corrections

If embedded corrections are opportunities for native speakers to position themselves as experts implicitly, then they may offer chances for learners to position themselves as novices implicitly by the same token. By comparing the structure of exposed corrections (trouble source – correction – uptake), one can find that embedded corrections match this prototypical structure, too.

In both exposed and embedded corrections, learners may take up the correction immediately or later. The repaired version of the trouble source was used by learners in my dataset later than immediately after the embedded correction. Delayed (later in the same conversation) or postponed (in a different chat session) uptake make the analysis of learning difficult.

Example 3.17. An embedded correction of a linguistic error.

`Chat from 11.06.12, correction`
228 20:15:33 L02 Dann brauchst du irgendetwas Beruhigungsmittel einzunehmen)))
Then you need to ingest something tranquilliser [* error] [smile]
Then you need to ingest something tranquillising
229 20:16:02 N01 Genau, zur Beruhigung meiner Nerven :-)
Exactly, to tranquillise my nerves

Chat from 14.06.2012, uptake

291 20:03:44 L02 Ja! Ist dein Herz in Ordnung?
Yes! Is your heart all right?

292 20:04:57 L02 Hast du keine Artzneien zur Beruhigung deiner Nerven eingenommen ?)
Did you ingest no remedy [* error: spelling] to tranquillise your nerves ?
You did not ingest any remedy to tranquillise your nerves, did you?

Example 3.17 shows an embedded correction with learner's postponed uptake. This sequence is spread over two conversations, one on 11th June and the other on 14th June 2012. In the conversation from 11th June, L02 uses a non-native-like expression in turn 228, which is implicitly corrected by N01 in the form of an acknowledgment in turn 229. In the conversation on the other day, L02 uses the correct expression in turn 292, as it was presented to her in the native speaker's embedded correction. This example also provides evidence that *noticing* (Schmidt, 1990), which is considered important for learning (Mackey, 2006), is possible even without focusing on errors explicitly. Consequently, embedded corrections provide opportunities for learning.

Example 3.18. The learner encourages the native speaker to correct linguistic errors.

130 19:01:18 L08 danke für Besonderheitn der Sprache=)für mich ist es sehr gut , dass du meine Fehler korrigierst)
*thank you for the specialities [*error: typo] of the language [smile] for me it is very good that you correct my errors [smile]*

131 19:05:01 N04 wenn es nicht nervt, gerne :-)
if it is not annoying, with pleasure [smile]

Because other-corrections are dispreferred and face threatening, face work becomes an important part of exposed corrections in the form of accountings. However, learners perceive error corrections as helpful, and encourage native speakers to correct them, as Example 3.18 illustrates.

Looking ahead at Example 4.5, page 117, we can see the following: After a preceding lengthy sequence of several repairs initiated by the learner and the native speaker, learner L08 encourages her partner N04 to correct her errors in the form of an expression of thanks while explicitly addressing her preference for correction. N04 agrees to correct "if it is not annoying", making visible that the dispreferred character of corrections is clear to him.

What else can be done by corrections

The dataset collected for this research contains only positive examples of chat users as helpful and supportive nice persons. This might be explained by the instruction to interact over many weeks, therefore chat participants paid attention to their relationships with their partners and handled the "face" of the others very carefully. The interaction setup in the study of Marques-Schäfer was different. The participants could come and go when they wanted and the chat was a group chat with many participants. The author reports cases of "mis-use" of exposed corrections for aggression in an untutored session (non-native speaker-non-native speaker group chat) (Marques-Schäfer, 2013, p. 192).

Example 3.19. Aggression in the form of an exposed correction. Example taken from (Marques-Schäfer, 2013, p. 192, Excerpt 67), turn numbers added.

1 19:14:53 L S: ich ja nicht so schlimm oder?)
*S:I [*error: typo] surely not so bad, or? [smile]*
2 19:15:00 L *ist
**is*
3 19:15:34 S nee. ich wusste es eigentlich schon - und es gibt auch schlechtere maniere :)
*nope. Actually, I knew it already - and there are also worse manners [*error: wrong plural]*
4 19:15:36 N ich bin*
*I am**
5 19:15:54 L N: halt deine klappe ok?
N: shut your trap, ok?
6 19:16:00 N er ist*
*he is**
7 19:16:07 N ich schreibe ich spreche nicht
I am writing, I'm not speaking
(...)
8 19:16:26 N dazu lehre ich dich kostenlos
in addition, I am teaching you for free

In Example 3.19, the learner L makes an orthographic error (probably just a typo) in turn 1, which L self-corrects in turn 2. Typos are considered unimportant and are normally not corrected in chat. However, the result of the typo is a legal German word, and it provides the other learner N room to interpret it as a morphosyntactic error (missing verb) and to produce a correction. The other-correction in turn 4 contains a correct pair of pronoun + verb "sein" in Präsens Indikativ (present simple indicative), which is the very basic level of German and is taught in the very beginning when people start learning German. From turns 1 and 2 it is clear that L has already mastered this level and is more advanced. When N teaches L how to conjugate "sein" in turn 4, it cannot be interpreted by L as "help to learn the language" but rather as face threatening and aggressive. It is not surprising that L reacts with aggression in turn 5. N continues to teach L how to conjugate the verb "sein" in turn 6, referring to this activity as "teaching for free" in turn 8, which is pure provocation.

With the correction in turn 4, N positions himself as a language expert and makes the differential language expertise relevant in conversation. With this positioning, he presents himself as more advanced and more knowledgeable than L, which does not correspond to the actual situation and is not accepted by L. The correction in turn 4 was not meant as "willingness to help to learn" as was the case in all the corrections in the dataset that we use in this book.

There might be different reasons for this behaviour of N that are not analysable from this excerpt. For this research it is important that there are also other things which can have the *form* of a correction, but have a completely different *function*. Similarly, there are structures in talk that do not have the form of a correction, but they function as corrections. For instance, other-corrections can have the form of repair other-initiations, as the reader will see in Section 5.3.4.

3.5 Results and discussion

This chapter presented a microanalytic study of how linguistic identities of a language novice and a language expert emerge in a chat-based Conversation-for-Learning between native speakers of German and advanced learners of German as a foreign language. Although sequences of repair with linguistic trouble source are the most obvious way to construct linguistic identities of language novices and language experts, other forms of orientation to linguistic identities can be found in instant messaging dialogues between language learners and native speakers. These forms include face work, evaluation, meta-talk about learning and collaborative learning.

This analysis was performed with the purpose to prepare an empirical basis for data-driven modelling of conversations between language learners and an artificial conversation partner. Therefore, the discussion in this chapter needs to address at least two points:

1. The empirical findings and what we learned about native/non-native speaker chat;
2. Possibilities for building computational models for conversation based on these findings.

Section 3.5.1 will summarise and discuss the findings. Section 3.5.2 will make a first attempt to transfer them into the context of computational modelling of an artificial conversation partner that helps a language learner to practice conversation. The concept of *interaction profiles* introduced by Spranz-Fogasy (2002) will be used in order to build a bridge between empirical reality and the world of computing. Section 3.5.3 will compare the findings to the results discussed in Chapter 2.

3.5.1 Participants' orientation to their linguistic identities

This chapter described and analysed three major types of practices where linguistic identities of a language expert and a language novice are co-constructed in text-based instant messaging dialogues between advanced learners of German and German native speakers. These three major types are:

1. Face work and evaluation:
    a) Learners make self-deprecating remarks about their language knowledge (*My German is not so good*). Native speakers respond with encouragement and positive evaluation (*You are doing a good job*).
    b) Learners apologise for their "bad" language knowledge (*Sorry for all my small mistakes*). Native speakers respond with encouragement and evaluation (*For now, I did not see any mistake*).
    c) Learners express anxiety about potential difficulties in comprehension (*I hope I understand everything, otherwise you will have to explain*). Native speakers position themselves as willing to help and provide responses designed to reduce anxiety.
    d) Native speakers evaluate learners' specific achievements in the form of compliments and praise.

2. Meta-talk about learning and collaborative learning:
   a) Comparison of grammar of shared languages.
   b) Discussion of (potential) difficulties in a particular language.
   c) Discussion of potential exam topics for exam preparation.
   d) Role play to rehearse exams.
3. Repair with linguistic trouble source.

Independently of sequences where participants orient to their linguistic identities in conversation, participants can choose to present themselves as members of a specific category. For instance a native speaker can mark their own membership in the category of fully proficient language users and become a role model for the learner.

Face work and evaluation

Learner-initiated face work sequences frequently exploit practices of apology: learners apologise for their L2 errors. The purposes of these excuses include fishing for compliments, warnings in order not to be laughed at (face preservation), justifications of errors and correction post-work. Native speakers handle the apologies not only as apologies doing nothing else but apologise, for which an accepting or a disaccepting response may be the preferred next. Instead, native speakers position themselves as more knowledgeable language users and helpful and encouraging interaction co-participants. They do this in the form of a positive evaluation and assessment of the learners' language proficiency, which frequently has the function of encouragement and empowerment. A ritualised "no problem" was rarely a response to such an excuse.

In addition, learners put their limited linguistic competences in focus in the form of a negative evaluation of their production and comprehension abilities. The social actions wrapped in these practices are mostly related to face work. Learners check whether they are accepted as competent interactants despite their limited linguistic competence. They present themselves as not yet fully proficient but willing to learn the native language of their partners.

Table 3.1 presents a summary of adjacency pairs in the sequences of face work and evaluation. In addition to the positive evaluations in a second pair part in face-work sequences initiated by the learner, there are teacher-like performance evaluations initiated by the native speaker after special "achievements" and at the end of the communication. Examples of negative evaluation provided by native speakers to learners are not contained in the dataset.

This analysis helped to determine how sequences of face work are locally organised. However, it does not explain how such sequences may be globally connected to other sequences in conversation. Therefore, which metrics for the evaluation can be used in a free chat and where in conversation such evaluations are appropriate need further analysis in a separate study. For the models of long-term interaction sequences of sequences as shown in Examples 3.5 and 3.6 on page 83, raise specific questions in terms of turn design with back links to events in the past (like *noch mal* in turn 406 of Example 3.5, page 83).

First pair part: learner	Second pair part: native speaker
Excuse for mistakes	Positive evaluation, encouragement Positioning as language novice in learner's mother tongue Compliments Ritualised "no problem" (rarely)
Negative self-assessment in production	Encouragement, empowerment Compliments Positive evaluation
Negative self-assessment in comprehension	Promise to explain Encouragement, empowerment

Table 3.1: Adjacency pair prototypes for learner-initiated apology-based and self-assessment-based face work

In addition, participants may negotiate what the conversation should be. Is it expected to be more focused on form and accuracy or do only the content and the fluency matter? Are errors and error corrections acceptable? Every answer to these questions leads to a specific variation of the speech exchange system and to a different "incarnation" of linguistic identities of a language novice and a language expert, and a different *interaction profile* (Spranz-Fogasy, 2002).

Meta-talk about learning and collaborative learning

Section 3.3 presented many examples in which language learning becomes the subject of the talk. Such sub-dialogues include:

- talk about comparison of languages spoken by participants of the conversation,
- talk about conversation practice and language study and
- doing exam preparation in the form of a role play and question discussion.

Three distinct corresponding roles emerge for the native speakers: a peer, a more knowledgeable peer and an examiner in a role play, respectively. The learners may take one of the three complementary roles: an equally knowledgeable peer, a less knowledgeable peer and a student in a role play. However, the participants might not always accept the roles assigned to them by their partners, as Example 3.8 on page 85 shows.

Role play differs from the other two types of talk in the following way. The practices deployed in examiner-student role play are restricted to interview-like talk. Then the "examiner" has the right to ask questions and to evaluate, and the "student" has the obligation to answer. In other words, participants simulate a non-equal-power speech exchange system of an exam within their equal-power speech exchange system. They embed a classroom-like talk in a Conversation-for-Learning, which does not oblige them to such a form of talk by itself.

When learners and native speakers talk about differences in their mother tongues or about particular difficulties in languages that they speak as foreign languages, they become sensitive to specific issues in grammar or lexicon. However, they do it in chat in a very "light" form; they do not discuss rules of grammar for hours, as sometimes happens in a language classroom. In contrast to short face-work sequences described in the preceding paragraphs, sub-dialogues where learning becomes the subject of the talk can become very long. Models of such sub-dialogues can be created similarly to models of task-based dialogues for dialogue systems. However, an artificial conversation partner will need to determine when such a sub-dialogue or topic becomes relevant. The dataset used for this work may provide the necessary information for the model.

The participants engaged in lengthy discussions of properties of shared languages when:

- They collected information about their partner at the beginning of the communication and wanted to know which other languages their partner speaks.
- They mentioned events related to language learning, such as exams at the university or travel plans.

Lengthy sequential continuations of the topic such as topicalisation and reworking of the first pair part or the second pair part have been described in the CA literature as *non-minimal post-expansions* (Schegloff, 2007, pp. 155-168).

Practicing specific conversational situations becomes relevant when events related to performance and evaluation of learners' language performance outside of the chat become relevant. For instance, when the learners have to prepare for language tests or exams, it might be appropriate to offer help in preparation and to practice in the form of a role play. Results in the area of task-based dialogue systems (Hjalmarsson et al., 2007), serious games (Wik and Hjalmarsson, 2009; Sagae et al., 2011) and micro-worlds (DeSmedt, 1995) for SLA can be applied for designing such sub-dialogues. Topic identification, topic tracking and generation of topical talk are also related research areas (Makkonen et al., 2004; Breuing et al., 2011; Breuing and Wachsmuth, 2012).

Repair with linguistic trouble source

The examples in Section 3.4 present various types of repair where the linguistic identities of a language novice and a language expert have been made relevant. Repair with linguistic trouble source was found in all types of repair (self-initiated, other-initiated, self- and other-repair). Different types of repair discussed in Section 3.4 have different purposes in dialogues with learners. The following was observed:

1. Native speakers' self-correction pro-actively repairs potential trouble, anticipating learners' difficulties in comprehension.
2. The learner self-corrects errors of form.
3. Other-initiated self-repair. Depending on the trouble-speaker, such sequences have different purposes.

   a) The learner is the trouble-speaker, the native speaker corrects errors.
   b) The native speaker is the trouble-speaker, the learner seeks explanation of unclear expressions.
4. Self-initiated other-repair (the learner is the trouble-speaker). The learner addresses their own difficulties in production, initiating various kinds of definition work.
5. Other-correction (the learner is the trouble-speaker). The native speaker provides implicit or explicit corrective feedback on the learner's linguistic errors.

These observations are summarised in Tables 3.2 and 3.3. The tables show that while native speakers are eligible to initiate and carry out repair caused by their own and learners' linguistic choices, learners are only responsible for their own linguistic troubles and do not correct native speakers' language.

RI\ RCO	Self	Other
Self	Correct errors of form and typos	Word searches and definition work
Other	*OISR-based corrections of learner errors*	*Corrections of learner errors*

Table 3.2: Types of repair with linguistic trouble source when the learner is the trouble-speaker. RI: repair initiation, RCO: repair carry-out

RI\ RCO	Self	Other
Self	Pro-active explanations of potential troubles	
Other	*Explanations of unknown words and not completely understood expressions*	

Table 3.3: Types of repair with linguistic trouble source when the native speaker is the trouble-speaker. RI: repair initiation, RCO: repair carry-out

Different strategies can be used by language learners to deal with trouble with understanding in text chat: they can search for translations and explanations using various online and offline resources, and they can ask their partners for help. Section 3.4.2 illustrates how learners may initiate repair to elicit an explanation of an unclear idiomatic expression in the form of a repair proper (Example 3.12, page 90). On the other hand, the environment of other-initiation of repair may be used by native speakers for the purpose of correction of linguistic errors (Example 3.13, page 91). In both cases, the environment of other-initiated self-repair is used to construct linguistic identities. However, depending on who initiates and who carries out the repair, the emerging linguistic identities are different. The learner initiates the repair in Example 3.12 and positions herself as a language novice. The native speaker initiates the repair in Example 3.13 and positions himself as a language expert. The corresponding repair carry-outs are different with respect to their function and the speaker's linguistic identity.

Language learners may use different strategies to deal with problems in production. Similarly to dealing with troubles in understanding, learners may use various online and offline information resources, machine translation tools and dictionaries to find the word that would in their opinion express their thoughts and emotions as closely as possible. In addition, language learners may choose to ask their more knowledgeable conversation partners to help them. Multiple instances of word searches and definition work document that the sequential environment of learners' self-initiated other-repair may be used by the learners to find the required vocabulary. Linguistic identities of a language novice and a language expert emerge in this way in informal conversations.

Native speakers appear as more knowledgeable language users in sequences of other-corrections of different types. If a deviation from standard language is worth a correction from the perspective of a native speaker, the native speaker may initiate and carry out a repair of such an error. They may do it in a more explicit (exposed corrections) or a less explicit form (embedded corrections). Although other-corrections of linguistic errors are generally dispreferred in informal conversations, learners perceive them as helpful. Nonetheless, the participants share the understanding of the face-threatening potential of such corrections. This becomes visible in the form of accountings and explicit negotiations, where participants make clear that corrections are acceptable and even desirable.

In addition to sequences where participants orient to their linguistic identities in talk, other possibilities exist for showing linguistic identities. Specifically, native speakers may position themselves as role models and proficient language users throughout all conversations by constantly paying specific attention to their own language production. Conversational Agents and Natural Language Interaction: Techniques and Effective Practices

Native speaker as a role model

Text-based instant messaging conversations with language learners may raise the question: "What is the most appropriate language form to be used across conversations?" The answers that the native speakers who participated in the data collection chose were different, for instance:

1. We use instant messenger; chat is the same as "talk in written". Then more oral style in syntax and orthography was chosen, and a faster typing pace had a higher priority than correct orthography. This strategy of language use was chosen by the majority of the native speakers in the dataset and is frequently reported in the literature.
2. I communicate with a language learner and want to use the language as correctly as possible to provide positive examples for the learner. Then the correct form of the language has a higher priority than faster typing.

In both cases, native speakers become role models: the former shows the learner how to do informal text chatting in German, the latter emphasises the importance of the language standard. However, the decision what is better for the learner is not just a simple selection between these two variants of language form. As the reader will see in Chapter 8, orthography is an interactional resource that can be used in chat to regulate social closeness.

3.5.2 Doing being a language expert: towards interaction profiles for an artificial conversation partner

Correction of L2 errors is not the only way for an artificial agent to construct the identity of a language expert. Other types of sub-dialogues described in this chapter need to be taken into account, too. However, the identity construction is a joint product of the machine and the user. If the user does not accept the machine as an expert, the machine cannot do much.

The identity of a language expert is constructed by two things simultaneously: 1) doing being expert - as discussed in this chapter, and 2) applying one's own expertise in overall doing (e.g. overall correct "native-like" language use - whatever it is). The grade of acceptance of the artificial conversation partner as a language expert by the user can be seen in the user's reaction to corrections and explanations, but also in presence or absence of other forms of orientation to linguistic identities in talk, as we described in this chapter. Technical limitations in language understanding and generation methods that are available in the current dialogue technology, such as conversation agents, dialogue systems and chatbots, will play a role in interaction. Learners accepted the native speakers as "role models", and therefore they took up corrections, asked for explanations and engaged in definition work sequences. It needs to be investigated in a separate study whether users of an artificial conversation partner would accept it as a more knowledgeable user of the language that they learn. However, further analysis of long-term interaction between language learners and native speakers may be required prior to setting up such a study.

All of the native speakers became language experts in conversations with learners, but the specific language expert "shape" was different for each of the native speakers. The concept of *interaction profiles* introduced by Spranz-Fogasy (2002) and discussed in Section 2.3.4 can help to build a bridge between the empirical reality and the technology. The work on interaction profiles was an attempt to grasp and to operationalise the individual factors of each interaction participant and the adaptive behaviour of the interaction participants towards other participants taking into account the interaction history. One of his findings has a special relevance for this work. He showed that each participant of the interaction has only a *limited* influence on his own interaction profile and image. As Spranz-Fogasy (2002) puts it, if someone becomes an outsider, it is less the result of her or his own interactional activities but rather a product of interactional activities of *others*. Spranz-Fogasy (2002) illustrates with his analysis of a TV debate how a participant of the debate becomes a troublemaker in interaction through the contributions of the other participants, and not through his own talk (Spranz-Fogasy, 2002, Sec. 2.1). The consequences for computational models of a conversational partner that simulates a language expert are that the conversational system will have to decide on one hand which "incarnation" of a language expert to choose from all the available options, and on the other hand to adapt to the possibilities provided by the user in the interaction and the opportunities for such behaviour that emerged through the interaction history.

Every native speaker in the dataset can be characterised in terms of practices chosen to orient to the linguistic identities. All of them positioned themselves as language experts in conversation or were put in this position by learners. However each of them used different resources for that and combined the resources in different ways. This, in turn, led to different images of the person behind the identity. The arsenal of resources that can be used to position oneself as a language expert in conversation was described in the previous chapters of this part. Now it can be summarised how different interaction profiles can emerge in conversation by using parts of the arsenal.

The Teacher has the following characteristics:

1. Writes full sentences all the time, does not change this even if the learner makes it more "oral". Is a role model with his correctly formed German, very polite and politically correct.
2. Evaluates the learner's performance from time to time.
3. Creates environments in conversation for language-learning tasks, e.g. uses difficult idiomatic expressions consciously with the goal to give the learner a chance to learn them. Checks their understanding with comprehension checks. Tells jokes with double word meaning (= elicitations of repair initiation).
4. Selects topics for talks related to German language and German literature.
5. Recommends books for reading.
6. Corrects errors sometimes.

The Adaptive profile includes the following features:

1. Very reactive to the learner's style. Imitates learner's self-repair formats, turn length, orthography.
2. Very reactive to the learner's emotions. Uses more emoticons if the learner uses them a lot, and fewer emoticons, if the learner does not use them much.
3. Prefers to let-it-pass. Mutual understanding is more important than form and accuracy.
4. Corrects either in embedded form or by repair-initiation formats when the learner's errors make understanding difficult.
5. Reacts to the learner's fishing for compliments by compliments, positive evaluation of language proficiency and encouragement.
6. Reacts to the learner's apologies for errors by confirmation of comprehension.

The Chaotic profile can be described as follows:

1. Is always in hurry, no time to talk and establish a kind of closeness, making appointments is the most frequent activity.

2. Is not consistent in spelling and does not commit to conventions (writes sometimes ue instead of ü, sometimes ü, sometimes nouns with an initial capital, sometimes everything lower case).
3. Consciously smuggles grammar errors into his messages, but does not react to the learner's repair initiations.
4. Error corrections are rather random and formatted without any visible system.
5. Very creative in self-repair carry-outs after learners' other-initiations.
6. Embeds language-learning tasks into the conversation in the form of exam rehearsal.

The More Knowledgeable Friendly and Helpful Peer behaves as follows:

1. Writes very "oral" utterances, writes lower case mixed up with correct spelling and grammar, uses word stretches and emoticons to express emotions.
2. Regularly offers help in learning tasks and exam preparation.
3. Corrects many errors in both exposed and embedded way.
4. Encourages the learner in the form of positive evaluation, diminishing the errors.
5. Provides detailed explanations for requests for definitions and word searches.
6. Helps the learner to remember spelling of difficult cases with memos.
7. Reacts to excuses for errors with positive evaluation and encouragement.
8. Uses rich palette of means for repair carry-outs: metalinguistic information, examples, paraphrasing, hyperlinks to examples, code switching.

The construction of linguistic identities is an interactional achievement and the product of joint activities of both participants of each dialogue. As (Hosoda, 2006) reports, it is normally the learner who starts making the differential language expertise relevant, and sometimes the learner needs several re-initiations of such "doing being novice" before the native speaker accepts the role of expert. While native speakers N02 and N03 rather confirm (Hosoda, 2006)'s finding, native speakers N01 and N04 show deviant patterns and disconfirm (Hosoda, 2006)'s finding. The learners L03, L04 and L05 did not ask their partner N02 much. They preferred to search for words in online dictionaries instead of repair initiation. These three learners did not position themselves as novices. This is why N02 did not have a chance to position herself as a language expert.

However, N01 and N04 are deviant cases in the dataset collected for this research. N01 *proactively* introduced more complex linguistic material to provoke repair initiations; he initiated assessments of learners' linguistic performance and praised the learners for their high level of proficiency. This may be explained for N01 by his profession of teacher of German. N04 corrected a lot of errors without being asked, which contradicts (Hosoda, 2006)'s observation and the correcting behaviour of the other three native speakers in the dataset. This might be explained for N04 by his previous experiences with learners of German in chat. In addition, N04 and L08 explicitly negotiated that corrections of linguistic errors are allowed (Example 3.18, page 96). This information may have been transferred to conversations with his other partners. As a result, N04 engaged in other-corrections with L09 without being invited to correct. In the retrospective interview, N04 said that he sometimes confused L08 with L09 “because they come from the same town" (orig.: *glaube, ich hab die beiden am Anfang sogar miteinander verwechselt, weil sie beide aus der gleichen Stadt kommen).* All these factors may explain why N04 started to correct L09’s errors without her invitation or prior negotiations, as opposed to Hosoda’s findings (Hosoda, 2006) and other native speakers’ behaviour in the dataset.

To summarise, there is no such thing as *the* language expert and *the* language novice. There are various practices where participants of native/non-native speaker conversations make their linguistic identities relevant in talk. Linguistic identities emerge in conversation in the form of face work, meta-talk about learning, role-play and repair with linguistic trouble source. Different practices can be deployed to realise them, as examples in this chapter illustrate. Each combination of these practices will lead to different interaction profiles of the conversation participants; however, all these different profiles will fall into the bigger categories of language novices and language experts.

These findings provide an opportunity for an implementation of an artificial conversation partner that behaves “like a language expert". Given a pool of practices for orientation to the differential linguistic expertise in conversation, the artificial agent needs in addition a decision mechanism that allows it to make use of specific practices from this pool at specific points in conversation with the user. How complex this decision mechanism may be can be seen in Chapter 8, where we will talk about a decision model for error corrections.

3.5.3 Discussion

Chat participants may choose to present themselves as members of the social category of language experts throughout the entire communication. The forms of presentation include participants’ choice of linguistic resources such as orthography, vocabulary and syntax. Similar types of orientation have been described in previous publications (Kasper, 2004; Hosoda, 2006; Tudini, 2010; Dings, 2012; Vandergriff, 2013).

Meta-talk about language learning as a form of orientation to linguistic identities was also found by Dings (2012). She reports cases of learner-error correction initiated by non-native speakers, which could not be found in the dataset used for this research. Dings (2012) observed changes from more form-focused to more meaning-focused repairs with time. This finding could not be confirmed by the dataset used for this research. This may be explained by the study duration and the number of corrections. The present study was much shorter than the study described by Dings (2012). It took several weeks as opposed to one year in (Dings, 2012). Some of the native speakers in our dataset corrected only once, therefore changes of correction forms are not observable. However, we do find changes in correction formats from more implicit and more polite to more explicit but with fewer accountings. Native speakers tend to reduce the interaction management required for corrections with rich accountings when they become more familiar with the non-native speakers. This, in turn, confirms the dependencies between the selection of correction formats and the grade of social proximity.

Vandergriff (2013, p. 395) points out that "the most prevalent way of indexing identity is by evaluating something". She found that stance-taking in native/non-native speaker chat dialogues may have the form of accountings (learners critically evaluate their linguistic competences), explicit labelling of interactional roles, evaluations and taking certain interactional structures (typographic markers, lexical items). The orientations to linguistic identities in Vandergriff (2013)'s data were primarily invoked by non-native speakers. Native speakers, in contrast, made differential language expertise relevant only in response to non-native speakers' "self-deprecating remarks". With regard to this, Vandergriff (2013)'s findings are in line with those reported by Tudini (2010) for chat and Kasper (2004) for face-to-face interactions. The research described in this book completes these findings in the following ways:

- Native speakers oriented to differential language expertise in the form of compliments where they took a positive stance toward the learner's linguistic knowledge (praise for extraordinary knowledge of language and literature).
- Learners made "self-deprecating remarks" primarily at the beginning of the interaction (first 10 minutes of the first session).
- Learners' negative assessment of their own L2 proficiency in the continuation of the interaction was usually triggered by other troubles with production or comprehension.
- There are huge differences in pair-by-pair analysis. While pairs of participants involving N02 and N03 only rarely engaged in teacher-student-like sub-dialogues of linguistic repair, N01 and N04 did it more frequently. In dialogues between N04 and L08, teacher-student-like sequences of linguistic repair can be found more frequently than the other two types of orientation to linguistic identities.

However, this dataset does not confirm the role of the interaction managers dedicated to native speakers as described by Vandergriff (2013). Non-native speakers showed themselves to be equally competent in initiating and closing sequences as native speakers.

Regarding the implementability of the findings in an ICALL application, we may come to the following conclusion. While the first two classes of sub-dialogues (face work and evaluation, and meta-talk about learning) can be transferred to a Communicative ICALL application in a relatively simple way by creating small dialogue scripts and using existing task-based dialogue models, repair with linguistic trouble source requires new models for dealing with different kinds of trouble in conversations with learners. Relatively simple means that local models of sub-dialogues belonging to these two classes already exist or can be covered even by pattern-based language-understanding techniques such as Artificial Intelligence Markup Language (AIML) (Wallace, 2003; MacTear et al., 2016). Recognition of user-initiated face work as face work (e.g. distinguishing between excuse-based face work and real excuses) and a decision when meta-talk about learning and collaborative learning is appropriate remain a challenge.

3.5.4 Conclusions

In light of the discussion started in Section 1.3 and extended in this chapter regarding participants' orientation to their linguistic identities, the following conclusions can be stated:

- Modelling interactional practices where participants of an interaction orient to their linguistic identities can be attempted independently of the question of "real" expertise.
- Although it depends largely on the user (language learner, non-native speaker) which of the local models of those practices will finally be activated, the machine needs the ability to recognise them and to react appropriately.
- The activation of specific local models will be different for each user, and will lead to a different interaction profile emerging in each case.

Chapter Summary

This chapter reported the findings with regard to the types of participants' orientation to their linguistic identities in longitudinal native/non-native speaker instant messaging dialogues in German. The identified types of behaviour in focus have been illustrated by multiple examples with turn-by-turn analysis. From the perspective of an implementation of a machine that behaves "like a language expert", the longitudinal behaviours of every native speaker have been stereotyped. The concept of interaction profiles has been used to prepare the findings for a design of a Communicative ICALL system.

4

Other-Initiated Self-Repair with Linguistic Trouble Source

Abstract This chapter focuses on learner-initiated explanations of unclear linguistic material used by the native speaker in chat, that is, repair with linguistic trouble source where the non-native speaker is the recipient of the trouble-talk. A detailed analysis of a collection of repair sequences in chat will be illustrated by multiple examples. A generalised model will be build upon the findings. The results will be discussed in comparison with recent academic publications on repair from various related disciplines.

4.1 Introduction

Participants in a conversation sometimes need clarification in order to be sure that they understand their partners correctly. As was shown in Chapter 3, non-native speakers of a language may have the additional need to clarify the meaning of particular, unknown linguistic constructions. By clarifying the meaning of new linguistic material learners advance their learning and fill gaps in their foreign language. We will use the term *linguistic trouble source* to refer to this type of trouble and to distinguish repair addressing linguistic matters from conversational repair as it may be found in native/native speaker ordinary conversation. Repair with a similar function can also be found in native/native speaker interaction if, for instance, a participant is not familiar with specific terminology and asks for an explanation (a form of definition work).

A prototypical sequential organisation of repair in oral and face-to-face settings has the following structure:

1. Participant A produces a turn with a unit that participant B cannot understand;
2. Participant B initiates a repair sequence asking for clarification or explanation;
3. Participant A carries out the repair providing a clarification or an explanation;
4. Participant B accepts the explained meaning explicitly or implicitly.

This prototypical structure has already been described in the academic literature for oral data: so-called negotiations of meaning in the language classroom context (Va-

S. Höhn, *Artificial Companion for Second Language Conversation*,
https://doi.org/10.1007/978-3-030-15504-9_4

ronis and Gass, 1985) and repair organisation in ordinary conversation (Schegloff, 2007). The same prototypical structure exists in chat, as confirmed by the dataset that was collected for this research. However, differences in resources made available by participants for trouble identification may occur due to the *virtual adjacency* in text chat (Tudini, 2010). That is, turns that are normally adjacent in oral communication may appear in chat with other turns between them. This happens because of the possibility to discuss multiple things at the same time (multiple conversation threads).

From all possible constellations, this chapter will focus on the case where the native speaker of German produces a turn containing a linguistic trouble source, the learner of German initiates repair, and the native speaker carries out the repair. This type of repair is *other-initiated self-repair (OISR) with linguistic trouble source when the native speaker is the trouble-speaker.*

The analysis in this chapter will show which interactional resources learners make use of (and make them available in this way) in chat in order to other-initiate repair with linguistic trouble source, that is to signal trouble and to reference the trouble source. Turn formats for repair initiation are of special interest, because this is important for the future recognition of such sequences by conversational agents. Section 4.2 illustrates the use of interactional resources for repair other-initiation on multiple examples from the dataset. The interactional resources used by native speakers in order to carry out self-repair need to be examined, because this is required to model the responses of the conversational agent. Section 4.3 is therefore dedicated to various ways of carrying out self-repair after an other-initiation in chat. Section 4.4 will summarise the preliminary empirical findings and discuss the insights as illustrated by examples.

Further, this chapter presents a computational model of other-initiated self-repair when the artificial agent is a trouble-speaker. The artificial agent will need to do the same as native speakers, namely, recognise repair other-initiations and carry out self-repair after that in order to resolve the trouble in the learner's comprehension.

Although the main focus is on German, possibilities to use the same model for other languages are of interest. This might be possible because repair other-initiations are structured very similarly in all languages for which other-initiated repair was studied until the present (Dingemanse et al., 2014, 2015). Therefore, one of the challenges in the modelling phase is to decouple language-specific devices (e.g. specific tokens used for repair initiation in German) from sequential models and turn formats that might be used across languages (e.g. repeats and specific symbolic resources available in chat).

Building on the prototypical structures in sequences of other-initiated self-repair (OISR), the second part of this chapter aims at designing a sequential computational model of other-initiated self-repair when the machine is the trouble-speaker (OISR_M). Section 4.5 describes a local model of OISR_M for German text-based chat dialogues with language learners. The model is divided into two steps:

1. Recognition of repair initiation and extraction of the trouble source, described in Section 4.5.1.

2. Generation of a repair proper (repair carry-out), explained in Section 4.5.2.

Later, in Chapter 10, we will look at an implementation case study where the proposed model of OISR_M will be realised as a repair manager in a simple conversation programm - a chatbot. The purpose of the present chapter is also to understand what is required from the computational perspective to simulate sequences of OISR_M. Specifically, it is important to know for an implementation what kind of metalinguistic information might be required, what kind of NLP tools might be helpful, and where the limitations are. We will discuss the results and the issues in Section 4.6.

4.2 Repair initiation: signalling trouble in chat

The majority of the repair other-initiations in the dataset belong to one of two abstract types of repair other-initiations:

- statements of *non-understanding*, where a part of the partner's utterance is marked as unclear, and
- *meaning checks*, where the own version of understanding of the problematic unit (candidate understanding) is provided in the repair initiation.

The responses to these different repair initiations require different types of answers. A non-understanding is usually formed as a *content question* and requires an explanation of the trouble source in the repair. A meaning check usually has the form of a *polar question* and requires a yes/no answer which confirms the candidate understanding or rejects it, and then probably explains the original meaning. The interactional resources that the learners use to implement these two types of repair initiation will be analysed here in detail.

There are two distinct types of position for repair other-initiations in the dataset. The first type comes immediately after the trouble source turn (adjacent position). The second type comes later than the adjacent turn. In this case, one or many turns produced by the trouble-speaker or trouble-talk recipient may be between the trouble turn and the repair initiation. The former will be termed *immediate* and the latter *delayed* repair initiation. However, sequentially both correspond to the next-turn repair initiation or second-position repair described in Conversation Analysis (CA) as the first structurally specified place for other-initiated repair (Schegloff, 2000; Liddicoat, 2011). Delayed repair initiations may occur because participants can produce turns simultaneously and follow multiple distinct conversation threads so that the threads are interleaved (virtual adjacency).

This section will argue that there is a dependency between the position of the repair initiation and the interactional resources that need to be involved to produce a repair initiation. We will see that some sorts of resources are dedicated to initiating repair in the immediately adjacent position and cannot be used in the delayed position.

4.2.1 Interactional resources available in chat for repair other-initiation

In the dataset, similarities between the resources for repair initiation described in the CA literature for face-to-face interaction and chat conversations were observed. The reader is invited to look again to Section 2.3.5, specifically open-class repair initiations and specific repair initiations, for a better comparison. However, there are also specific interactional resources in chat influenced by the sequential organisation of the chat (virtual adjacency) and medially written mode of communication. It is also observable that the repair initiations conform to the conversation quantity rule suggested by Grice: they are as short as possible but as informative as needed to understand the problem (see (Auer, 1999) for a short summary). Dingemanse et al. (2015) describe a similar principle with regard to repair other-initiations, which they call the *specifity principle*:

> People choose the most specific repair initiator possible, and the choice is affected by the same kinds of factors in the same way. (Dingemanse et al., 2015, p. 7)

In Example 4.1, the learner initiates a repair by posting three question marks (and nothing else) directly after the trouble source turn. The native speaker N04 is able to locate the trouble source, which is the abbreviation. Why does this work?

Example 4.1. Open-class repair initiation expressed through symbolic means.

615	20:41:24	L08	danke. good night) *thank you. good night*
617	20:41:38	N04	gn8 :-)
618	20:41:48	L08	???
619	20:42:58	N04	gn8 ist ein zusammengeschrumpftes "gute Nacht" (lies: "g" = "gut" und "n8" = "N-Acht") *gn8 is an abbreviation of "good night" (read: "g"="good" and "n8" = "n-ight")*
620	20:43:27	N04	oder englisch, g=good, n-eight *or English, g=good, n-eight*
621	20:43:29	L08	aach sooo)) *I see*
622	20:43:42	N04	:-)

The abbreviation “gn8" is a second pair part of the farewell adjacency pair. Three question marks do not contain any reference to anything that has been said before; therefore, they are interpreted by the native speaker as a signal of non-understanding of the whole previous turn, which contains only the abbreviation and an emoticon. The symbolic resource - question mark - is normally used to mark something as a question, which is something that requires a clarification or an explanation or more information. The native speaker makes his interpretation of the reading of “???" by providing an explanation of the abbreviation in turns 619 and 620. The learner accepts the explanation with a news receipt token in turn 622.

Example 4.2 shows an alternative possibility of a repair initiation referring to the whole previous turn. It is done by an explicit statement of non-understanding accompanied by a sad emoticon "(". The learner L08 makes visible in turn 505 that something in turn 504 is problematic for comprehension, which is, in fact, the whole turn containing colloquial tokens such as *halt* and *nix*. N04 paraphrases the whole message because he interprets the repair initiation as referring to his whole previous turn.

Example 4.2. Open-class repair initiation: lexical means.

504 18:13:50 N04 ich war halt arbeiten, da gibt's nix zu berichten
I was just at work, there is nothing to report
505 18:15:01 L08 ich verstehe nicht(
I do not understand [sad emoticon]
506 18:15:46 N04 damit wollte ich sagen: ich war bei der Arbeit und habe nichts erlebt, was man erzählen könnte
with this I wanted to say: I was at work and did not experience anything that one could tell
I just wanted to say: I was at work and nothing happened that would be worth telling

Repair initiations of this type correspond to open-class repair initiations or unspecific initiations described in the CA literature and discussed in Section 2.3.5. In the dataset, they occur always in the turn immediately following the trouble source turn and refer to the whole trouble source turn. A trouble source turn may contain only one token, but also a longer utterance. This shows that the research results on repair described in Section 2.3.5 for oral conversation are also valid for Conversation Analysis of chat. More specifically, open-class repair initiations can be used in chat in immediate next-turn repair initiations and work in a similar way as in face-to-face conversations. However, delayed next-turn repair initiations do not exist in face-to-face talk and need to be studied more precisely.

Repair initiations can be realised by using demonstrative determiners and demonstrative pronouns, as Example 4.3 illustrates. In turn 168, the learner asks for clarification of the expression that the native speaker posts in turn 167. In addition, L02 provides her own understanding in turn 169, which relates to the topic "dance" discussed in the previous conversations.

The reference to the trouble source *dieser Ausdrück** (En.: *this expression*) in turn 168 points to the entire preceding turn as unclear. In such cases, the use of demonstratives does not make repair initiations more specific than open-class repair initiations.

Example 4.3. Use of a demonstrative determiner to reference the trouble source.

167 20:01:24 N01	Was macht die Kunst? What makes the art? *How are you?*
168 20:03:29 L02	Was bedeutet dieser Ausdrück? Ich verstehe nicht (((*What does this expression [* error] mean? I do not understand*
169 20:04:09 L02	Meinst du Tanzen? *Do you mean dance?*
170 20:04:44 N01	Das habe ich mir schon gedacht :-) Wir verwenden diesen Fragesatz in Deutschland als Synonym für "Wie geht es dir?". Man könnte auch sagen "Was macht die Kunst (des Lebens)?" *That's what I was already thinking about* *We use this question in Germany as a synonym for "How are you?"* *One could also say "How is the art (of life) going?"*
171 20:05:32 L02	Ach so! Ich habe das nicht gewußt)) *I see! I did not know this*

However, it is not always necessary to mark the whole turn produced by the native speaker as a problem. If the learner is able to identify a smaller segment of a trouble turn as problematic, they use more specific references to the trouble source in their repair initiations. Such specific references contain all required information about the nature of the trouble. In Example 4.4, in turn 640 the native speaker uses a word to describe his kinship relations that the learner does not understand. This turn is followed by a counter question *Und du?* (En.: *And you?*) in turn 641. Even without the hidden insertion sequence in turns 642-646, an open-class repair initiation after the counter question in turn 641 would not address the problem with the token *halbBruder* because of the delayed position. Therefore, something more specific is needed to mark the particular turn or even part of it as unclear. The learner reuses the term used by the native speaker, adding a question mark to it, in turn 647. The question mark signalises the need for more information with regard to this particular term. This request is interpreted by the native speaker as the need for an explanation of the meaning of this word. The explanation is delivered in turn 648.

Recycling of one or many tokens combined with symbolic means (mostly question marks, but also combined with dashes and quotes) to signalise trouble with one word or a part of a message is frequently used by chat participants in the dataset. However, lexical means to signalise trouble are also present in the corpus (explicit statements of non-understanding), as shown in Example 4.5. The learner L08 copies a part of the partner's message and adds an explicit statement of non-understanding in a new line of her message followed by a smile (the closing parenthesis) in turn 120.

Example 4.4. Using repetitions of the trouble source to initiate a repair (simplified).

634 19:45:33 L07 und hast du geschwister?
and have you brothers and sisters?
639 19:47:05 N03 Einen älteren Bruder
An older brother
640 19:47:34 N03 Und einen jüngeren halbBruder
And a younger half-brother
641 19:49:29 N03 Und du?
And you?
`[turns 642-646 build an insertion sequence]`
647 19:53:35 L07 halbbruder??
half-brother?
648 19:54:56 N03 Sohn meines leiblichen Vaters und der Lebensgefährtin nach meiner Mutter
Son of my biological father and his partner for life after my mother
649 19:55:53 L07 aaa... dann ich habe auch einen... und wie ich schon geschriben habe eine schwester..))
aaa ... then I also have one... and as I already have written one sister

Example 4.5. Reuse part of a message (simplified).

118 18:50:30 N04 Ja, Kommissar Rex hab ich früher auch geschaut... Das muß 15 Jahre her sein, da kannst Du dich dran erinnern?
Yes, Kommissar Rex have I earlier also watched... This must 15 years back be, there can you yourself on recall?
Yes, I used to watch Kommissar Rex, too... This must be already 15 years ago, you can still remember that?
120 18:52:53 L08 her sein, da kannst Du dich dran erinnern?
verstehe nicht)
back be, there can you yourself on recall?
understand not
back be, there can you yourself on recall?
don't understand
121 18:53:33 L08 her=früher
back=earlier
122 18:54:26 N04 etwas ist schon lange her = "etwas ist vor langer Zeit passiert"
something is already long back = "something happened a long time ago"
123 18:55:57 N04 und "dran" (umgangssprachlich) = "daran" (hochdeutsch)
and "dran" (colloquial) = "thereon" (hochdeutsch)
124 18:56:29 L08 aha...nun in Belarus wurde es später passiert.
I see... well, it was happened later in Belarus.
125 18:56:59 L08 oh danke für solche Erklärungen))
oh thank you for such explanations

To sum up, Examples 4.1 to 4.5 in this section illustrate a common prototypical structure of next-turn repair initiations where a unit of the trouble source turn is marked as unclear by lexical or symbolic means (signalling non-understanding):

reference to the trouble source + signalling non-understanding

Candidate understanding or meaning check is another possibility to mark a unit of an utterance as not (completely) clear. In this case the repair other-initiation is designed as a polar question requiring a confirming or a disconfirming answer. It may be necessary to check the similarity of two different descriptions of an object in order to generate a response to such a question automatically.

Example 4.6. Many many people.

221	18:45:26	L08	ja ich habe über Oktoberfest gehört, etwas lustiges und buntes)) *yes I have heard about Oktoberfest, something funny and colourful*
222	18:46:25	N04	ja, und teures und überfülltes ;-) *yes, and expensive and overfilled*
223	18:47:48	L08	))überfülltes bedeutet "viele viele Leute"? *overfilled means "many many people"?*
224	18:48:14	N04	genau *exactly*

Example 4.6 shows a fragment of a chat where the native speaker N04 uses the word *überfülltes* to describe an event in Munich (turn 221). The learner L08 checks her understanding of this term in turn 223 by copying the trouble source and providing her own candidate understanding of the word. A confirmation follows in turn 224. In this way, Example 4.6 illustrates a prototypical repair initiation format for a meaning check:

left-hand part + EQUALS-*token* + *right-hand part* + *turn-final element*

The EQUALS-tokens that can be found in the dataset are either lexical such as *bedeutet* and *heisst* or symbolic such as "=" and "-". The borders of the left-hand part and/or right-hand part may also be marked in addition with quotes (*framing*) or uppercase (*highlighting*). The turn-final element may be symbolic, such as one or many questions marks, or lexicalised, like for instance the question *habe ich das richtig verstanden?* (En.: *did I understand it correctly?*). The turn-final element has the function to mark the turn as a question seeking confirmation.

The repair initiations produced by the learners in the dataset always try to resolve problems with the meaning of something in the native speaker's utterance. None of the repair initiations was concerned with the form by itself. Given that repair other-initiations can occur anywhere in conversation because anything can potentially cause problems with understanding of the talk by the recipient, there are some specific units in every language that become likely trouble sources for non-native speakers. These are in particular idiomatic expressions and abbreviations. These two categories of lexical units frequently cause repair other-initiations in the dataset. Sometimes the learner marked the whole message of the native speaker as unclear because they were not able to identify the problem more specifically. Examples 4.2 (page 115) and 4.13 (page 125) contain instances of such repair initiations. However, as soon as the learners understand what exactly is the problem in the native speaker's turn, they make their repair initiations very specific; see for instance Example 4.4 on page 117 (*halbbruder*) and Examples 4.9 and 4.10 on page 123 (*eckball*, *in sachen essen*).

To sum up, the following types of trouble sources have been identified in the dataset:

1. The whole one-word message.
2. The whole longer message.
3. A part of a longer message.
4. An idiomatic expression which is a part of a message or the entire message.
5. A single word which is a part of a longer message.
6. A single word which is the entire message.

These types will play a role in the production of repair by native speakers, as the reader will see in Section 4.5.2.

4.2.2 When the recognition of the repair other-initiation fails

As Schegloff pointed out, "there appears to be a determinate set of turn formats used to initiate such [other-initiated] repair" (Schegloff, 1993). In addition, it has been shown that other-initiated repair is present in all languages, meaning that no language is known until now that does not have other-initiated repair (Dingemanse et al., 2014). It has also been shown by Dingemanse et al. (2014) that the majority of repair formats exists in all analysed languages. Learners of a language, however, sometimes have difficulties formulating a repair initiation properly in the foreign language. This makes the correct interpretation of the repair initiation difficult for the native speaker. It also increases the variance in referencing and signalling and makes the intended natural language understanding task more challenging. Example 4.7 invites us to look closer at one such repair sequence.

There are several problems with the repair initiation in turn 304 of this example. First, L03 wrongly identifies the part of the native speaker's turn *zwei Tage krieg* as an idiomatic expression. However, she refers to this trouble source as *dieses* Phraseologismus* (En.: *this phraseologism [* wrong determiner-noun congruence]*). The reference cannot be resolved by the native speaker; therefore, she starts a nested repair initiation sequence in turn 305, which also contains an exposed correction (see Chapter 5 for a detailed discussion of exposed corrections and this example in particular). Turn 306 contains an uptake of the corrected congruence error. Due to a small difference in time stamps of turns 305 and 306 it is hard to say whether it was a self-correction or an acceptance of the explicit correction provided by the native speaker. Second, even the explicit repair initiation in turn 307 does not properly locate the trouble source because the learner segmented the utterance wrongly, *zwei Tage krieg* (possibly En.: *two days of war*) instead of *zwei Tage rumkriegen* (En.: *to get around two days*).

In addition, by using the term *Phraseologismus* to refer to the trouble source in turns 304 and 306, L03 positions herself as an expert in linguistics, and, at the same time, she produces a grammatical error combining a neutral gender determiner with the male gender noun. This might be one of the reasons why the native speaker refuses to provide a proper clarification until the end of this sequence: two contradictory identities of L03 are interleaved, one of the language expert and one of the language novice. L03 provides an explicit reference to the trouble source, repeating the problematic unit in turn 307. However, the native speaker still does not provide any repair of the linguistic trouble source, commenting on learning in turn 308 instead. In order to explain the part of the message that really caused the problem, the native speaker would have to show the learner that she is *not* an expert (she wrongly identified the expression as idiomatic and she even wrongly segmented the utterance), which might be too much face threatening. The native speaker prefers to let it pass.

Example 4.7. Learner failed to reference the trouble source properly.

303	17:10:14	N02	Danke, bis Dienstag ist noch Schule und dann sind endlich Ferien :) aber die zwei Tage krieg ich jetzt auch noch rum! Thanks, till Tuesday is still school and then are finally holidays but the two days get I as well around! *Thanks, we have classes till Tuesday, but then we have holidays finally but the two days will pass as well!*
304	17:12:11	L03	ach so, ja, ab dem 1. August, ich erinnere mich jetzt... dieses Phraseologismus habe ich noch nie gehört :) oh so, yes, from the 1st of August, I recall now... this* [neutrum] phraseologism [maskulinum] have I yet never heard *oh, I see, yes, beginning on the 1st of August, I recall now... I have never heard this phraseologism*
305	17:12:26	N02	welchen? ;) which [maskulinum] one? *which one?*
306	17:12:32	L03	dei Phraseologismus :) [typo: intended "den" - determiner maskulinum] phraseologism *the phraseologism*
307	17:12:51	L03	über zwei Tage krieg *about two days war*
308	17:13:10	N02	oh ach so ;) haha, dann lernst du hier ja sogar noch etwas :) *oh I see, then you will even learn something here*
309	17:14:38	L03	hahaha, aber ich zweifele jetzt, ob es wirklich eine Idiomatische Wendung ist ist hahaha, but I doubt now if it really an idiomatic phrase is is* *hahaha, but I doubt now if it is really an idiomatic expression*
310	17:16:52	N02	nein, das ist wohl eher Dialekt... *no, this is rather dialect...*
311	17:16:53	N02	;)
312	17:18:27	L03	ach so... in jedem Fall interesant. *oh, I see... interesting anyway.*

4.3 Repair carry-out strategies

This section describes the strategies that the native speakers deployed to carry out repair with linguistic trouble source in response to repair initiations. Repair carry-out strategies depend on the type of the trouble source and the repair initiation format. As explained earlier, in Section 4.2, some of the repair initiations require a yes/no answer, and some of them require definition work or paraphrasing of the trouble source. Both yes/no answers and definition work can be carried out in different ways, as the reader will see in the remainder of this section.

If the trouble source is an abbreviation, the definition work carried out by the native speaker normally contained a full spelling of the abbreviated words and their explanation. For chat abbreviations, a full reading of the abbreviation was normally provided. Normally, this was also sufficient for an explanation, as Example 4.1 demonstrates. The problematic abbreviation is always repeated in all relevant examples in this dataset, then a full spelling or, as for chat jargon, an intended reading is provided.

If the trouble source is one semantic unit (e.g. one word or an idiomatic expression), a dictionary-like definition is often selected to provide a repair. A dictionary-like definition may contain synonyms and examples. For longer messages or longer parts of longer messages, a strategy of splitting the message into smaller semantic units and separate explanation of each unit can be chosen, as illustrated in Example 4.5 on page 117, turns 121-123. Paraphrasing is also one of the strategies used by the native speakers to explain longer messages; see Example 4.2 on page 115, turn 506.

4.3.1 Providing definitions, paraphrases and synonyms

Examples 4.3 and 4.4 in the preceding section (page 116) and 4.8 below show instances of repair where the native speaker tries to resolve troubles in understanding by providing definitions, paraphrases and synonyms for the trouble sources. For instance, turn 170 of Example 4.3 contains a synonym of the problematic expression. Turns 172 and 173 provide in addition an explanation about the use of the expression. In Example 4.4, the trouble in understanding the word *Halbbruder* (En.: *half-brother*) is resolved by an explanation of the family relations.

Example 4.8. Ins Auge fassen (prev. Ex. 3.12).

122 13:08:39 N04 zugegeben, ich war dieses Jahr auch noch in keinem See, aber so langsam könnte man das mal ins Auge fassen :-)
admitted, I was this year not in a lake, either, but slowly one could reach this into the eye
I admit I was this year not at a lake, either, but I could slowly consider it
123 13:10:47 L09 ins auge fassen?
reach into the eye?
124 13:11:56 N04 das heißt _hier_ etwa soviel wie "planen" oder "bald mal machen"
it means here something like "to plan" or "to do soon"
125 13:12:16 L09 :) :)
126 13:12:22 L09 klar
I see

Example 4.8 illustrates another sequence where the learner has problems understanding an idiomatic expression. This excerpt was already discussed in Section 3.4.2

from the perspective of all potential types of repair as a means for making differential language expertise relevant in talk; see Example 3.12 on page 90. The excerpt is repeated here for convenience. In this sequence, turn 123 contains a repair initiation produced by the learner. The native speaker N04 uses synonyms to construct an explanation for an idiomatic expression in turn 124. He emphasises in addition that this expression was used with this meaning in this particular context (_*hier*_, En.: *here*).

4.3.2 Translations and demonstrations

Other strategies implemented by the native speakers for definition work that can be found in our dataset include translations into a different language and hyperlinks to examples of the objects referenced by the trouble source expressions. The translations were done manually into a shared foreign language or automatically into the native language of the learner using a machine translation service. Hyperlinks as an explanation strategy were used in combination with textual explanation of the trouble source expressions, or on their own. The reader is invited to analyse these four strategies for repair carry-out below on examples from the dataset.

Example 4.9 illustrates how a translation into English, which was a shared foreign language for N04 and L08, can be used in addition to a textual explanation of the problematic unit in a native speaker's talk. Turn 528 contains a trouble source *Eckball*, which is made visible in turn 530 by the learner in the form of a repair initiation. Turn 531 contains the English translation of the German word *Eckball*. The following turn 532 provides in addition an explanation in German how the ball must be played in this situation.

Example 4.9. Use English translation to repair.

528	18:47:09	N04	und schon ein Eckball für Deutschland! *and already a corner kick for Germany*
529	18:47:28	N04	doch nicht :-(*not yet*
530	18:47:29	L08	eckball? *corner kick?*
531	18:47:42	N04	corner kick auf englisch *corner kick in English*
532	18:48:05	N04	der Ball wird von einer Ecke des Spielfelds vor's Tor gespielt *the ball is being played from a corner of the field of play to the goal*
533	18:48:22	N04	aber diesmal noch nicht, denn der Schiedsrichter hat sich noch mal umentschieden *but this time not yet, because the referee changed his decision again*
534	18:48:25	L08	aga, etzt klar) [acknowledgement token], now [*error: typo, missing verb] clear *I see, now it's clear*

Example 4.10 shows how a machine translation service can be used for definition work. It might be important to know for the analysis of this sequence that N03 is learning Russian as a foreign language, but he has just started and cannot converse in Russian.

Example 4.10. In Sachen Essen: repair is carried out using machine translation.

376 07:40:24 N03 gibt es irgendwas moskau typisches in sachen essen?
is there something typical for moscow in things food?
is there some kind of food which is typical for moscow?
377 07:41:03 L07 in sachen essen???
in things food???
378 07:41:31 L07 übersetze bitte)))
translate please [smile]
379 07:44:36 N03 какая пища является типичным Москве?
which food is typical [* wrong noun-adjective congruence] [* missing preposition] Moscow?
which food is typical for Moscow?

Turn 376 contains an expression that the learner does not (fully) understand: *in sachen essen*. This expression is marked as a trouble source in the repair initiation in turns 377 and 378. Turn 377 locates the trouble source and marks the expression as unclear. Turn 378 contains an instruction for what kind of explanation is desired.

The learner is aware of the fact that N03's level of knowledge in Russian is not enough to translate this, but she challenges him in her repair initiation; however, the word *translate* can also mean *say it in a language that I understand*. The native speaker chooses the playful version of translation and translates his question using an online machine translation service despite having no idea about the quality of the translation.

Example 4.11. Demonstration in addition to the textual definition work.

541 18:52:01 L08 du bist heute ein internationaler Fussballkommentator)
today you are an international football commentator
542 18:52:43 N04 ja, ich bin grad sowas wie der Live-Ticker
yes, I'm now something like a live-ticker
543 18:54:49 L08 Ticker–nicht besond. verstehe Bedeutung
Ticker - I don't exactly understand the meaning
544 18:57:19 N04 der Begriff kommt vom "newsticker", den man früher in Zeitungsredaktionen stehen hatte
The term comes from "newsticker", which they had in the past in newspaper editorial offices
545 18:57:30 N04 und heute meint man damit sowas: HYPERLINK
and today we mean with it something like: HYPERLINK
546 18:57:37 N04 oder sowas: HYPERLINK-11freunde
or something like: HYPERLINK-11freunde
547 18:58:13 N04 (der 11freunde-Ticker ist allerdings nicht ganz so ernst gemeint)
the 11freunde-ticker is however not meant very seriously
548 18:59:23 L08 nun im großen und ganzen verstehe ich)
well, in general, I understand

As already mentioned, participants in the chat conversation may use hyperlinks to further information resources on the Web for repair carry-out. In Example 4.11, the learner compares the native speaker to an international football commentator (turn

541) because he comments in chat on everything that is happening on the TV in a football game (before turn 541). However, the term *Live-Ticker* is from N04's point of view conceptually closer to what he was doing (textual comments instead of oral comments as usually done by commentators on the TV); therefore, an embedded correction is performed in turn 542: the term *Fussballkommentator* (En.:*football commentator*) has been replaced by the term *Live-Ticker*. Unfortunately, the learner does not understand the term *Live-Ticker* and initiates the repair in turn 543, marking only a part of the term as unclear (*Ticker*) and producing L2 errors in her repair initiation in addition. The native speaker explains the origin of the word in turn 544 and provides in turns 545 and 546 two hyperlinks to websites with live-ticker examples to demonstrate what they look like. Turn 547 explains how the learner should interpret the demonstration from turn 546.

Example 4.12 illustrates how explicit definition work can be avoided while still providing a preferred response to a repair initiation. In this case it is just a demonstration of an instance of a *live stream*. Indeed, it is not easy to explain what a life stream is. The term *Livestream* is used by the native speaker in turn 653. The learner marks this term as unclear in turn 656 (delayed repair initiation). The native speaker provides a link to the live stream that he is watching. This action is implicitly accepted as an appropriate clarification by the learner in turn 659.

Example 4.12. Use of a hyperlink to an example.

653	19:22:14	N04	[elided] ich schau mir gerade den Livestream von einer Preisverleihung an *I am watching the live stream of an award at the moment*
654	19:22:43	N04	es geht da um einen Preis für Unternehmensgründer *it is about a prize for the company founder*
655	19:22:59	N04	meine Chefs haben auch etwas bekommen :-) *my bosses got something, too*
656	19:23:22	L08	Livestream? *Live stream?*
657	19:23:28	N04	der interessante Teil ist vorbei, aber hier ist der Link: *the interesting part is over, but here is the link:*
658	19:23:34	N04	HYPERLINK
658	19:24:23	N04	was gerade läuft ist ein Portrait des Preisträgers in der Kategorie "Lebenswerk" *what is running now is a portrait of the winner in the category of "lifetime achievement"*
659	19:28:18	L08	und wo sind deine Chefs?)oder sie fehlen) *and where are your bosses? or they are missing*

4.3.3 Non-present repair carry-out after other-initiation

Repair carry-out is a preferred response to a repair initiation, but not the only one possible. Example 4.7 showed that not every repair initiation contains a proper reference to the trouble source and therefore such repair requests have little chance of being satisfied in the repair response. Example 4.13 shows another case where a dispreferred response to a repair initiation is provided, namely, a comment on the topic of the talk, but not the expected next which would be a repair.

Example 4.13. Non-present self-repair carry-out after other-initiation.

395	20:43:29	L08	oh, Spiel ist am Ende od. am Anfang?
			oh, the match is at the end or at the beginning?
396	20:43:43	N04	ist in etwa 5 Min. aus
			is over in about 5 min.
397	20:44:04	L08	unklar
			unclear
398	20:44:07	N04	Schweden 2:3 England
			Sweden 2:3 England

The problem with the trouble source - the whole turn 396 - is never clarified in the chat between L08 and N04. An explanation of the linguistic trouble is omitted by the native speaker. Instead, he provides information about the state of the game, addressing a potential problem with understanding the situation in the game.

The explanation *why* the repair has not been carried out may be very simple: there are only 3 seconds between the repair initiation in turn 397 and the next turn of the native speaker. It is very likely that there was an overlap in production of the turns 397 and 398. The native speaker probably did not want to ignore the repair initiation. However, the turn containing the comment on the topic "Sweden 2:3 England" came just *after* the repair initiation and could be interpreted by the learner as a response to it, even though it does not explain the problem. The fact *that* a repair carry-out is non-present (or maybe even missing) and the problem is not clarified seems not to have any impact to the continuation of the interaction. The learner does not re-initiate repair, and with the continuation of the talk, the problem becomes irrelevant. Thus, the non-present repair carry-out does not have any sequential consequences in this case.

4.4 Empirical findings and discussion

The preceding sections analysed a collection of other-initiated self-repair sequences where native speakers produced something in their turns that non-native speakers could not (completely) understand, so asked for explanation or clarification. Specifically, the reader was invited to look at interactional resources that language learners made available in text-based instant messaging dialogues in German to produce repair other-initiations, at the positions relative to the trouble turns where the repair other-initiations were placed, and at the types of troubles addressed. This analysis was performed with the purpose of computational modelling of such sequences; therefore, turn formats for repair other-initiations in chat are of special interest. In particular, the intended model needs to distinguish between repair other-initiations and all other turns, and to identify the trouble source in a given repair initiation.

Repair initiation formats combining interactional practices and devices were analysed. Specific devices are used to signal trouble and other devices are used to reference the trouble source. More specifically, it was found that:

- Questioning is *the* practice to initiate repair in chat, confirming the results in the academic literature for oral interaction (Dingemanse et al., 2014). Other practices are declarations of lack of understanding such as *unklar* and *ich verstehe nicht* (labelling).
- Devices for signalling trouble are question marks, dashes, explicit statements of non-understanding and presenting candidate understandings.
- References to the trouble source may be realised through adjacent position, demonstrative proterms and repetitions.
- Delayed repair initiation requires more specific referencing of trouble source; open-class repair initiations cannot be used in a delayed second position.
- Repetition-based repair initiations may contain repetitions of one specific unit from the previous turn or contain a copy of a piece of the preceding turn regardless of the unit boundaries. The latter may be placed between open-class and restricted-class repair initiations. Such types of repetitions have not previously been described in the academic literature and must be typical for non-native speakers.
- Communication medium influences repair initiation types and formats. In particular, repair initiations eliciting a repetition of the trouble source are uncommon in chat. Misreadings are possible, but they are made visible through misproductions in repetition-based repair initiations.
- Non-native speaker identity influences the format of candidate understandings, which differ from those in L1 talk.
- Repair initiation is one option to deal with trouble in comprehension. Learners may make use of other options, too (dictionary look-up, let-it-pass...). The learner's interactional and linguistic competence influence the selection of a repair initiation format and its successful recognition.

Repair carry-out is the preferred and the most frequent response to a repair initiation but other forms of responses are also possible. For instance a new repair sequence may be initiated in order to deal with difficulties in identification of the trouble and responses which do not address the trouble. The following was found with regard to repair carry-out formats:

- Explanations of the meaning, translations and demonstrations are the most frequent forms of repair carry-outs.
- Repair design is linked to expectations of what is known to the repair recipient. Consequently, repairs are designed to target the language learners' difficulties in linguistic matters.
- Repair carry-outs may be immediate or delayed.
- References to the trouble source may be realised by the same resources as for repair initiations.
- There are dependencies between types of trouble source and participants' selection of resources for referencing the trouble source. For instance, abbreviations are usually repeated.

It was shown that each repair initiation contains some symbolic or lexical signs that are dedicated to *signal* the trouble, and other resources that are used to point to the trouble source, so-called *referencing*. Depending on the position of the repair other-initiation relative to the trouble turn, different sets of resources may be used to reference the trouble source. Normally, the next turn position is dedicated for repair other-initiation, after which a self-repair follows (Schegloff, 2000). Because text-based chat allows for virtual adjacency (Tudini, 2010), next-turn repair initiations may appear immediately after the trouble turn, as in oral talk, or a few turns later, where turns belonging to a different thread in conversation may intervene.

Open-class repair initiations do not contain an explicit reference to the trouble source. The referencing is signalled by the adjacent position immediately after the trouble turn. Use of demonstrative pronouns and determiners makes sense only in immediate repair initiations, too. In both cases, the complete trouble turn is marked as problematic. More precise references use a copy (reuse) or a modified copy (re-cycle) of a part of the trouble turn to reference the trouble source. Such repeat-based references to the trouble source can be used in immediate and in delayed repair other-initiations. Various means to frame (e.g. by quotation marks) or to highlight (e.g. by upper case) the trouble source in repeat-based repair initiations may be used in addition to make the turn format more clear and to emphasise its social action and interactional function, namely, repair other-initiation.

For signalling the trouble, a variety of symbolic and lexical means were used by language learners. Symbolic means include question marks, dashes, quotation marks and equal signs. Lexical means include explicit statements of non-understanding such as *Ich verstehe nicht* or *unklar*. Lexicalised equivalents of paralinguistic cues were not used by language learners to initiate repair, as opposed to native speakers' *hä?* used for this purpose. This confirms that models based only on native speaker data may not reflect reality in interaction with learners.

The dataset contains examples where native speakers had difficulties with recognition of learners' turns as repair initiations because learners had problems with referencing the trouble source. Such cases will make automatic recognition of repair initiations even more difficult. Sometimes, native speakers failed to produce a repair proper. However, it is very likely that they simply did not notice the learner's repair initiation.

Repair carry-outs provided by the native speakers were tailored to the type of the trouble source. If it was an abbreviation, the trouble was resolved by a complete writing of the abbreviated words. If a word or an idiom caused trouble in understanding, an explanation of the meaning of these items was provided. If a longer part of a turn or a longer turn caused a problem with comprehension, it was paraphrased or only a few words, which were supposed to be the trouble source, were explained. Sometimes translation into other shared languages was used to explain unknown terms.

Native speakers were very creative in providing explanations of unknown terms. Although using synonyms, examples and paraphrasing is a frequently used form of self-repair carry-out, various external resources from the internet were involved in explanations. Native speakers used hyperlinks to show examples of entities referred to by words that were unknown to the learner, such as *Liveticker*. In addition, machine translation tools were used to present a translation of unknown expressions to the learner. to summarise, various information resources from the Internet were used by native speakers in instant messaging dialogues *as an interactional resource*. This is impossible in a face-to-face interaction without technology.

In order to "serve computational interests" (Schegloff, 1996), the following needs to be taken into account for the purpose of modelling. Because repair initiations may occur *anywhere*, each user utterance may be a repair initiation. Therefore, a repair initiation recognition routine needs to be activated after *every* user turn. Two essential problems must be solved by a computer program in order to react to a repair initiation properly:

1. Recognise that the user's utterance is a repair initiation,
2. Recognise the source of trouble and the kind of the problem.

Repair initiation formats need to be "translated" into computational models of repair initiations to make the findings applicable for computational purposes. The next section will focus on this task.

4.5 A local model of other-initiated self-repair

Repair initiations normally contain all the necessary information for human participants to understand that there is a problem with comprehension, to locate the trouble source (TS) and to identify the type of trouble. However, sometimes additional work is required for the participants to clarify what exactly is unclear. This process can become very complex and the trouble source may or may not be identified at the end of the clarification sequence. However, such nested repair sequences where repair initiation itself becomes a new trouble source still have the same prototypical structure. There is something in a preceding turn that is marked as a trouble source in the ongoing turn and is resolved in the subsequent turn. The basic structure including a trouble source, a repair initiation and a repair carry-out is kept in nested repair sequences as well. Therefore, for simplicity, we focus here only on repair sequences where no additional work for the identification of the trouble source is needed.

Because every repair other-initiation also contains information about the kind of trouble that the trouble-talk recipient has, it is possible for the recipient of the repair other-initiation (who is also the trouble-speaker) to recognise *that* there is a problem with understanding and *what kind* of problem occurred. A repair proper is delivered after that. Because nothing in conversation is dedicated to be a trouble source by itself, but everything in conversation may appear to be a source of trouble for the recipient of a piece of talk, repair initiations may occur after each turn. For chat-based communication with an artificial agent, this means that every message of the user may be a repair initiation. Therefore, each user's turn needs to be checked to see whether it is a repair initiation.

With this motivation, we will divide the handling of $OISR_M$ in two steps:

1. Recognition of repair other-initiation and extraction of the trouble source;
2. Self-repair carry-out.

The model described in this chapter specifically concerns OISR_M sequences with linguistic trouble source, i.e. when troubles in the learner's comprehension occur due to their not yet fully proficient level of knowledge of the foreign language.

4.5.1 Modelling recognition of repair initiation and identification of the trouble source

In the dataset, the most frequently used device for marking the trouble source and signalling a problem with understanding was reusing the problematic token or phrase and appending one or more question marks to it. In such repair initiations, the question marks are used to signal that something is wrong with the copied part of the trouble- turn. The copied part is used to point to the trouble source. Each class of repair initiations discussed in Chapter 2 also contains a specific way of referencing the trouble source. To extract a trouble source from the repair initiation and the corresponding trouble-turn, we will look at possibilities to reference the trouble source that we found in the dataset. The following types of referencing appear in the OISR_M sequences with linguistic trouble source:

1. Repeat-based initiations: *reuse* (a 1:1-copy of the trouble source), *recycle* the trouble source (rewriting it in a slightly different way),
2. Demonstratives-based initiations: using demonstrative adverbs, determiners and pronouns, such as *dieser Ausdruck* or simply *das*,
3. Open-class initiations: referencing by placing a statement of non-understanding in a turn adjacent to the trouble source turn. The adjacent position of the repair initiation references the whole preceding turn as a trouble turn. Therefore we refer to this type of referencing as *reference by position.*

To extract the trouble source from a repair initiation, it is good to know how big the trouble source is and what is the scope of the search. Each class of repair initiations listed just above is dedicated to reference trouble of a particular size: either it is the whole preceding message (open-class and demonstratives-based repair initiations) or it is only a part of it (repeat-based and recycle-based initiations). Then, there are three cases of trouble sources: a single word (part of a longer message or a one-word message), part of a message (PoM) of two or more words, and a whole message consisting of two or more words.

As we discussed in the preceding sections, signalling trouble involves symbolic and/or lexicalised means of signalling and a specific format designed either to mark something as unclear or to compare the trouble source with the initiator's own version of understanding. We will call the combination of these resources the *signalling format*.

Table 4.1 summarises the different possibilities to reference the trouble source and to signalise troubles with comprehension that were found in the dataset. Demonstrative determiners (DD) or demonstrative pronouns (DP) may be used in combination with the adjacent position to point to the trouble source. The architecture of the repair initiation (RI) for this type of OISR can be formalised as follows. Depending on the time, different formats for the repair initiation may be used:

Time	Ref.	Signalling	Used for
Immediate	Reuse, recycle	One or more "?" also combined with one or more "-", explicit statements of non-understanding, lack of knowledge, requests for help, candidate understandings	Single word, PoM
	Position	Multiple "?", non-lexical tokens of non-understanding, explicit statement of non-understanding, requests for help	Entire message
	Position, DD/DP	DD/DP in combination with explicit statements of non-understanding, candidate understandings	Entire message
Delayed	Reuse, recycle	One or more "?" also combined with "-", explicit statement of non-understanding, lack of knowledge, ask for help, candidate understandings	Entire message, single words, PoM

Table 4.1: Referencing trouble source and signalling trouble

$$RI = TIME \times RIFormat \tag{4.1}$$

Time may be immediate or delayed: $TIME = \{immediate,\ delayed\}$. A repair initiation format is a combination of a reference to the trouble source and a selected signalling format:

$$RIFormat = REF \times SignalFormat \tag{4.2}$$

As mentioned earlier, repeat-based references such as reusing $reuse(x)$ and recycling $recycle(x)$ include the trouble source. References can also be based on demonstrative determiners DD or demonstrative pronouns DP. In addition, adjacent position-based AP references may be used to refer to the trouble source in the repair initiation. The signalling format may mark something in the trouble turn as unclear $unclear(x)$ or present a candidate understanding in comparison to the trouble source $equals(x, y)$. The trouble source x and the candidate understanding y may be a single word, an idiomatic expression, part of a message or a complete turn (utterance).

$$REF = \{reuse(x),\ recycle(x),\ AP,\ DD,\ DP\} \tag{4.3}$$

$$SignalFormat = \{unclear(x),\ equals(x, y)\} \tag{4.4}$$

$$x, y \in \{word,\ idiom,\ PoM,\ utterance\} \tag{4.5}$$

For each repair initiation, if only the adjacent position or only a demonstratives-based reference was used in the repair initiation to point to the trouble source, then the scope for the trouble source extraction is limited to the preceding turn.

if $REF \in \{AP,\ DD,\ DP\}$ **then**
| $TIME = \{immediate\}$;
else
| $REF \in \{reuse(x),\ recycle(x)\}$;
| $TIME \in \{immediate,\ delayed\}$;
end

This repair recognition procedure is also expected to differentiate between ordinary questions related to the subject of the ongoing talk and repair initiations. It works because ordinary questions are not formatted as $unclear(x)$ or $equals(x, y)$.

If a complete turn is recognised as a trouble source and this turn is a longer message, further filters may be applied to identify more precisely which of the parts of the longer message may cause a problem with comprehension. Such more precise trouble source identifications may be influenced by the learner model (which words the learner is supposed to understand), but also by the system's capabilities to generate a repair proper (are paraphrases available or only synonyms for single words). We will address this problem in Section 10.3, providing examples of possible further filters.

After a successful identification of a repair other-initiation and a trouble source extraction, generation of a repair proper is required. The next section will describe the model for repair carry-out.

4.5.2 Modelling self-repair carry-out

Repair carry-out in conversations with learners differs depending on the trouble-speaker and repair initiator. As illustrated on multiple examples in this chapter, different types of repair proper are designed to solve the learner's problems with comprehension of the native speaker's talk, and the other way round. While explanations of the meaning of the trouble source are delivered to the learner (the trouble source is not replaced), *different* descriptions of the objects or actions are delivered to the native speaker (the trouble source is replaced).

Similarly to repair initiations and their relative position to the trouble source, the repair carry-out part of a repair sequence can occur immediately after the repair initiation or a few turns later. Additionally, it can contain a lexical reference to the trouble source, such as repeat-based and demonstratives-based references, or point to it just by occurring in the adjacent position just after the subsequent repair initiation. The format of the repair proper depends on the format of the repair initiation and on the type of the trouble source.

Table 4.2 contains dependencies between repair other-initiations and the subsequent self-repairs that were identified in thedata set. We use the abbreviation RI to refer to repair initiation, and the abbreviation RCO to refer to repair carry-out in the table and in the remainder of this chapter. *Split-reuse* is a type of reference to the

TS Type	RI Signaling	RCO Time	RCO Reference	RCO Type
Abbreviation	$unclear(x)$	immediate	reuse	spell out, synonym, example
		delayed		
Single word or idiom	$equals(x, y)$	immediate	position	confirm, disconfirm
		delayed	reuse	
	$unclear(x)$	immediate	position	definition, synonym, example, translation
		delayed	reuse	
Long turn, long part of a turn	$unclear(x)$	immediate	split-reuse	$explain(x)$ for all x
			position +/- DP	paraphrase

Table 4.2: Dependencies between repair other-initiations and self-repair carry-out

trouble source which did not appear in repair other-initiations but was found in corresponding self-repair carry-outs. This way of referencing corresponds to self-repairs where native speakers only explained a few words from a longer turn or longer part of a turn marked as a trouble source. The trouble source was split into tokens, and only tokens that were supposed to cause the trouble were explained. This is shown in Table 4.2 in the form of the $explain(x)$ function where x is the extracted trouble source. The corresponding trouble-signalling format is denoted by $unclear(x)$ and $equals(x, y)$, as in the preceding section.

All repair other-initiations in repair sequences with linguistic trouble source that were found in the dataset can be interpreted as either a content question “What does x mean?" or a polar question “Does x mean y?" Table 4.2 reflects this observation. A confirmation or a disconfirmation is an appropriate type of self-repair carry-out after a repair other-initiation presenting candidate understanding $equals(x, y)$. All other self-repair carry-outs are expected to provide an explanation of the unit that is marked as problematic: a simple yes or no would not be sufficient.

The following decision routine for self-repair carry-out results from the dependencies summarised in Table 4.2. Because different options are available for referencing trouble source in immediate and delayed self-repairs, time needs to be taken into account in the abstract description of the self-repair carry-outs:

$$RCO = TIME \times RCOFormat \tag{4.6}$$

As for the repair other-initiations, time may be immediate or delayed:

$$TIME = \{immediate,\ delayed\} \tag{4.7}$$

A self-repair carry-out is a product of a reference to the trouble source and the function which it is expected to perform: confirming/disconfirming answer or explanation:

$$
\begin{aligned}
RCOFormat &= REF \times RCOFunction && (4.8)\\
REF &= \{reuse(x),\ recycle(x),\ AP,\ DD, DP, && (4.9)\\
&\quad splitReuse(x),\ splitRecycle(x)\} && (4.10)\\
RCOFunction &= \{explain(x),\ confirm(equals(x,y))\} && (4.11)
\end{aligned}
$$

Depending on the timing of the self-repair production, different types of referencing may be appropriate: delayed self-repairs need to update the focus of the talk, and therefore a repeat-based reference makes more sense than other types of referencing.

if $TIME = \{immediate\}$ **then**
| $REF \in \{reuse(x),\ recycle(x),\ AP,\ DD,\ DP\}$;
else
| $REF \in \{reuse(x),\ recycle(x)\}$;
end

In practice, the function $explain(x)$ needs to be implemented differently for different types of trouble source (see column RCO Type in Table 4.2). For instance, abbreviations from chat jargon are typically explained by spelling out the intended reading of the abbreviation. For all other abbreviations a full version of the word(s) is presented, sometimes in combination with examples, synonyms and comments on the topic. Practices used to explain whole messages consisting of two or more words include splitting the message into single words and explanation of a couple words of the message and paraphrasing. The quality of the response is highly dependent on the linguistic resources available for the artificial conversation partner.

4.6 Results

Because repair is a building block of conversation, it is absolutely reasonable to expect conversational software to be able to perform proper handling of repair initiations and distinguish between questions with the function of repair initiation and all other questions. However, the great majority of conversational agents and dialogue systems were designed with the assumption that the user understands everything, and only the machine might have difficulties in language understanding due to technological limitations. We discussed a number of studies targeting these issues in Chapter 2. However, if a language learner is involved in a dialogue with a conversational agent or a dialogue system, the assumption that the user understands everything may no longer be valid. This work made a step towards closing this gap.

This chapter analysed a collection of sequences of other-initiated self-repair when the native speaker is the trouble-speaker to create an empirical basis for computational modelling of this repair type. The resulting computational models were presented in Section 4.5. This section synthesises the results with regard to the following two research questions:

RQ1 Which interactional resources do language learners use in a chat-based Conversation-for-Learning with native speakers to initiate repair in order to deal with trouble in comprehension and how do native speakers deal with these repair initiations?

RQ2 How can other-initiated self-repair when the machine is the trouble-speaker be handled in a chat-based Communicative ICALL system?

We specifically looked at interactional resources that are used to tell the trouble-speaker *that* there is a problem with a previous utterance and to show *what kind* of trouble occurs. In this way, this work is close to studies described by Egbert (2009) for naturally occurring German oral interaction and a cross-linguistic study described by Dingemanse et al. (2014). We discuss the results and the contribution of the work to CALL and ICALL using a comparison of the findings of this study with studies of repair in native/non-native speaker chat (Tudini, 2010; Marques-Schäfer, 2013). The findings and the contribution are discussed in Section 4.6.1. The applicability of the models and the contribution of this work to Communicative ICALL and NLP in a broader sense are discussed in Section 4.6.2.

4.6.1 Repair initiation and resolution in chat with language learners

In the analysis of repair initiation formats, we distinguished between resources used to reference the trouble source, and resources used to signal trouble in comprehension. This was a necessary abstraction to prepare a basis for computational recognition of repair initiations and trouble source extraction. We argued that the selection of a specific format for a repair initiation may be influenced by the type of trouble, communication medium, turn adjacency in chat and learner's level of language proficiency. Repair carry-outs depend on repair initiations in terms of format, referencing trouble source, type of information required to solve the problem and interactional resources that may be employed for that. The information provided in the repair projects the expectations of the trouble-speaker toward what is known to the repair-initiating speaker.

This work focused only on repair initiations with linguistic trouble source in text chat-based dialogues. The following formats of repair initiations produced by the learners to point to a linguistic trouble source were found:

1. Open-class repair initiations realised through symbolic and lexical means, for instance *unklar* (unclear), *ich verstehe nicht* (I don't understand) or simply *???*.
2. Demonstratives-based repair initiations, such as *Was bedeutet das?* (What does it mean?).
3. Repetition-based repair initiations.

We will use here the concept of an *action ladder* to start a discussion about repair initiation formats in text chat. Repair initiations signal that there is a problem with a previous utterance, and they allow the trouble-speaker to understand what kind of trouble the recipient of the trouble-talk may have with it. Dingemanse et al. (2014) describe the problem space building on previous work by Austin (1962) and Clark (1996) in the form of a so-called *action ladder*.

In the action ladder presented in Table 4.3, higher levels of comprehension can only be reached if the lower levels are passed: one needs to attend to the speaker's

Level	Speaker A's actions	Addressee B's actions
4.	A is proposing joint project w to B	B is considering A's proposal of w
3.	A is signalling that p for B	B is recognising that p from A
2.	A is presenting signal s to B	B is identifying signal s from A
1.	A is executing behaviour t for B	B is attending to behaviour t from A

Table 4.3: The Austin/Clark action ladder aids understanding of the problem space. Adopted from (Dingemanse et al., 2014, p. 8)

talk, correctly recognise the speaker's words, find an interpretation of the speaker's words and recognise the intended social action. As Dingemanse et al. (2014) note, "all four levels are involved in building mutual understanding, and each of them can be a locus of trouble" (p. 9). Moreover, the levels of trouble determine the selection of formats for repair initiation.

> Repetition is a commonly used device in the other-initiation of repair, but if something was imperfectly produced by A or not attended to by B (level 1), repetition-based formats will not be available. Conversely, the format selected by B can be inspected by A for its downward evidence. An interjection like *huh?* entails at least that some expressive behaviour was perceived (level 1), but not much more than that, and therefore indicates that there was likely a low-level problem. A question word like *who?* entails not only that some words were perceived, but also that they were identified by B as a person reference, and therefore indicates that the problem likely lies at the level of signalling and recognition. (Dingemanse et al., 2014, p. 9)

While a repetition of the trouble turn is an appropriate repair after an open-class repair initiation in oral talk (the problem is located on level 1), our dataset does not contain any example of such repairs. Probably for the same reasons, repair initiation formats based on question words are not present in the dataset. However, *WHAT?s* can be found in chat to express surprise. This might be explained by the influence of the medium giving the possibility to re-read and making repetitions to repair mishearings unnecessary. Similarly, the formulaic German *bitte?* or *wie bitte?* does not occur in the dataset, because the relevant next action after this repair initiation is a repetition of the trouble turn. Repair initiation formats based on *Wie + repetition* described by Egbert (2009) were not found in the dataset, either. This may be explained by language classes not covering such repair initiations, which, in turn, can be only be acquired in interaction with native speakers. Sometimes language learners fail to produce an appropriate repair initiation. This may be caused by, for instance, their inability to identify the unit where the trouble source is located and selecting a wrong reference to it (Example 4.7, page 120). This, in turn, may lead to problems in trouble source identification by the native speaker and, consequently, in repair carry-out. Hence, the non-native speaker's interactional and linguistic competence influence the selection of a repair initiation format and its successful recognition.

In contrast to oral communication analysed in (Egbert, 2009; Dingemanse et al., 2014), repetition-based repair initiation formats obscured that the source of trouble was on a lower level than normally required in oral talk to produce a repetition-based repair initiation. Namely, in a repetition-based repair initiation the repeated trouble-source was repeated with an error: *Frage machen* instead of *Fliege machen*. The original idiom used by the native speaker seems to be misread, although text chat allows the user to re-read all previous turns. There are for sure explanations in psycho-linguistics or cognitive linguistics for how such errors may occur. For the study of computer-mediated communication it might be important *that* problems on the lowest level of attention may occur in text chat, too, and that they can be detected through other means than in oral communication.

Another difference as compared to Dingemanse et al. (2014)'s and Egbert (2009)'s results is that candidate understandings are formatted differently in repair initiations with linguistic trouble source. Meaning check is a typical repair initiation format based on a candidate understanding: the trouble source is repeated (usually left-hand side), followed by a comparison token, and the candidate understanding is presented (usually right-hand side). Candidate understandings are usually formatted as polar questions, which require a confirmation or a disconfirmation of the hypothesis. *You mean*-based candidate understandings were produced by learners in my dataset only as an additional resource for repair initiation following another, less specific repair initiation (Example 4.3). Candidate understandings for linguistic trouble sources seem to require additional resources in order to mark the trouble source as a *linguistic* trouble source.

Open-class repair initiations such as lexicalised equivalents of an oral *hä?* are not used by learners, but only by natives. This may obscure learners' lack of familiarity with oral open-class repair initiations in German, and therefore, the level of communicative competence. However, learners used multiple question marks *???* to initiate unspecific repair. The majority of all repair other-initiations produced by the learners are repetition-based. These repair initiations always entailed repair resolutions presenting explanations of the meaning of the trouble source. Dingemanse et al. (2014, p. 24) explain a similar phenomenon in native speaker data as follows:

> A difference in the type of repair solution provided in response to a repeat-formatted repair initiation is not always directly linked to a difference in formatting, but may also be linked to expectations about what is known. [...] Partial repetitions of terms clearly known to both speakers never result in clarifications of the terms, but are treated as taking an epistemic position that calls for another type of response, for instance a justification.

In conversations with language learners, not a conceptual clarification of the terms is required, but an explanation of some lexical material in the language-to-be-learned. This need may be satisfied by paraphrasing, synonyms, examples and translations. The latter are rather untypical for native/native speaker talk.

Further, differences in repair initiation formats were found that were caused by the timing of repair initiations relative to the trouble source. Although all repair initiations with linguistic trouble source correspond to second-position repair initiations, they may occur immediately after the trouble source turn in the timeline (adjacent position) or more than one turn after the trouble source (virtual adjacency (Tudini, 2010)). Virtual adjacency provides a constraint on open-class repair initiations. A more explicit reference to the trouble source is needed if a repair initiation does not immediately follow the trouble turn.

With regard to interactional resources used to signal troubles in comprehension, question mark is an important and effective device; it is involved in the majority of repair initiations in chat. Dingemanse et al. (2014, p. 21) explain it as follows:

> At the most general level, questions are next-speaker selection devices [...]. They are well-fitted to the other-initiation of repair because they put the ball in the court of the trouble-source producer.

Besides the practice of questioning, declarative utterances labelling the preceding turn explicitly as unclear were found.

The types of trouble sources addressed in sequences of other-initiated self-repair with linguistic trouble source were classified by length and unit integrity:

1. One unit: a single word, an abbreviation, an idiomatic expression or an utterance.
2. Copy-paste of a part of the trouble turn containing the trouble source regardless of unit boundaries.

Copies of turn parts regardless of unit boundaries may imply that learners sometimes are not able to identify the problematic unit and copy a random part of the native speaker's turn that contains the trouble source. Such repair initiations may be placed between open-class and restricted-class repair initiations, because they restrict the search space, but do not completely specify the problem.

Repair carry-outs contain references to the trouble source. The selection of a proper referring expression depends on the reference to the trouble source in the repair initiation, the type of the trouble source and the timing of the repair carry-out. For instance, abbreviations are usually repeated in both repair initiation and repair carry-out.

Marques-Schäfer (2013, Ch. 8) does not explicitly analyse repair sequences in chat, but she classifies *questions with linguistic matter* (orig.: *sprachbezogene Fragen*). She classifies question content as related to form and related to meaning. She distinguishes between triggers for questions that are related to the interaction and that are not related to the interaction. Responses to questions with linguistic matters are classified as zero-response, direct response, translation, synonym, paraphrasing, example and hyperlink to a web page. With regard to this classification, repair other-initiations in response to NS's turn with linguistic trouble source in our dataset correspond to questions related to interaction. All question-based repair initiations were meaning-related. Form-focused repair initiations are not present in the dataset used in this book. This may be explained by the absence of a pre-assigned role of a tutor who is responsible for all linguistic issues and by the learners' advanced level of L2 proficiency. With regard to repair carry-outs, the dataset contains the same types as the dataset used by Marques-Schäfer (2013). Both translations into a different shared language and machine translation into the learner's native language belong to interactional resources for repair in native/non-native speaker chat.

Tudini (2010) applied CA methods to analyse different repair types in native/non-native speaker chat. She concludes that learners have various opportunities to improve their foreign language skills in a Conversation-for-Learning. However, interactional resources for dealing with trouble in chat as they are made available by participants were not in the focus of her study. In this sense, the present study continues the CA-informed analysis of native/non-native speaker chat started by Tudini (2010) and Vandergriff (2013). Since language learners are expected to benefit from a conversation with an artificial chat partner, aspects of learning are an important issue for communicative ICALL. It needs further investigation whether language learners will make use of the same opportunities to engage in repair with linguistic trouble source with an artificial conversation partner as they do with a native speaker.

Relying on the SLA-theoretic results on the influence of specific interactional routines on language acquisition, Marques-Schäfer (2013) argues that negotiations with regard to questions about linguistic matters support language learning and help learners to improve their knowledge of L2. Tudini (2010) concludes more generally that learners' engagement in repair sequences supports learning. However, repair initiation is one option to deal with troubles in comprehension, but not the only one. The participants of the present study reported that they used online dictionaries and machine translation if they had difficulties in comprehension. Such strategies belong to learning strategies, too. The selection of a strategy to deal with trouble depends on many factors, and the learner's choice to position herself in the weaker position of a language novice may be one of them. Strategies to deal with trouble in comprehension not visible in the chat protocols need to be targeted in the research design phase in order to assess their influence on learning.

4.6.2 Computational models of other-initiated self-repair

In this research we made the first step towards closing the gap in modelling repair initiated by the user, specifically targeting language learners. Related academic literature has been discussed in Section 2.4.2.

The new model of other-initiated self-repair when the machine is the trouble-speaker ($OISR_M$) allows us to recognise learner repair initiations and to extract the trouble source based on a description of language-specific and medium-specific resources for repair initiation. The model is created on a level of abstraction necessary for it to be applicable for text chat interaction in languages other than German. This assumption builds on Dingemanse et al. (2014)'s finding that similar repair initiation formats exist across languages. Therefore, when provided with a set of language-specific devices for repair initiation (such as lexicalised unspecific signalling resources and demonstratives), it can be implemented for other languages. The extraction of the trouble source is based on abstract features such as repetition of parts of the trouble turn and adjacent position. These features are language independent.

The problem of trouble source extraction is related to referring-expression recognition or reference resolution described in NLP textbooks (Martin and Jurafsky,

2009, Ch. 21), which is addressed in a large number of scientific publications (Dahan et al., 2002; Iida et al., 2010). Usually only noun phrases or their pronominalised alternatives are considered for reference resolution in NLP. These are usually definite and indefinite noun phrases, pronouns, demonstratives and names. The analysis of repair initiations shows that verbs or parts of utterances may be used to refer to the trouble source. The model of OISR_M implicitly includes a local *discourse model* which "contains representations of entities which have been referred to in the discourse" (Martin and Jurafsky, 2009, p. 730). The local discourse model in OISR_M sequences is restricted to the possible representations of the trouble source.

Compared to the model of clarification requests proposed in (Purver, 2004), the model introduced in this work has the following advantages. First, the inconsistencies from the CA perspective found in (Purver, 2004)'s classification (see Section 2.4.2 for critiques) do not exist in the model presented in this work because of a close cross-disciplinary connection with CA. The model for repair initiations presented here strictly differentiates next-turn repair other-initiations from all other types of repair and describes only these repair initiations. Second, (Purver, 2004) introduced a model for clarification requests with a strong connection to the HPSG formalism. He lists technological requirements regarding language-understanding capabilities, including:

- The representation of utterances must include information at phonological, syntactic and semantic levels.
- This representation must have an appropriate semantic structure: it must be made contextually dependent, with words and certain phrases contributing elements which must be contextually identified during grounding.
- Both user and system utterances must share this representation, as both may be subject to clarification (Purver, 2004, p. 236) .

As opposed to these strong requirements, the model presented in this book is already implementable with such simple language-understanding technology as AIML-based chatbots, as we will see in Chapter 10. The separation between resources for signalling trouble and resources for referencing a trouble source allows the creation of a rule-based abstract description that can be implemented in dialogue systems and conversational agents with different levels of complexity in language understanding.

With regard to the analysis of causes of trouble in understanding introduced in (Schlangen, 2004) and discussed in Section 2.4.2, problems on the third level (Meaning and understanding) were the usual subject of learner's repair initiations. Consequently, the modelling was approached in this work with the assumption that the required kind of clarification is mainly determined by the user model targeting non-native speakers. Similarly to (Schlangen, 2004)'s approach to map the variance in form to a small number of readings, repair initiations in this work are mapped either to a content question *What does X mean?* or to a polar question *Does X mean Y?* where X is the trouble source and Y is the candidate understanding. In this way, the two approaches to modelling repair initiations are similar.

Models of repair covering repair initiations proposed in (Purver, 2004) and (Schlangen, 2004) and extended in follow-up work (Purver, 2006; Ginzburg et al., 2007; Ginzburg, 2012) were motivated by Conversation Analysis research. However, other approaches for modelling were preferred because of the insufficient operationalisation of CA findings for computational modelling. Consequently, the factors influencing the interaction that have been identified as important in CA studies and building a *system* did not become part of the baseline models in (Purver, 2004) and (Schlangen, 2004). Such factors include repair, turn-taking, membership categorisation, adjacency pairs and preference organisation. In contrast to the previous models of repair (Purver, 2004; Schlangen, 2004) this work analyses repair initiations in a system of interconnected factors in conversation. More specifically, the proposed model of repair initiations explicitly takes turn-taking and sequential organisation of interaction into account by distinguishing between immediate and delayed repair initiations, and respective options for trouble source extraction. In addition, the new model takes virtual adjacency in chat into account. It explicitly differentiates repair initiated by the user from repair initiated by the system, taking the sequential organisation into account. Finally, the preference organisation and recipient design were taken into account by the user model. Based on the findings from the dataset, the user model assumes that language learners will request a special kind of clarification.

While recognition of repair initiations and trouble source extraction can be implemented using the simplest type of language understanding, namely pattern-based language understanding, most repair carry-outs require more sophisticated linguistic capabilities. We will now go through all of them based on the list of identified repair carry-out types.

Definitions provide an explanation of the trouble source. Existing online dictionaries such as Wiktionary or Wikipedia may be used to create linguistic knowledge bases. Because one term may have multiple meanings, a link to the correct meaning may be required. This problem has been addressed in NLP mainly in the area of lexical ambiguity resolution, also known as meaning resolution (Small et al., 1987), and is part of a larger area of computational lexical semantics (Martin and Jurafsky, 2009, Ch. 20).

Paraphrasing provides a reformulation of the trouble source. A lot of efforts have been put into automatic paraphrase generation and recognition. Several recent publications are (Metzler et al., 2011; Regneri and Wang, 2012; Marton, 2013).

Synonyms provide a short reformulation of the trouble source. Existing language resources include WordNet (Fellbaum, 2010) and GermaNet (Hamp et al., 1997). Similarly to definitions, multiple meanings of a word may need to be resolved.

Translations may be generated by using existing machine translation systems (Burchardt et al., 2014; Avramidis et al., 2015). Open-source statistical machine translation systems such as Moses[1] make experimental implementations feasible. Commercial machine translation API can be integrated into the dialogue manager, for instance Google Translate API[2].

[1] http://www.statmt.org/moses/

[2] https://cloud.google.com/translate/docs

Demonstrations include hyperlinks to websites containing relevant information or as a way to show one example of an object referenced by the trouble source. For instance, objects and concepts related to web technologies such as *live ticker* and *live stream* may be explained by an example of such objects. Using search engines to find relevant websites may be one way to find relevant information in real time. However, only one of the found documents can be presented to the user. For semi-automatically created databases of linguistic knowledge, such information may be included in examples. Wikipedia articles sometimes also contain links to example websites and pictures that may be used as examples of concepts described in the article.

Because anything may become a trouble source in conversation, repair initiations may come after *any* utterance and even after silence. For human-machine dialogues, this means that the machine needs the ability to distinguish the action of repair initiation from all other actions that may come routinely after a system utterance. This research made a contribution to the computational dialogue and conversational agent research by proposing a local model for OISR_M. Explicit handling of repairs targeted for language learners allows an implementation in a Communicative ICALL system mimicking Conversations-for-Learning. Other types of tutorial dialogues where a clarification of the terminology may be necessary, would also benefit from the presented model.

With regard to the areas of applicability of the proposed model, similar types of repair carry-outs can be found in professional talk, where novices in other areas than foreign language acquire professional terminology. It can be tested in a separate study whether the model presented here for SLA application can be transferred (maybe with modifications) into other domains where conversational agents are used, for instance as tutors. Taking into account the recent developments in NLU services

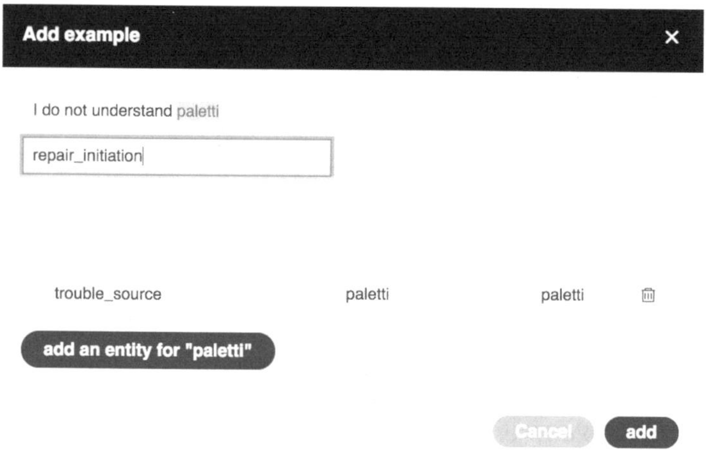

Add example ×

I do not understand paletti

repair_initiation

trouble_source paletti paletti

add an entity for "paletti"

Cancel add

Fig. 4.1: Entering a training example in the RASA NLU Trainer tool

discussed in Section 2.5.1, it might be interesting to find a way of using these services for the recognition of repair initiations. One can see repair initiations as a specific type of intent and a trouble source is a special type of concept contained in this intent. We took RASA as an example, but the other services discussed in Section 2.5.1 would require a very similar pipeline. First, a set of annotated examples needs to be provided to the system in order to train the model. Then, the trained model can be used for a service, for instance, a chatbot. NLU services are designed to help chatbot developers to maintain a task-based conversation with bot users. Therefore, all user utterances are seen as intent declarations containing requests for specific services. What happens if we define a repair initiation as a specific type of intent?

Figure 4.1 shows an example of data that can be used to train an NLU system. In this example, we use a tool called RASA NLU Trainer[3] to visualise the dataset and to edit the training dataset.

Then, after adding a large number of such examples or automated training-data conversion into RASA .json format, we can train the RASA NLU model as described in the RASA tutorial[4]. The RASA NLU model runs on the local device after the installation. In contrast to most other NLU services, we do not need to communicate over https with an API. Then, if we test the trained model with the same utterance "I do not understand paletti", something similar to the following .json structure should appear on the screen:

```
{
    "entities": [
{
            "end": ,
            "entity": "trouble_source",
            "extractor": ,
            "start": ,
            "value": "paletti"
 }
],
    "intent": {
        "confidence": a numerical score,
        "name": "repair_initiation"
    },
    "intent_ranking": [],
    "text": "I do not understand paletti"
}
```

The following difficulties occur with intent-based NLU services. First, in our example the trouble source is contained in the repair initiation (a repeat-based repair initiation). However, as we have seen in this chapter, many other types of repair initiations use only pointers to the trouble source or even do not contain any reference

[3] https://github.com/RasaHQ/rasa-nlu-trainer

[4] https://nlu.rasa.ai/tutorial.html

(open-class repair initiations that reference the trouble source by its adjacent position). Second, the training data that such NLU services expect need to contain a set of independent utterances with intents and concepts labelled in each of them. However, as we have seen in this chapter, repair initiations *always* contain a link to what happened before in the interaction. Such long-term and cross-turn dependencies cannot be annotated within single utterances.

Thus, it requires further investigation to what extent NLU services discussed in Section 2.5.1 can be used for chatbots that behave like language experts and, more specifically, properly handle the whole range of repair initiations as they occur in natural data.

4.6.3 Conclusions

The study of other-initiated self-repair leads to the following conclusons:

- Because repair initiations to deal with trouble in comprehension is a frequent form of orientation to linguistic identities, it has to be an integral part of each conversational system designed to interact with language learners.
- Repair initiations are closely connected with the complex of other factors in interaction, such as turn-taking, adjacency pairs, virtual adjacency in chat, membership categorisation and preferences. Therefore, repair initiations need to be analysed and modelled as part of this system.
- Responses to learners' repair initiations reflect the assumption that difficulties in comprehension caused the repair initiation. However, it cannot be excluded that learners also may initiate conversational repair not related to difficulties with the second language. In such cases, other strategies for repair carry-outs are needed.

The model can also be applied in other domains where professional talk is mimicked by an artificial agent in conversations with novices, for instance, to help learners of various professions to acquire professional terminology.

Chapter Summary

This chapter presented an analysis of a collection of sequences of other-initiated self-repair when the native speaker is the trouble-speaker in conversations with a non-native speaker. Based on this analysis, it introduced an abstract computational model of other-initiated self-repair when the machine is the trouble-speaker tailored for conversations with language learners. The conversation-analytic concept of *recipient design* is reflected in this model in the way that the self-repair carry-outs are tailored for non-native speakers: the delivered explanations clarify the meaning of the used words and expressions. A comparison with related academic publications was provided. Technical feasibility of the proposed model was analysed.

5

Exposed Corrections

Abstract This chapter presents a microanalytic study of exposed corrections. After the analysis of the relationship between the error types and correction types, this chapter will focus on the turn design and turn-taking in exposed-correction sequences. This will be followed by an analysis of accountings and emphasis means accompanying and highlighting the corrections. Finally, empirical findings will be discussed and a comparison with state-of-the-art publications will be presented.

5.1 Introduction

Exposed corrections of linguistic errors are dispreferred in both native and non-native speaker conversations. However, they occur in non-native speaker conversations more frequently and are perceived by language learners as helpful for learning. This has been reported in multiple academic publications discussed in Section 2.3 and confirmed by the participants of the data collection that was later used for this research, in the retrospective interviews. The position of the native speaker as more knowledgeable in linguistic matters and the asymmetric relationship with the learner in those matters make corrections possible. However, the asymmetry by itself does not explain why or when they occur (Kurhila, 2006, p. 35). Moreover, no dependencies were found in the previous research on exposed corrections between the error and the correction (Schegloff, 1987b). Error taxonomies and automatic error recognition are considered to be a preliminary step for error correction. However, as pointed out by (Schegloff, 1987b, p. 216),

> the occurrence of repair is not prompted only by the occurrence of error, an important step was taken in disengaging trouble (error and nonerror) from the practices employed to deal with it.

For these reasons, we need to look at correction practices, decoupled from the errors and other reasons for correction aside from the occurrence of an error. This will be the main business of this chapter. Nonetheless, we will need to come back to the analysis of the factors influencing the occurrence of a correction other than just the

S. Höhn, *Artificial Companion for Second Language Conversation*,
https://doi.org/10.1007/978-3-030-15504-9_5

occurrence of an error. We will do so in Chapter 8. A conceptual definition of an error in chat will be included in the discussion and will be the subject of Section 8.2.

With regard to sequential organisation of talk containing a correction, Jefferson (1987, p. 88) made the observations that first, "whatever has been going on prior to the correcting is discontinued" and "correcting is now the interactional business", and second, there are such "attendant activities as e.g. instructing, complaining, forgiving, apologising, ridiculing". She introduced the term *accountings* for this class of activities. However, not all corrections are accompanied by such side activities. Kurhila (2006) describes a type of correction in face-to-face communication in which a correction is provided without accountings and the talk in progress is continued immediately so that there is no space left for the non-native speaker to start any kind of negotiations. Kurhila (2006) calls this type of repair the *en passant* correction. Tudini (2010) observed a similar type of correction in her study of intercultural chat that she called *on the fly*. In this book, we will use the term correction *on the fly* suggested by Tudini (2010).

In corrections *on the fly*, the social talk immediately follows the correction so that there is no space left for the learner to contribute to the correction sequence. As opposed to this, in explicit exposed corrections with accountings the learner has a chance to contribute to the correction side sequence. We already had a very short contact with these two types of exposed corrections in Section 3.4 from the perspective of construction of identities of experts and novices in chat. In this chapter, we will come back to them from the perspective of correction practices and formats.

Section 5.2 shows that there are some dependencies between the type of error and the type of trouble caused by it, and the correction format chosen by native speakers to deal with it. We will discuss the variations in turn design and the influence of the turn-taking on the turn design in exposed corrections in Section 5.3. We will take various types of accountings under the loupe of our analysis in Section 5.4. We will summarise and discuss the empirical findings in Section 5.5.

5.2 Types of corrected errors

The participants of conversations in the analysed dataset engage in sequences of exposed corrections of orthographic, grammatical and lexical errors. However, the majority of all corrections in the dataset deal with lexical errors. In total, 22 instances of exposed corrections were found in the dataset. The corrections are not equally distributed throughout all conversations. Some of the native speakers corrected learner errors more frequently than others. Nevertheless, corrections were produced by every native speaker. As already mentioned in Chapter 3, different native speakers selected different strategies in interaction, sometimes correcting a lot of different errors and sometimes choosing to let it pass although some of the learners made a lot of mistakes.

Schegloff (1987b) examined problematic references and problematic sequential implicativeness as classes of trouble based on a collection of third-position repairs.

He described his study as "a brief account of several such trouble sources" and "neither an exhausting nor a systematically representative display" (Schegloff, 1987b, p. 204). He observed that "there do not seem to be systematic relationships between the types of trouble source and the form taken by repairs addressed to them"(Schegloff, 1987b, p. 216). However, some dependencies between the error types and their corrections can be seen in the dataset that we use for this research, as this section will show by discussing the types of corrected errors. Corrections of lexical errors will be in focus in Subsection 5.2.1. Subsection 5.2.2 will analyse corrections of morpho-syntactic errors. Finally, Subsection 5.2.3 will focus on corrections of spelling errors and typos.

5.2.1 Corrections of lexical errors

Lexical errors have been corrected by native speakers both in situations where misunderstandings occurred and where intersubjectivity could still be maintained despite suboptimal lexical choice. Example 5.1 shows a case where intersubjectivity is not in danger however the native speaker chooses to correct the wrong lexical choice.

Example 5.1. Pedagogical repair: the native speaker corrects a wrong lexical choice in the absence of a communication problem.

150 13:32:57 L09 jeztz ist dein gesichtskreis mehr)
now is your horizon more [error: lexical choice]*
151 13:33:15 N04 größer :-)
wider
[Turn 152 hidden as it belongs to a different thread.]
153 13:33:35 L09 ok))grösser)
ok [smile] wider [smile]

In contrast, Example 5.2 shows one of the instances of a correction where the learner's turn is ambiguous due to a lexical error. In turn 135, L09 uses the non-native-like expression *leicht gefallen*. This erroneous expression may have (at least) two correct targets: *gefallen* (En.: *to like*) or *leicht fallen* (En.: *to be easy for someone*). This trouble is resolved by N04 by means of contrasting two possible interpretations of the erroneous expression. Thus, the type of trouble (ambiguity of the learner's expression) required a repair strategy that allows a disambiguation.

Example 5.2. A correction of a lexical error: the non-native-like expression leads to ambiguities and has sequential consequences.

135 13:21:09 L09 gefiel dir das studium leicht?
did you like [* error] your study easy [* error]
did you like your study? / was your study easy for you?
136 13:21:45 N04 es gefiel mir, aber es fiel mir nicht immer leicht ;-)
I liked it but it was not easy for me [smile]
137 13:22:14 N04 ("gefallen" = "etwas schön finden",
("to like" - "to find something pretty",
138 13:22:41 N04 etwas fällt jemandem leicht = man hat keine Mühe damit)
something is easy for someone = one has no trouble with it)

Example 5.3 illustrates the case where a real communication problem exists and a lexical error (a creation, the word does not exist in German) needs to be corrected. It is not completely clear from the data whether the communication problem is resolved in this repair sequence.

Example 5.3. The native speaker produces a correction formatted as a repair initiation. The communication problem remains (probably) unresolved.

119 17:31:47 L04 es kommt manchmal vor, dass einige Studenten viele Male ihre Diplomarbeit wiederdrücken müssen!!
it happens sometimes that some students many times their diploma thesis againpress [* error: creation] must!!
it happens sometimes that some students must re-print their diploma thesis many times
120 17:32:25 N02 meinst du wiederholen? also nochmal schreiben?
you mean repeat? well, write again?
121 17:32:43 L04 jja! mit Korrigierungen
yes! with correctings

L04 creates the word *wiederdrücken* (En.: *wieder - again, drücken - press*). Probably, the word *re-print* (*print once again*) was intended. However, from the repair initiation by the native speaker in turn 120 it is analysable that the native speaker's interpretation of the creation is *to write again*, so to start the entire work from the beginning and to write the whole thesis once again. The learner accepts the correction of the word in turn 121, adding the clarification *with correctings* (*re-write the thesis with corrections*). It is not clear from the data whether the communication problem was resolved and whether the native speaker understood the intended target meaning first expressed with the creation.

Example 5.4. Correction of a lexical error in the form of repair other-initiation.

286 08:47:07 N03 alle pruefungen ueberstanden?
got through all examinations?
287 08:49:32 L07 am montag hab ich englisch abgegeben.... für eine 10.... es sind jetzt 2 letzte geblieben..und endlich sommerferien...!! die sibd auch die letzten— nachstes jahr absolviere ich DIE UNI-)))
on Monday I delivered English.... for a 10.... there are the last 2 left.. and finally summer vacations...!! but they arethe last ones— next [* error: typo] year I complete [* error: lexical choice] THE UNI
I passed English on Monday... I got a 10.... there are 2 more left.. and finally summer vacation...!! but they are the last ones— I'm graduating from university next year
288 08:58:43 N03 wow.
289 08:58:56 N03 was heisst das, absolviere ich die uni?
what does it mean, I complete the uni?
290 08:59:04 N03 bist du fertig, schliesst du ab?
are you done, are you finishing?
291 08:59:52 L07 ja... du bist ein guter übersetzer..))))))
yes... you are a good translator
292 09:00:23 N03 hahaha

In contrast, a lexical error is successfully corrected in the form of a repair other-initiation in Example 5.4. The learner uses the word *absolvieren* (En.: *to complete, to work through*) in a wrong context in turn 287; however, the native speaker guesses the intended meaning. He “wraps" the correction of this error into a repair initiation in turn 289, suggesting the correction in turn 290.

5.2.2 Corrections of morpho-syntactic errors

Errors in syntax and/or morphology bcompriseuild the second largest category of all explicitly corrected errors. The errors in word order, verb tenses and conjugation, noun-determiner congruence and government are examples of trouble on the morphosyntactic level that have been made relevant for corrections by the native speakers in the dataset. All instances of corrections of morphosyntactic errors in our dataset deal with pure pedagogical repair in the absence of any communication problems.

Example 5.5 illustrates an exposed correction of a wrong use of an infinite verb form. The learner produces the error in turn 323. The error does not have any sequential implications for the next relevant action. The native speaker produces the response turn, which also incorporates the correction. The response is not formulated as a projected next after a good-wishes-expression (*relax well, too*, for instance), but as an explicit correction with the form of the verb that should be used from the perspective of the native speaker highlighted with quotes. The emoticon belongs to the class of accountings.

Example 5.5. A correction of an error in grammar, use of the infinite verb form is replaced by the imperative.

323 17:55:04 L08 alles Gute)und sehr gut sich erholen!!))
all the best and to relax [error] very good!!*
324 17:55:51 N04 Danke, und "erhol Dich gut" ;-)
Thank you and "relax very good"
325 17:56:02 L08 =))

However, morpho-syntactic errors can lead to problems with maintaining intersubjectivity and therefore have sequential consequences. A situation of this kind but with the native speaker as the trouble-speaker and the learner initiating repair is discussed in Example 5.6. We analyse it from the perspective of the relationship between the error and the chances to produce the next relevant turn for the trouble-talk recipient.

Example 5.6. A morpho-syntactic error produced by the native speaker leads to a communication problem but remains unresolved.

652 19:57:33 N03 Der hast auch einen halb Bruder?
Determiner [maskulinum III p. sg.] aux. II p. sg. too one half brother?
He has a half-brother, too?
653 19:58:17 L07 r hat oder du hast??
r [probably the end of der = he] has or you have?
he has or you have?
654 19:58:28 L07 wer von uns?
who of us?

The native speaker produces an error in turn 652 in a question. The wrong subject-verb congruence does not allow the intended meaning of the question to be understood. The learner cannot produce the next relevant action (an answer to the question) and has to initiate a repair sequence in turn 653. The repair initiation contains both variants of possible correct readings of the erroneous pronoun-verb pair. Turn 654 is a repair re-initiation that explains the kind of trouble more precisely, and this appears to be an attempt to resolve an ambiguous reference to a person. However, the native speaker never produces an answer; the trouble remains unresolved.

5.2.3 Corrections of spelling errors and typos

Typos are normally not considered to be errors in instant messaging. Chat communication requires fast typing. As a consequence, mis-typings happen quite often to both learners and native speakers. Normally spelling errors have been ignored, too, or corrected in the form of embedded corrections, but there are two cases when they have been corrected in form of exposed corrections. We will discuss them in detail here and try to find an explanation in which situation an exposed correction in an informal conversation might be appropriate for the class of “unimportant" errors.

One of the cases is when the spelling of a word is difficult to learn even for the native speaker, and a sort of memo expression exists for native speakers to remember the spelling better. Example 5.7 illustrates one such case.

Example 5.7. Ziemlich ohne h (simplified).

167	18:54:38	L08	ja, bin ich ziehmlich einverstanden yes, am quite [* error] agreed *yes, I agree pretty much*
168	18:55:11	N04	ziemlich ohne h ;-) *ziemlich without h* [Turns 169 omitted.]
170	18:57:06	L08	ich zweifelte daran)mit oder ohne=) *I questioned whether it was with or without*
171	18:57:51	N04	es gibt da so einen Merkspruch, aber der ist fast ein bißchen unverschämt... *there is a mnemonic, but it is almost a little bit rude...*
172	18:58:02	N04	ich schreib’s Dir trotzdem, nicht böse sein: *I write it nonetheless, don’t be angry:*
173	18:58:27	N04	wer ziemlich oder nämlich mit h schreibt ist dämlich *He who writes ziemlich or nämlich with h is stupid*

The second case of an exposed correction of a spelling error concerns a repeated deviation in spelling of the same word twice in one turn. Because the word *Theory* was wrongly spelled *twice* in one turn, the native speaker did not consider this error to be a simple typo any more. The error was corrected in turn 348.

Of course there are cases in many languages where the edit distance between two different words is very small and mis-typing can lead to funny sequential implications. The two errors analysed above are not of this kind; there is no misunderstanding or problem in communication. Both cases of exposed correction of spelling errors are instances of pedagogical repair.

Marques-Schäfer (2013, Sec. 7.3) discusses the difference between errors and mistakes. In her understanding, errors are gaps in the learner's interlanguage, and mistakes are lapses. One of the possibilities to test whether a deviation is an error or a mistake is to see continuously whether the learner produces the same deviation constantly or only occasionally. In Example 5.8, the learner repeats the deviation in spelling twice within one short turn. Therefore, it seems natural to assume that the native speaker interprets this deviation as an error, and not as a mistake.

Example 5.8. A repeated occurrence of a typo is considered to be a lack of knowledge in spelling and corrected.

346	18:37:10	L08	Teorie der Literatur und Teorie der Sprachwissenschaft teory [* error: orthograpy] of literature and teory [* error: orthograpy] of linguistics *theory of literature and linguistic theory*
348	18:38:57	N04	Sehr gut. Und "Theorie" mit "h" :-) *Very good. And "theory" with "h"*
349	18:39:30	L08	of course)ich bin nicht aufmerksam wie immer) *of course I am not attentive as always*
351	18:40:13	N04	doch, du machst das gut *no, you are doing a good job*

Having more examples would be an advantage for a reasonably generalised model of exposed corrections of spelling errors. However, a simple rule-based heuristic based on these two examples would be a good start. Since spelling errors and typos normally were not addressed in corrections, having fewer exposed corrections of spelling errors in conversations with an artificial chat partner would be better than having too many.

5.3 Turn design and turn-taking in exposed corrections

This section analyses whether there are any structural relationships or dependencies in the format of the trouble source turns and the corresponding correction turns. The properties of the turns containing corrected errors may be relevant for the intended modelling of exposed corrections for an artificial conversation partner. Correction turn formats are of interest, specifically possibilities to reference the trouble source, to present the correct version, and accountings. Finally, the relationship between the trouble turn and the correction turn(s) in terms of turn design is also relevant for the intended modelling.

The dataset contains the following types of exposed corrections:

1. Simple explicit corrections only presenting the correction. Corrections *on the fly*, simple explicit corrections with minimal accountings and with rich accountings are the variations that I found in this class.
2. Explicit correction by means of contrast comparing the wrong and the correct item.

3. Exposed corrections integrated into the next relevant turn.
4. Exposed corrections formatted as other-initiations of repair.

We will discuss the identified correction types below. The findings will be illustrated by examples.

5.3.1 Simple explicit corrections

The examples in this section will be ordered according to the grade of explicitness of the correction. The types are corrections on the fly, explicit corrections with minimal accountings, and explicit corrections with rich accountings. Corrections on the fly are the least explicit of all exposed corrections that have been described in the literature and occur in the dataset. Example 5.9 shows how a correction on the fly is organised.

The design of the correction turn 445 can be characterised as minimal: only the correct version is presented, and symbolic means are used to mark it as a correction. The correction turn is followed by a turn containing minimal accountings - a smiley (turn 446). The turn design of the correction sequence does not leave any space for the learner to react to the correction turn. The correction and the accountings turns are immediately followed by turns relevant for the interpersonal trajectory. In this way, it is the native speaker who makes the reaction to the correction into a non-relevant action in turns 446-449.

Although the academic literature describes corrections on the fly as something that does not have space for accountings, their main characteristic is that they do not leave any space for a learner's reaction to the correction. The interpersonal trajectory remains the most important and the side correction sequence is kept as short as possible and managed by the speaker who produces the correction.

Example 5.9. A simple correction on-the-fly with minimal accountings.

444 08:06:25 L07 es wäre prima... aber wir haben hier nur seen... die gibt es mehrere in unserer umgebung...) man kann zu fuß gehen oder mit dem auto fahren ein bisschen weiter...weil sich so viele leute jetzt zum strand begeben))
it would be great... but we have here only lakes... they [* error] there are many in our area... one can walk or go by car a little bit farther... because so many people betake themselves now to the beach
it would be great... but we only have lakes here... there are many of them in our area... one can walk or go by car a little bit farther... because so many people go to the beach now

445 08:07:16 N03 [[von denen gibt es mehrere]]
[[of them there are many]]
[[there are many of them]]

446 08:07:19 N03 :-)

447 08:07:25 N03 ach so
I see

448 08:07:37 N03 wenn du meer haettest waere ich mal vorbei gekommen
if you had a sea, I would come over

449 08:07:40 N03 :-)

Examples of corrections on the fly provided by Tudini (2010, Chapter 5) show similar sequences; however, the correction turns in her examples do not contain any accountings and the interpersonal trajectory is continued in the same turn as the correction. It seems important that the participant who positions himself as a language expert in the form of an exposed correction on the fly, immediately continues the interpersonal trajectory, with or without accountings, and the accountings should be minimal.

A prototypic sequential structure of corrections on the fly is:

T1 The non-native speaker produces an error.
T2 The native speaker produces a correct version. It may come with minimal accountings, but does not have to.
T3 The native speaker continues the interpersonal trajectory.

In Example 5.10, the learner tells the native speaker about her hometown and the city where she studies, and the capital of Belarus. Turn 150 contains a trouble source which is corrected in turn 151. The native speaker produces a correction with minimal accountings. The turn consists of the correct version not specifically marked and the smiley. Here, in contrast, the learner reacts to the correction. Turn 152 is produced by the learner and continues the interpersonal trajectory started earlier (Belorussian geography). In turn 153, the learner reacts to the correction of the error (with one turn intervening between the correction and the reaction).

Example 5.10. Simple explicit correction with minimal accountings.

148	13:30:39	L09	schaust du google map?)) *are you looking up google map?*
149	13:31:29	N04	ja, um mal einen Überblick zu kriegen :-) bisher kannte ich nur Minsk, weil es halt die Hauptstadt ist. *yes, to get an overview till now I knew only Minsk because it is the capital.*
150	13:32:57	L09	jeztz ist dein gesichtskreis mehr) *now [* error: orthography] is your horizon more [* error: lexical choice]*
151	13:33:15	N04	größer :-) *wider*
152	13:33:25	L09	Vitebsk ist gebietstadt)) Vitebsk is a provincial city
153	13:33:35	L09	ok))grösser) *ok wider*
154	13:34:27	N04	ja, wenn man "Vitebsk" in googlemaps eintippt, leuchtet der ganze Norden Weißrusslands rot, aber die Stadt hab ich auch gefunden :-) *yes, if you type "Vitebsk" in google maps, the whole North of Belarus shines red, but I found the city, too*

Accountings highlight the correction in addition to their primary action such as excuse, justification etc. This kind of highlight can be of different intensity, for instance, minimal like in Examples 5.10 and 5.9, or "rich" like in Example 5.11, which presents a sequence where the participants are making an appointment.

In Example 5.11, the learner produces an error in turn 148 (incorrect future form) in her inquiry about the native speaker's availability. The native speaker chooses first to produce the next relevant turn continuing the interpersonal trajectory in turn 149. This is a repair initiation, because clarification is needed with regard to the intended time slot. After the appointment has been made in turn 152, the native speaker renews the context of the error turn by marking his turn as something additional, coming with a delay ("PS:"). He recycles a part of the learner's utterance and uses symbolic and lexical means to frame the correct version (*es sollte heißen "..."*, En.: *you should say "..."*).

Example 5.11. Explicit correction with rich accountings.

148	18:31:40	L08	NATIVE04_FN, wirst du hier um 23:00 d.Z? NATIVE04_FN, will you [* error: missing main verb] here at 23:00 G.t? *NATIVE04_FN, will you here at 23:00 German time?*
149	18:31:59	N04	heute? *today?*
150	18:32:04	L08	ja *yes*
151	18:32:19	N04	keine Ahnung, mal sehen, schreib dann einfach mal, falls ich da bin, antworte ich *no idea, let's see, just write to me, if I'm there, I will reply*
152	18:32:34	L08	ok)abgemacht!) *ok agree!*
153	18:33:08	N04	PS: Verzeih mir, aber es sollte heißen: "... wirst Du hier SEIN um ..." *PS: I'm sorry, but you should say: "... will you BE here at ..."*
154	18:35:47	L08	klar)das große Problem der d-en Sprache ist: man vergißt am ende des Satzes, was man am Anfang sagen wollte) *clear the big problem of the G-n language is: one forgets at the end of a sentence, what one wanted to say in the beginning*
155	18:36:10	N04	verstehe, diese zweigeteilten Verben sind sicher verwirrend *I see, these split verbs are surely confusing*

Since the correction is not made immediately after the error and the context of the error had to be renewed, more interactional management has to be done in order to make the correction recognisable as a correction. In addition to making the correction recognisable, the native speaker highlights the action of correcting by symbolic means such as quotations and upper case. The accountings (*Verzeih mir, aber...*, En.: *I am sorry, but...*) make the correction even more prominent.

A prototypical structure of simple explicit corrections with minimal accountings is:

T1 The non-native speaker produces an error.
T2 The native speaker presents the correct version accompanied by minimal accountings.
T3 The non-native speaker continues either on the interpersonal trajectory or by an uptake.

We need to differentiate between immediate and delayed correction in the prototypical turn structure for corrections with rich accountings. For an immediate correction:

T1 The non-native speaker produces an error.
T2 The native speaker presents the correct version accompanied by rich accountings.
T3 The non-native speaker continues either on the interpersonal trajectory or by an uptake.

A delayed correction will appear a few turns later. The exact number of turns is not given in advance, therefore we will just assume that it appears i turns later. A prototypical structure for a delayed correction will have then the following form:

T1 The non-native speaker produces an error.
T+i The native speaker presents the correct version with rich accountings and back-links.
T+i+1 The non-native speaker continues either on the interpersonal trajectory or by an uptake.

These prototypes will be taken into account for the description of local models of exposed corrections in Chapter 7 of this book.

5.3.2 Contrasting explicit corrections

The examples discussed earlier in this section deal with corrections that only present a correct version of the trouble source. However, a direct comparison between the trouble source and the correct version in the correction turn is also a possible way to present the correction.

Example 5.12 illustrates this type of turn design for exposed corrections. The learner produces an error in turn 49. The native speaker corrects the error in turn 51 (turn 50 is a sequence closing of a different thread in talk). The correction turn contains accountings, a turn-initial request for permission to correct and a turn-final smile. Both the original trouble source unit and the replacement are part of the turn. They are both marked with quotes and the erroneous unit rejected by the negation (you X not Y).

Example 5.12. Contrasting the error and the correction (prev. Ex. 3.16).

49	19:40:59	L09	Zur Zeit bin ich frei um Diplomarbeit zu schreiben at this time I am [* error] free in order to write [* error: 0-determiner] diploma thesis *at the moment I have free time to write my diploma thesis*
50	19:41:15	L09	danke schön! :) *thank you very much*
51	19:41:58	N04	Falls ich das korrigieren darf: Du "hast" frei, nicht "bist". :-) *If I may correct you: you "have" free, not "are".*
52	19:42:48	L09	Danke *Thank you*
53	19:43:16	L09	Ich habe frei :) *I have free* I have free time

This turn format allows the correct version to be highlighted and the action of correction to be made more prominent. The learner expresses thanks for the correction in turn 52 and repeats a part of her original utterance taking up the correct word.

The prototypical structure of corrections based on contrasting is the same as for simple corrections with rich accountings, with a difference in the native speakers' turn T2 in an immediate correction (or T+i+1 in a delayed correction):

T2 Native speaker presents the correct version as opposed to the original version with deviations accompanied by rich accountings.

5.3.3 Explicit corrections integrated into the next relevant action

Embedded corrections as discussed in Chapter 6 do not contain accountings. Examples discussed in this section do. However, they integrate (or embed) the corrections into the next relevant action, similarly to embedded corrections. The corrections are not explicitly made to the new interactional business (compare Sections 5.3.1 and 5.3.2), but they contain accountings and explicit markers for the corrected unit, which is not characteristic for embedded corrections as defined by Jefferson (1987). The majority of examples of corrections integrated into the next relevant action are located in the second pair part (SPP) of an adjacency pair (question-answer, farewell-farewell).

Example 5.13. The native speaker other-initiates the learner's self-repair and corrects a grammar error (prev. Ex. 4.7).

303 17:10:14 N02 Danke, bis Dienstag ist noch Schule und dann sind endlich Ferien :) aber die zwei Tage krieg ich jetzt auch noch rum!
Thanks, till Tuesday is still school and then are finally holidays but the two days get I as well around!
Thanks, we have classes till Tuesday, but then we have holidays finally but the two days will pass as well!

304 17:12:11 L03 ach so, ja, ab dem 1. August, ich erinnere mich jetzt... dieses Phraseologismus habe ich noch nie gehört :)
I see, yes, from the 1st of August, I recall now... this* [neutrum] phraseologism [maskulinum] have I yet never heard
I see, yes, beginning on the 1st of August, I recall now... I have never heard this phraseologism [smile]

305 17:12:26 N02 welchen? ;)
which [maskulinum] one? [smile]
which one?

306 17:12:32 L03 dei Phraseologismus :)
[typo: intended "den" - determiner maskulinum] phraseologism
the phraseologism

Example 5.13 illustrates this type of correction in a location other than an SPP. Turn 304 is a repair initiation, and it contains a congruence error: neutral determiner *dieses* (En.: *this*) combined with male noun *Phraseologismus* (En.: *phraseologism*). However, the native speaker does not understand what is meant by this referring expression, because she did not use any phraseological expressions in her previous turn.

Therefore, the next relevant action for the native speaker is not a repair proper, but another repair initiation, which is produced in turn 305.

The question word in the repair initiation is put into the correct congruence form with the word *Phraseologism* (correction) and accompanied by an emoticon (accountings). Without accountings it would become an embedded correction. The correction is noticed by the learner. She starts an attempt to self-correct in turn 306 and produces a typo, so that the error cannot be self-corrected in this case. It is not fully clear from the data, whether it was a self-initiated self-repair by the learner in turn 306 or whether it was an uptake after the correction turn 305, because the difference in the time stamps for these two turns is very short. Parallel production of these two turns might be possible.

The correction turn is designed in order to perform the next relevant action. The correction is integrated here into a repair other-initiation, but the trouble source addressed by the repair initiation (the idiomatic expression) is not the same as the trouble source addressed by the correction (determiner-noun congruence). As opposed to this, in the next section we will discuss variants of exposed corrections by means of other-initiations of repair where the trouble source addressed by the repair initiation is the same as that addressed by the correction.

Minimal accountings are characteristic of integrated corrections; however, metalinguistic information may be provided after the correction. We will analyse possibilities to integrate a correction into the next relevant turn without accountings in Chapter 6, which is dedicated to embedded corrections. Integrated corrections can be seen as a variation of embedded corrections with accountings in terms of their integration into the relevant next action. However, due to the present accountings, they are explicit, and can be classified as a type of exposed corrections.

5.3.4 Other-corrections by tools of OISR

Some of the corrections are delivered by the native speaker in the form of repair other-initiations, which are responded to by the learners' self-repair. In Example 5.14 the learner produces a problematic lexical unit in turn 420. This unit is marked as a trouble source by the native speaker in turn 421. There is no explicit correction (no explicit correct version of the trouble source) in this turn; however, we can assume that the native speaker understands the meaning of the word itself.

Example 5.14. Repair other-initiation as a correction format (prev. Ex. 3.13).

420 21:02:32 L08 ja, ich war dort. es ist sehr maßstäblich
I was there. it is very full-scale [error: lexical choice]*
421 21:03:30 N04 maßstäblich?
full-scale?
422 21:04:02 L08 hmm...sehr sehr groß, umfangreich
hmm...very very big, wide
423 21:07:34 N04 ah, ok!

This type of correction has been described in language classroom research as repetition (Lyster et al., 2013) where the teacher repeats the problematic part of the learner's utterance, adjusting intonation to draw learner's attention to the error. The rising intonation can be marked in chat by adding a turn-final question mark (as in turn 421). It is not analysable from the data whether the target meaning was clear to the native speaker or not.

The format of this repair sequence is equivalent to one of the formats for repair other-initiation when the native speaker is the trouble-speaker, as discussed in Section 4.2 (e.g. Example 4.4), but with the difference that the learner is the trouble-speaker here. The main difference here is in the design of the repair proper. The learner does not explain the meaning of the original reference to an object or action that caused the trouble, but tries to express the intended meaning in a different way by a different reference. Thus, recipient design plays a role in how repair carry-outs are designed after other-initiations. The identified prototypical sequential structure for repair other-initiation-based error corrections is the following:

T1 The non-native speaker produces a turn x_1 ... TS ... x_n.
T2 The native speaker marks a part of the trouble turn as unclear: $unclear(TS)$.
T3 The non-native speaker selects a different reference to the object or action instead of the trouble source.

Candidate understandings can be made part of repair other-initiation-based correction formats. For instance, Example 5.4, discussed earlier in this chapter (page 148) from the point of view of error types, contains a correction of a lexical error produced by the learner in turn 287. The native speaker first produces the next projected action - a news marker in turn 288 confirming the receipt of new information and a kind of astonishment (so, the message is clear, there is no problem with the intended meaning of turn 287). The contribution to the interpersonal trajectory is immediately followed by a repair initiation marking a part of the learner's utterance as problematic (recycling), which, in turn, is followed by candidate understandings. The sequential prototypical structure can be described as follows:

T1 The non-native speaker produces a turn containing an error TS.
T2 The native speaker corrects the error by providing a candidate understanding.
T3 The non-native speaker confirms or disconfirms.

The learner only needs to produce a confirming or a disconfirming answer to a correction formatted as a polar question. There is no difference compared to repair sequences where the learner produces a repair initiation containing a candidate understanding and the native speaker just needs to confirm or to disconfirm.

5.4 Types of accountings and emphasis on correction

Native speakers used a variety of interactional resources in chat to emphasise corrections. All such resources can be categorised as for framing or for highlighting. Framing resources were typically quotes, dashes, brackets and parentheses, which were put on the left-hand side and on the right-hand side of the copy of the trouble source. In contrasting corrections, framing was also found to mark the corrected trouble source. Highlighting was typically realised by upper case typing of the correction. Various examples discussed in the preceding sections contain instances of the two classes.

Non-symbolic highlighting was found only once in the dataset after an integrated correction. The trouble source and the correction were spelled in a similar way and differed in only one symbol. To highlight the correct version, the native speaker posted an increment to the correction where the correct version was highlighted. Example 5.15 shows the sequence from the dataset where a native speaker produces a correction in turn 442. However, he adds accountings to emphasise the correction in the subsequent turn 443, which makes the correction an exposed correction.

Example 5.15. Accountings highlight the correction.

441	21:24:34	L08	ach, ja)so, ist das richtig:du kannst mit dem Auto fahren, d.h. du hast ein Fahrerschein. ich habe richtig verstanden? oh yes well, is it correct: you can drive a car, this means, you have a driver licence [*errors: gender, lexical]. I understood correctly? *oh yes well, is it correct: you can drive a car, this means, you have a driving licence. Did I understand correctly?*
442	21:25:50	N04	ja, ich habe einen Führerschein und ich fahre selbst :-) *yes, I have a driving licence [correction] and I drive by myself*
443	21:26:08	N04	(kein blöder Witz: es heißt wirklich "Führerschein") *(this is not a stupid joke: it is called really "Führerschein")*

Regarding a classification of accountings, we discussed in this chapter the following types:

1. *Minimal accountings*: found in correction formats accompanied only by emoticons;
2. *Rich accountings*: found in corrections where several other social actions were performed in the form of accountings, such as requests for permission to correct, excuses for corrections and justifications of corrections

Some of the types of rich accountings are typically correction-initial, such as requests for permission, correction announcements and instructing. Other types are found to be typically correction-final, such as encouragements, justifications of correction and declarations of intentions.

5.5 Results

In this section we discuss research results in the field of exposed corrections to answer the following research question:

RQ3b. Which types of exposed corrections of linguistic errors exist in the dataset representing a chat-based Conversation-for-Learning?

To make the contribution of this work to CA-for-SLA and CALL clear, we compare our findings with the results described by Markee (2000), Kurhila (2006) and

Tudini (2010) and the study of German native/non-native speaker chat described in (Marques-Schäfer, 2013). In addition, we compare the types of exposed corrections with the classification of corrective feedback obtained from language classroom data (Lyster et al., 2013).

Conversation-for-Learning as a speech exchange system, with which we had to deal during this analysis, turned out to be a supportive environment for exposed corrections. They probably would occur less frequently and be less preferred in other native/non-native speaker communication contexts, such as for instance online dating. The participants of the chat conversations engaged in exposed corrections of various types of errors on the levels of orthography, morpho-syntax and vocabulary.

The organisation of corrections has been seen in the CA literature as turn-by-turn organisation, for instance (Jefferson, 1987). The prototypical structure of a correction is then the following:

1. Speaker A produces an item X;
2. Speaker B produces an alternative item Y;
3. Speaker A accepts Y or rejects Y by using X again.

How each turn is formatted did not play a role in this sequential model. However, in addition to X and Y, corrections may contain various types of accountings and refer to earlier points in interaction in some way. In order to provide a conversational agent with a detailed instruction how to use all these parts to generate a correction of a particular type, a detailed analysis of correction turn formats was required, which we performed in this chapter.

Native speakers corrected learners' lexical errors if they caused a communication problem, but also in the absence of communication problems. Different correction formats were used by native speakers to deal with different levels of trouble caused by wrong lexical choices. Correction formats designed as information requests (repair initiations) are preferred if the intended meaning is not (completely) clear. Pedagogical corrections presenting multiple target hypotheses in one correction are suitable for dealing with ambiguity errors. Simple corrections are chosen by native speakers to deal with lexical errors in the absence of a communication problem, thus, for barely pedagogical purposes.

Compared to the turn sequence in Example 5.2, page 147, the strategies applied by the native speaker and the learner to resolve ambiguities can be different. This is because some parts of turns become trouble sources for different reasons. For instance, lack of knowledge causes the production of an error in Example 5.2 as opposed to accidental deviations in spelling in Example 5.6, page 149. In addition, participants' stances and identities are relevant for the formulation of the repair.

The following correction formats were used by native speakers for corrections of linguistic errors produced by the learners:

- Simple explicit corrections presenting only the correct target to the recipient of the correction. Such corrections can be accompanied with *minimal or rich accountings*. The turn-taking can be organised in such a way that the learner does not have a space to react to the correction, so-called correction on the fly.

- Contrasting explicit corrections presenting to the recipient of the correction both the initial deviation and the correct target. This type of correction can also be accompanied by minimal or rich accountings.
- Exposed corrections integrated into the next projected turn are those corrections which syntactically and semantically incorporate the correct target but highlight it by symbolic means and expressions of contrast.
- Exposed corrections by means of other-initiated self-repair. These corrections are formulated as clarification requests providing the trouble-speaker the opportunity for self-correction. Candidate understandings can also be presented to the trouble-speaker, replacing the reference with deviations with a correct one.

Previous academic literature distinguished between exposed an embedded corrections. Exposed corrections are delivered in a separate side sequence and may include accountings. Embedded corrections are delivered as part of the relevant next action to the trouble turn and do not permit for accountings or any other form of focusing on correcting. In this work we found a type of corrections not previously described as a separate correction type, which we named *integrated*. We argued that integrated corrections are a distinct type of corrections combining features of exposed and embedded corrections. Integrated corrections do initiate a separate side sequence but they are fully semantically and syntactically integrated into the next action. They may contain accountings and usually emphasise the correction, and become an exposed correction through accountings and/or emphasis. The existence of integrated corrections extends the understanding of the correction types and takes us away from the dichotomy of embedded as opposed to exposed correction types.

OISR-based error correction formats have previously been described in classroom research (e.g. initiations of meaning negotiations (Varonis and Gass, 1985)) and in the CA-for-SLA literature (Kurhila, 2006). Such correction formats explicitly initiate a repair side sequence to deliver a correction; however, they formally provide the learner the opportunity to self-correct. In addition, repair initiations are potential relevant nexts after each turn. On the other hand, the correction in this case is not integrated into a preferred or sequentially projected response, as opposed to embedded or integrated corrections. Therefore, these formats have features of both exposed and embedded corrections. They hide their face-threatening effect behind the preference for self-correction. Nevertheless, they are exposed because they clearly do correction and are taken up as exposed corrections by non-native speakers.

Consequently, integrated and OISR-based corrections open a third dimension in the classification of correction formats, namely grade of relevance (projectedness, preference).

Accountings help the speaker and the recipient to deal with dispreferred social actions performed by corrections of linguistic errors. As in face-to-face interaction, various types of accountings occur in text-based chat. There are corrections where accountings are minimal and are expressed first of all by symbolic means of highlighting the correct target such as upper case spelling, quotes or winking smileys. In contrast, corrections with rich accountings include expressions of apology, instructing, justification of correction and similar.

The dataset contains explicit corrections of lexical, morphosyntactic and orthographical errors; however, the majority of all exposed corrections were produced to correct lexical errors. The lexical errors that became trouble sources in conversations in our dataset are of two types:

1. Problematic references to objects, their attributes or actions so that the native speaker is still able to guess what object or attribute was intended (e.g. more vs. wider, astrology vs. astronomy); see Example 5.1 on page 147. This type makes no restriction on correction types.
2. Problematic references to objects, attributes or actions that make it difficult to guess what was intended and have sequential consequences: the recipient of the trouble-talk needs clarification of what is the next relevant action for the response to the trouble turn. These errors, in turn, can be classified further into those which allow the recipient to project a small number of alternatives (e.g. Example 5.2), and those which leave the intended meaning completely open.

Since the collection of errors is - similarly to that by Schegloff (1987b) - neither systematically representative nor exhaustive, general conclusions would not be valuable; however, we can identify the following tendencies. First, the projection only restricts the corrections to those involving the projected alternatives and those that are formatted as repair other-initiation. Second, for the open type, corrections formatted as repair other-initiations (with or without the candidate understanding) are the preferred type of correction. To summarise, the correction type involves some sort of target hypothesis (what the learner is supposed to mean). The following variants are observed in the dataset:

1. A unique target hypothesis,
2. Multiple target hypotheses from a small set of possibilities,
3. Unclear targets.

Strategies to deal with multiple target hypotheses include disambiguation attempts and clarification requests. Our dataset does not include cases where an unclear target had sequential consequences and had to be resolved “at any cost". Let-it-pass was the preferred strategy for the continuation of the conversation and was chosen by the native speakers. The problem with determining a correct target hypothesis will be discussed from the perspective of learner language annotation in Section 7.2 and will play a role in the application design phase in Section 8.5.2 .

Sequential positions of the trouble turn are relevant for the selection of the correction format. In the analysed examples, corrections on the fly are preferred after questions containing errors. Such corrections allow the native speaker to deal with the error and immediately deliver a projected turn type, thus an answer. Delayed corrections are an alternative form to corrections on the fly, because they allow the speakers to close the open sequence first and then to come back to the linguistic matters, as in Example 5.11, page 154. Participants' choice of a correction format is influenced by the sequential position of the trouble turn and the projected next action. This is especifically important for correction formats that are integrated into the next relevant turn. The correction in this case is repetition-based, but the repeated unit contains modifications which correct the error.

Marques-Schäfer (2013) found that most corrected errors are either orthographical errors or morpho-syntactic errors. She concludes that the tutors and the chat participants perceive the corrections of orthographic and morphosyntactic errors to be more important than the "way of expression" (orig.: *Ausdrucksform*, p. 195). The dataset chosen for this research does not confirm this finding. The majority of all corrected errors in our dataset were lexical errors. This can be explained by the speech exchange system. Due to the study setup, the obtained Conversation-for-Learning appears less formal and less focused on learning (more focused on communication) than the group chat in *JETZT Deutsch lernen*. The chat participants in the study by Marques-Schäfer (2013) must have oriented to the didactic purpose of the learning platform through error correction.

Corrections *en passant* identified in oral talk (Kurhila, 2001), also called *on the fly* in native/non-native speaker chat (Tudini, 2010) allow explicit correction without making correcting a big interactional deal. The same two types of corrections on the fly described by Tudini (2010) were found in the dataset chosen for this work. Either correction and interpersonal trajectory are contained in one turn, or the correction turn produced by the native speaker is immediately followed by another turn continuing the interpersonal trajectory.

Speaker	Repairs by type				
	Conversational recast	Didactic recast	Clarification request	Explicit correction	Explicit corr. with MLE
N01				1	
N02		1	1		
N03		2	1	1	1
N04	2	2	1	9	
TOTAL	2	5	3	11	1

Table 5.1: Classification of exposed corrections according to the classification of corrective feedback proposed by Lyster et al. (2013, p.4); MLE: meta-linguistic explanation

Table 5.1 shows the result of classification of all exposed corrections from our dataset according to the classification of corrective feedback suggested by Lyster et al. (2013). The dataset does not contain any repetitions, metalinguistic cues, paralinguistic signals or elicitations. These types of corrective feedback seem to be typical for classroom interaction (typical teacher's expressions) but too teacher-like for a Conversation-for-Learning. Paralinguistic signals do not occur in the dataset to signalise an error. This result confirms the hypothesis that classifications obtained from a different speech exchange system may be not applicable to a Conversation-for-Learning.

In addition, the classes of corrective feedback are not disjoint. This has already been criticised in the CA literature (Markee, 2000; Kurhila, 2006). Especially recasts were frequently selected for analysis in Communicative ICALL. However, recasts as a form of correction cover several *different* types of corrections with *different interactional import* found in the dataset and described in earlier CA-driven SLA studies. Recasts may have the form of an embedded correction or of an exposed correction. Subsequently, different next actions may be expected after them. This research showed how CA-for-SLA may be an effective methodology on the way to create a consistent classification of disjoint categories of exposed corrections. The proposed classification of error correction formats contains only disjoint classes based on interactional resources employed in their construction.

With regard to the variance within correction formats, the following has been observed. The native speakers rarely changed their correction variants within one format. Some of the native speakers preferred upper case for emphasis, other users preferred quotes. However, native speakers preferred not to use the same correction format twice in a sequence. A small number of preferred correction variants for each format may provide the machine with a personal style. Using the full palette of available correction formats would provide the learners with examples of "doing correction" in chat, which would support learning by imitation (Aguado Padilla, 2002).

While stress and laughter were found in oral data as devices for accomplishing corrections (Hauser, 2010), other medium-specific resources are at participants' disposal in chat to perform a correction. These resources are upper case writing, quotes, dashes and emoticons. Repetitions of errors and explanations are common to oral and chat data as devices for correction. The role of the specific correction devices for construction of different correction formats in chat needs to be taken into account for design of chat-based Communicative ICALL applications. The proposed correction format classification serves this purpose.

Chapter Summary

This chapter presented a detailed analysis of exposed corrections of linguistic errors in Conversations-for-Learning between native and non-native speakers of German using instant messaging. The analysis focused first on possible dependencies between error types and corrections. It was shown that a correction is rather likely to occur if the error has sequential consequences and influences comprehension. Further, error correction formats were discussed. Turn design and turn-taking options for production of corrections of different types were systematically analysed. Various types of accountings and correction emphasis were inspected. Finally, preliminary findings were summarised and discussed.

6

Embedded Corrections

Abstract This chapter prepares an empirical basis for computational modelling of embedded corrections in native/non-native speaker chat. First, embedded corrections of various types of linguistic errors will be discussed. The sequential places where embedded corrections can occur will be analysed. Further, embedded correction addressing trouble other than linguistic errors will be introduced. The working mechanism of embedded corrections will be then under the loupe. Finally, the findings will be summarised and discussed.

6.1 Introduction

As already discussed in Section 2.3.6, embedded corrections are constructed in a way that allows loss of face to be avoided and replaces the erroneous item with a new one in a discrete way. In this way, "... correction occurs, but is not what is being done interactionally" (Jefferson, 1987).

To understand the phenomenon of embedded corrections we need to look again at possibilities to reference objects in conversation. Jefferson (1987, pp. 90-93) mentions three possibilities for referencing:

1. use proterms,
2. repeat the term, and
3. replace the term with a different one.

Jefferson's hypothesis is that "when a next speaker produces, not a proterm or a repeat, but an alternative item, *correction* may be underway."

Examples 6.1 and 6.2 illustrate how an incorrect spelling of a word may be corrected without making the correction interactional business (Example 6.1), and how the error can be ignored (so-called let-it-pass strategy) and replaced with a preposition pointing to the object (Example 6.2).

Example 6.1. Embedded correction: the learner L04 uses a non-German version of the name of Rome (probably Italian). The native speaker N02 replaces it with the

S. Höhn, *Artificial Companion for Second Language Conversation*,
https://doi.org/10.1007/978-3-030-15504-9_6

German version.

163 18:06:05 L04 ich habe 2 Wochen in Roma verbracht))
I spent 2 weeks in Roma [error: spelling]*
164 18:06:12 L04 das war wunderschön
it was wonderful
165 18:06:32 N02 oooooooooooooooooooh, Rom ist die schönste Stadt der Welt!!!
oh, Rome is the most beautiful city in the world!!!
166 18:06:53 L04 jaja!!
yes yes!!

Thus, a replacement can be used as an option to correct in an embedded way; however, not every replacement is an embedded correction of a linguistic error. Jefferson (1987, p. 93) provides examples of embedded corrections where the term *nigger* is replaced by the term *Negro*, and the word *police* is replaced by the word *cops*. These replacements are rather of a stylistic or conceptual nature, and do not correct any errors in orthography or grammar or non-native speaker lexical errors. However, it is apparently the lexical choice that is corrected in Jefferson (1987)'s examples. We can see replacements similar to Jefferson (1987)'s examples in the dataset chosen for this research. However, the majority of all embedded corrections in our dataset is composed of embedded corrections of linguistic errors (ca. 70%).

Example 6.2. Let-it-pass: the learner L04 uses a non-German version of the name of Rome (this time the English version). The native speaker N02 uses a pronoun *das* (En.: *it*) to refer to it in the response.

417 16:49:33 N02 in welcher Stadt in Italien bist du denn?
in which city in Italy are you now?
418 17:04:09 L04 in Rome
in Rome [error: spelling]*
419 17:05:36 N02 ach super, das ist sooooooooooooooooo eine schöne Stadt!
ah super, it is such a beautiful city!
420 17:05:43 N02 Da wünsch ich dir ganz viel Spaß!
Enjoy it there!

In this chapter, we will describe the types of embedded corrections that occur in the dataset. We will discuss types of errors corrected in this way. We will analyse the sequential environments where embedded corrections occur. In addition, we will argue that opportunities to produce embedded corrections depend on the sequential position of the trouble turn and the unit of the trouble turn where the error occurs, and the error type.

The next Section 6.2 provides a detailed analysis of embedded corrections of linguistic errors. Section 6.3 describes other types of embedded corrections that are designed to handle other types of trouble sources and are similar to embedded corrections in native/native speaker talk. The working mechanism of embedded corrections is analysed in Section 6.4. The findings are discussed in Section 6.5.

6.2 Embedded corrections of linguistic errors

An embedded correction of a linguistic error is a pair of utterances of the form:

1. Speaker A produces an utterance a containing one or more linguistic errors;
2. Speaker B produces a response r reusing the unit from the preceding turn where the error occurred, and modifying this unit in such a way that the error is corrected.

Thus, embedded corrections are recognisable as *corrections* only in a direct comparison with the corresponding trouble turn.

To prepare the empirical basis for a computational model of embedded corrections, we need to examine different types of embedded corrections and errors corrected by them. The types of errors that were corrected implicitly will be described in Section 6.2.1. Turn design of sequences where embedded corrections occur will be analysed in Section 6.2.2.

6.2.1 Errors addressed by embedded corrections

The majority of all embedded corrections were produced for lexical errors. The collection of embedded corrections of lexical errors consists of 17 instances. In addition, there are 11 embedded corrections of morpho-syntactic errors and eight embedded corrections of spelling errors and typos. Table 6.1 summarises the numbers of corrections per error type.

	Embedded Corrections				
Error Type	Total	N01	N02	N03	N04
Lexical	17	4	4	3	6
Morpho-syntactic	11	3	3	2	3
Spelling & typos	8	3	1	2	2
Total all error types	36	10	8	7	11

Table 6.1: Types of errors addressed by embedded corrections in the dataset

Example 6.3 illustrates a possible way to correct a lexical error implicitly. The term *Lieblingsgemeinshaft* (Engl.: *favourite community*) produced by the learner in turn 366 is replaced by the native speaker by the term *Lieblingsmannschaft* (Engl.: *favourite team*) in turn 367. Despite the spelling error in the last part of the composite *Lieblingsgemeinschaft*, both the trouble source and the correction are legal German words. However, the latter is a common term in the context of sports, which is the topic of the talk[1].

[1] The interaction took place in the time of the European Cup in summer 2012.

Example 6.3. An embedded correction of a lexical error.

366 18:49:22 L08 und welche deine Lieblingsgemeinshaft für heute?)
and which [error: missing verb] your favourite community [errors: wrong lexem and wrong spelling] for today?)
and which is your favourite team today?
367 18:59:14 N04 hab heute keine Lieblingsmannschaft.
ich freue mich auf ein entspanntes Zuschauen und warte auf irgendetwas Spektakuläres oder Schönes oder Furchtbares oder sonst irgend etwas, wovon man noch in Jahren spricht
don't have today any favourite team [embedded correction]
I'm looking forward to a relaxed viewing of the game and waiting for something spectacular or beautiful or ugly or whatever that people will talk about for years to come

The first turn-constructional unit in the native speaker's response *hab heute keine Lieblingsmannschaft* documents more precisely the information requested in the learner's turn while filling the verb gap and correcting the lexical error. This part of the native speaker's turn is clearly doing more than simply producing the projected second pair part after the first pair part - the question.

Example 6.4 shows an embedded correction of a morpho-syntactic error. The native speaker replaces the erroneous plural form of the word Test - *Teste* - by the correct one *Tests* in turn 142. The repeat-based response to news re-formats the trouble source to a surprise source.

Example 6.4. An embedded correction of a wrong plural form.

141 18:29:10 L08 leider auch nicht(((morgen schreibe ich 2 Teste in Deutsch und Englisch. und wie du verstehst, habe ich noch nicht sie gelernt=))
unfortunately not, either tomorrow write I 2 tests [* error: wrong plural] in German and English. and as you understand, have I not yet they [*error] learned
unfortunately not, either. tomorrow I'm taking 2 tests in German and English. and as you understand, I haven't prepared for them yet.
142 18:30:02 N04 2 Tests? ok, klar, dann erstmal viel Erfolg dabei!
2 tests? ok, I see, then good luck with them for now!

Example 6.5 shows that spelling errors can be corrected implicitly. In this case, a farewell token *Tschüß* is replaced in the farewell reply by *Tschüss*.

Example 6.5. An embedded correction of a spelling error (only regionally used form).

82 20:53:17 L02 Gegenseitig und ja, Montag passt gut. Tschüß!
Mutually [* error: lexical choice] and yes, Monday suits good. Bye-bye [* error: spelling]!
For me too and yes, Monday suits me well. Bye-bye!
83 20:53:34 N01 Tschüss und gute Nacht!
Bye-bye [correction] and good night!

Embedded corrections of spelling errors, typos and some morpho-syntactic errors have the form of repetition with some editing, while embedded corrections of lexical errors are realised through replacements. In Examples 6.4 and 6.5, we see replacements *Teste→Tests* and *Tschüß→Tschüss*, which are repetitions of the same term with replacements in it. In contrast, embedded corrections of lexical errors replace the entire tokens or expressions, as Example 6.3 demonstrates: *Lieblingsgemeinschaft→Lieblingsmannschaft*.

Sometimes, a learner's utterance contains many errors. A complete correction of each of the errors might make the interaction too classroom-like. In addition, some errors are not easy to correct. The native speakers are fluent users of the language, but are not always experts in linguistic matters. If the meaning of the learner's utterance is clear, the strategy of partial correction can be selected. Then only the errors should be corrected that can be corrected *easily*. As opposed to this, some erroneous units may have sequential consequences. Then a correction might be necessary. Example 6.6 illustrates this strategy.

Line 145 of Example 6.6 contains multiple errors. One correct formulation of the question could be *Wie war dein Wochenende?* (En. *How was your weekend*). One more possible correct formulation is *Wie waren deine Wochenenden?* (En.: *How were your weekends?*). The native speaker N02 decides to *test the hypothesis* that only the last weekend was meant, not many of them. The purpose of the replacement is, in this case, not a didactic correction, but a precise formulation of the information in order to avoid misunderstandings.

Example 6.6. Partial embedded correction.

			L05 tells about problems with internet connection
145	17:18:41	L05	Wir waren deine Wochenende? We [*error: typo] were [*pl. aligned with weekends] your [*pl. aligned with weekends] weekend? *How was your weekend?*
146	17:21:59	N02	alles kein Problem! Ich hatte ein schönes, aber anstrengendes Wochenende. War in Darmstadt auf Wohnungssuche und hatte einen Termin nach dem anderen, das war nervig... aber abgesehen davon war es ganz schön, war abends mit Freunden weg (was trinken und - wie immer - Fußball schauen). Was hast du gemacht? *no problem at all! I had a nice but exhausting weekend [correction]. [...] What did you do?*

So far, there is no difference between exposed and embedded corrections in terms of their ability to correct errors of different types: lexical, morpho-syntactic and orthographic. Nevertheless, the following sections will show that the two classes of corrections are not equivalent.

6.2.2 Embedded corrections of linguistic errors and turn-taking

Examples 6.3 and 6.5 of the previous section have in common the high-level principle of embedding a correction in the second pair part (SPP) of an adjacency pair as a response to the first pair part (FPP). Examples of such pairs are greeting-greeting, question-answer, farewell-farewell. This is the most frequent sequential architecture of embedded corrections in the dataset chosen for this research. In addition, our dataset shows replacements in counter questions, acknowledgements, expressions of surprise, questions in positions later than an FPP and sequence closings such as assessments and evaluations. However, a replacement is not the only form of embedded correction of learner errors. Several cases of insertions are also contained in the dataset. In such embedded corrections, a syntactic position empty in the learner's utterance was filled in by the native speaker. Insertions of missing determiners and verbs are examples of such corrections. We will discuss the identified sequential environments supporting embedded corrections in the reminder of this section.

Embedded correction in a second pair part

Embedded corrections in the second pair part of an adjacency pair are the most frequent type of embedded correction in the dataset used for this work. One such instance is shown in Example 6.7. The learner L01 uses a non-standard German[2] spelling version of the farewell token *Tschüß* in turn 35. The native speaker N01 replaces the spelling version with a standard version *Tschüss* in turn 37. The correction is taken up by the learner in turn 38. We will refer to this type of embedded correction as an FPP-SPP correction.

Example 6.7. Insertion of a missing verb in the SPP-FPP position.

35	20:53:29	L01	Ja, das passt mir) Dann Tschüß! *Yes, this suits me Then bye [spelling error]!*
36	20:54:01	L01	Ja, das klappt bei mir *Yes, this works out for me*
37	20:54:22	N01	Okay, super! *Okay, super* Dann bis dahin. Tschüss. *See you then. Bye [embedded correction].*
38	20:54:44	L01	Tschüss. *Bye [uptake]*

Non-present auxiliary verbs and determiners are frequent learner errors. Embedded corrections of such omission errors are insertions. In Example 6.8 the learner L01 drops the verb *war* in her question (FPP) in turn 277. The native speaker N01 inserts the missing verb in his answer in turn 280.

A prototypical structure of this type of FPP-SPP correction consists of two steps:

1. Speaker A produces an FPP containing a problematic unit.
2. Speaker B produces an SPP containing a replacement or an insertion.

[2] Northern German according to the Duden online dictionary. The dictionary lists two correct versions of this farewell token, *tschüs* and *tschüss*.

Example 6.8. An insertion in the FPP-SPP sequence: an embedded correction of a morpho-syntactic error.

277 21:08:00 L01 Wie deine Arbeit?
How [error: missing auxiliary] your work?
How was your work?
278 21:08:04 N01 Wann hast du denn die Prüfung?
When do you have the exam?
279 21:08:27 L01 um 15.00
at 3 p.m.
280 21:09:57 N01 Meine Arbeit war ganz ok. Wie immer eigentlich. Die Schüler waren brav. Die Kollegen waren nett. Und es waren keine Eltern da, um sich zu beschweren ;-)
My work was [insertion] quite ok. As usually actually. The pupils were good. The colleagues were nice. And there were no complaining parents

Deletions of some tokens which may be present but not required by the utterance structure, such as zero-article errors, were not found in the dataset. Nonetheless, such deletions may also be produced by means of replacement in an SPP.

Embedded corrections in counter questions

Environments suitable for counter questions such as *and you?* provide opportunities to embed corrections of a linguistic errors. The sequential place of an embedded correction depends on who is the initiator of the initial question and who produces the counter question, which turn contains the trouble source, and which turn(s) can contain the correction. These sequential variants are seen in the following two examples.

Example 6.9. An embedded correction in a response to a counter question.

115 20:36:06 N01 Welche Bücher liest du gerne?
Which books do you like to read?
116 20:39:12 L01 ich lese historische Romana und manchmal Science-fiction, aber auch kann Krimis oder Liebesromane lesen. Alles hängt von dem Inhalt ab
*I read historical novels [*error: spelling] and sometimes science fiction, but can also read crime novels or love stories. Everything depends on the content*
117 20:39:32 L01 Und du???
And you???
118 20:41:59 N01 Klingt gut, historische Romane habe ich als Jugendlicher auch viele gelesen. In letzter Zeit lese ich aber eher keine fiktionalen Bücher, sondern eher wissenschaftliche Geschichtsbücher.
Obwohl...auf meinem Nachttisch liegt aber im Moment ein Sherlock-Holmes-Buch :-)
Sounds good, I read many historical novels [correction] when I was teenager. In recent times I do not read fiction books, but rather scientific books in History. However... on my night table is a Sherlock Holmes book now.

The first sequential variant can be mapped to the following prototypical structure:

1. The native speaker produces the initial question: Q_1.
2. The non-native speaker produces a response containing an error followed by a counter question: $R(Q_1)^{error}$, $Q_{counter}$.
3. The native speaker responds to the counter question with an embedded correction: $R(Q_{counter})^{correction}$. Even if $Q_{counter}$ in the ancestor turn is omitted, the response still has the form $R(Q_{counter})$ and contains a replacement.

Though the general question-answer pair makes this correction very similar to the FPP-SPP correction (the correction is in the answer to a question), the error is not necessarily located in the question. It can be located either in the counter question or in the answer to a preceding question.

A case of an embedded correction of this type is shown in Example 6.9. The native speaker posts a question in turn 115. The non-native speaker answers the question with an error in it where it is not clear, whether it is a spelling error or a morphology error: *Romana* instead of *Romane*. The answer in turn 116 is followed by a counter question in turn 117. The native speaker's response in turn 118 contains an embedded correction.

The second prototypical structure of a sequence involving embedded corrections in counter questions has the following form:

1. The non-native speaker produces a question containing an error: Q_1^{error}.
2. The native speaker responds to the question. The response is followed by a counter question. Both, the response and the counter question may contain an embedded correction: $R(Q_1)^{correction}$, $Q_{counter}^{correction}$.
3. The non-native speaker responds to the counter question. The response may contain an uptake $R(Q_{counter})$.

Example 6.10 illustrates this schema: L05 uses a word-by-word translation from Russian *Ausgehtage* (выходные дни, going-out days) instead of a standard German *Wochenende* (weekend). N02 replaces this token in her answer *Wochenende war toll* and reuses the same token in her return question *Wie war dein Wochenende?*

Example 6.10. Embedded correction in a counter question.

89	16:58:34	L05	Hallo! Wie geht es? Wie waren deine Ausgehtage? *Hello! How are you? How were your going-out days [error]?*
90	16:59:55	N02	Hallo! Danke, mir geht es gut, und dir? Wochenende war toll, war auf dem Geburtstag einer Freundin, gestern hab ich Wohnung aufgeräumt usw, also alles erledigt, was so angefallen ist, das musste auch mal sein. Wie war dein Wochenende? *Hello! Thank you, I am fine, and you? The weekend [replacement] was excellent, was at a birthday party of a friend, [continuing] How was your weekend?*

In some contexts, *Ausgehtage* could be a legal expression, for example if a speaker makes it relevant that an action of going out took place on a particular day. This expression is not restricted to weekends (*Der beliebteste Ausgehtag ist Donnerstag*, En.: *The most popular going-out day is Thursday*). However, the chat participants

L05 and N02 did not make the action of going out relevant in the previous dialogue. In addition, they met on the 13th of June, and the subsequent chat (from which Example 6.10 was taken) took place on the 18th of June. Thus, both participants knew that only one weekend was between their chats; neither of the participants could talk in this context about multiple weekends. In Russian, the phrase выходной день (vykhodnoy den') can denote any day when one does not have to work (weekend, legal holiday, a day off), but normally it is used to refer to the weekend. Therefore, this replacement is analysable as a correction of an error in lexical choice, and not as just a disambiguation.

To sum up, the counter question environment provides opportunities for embedded corrections regardless of who produced the first question. A successful production of an embedded correction in a counter question depends on the appropriateness of the counter question itself.

Embedded corrections in expressions of surprise

In the examples of embedded corrections in expressions of surprise, the trouble source is reused to become a surprise source. In Example 6.4, discussed earlier in this chapter, the non-native speaker produces a message containing a problematic unit *2 Teste*. The native speaker's response starts with a repetition of the trouble source formatted as the surprise source "2 Tests?" followed by a wish of good luck.

Example 6.11. Embedded correction instead of a 1:1-repetition in expressions of surprise.

186 19:37:51 L06 ich arbeite als Erzieherin in dem Kindergarten
*I work as a nursery nurse in the [*error] kindergarden*
187 19:38:12 L06 wie war dein Urlaub?
how were your holidays?
188 19:39:15 N03 Im Kindergarten? !Super.
In a [correction] kindergarden? !Super.
189 19:39:22 N03 Ich habe auch mal ein Jahr im Kindergarten gearbeitet
I worked for one year long in a kindergarden, too
190 19:39:34 N03 Der Urlaub war toll
The holidays were awesome

Example 6.11 shows another case of an embedded corrections formatted as an expression of surprise. Turn 186 contains the trouble source *in dem Kindergarten*. In turn 188, N03 recycles the trouble source to display surprise and corrects the error. The same turn contains an evaluation. The native speaker keeps the floor and provides information about himself, repeating the corrected version again in turn 189.

The prototypical sequential structure of using the surprise environment to embed corrections of linguistic errors can be described as follows:

T1 The non-native speaker tells some news (e.g. a new fact about herself) that contains a trouble source which is a potential surprise source.

T2 The native speaker produces an expression of surprise by reusing the trouble source from the preceding turn as a surprise source. An evaluation, a ratification, an assessment, an information request or a "me too" statement may continue the surprise turn.

An expression of surprise, like anything else, cannot be placed randomly in conversation. There are turns designed to elicit a surprise response, for instance "negative observations, and extreme case formulations are common components of turns treated as surprise sources" (Wilkinson and Kitzinger, 2006, p. 157). If a surprise reaction follows a turn not designed for a surprise reaction, an elaboration is needed; see (Wilkinson and Kitzinger, 2006, p. 159). An elaboration locates the surprise source (often a repetition or a paraphrase of the surprise source) and explains why it is surprising.

Corrections embedded in an information request

Repair initiations and counter questions provide opportunities for embedded corrections. Another type of question where embedded corrections were found is information request, as shown in Example 6.12. The non-native speaker L02 produces a problematic unit *Halbezeit* in turn 283 (En.: *half of the time*). The native speaker N01 requests more information about something related to the current topic of the talk. This information request contains a replacement *Halbzeit* (half-time) in turn 288.

Example 6.12. Replacement of the form "request more information".

283 20:00:15 L02	Hallo, NATIVE01_FN! Ich statte dir meinen Glückwunsch zum Sieg deiner Mannschaft ab! Ich habe gestern eine Halbezeit angesehen. ;) Hello, NATIVE01_FN! I am paying you my congratulations [* error: lexical] to the win of your team! I watched a half-of-time [*error: orthography] yesterday. *Hello, NATIVE01_FN! Congratulations on the win of your team! I watched until half-time yesterday.*
284 20:00:32 N01	Vielen Dank! Vielen Dank! *Thanks a lot! Thanks a lot!*
285 20:00:41 N01	Ich bin begeistert :-) *I am excited*
286 20:01:30 N01	Jetzt sind wir fast schon im Viertelfinale. *We are almost in the quarter-final.*
287 20:01:36 L02	Obwohl ich kein Profi bin, denke ich, dass die deutschen Fußballsieler gestern der Situation gewachsen waren. *Although I am not a professional, I think that the German football players [* error: spelling] were up to the task yesterday.*
288 20:01:54 N01	Hast du die erste oder die zweite Halbzeit angesehen? *Did you watch the first or the second half-time?*
289 20:02:04 L02	Erste *First*
290 20:02:38 N01	Gut, das war die bessere Hälfte. Mit zwei deutschen Toren :-) *Good, this was the better half. With two German goals*

A prototypical sequential structure for this type of embedded correction may be the following:

T1 The non-native speaker produces a second pair part containing an error.
T2 The native speaker initiates a post-expansion with an information request, which contains a correction.

Embedded corrections in information requests after an SPP represent embedded corrections in initiations of non-minimal post-expansions. However, embedded corrections may also occur at other places in post-expansions, as the next section shows.

Embedded correction accompanied by discourse markers

The example discussed in this section represents anembedded correction in a non-minimal post-expansion later than its initiation. Such non-minimal post-expansions are referred to as *topicalisation* in the CA literature (Schegloff, 2007). Example 6.13 shows how a turn with an embedded correction can be formatted. The non-native speaker produces a message containing a problematic unit. The native speaker replies with an acknowledgement/confirmation token followed by a repetition of the trouble source with correction. There are three sequences of this type in the dataset; however, more examples of this kind can be found in the CA literature; see for instance (Jefferson, 1987, p.94 (17), (18)).

Example 6.13. Embedded correction after an acknowledgement token (prev. Ex. 3.17).

228 20:15:33 L02 Dann brauchst du irgendetwas Beruhigungsmittel einzunehmen)))
Then you need to ingest something tranquilliser [* error] [smile]
Then you need to ingest something tranquillising
229 20:16:02 N01 Genau, zur Beruhigung meiner Nerven :-)
Exactly, to tranquillise my nerves

Although both the error turn and the correction turn are part of a non-minimal post-expansion, the correction turn is analysably a projected second pair part to the learner's suggestion, which is a first pair part. Such pair parts may also be placed elsewhere, not only in post-expansions. A prototypical structure of an embedded correction in combination with acknowledgement tokens can be specified as follows:

1. The non-native speaker produces a turn projecting agreement or disagreement in the response.
2. The expert produces a confirmation / agreement containing an acknowledgement token and a corrected version of the trouble source.

Similarly to an expression of agreement, variants with expressions of disagreement or rejection of an offer are potential candidates for embedding a correction.

Embedded corrections after assessments

Example 6.1, provided earlier in this section on page 165, contains an embedded correction in an assessment. A non-standard German spelling of the word *Rom* (En.: Rome) in turn 163 is replaced by the standard German spelling in turn 165. The native speaker shares her opinion about the place in the form of an assessment. The place is referred to by its full name in both turns. The correction of the spelling error is realised through the repetition of the full reference to the place that the participants were talking about. The correction is embedded in the projected next action after the action of telling in turns 162-164.

An instance of a similar type is shown in Example 6.14. In turn 248 a wrong plural form *Abenteuers* is produced and replaced by a correct plural form *Abenteuer* in turn 252. Sequentially it occurs in the talk on topic introduced by an evaluation in turn 249.

Example 6.14. An embedded correction after an assessment.

248	08:12:52	L06	manchmal sind die Träume erschrecklich. besonders mag ich nicht, wenn ich meine toten Verwandten sehe. aber meistens habe ich irgendwelche Abenteuers *sometimes the dreams are erschrecklich [*error: creation]. especially I don't like, when I see my dead relatives. but in the most cases I have some adventures [* error: wrong plural]*
249	08:14:26	N03	krass! *Gosh!*
250	08:14:41	N03	ich habe noch nie tote verwandte in traeumen gesehen! *I have never seen dead relatives in my dreams*
251	08:14:46	N03	das klingt schrecklich! *it sounds terrible [correction of the lexical error]*
252	08:14:53	N03	ich habe meist abenteuer *I have adventures [corrected plural form] in most cases*

Assessments and evaluations are frequently found in the position of a minimal post-expansion or "sequence-closing thirds" (Schegloff, 2007). The turn sequences analysed in Examples 6.1 and 6.14 are parts of non-minimal post-expansions referred to as topicalisation.

To sum up, two levels of analysis are required for embedded correction: first, on the level of turn pairs to find the mechanism of the "correcting", and second, on the level of the place of this turn pair within the larger turn sequence, such as post-expansion.

6.3 Other types of embedded corrections

This section supports the conceptual understanding of the error/correction dichotomy from the radically emic perspective on data analysis postulated by Conversation Analysis. From this perspective, particular units in talk are considered to be errors if they are *handled* as errors by interaction participants. More specifically, not only language errors can be handled by conversation participants as something that needs a correction. The recipient of the talk may find some features in style, political correctness, preciseness or emotional marking of a reference to an object, attribute or action to require replacement by another term that may be more precise, more polite or more neutral. Other such classes of corrections may be conceptual replacements and stylistic replacements. In this way, the types of embedded corrections discussed in this section are closer to the types discussed in (Jefferson, 1987)'s analysis of native speaker data.

6.3.1 Conceptual embedded corrections

In conceptual embedded corrections, a unit is replaced by a different unit, although the first unit does not contain any formal linguistic error. The examples below are provided for a better understanding of the difference between embedded corrections of linguistic errors and conceptual replacements.

In Example 6.15, the native speaker N01 replaces the neutral word *Anhänger* (supporter, follower) with the stronger concept *Fan* (very enthusiastic supporter, fan). This is even emphasised by the adjective phrase *sehr sehr großer* (very very big). It was not wrong to use the word *Anhänger* in this case. However, the native speaker chose to use a different concept, maybe reflecting more precisely his passion for soccer.

Example 6.15. Replacement of a concept by another concept with no linguistic error.

98 20:11:38 L02 Bist du Fußball-Anhänger, spielst du selbst?
Are you a football supporter, do you play yourself?
99 20:13:12 N01 Ja, absolut. Ich bin ein sehr sehr großer Fußball-Fan :-) Vor allem wenn eine Welt- oder Europameisterschaft stattfindet.
Yes, absolutely. I am a very very big football fan [smile] Most of all when a World or European Cup takes place.

There are three different kinds of conceptual replacements in the dataset:

1. Replacement of a concept by a more specific concept, for instance *read* $\rightarrow$ *read books*. Such replacements may be figurally described as zooming in or out.
2. Replacement of a concept by a stronger/weaker concept. Example 6.15 contains such a replacement. Other examples of this kind are *interesting* $\rightarrow$ *very interesting, exciting* and *you are today a ...* $\rightarrow$ *I am something like a ...* .

Further research on typology of replacements would probably discover more different kinds of what we call here conceptual replacements. Although this type of correction is closer to the embedded corrections in native speaker data described by (Jefferson, 1987), differences in comparison to native/non-native speaker data may exist and may be detected in a future study.

6.3.2 Embedded corrections of style

Instant messaging communication is a conceptually oral type of discourse where participants tend to use short phrases instead of full grammatically correct sentences. This is also a way to adjust the grade of social proximity. The regulation of social proximity may also be performed by the lexical choice where participants select among more formal or marked and more colloquial or unmarked expressions.

Two different kinds of stylistic replacements were found in the dataset used for this work:

1. Replacement of a marked expression by an unmarked expression, for instance *to take pleasure in something* → *to enjoy something*. Example 6.16 contains an instance of a replacement of this kind.
2. Replacement of more official, formal terms by more colloquial ones or vice versa, for instance *White Russia* → *Republic of Belarus*.

In Example 6.16 the non-native speaker uses a marked expression *an etwas Gefallen finden* (En.: *to take pleasure in something*). The native speaker replaces it with a more neutral, unmarked *hat mich auch gefreut* (En.: *I enjoyed it, too*). The use of the adverb *auch* makes the replacement analysably a correction saying "I did the same thing as you did, but I use a different name for it".

Example 6.16. Replacement of a marked expression by an unmarked one.

35	20:35:57	L05	OK, es passt mir ganz gut)))) So, bis morgen, ich fand Gefallen an unserem Chatten, gute Nacht!)) *OK, it fits me quite well [smile] Well, see you tomorrow, I took pleasure in our chat, good night! [smile]*
36	20:37:12	N02	ok schön, dann bis morgen, gute Nacht! :-) *ok great, then see you tomorrow, good night! [smile]*
37	20:37:16	N02	hat mich auch gefreut *I enjoyed it, too*

Non-native speakers tend to use additional language resources to deal with trouble in production. When using dictionaries, they may face the problem of selection of an appropriate expression to serve a particular pragmatic need. This may lead to an incorrect use of correct expressions in a second language, as illustrated in Example 6.16. Therefore, such cases may be also classified as linguistic errors.

6.4 The mechanics of embedded corrections

Repetitions and replacements do not happen incidentally, but perform a particular kind of work in conversation. Repetitions can be used, for instance, to formulate a topical focus, to confirm receipt of a prior turn (Tannen, 1987), to claim epistemic authority over the matter (Stivers, 2005), to initiate repair (Schegloff et al., 1977; Rieger, 2003) or to resist presuppositions generated by questions, to mark questions as problematic or display a problem in question comprehension (Bolden, 2009). To perform these types of interactional work, some particular parts of a preceding turn may need to be repeated, and some others should not. In addition, some units in a turn may exist that cannot be repeated for specific reasons. This, in turn, may influence the opportunities to embed a correction in the repetition. With this motivation, the question that this section seeks to answer is, whether there is any connection between the repeatable units and embedded corrections.

As discussed earlier in this chapter, there are various sequential environments in chat where an embedded correction can occur. However, the majority of embedded corrections were found in question-answer pairs. Therefore, the following specific questions are addressed in this section:

1. Which errors produced in a question can be addressed in an embedded correction in a response to the question?
2. Are there any properties of an error in a question that make an embedded correction of this error in the answer impossible?
3. Are there cases where embedded corrections are unavoidable?

We use a collection of question-answer pairs contained in our dataset to get an intuition from the data whether there are dependencies between error types and embedded corrections. The collection was composed of all questions produced by learners and responses to these questions produced by native speakers. Questions that did not receive any response were not included in the collection, because no correction can be embedded in a non-existent response.

6.4.1 A modified coding scheme for question-answer pairs

To decide what is a question and what is not a question but looks like a question we will use the question-coding scheme introduced by Stivers and Enfield (2010). According to their criteria for questions, an utterance qualifies to be coded as a question in the following cases:

1. It is a formal question if it employs lexico-morpho-syntactic interrogative marking.
2. It is a functional question if it effectively seeks to elicit information, confirmation or agreement regardless of the sentence type.
3. It is a news marker like "Really?" News markers qualify as formal questions because they are treated as seeking confirmation.

Other types of utterances formatted as questions (questions seeking acknowledgment, continuers, requests for immediate physical action or questions offered in reported speech) were not classified as questions. In addition, there are special cases of questions that we will not consider as separate questions, for instance, repetitions of the same question because of connectivity problems. Then, only the first occurrence of a question was included in the collection of questions.

We need to change the unit of analysis in order to answer this research question. The unit of analysis here will be a question, and not a message, because a question in chat can consist of multiple turns or be only a part of a turn. Due to the medially written communication mode, the following had to be added to the definition of questions:

1. Turns may contain phrases related to different threads. In this case only the phrase formatted as a question was considered as one question for the analysis, and not the complete message.
2. The opposite case is when many phrases from one or many messages form one question. In such cases, the question is frequently formed by a declarative utterance followed by a confirmation request or an element corresponding to a turn-final element (Stivers and Enfield, 2010). The response is then related to the whole question stretching over multiple turns, and not only to the part of it formally designed as a question. Such sequences of messages are handled as one question.

In total, 481 question-answer pairs that meet our requirements are contained in the dataset. All questions were independently annotated by two human annotators. The annotators were one native German speaker and one non-native speaker with a native-like fluency in German, both experienced users of messengers. The annotation was performed in the following way:

- Each of the annotators first marked all questions that contained some deviations compared to German language standard or non-native like constructions. The annotators used the Duden online dictionary as a reference.
- Because not all deviations from German language standard can be addressed in chat as linguistic errors, the annotators intuitively marked questions containing "real" errors with a "real" error flag.
- All questions containing "real" errors were coded as polar, content or multiquestion according to the extended question-coding scheme based on the scheme proposed by Stivers and Enfield (2010).

The intuitive "real" error annotation is sufficient for the purpose of this section; however, a proper definition of the concept of linguistic errors in chat is required for automatic error recognition and will be the subject of Section 8.2.

For each "real" error, the error types were annotated (what exactly is the problem), the trouble source in the original question and the references to the trouble source in the original NS's responses. Only 17 questions containing real errors received an embedded correction in native speakers' responses. Therefore, in order to enrich the collection of examples, a methodological change was introduced that is normally not applied in CA-driven research. In order to "simulate" an artificial dialogue system that should generate embedded corrections, native speakers' responses to questions that did not receive any embedded correction in the original corresponding response were modified in the following way. Embedded corrections were added to the responses while trying to preserve the social action of the original response.

This methodological modification was motivated as follows. First, embedded corrections were interspersed into answers to questions, which are *the* place in which embedded corrections have been found in naturally occurring data. Second, only repeatable units of the question could be reused in the answer, otherwise the modified responses were no longer valid answers. In addition, the analysis is restricted to the local question-answer pair; it does not address the reasons for a present or non-present embedded correction in a larger interactional context. Consequently, responses modified by the researcher could not be modified in a way, that could lead to a falsification of the result.

After the error annotation and response modification, the collection of the questions with “real" errors was partitioned into three parts:

1. EC question-answer pairs where a question is produced by the learner, and an answer is produced by the native speaker. These are answers that did not contain any corrections and that were extended by an embedded correction. This collection includes 74 examples.
2. $NOEC$ question-answer pairs where a question is produced by the learner, and an answer is produced by the native speaker without any embedded correction, but the answers could not be extended by an embedded correction. This collection includes 45 examples.
3. EMB question-answer pairs where a question is produced by the learner, and the answer produced by the native speaker contains an embedded correction of a linguistic error. This collection includes 17 examples.

Metrics	L01	L02	L03	L04	L05	L06	L07	L08	L09	Sum
Total questions	22	38	51	75	41	37	52	90	75	481
Errors Duden	11	13	46	73	35	38	50	87	75	428
Real errors	2	12	19	14	26	8	11	28	16	136
EC	0	9	15	6	15	3	5	11	10	74
$NOEC$	1	1	2	6	8	5	5	11	6	45
EMB	1	2	2	2	3	0	1	6	0	17

Table 6.2: Questions, errors and embedded corrections in responses

Table 6.2 summarises numbers of questions, questions with deviations from the German standard as specified by Duden, and “real" errors. Figure 6.1 illustrates the composition of the collection of questions with real errors. From 136 questions in total, six received a self-correction by the learner, and 21 received a response containing either an exposed or an embedded correction (Fig. 6.1a). The composition of the same set after the interspersal with embedded corrections is shown in Fig. 6.1b.

Responses to questions that received a self-correction were modified because self-corrections do not change the basic correctability of the *error type*. However, none of the self-corrected errors was other-corrected in the subsequent continuation of the interaction. This must be taken into account in the final decision model, which should determine whether a correction should be produced or not. We will come back to this problem in Section 8.2.3.

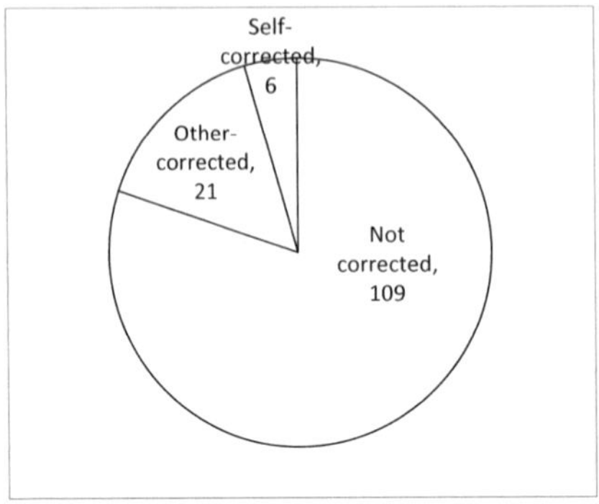

(a) Composition of the original collection

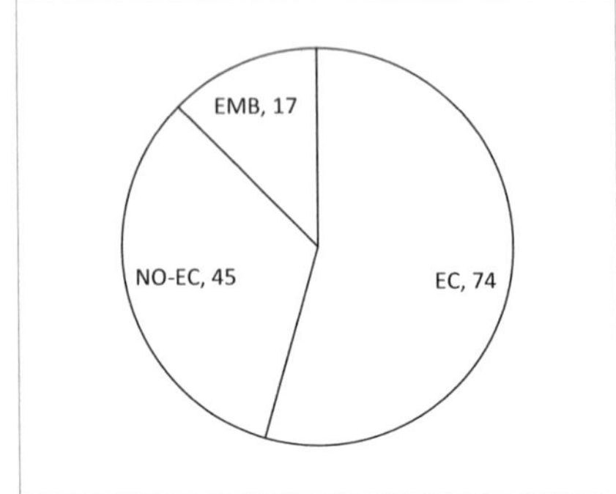

(b) Composition of the enriched collection

Fig. 6.1: Questions with real errors: partitions

To understand what distinguishes errors that can be corrected implicitly from those that cannot, we need to analyse error types in questions. We will describe below the properties of the errors for which an embedded correction can be produced as opposed to errors for which embedded corrections are not possible. In addition, there are examples of embedded corrections for errors that do not count as errors in chat. Such corrections appear when there is a need for a repetition of the reference to an object and the first mention of the object contained an error, for instance a typo. Thus, we will discuss possible, impossible and unavoidable embedded corrections in the remainder of this section. Because polar questions were the best operationalised type of questions covered in the coding scheme by Stivers and Enfield (2010), we focus only on *polar questions* and *answers* to them.

According to the question-coding scheme by Stivers and Enfield (2010), a polar question can receive a response which handles the question "as put" by a *confirming* or a *disconfirming* reaction regardless of form. Such responses are classified as *answers*. All other responses to polar questions, including I-dont-knows, indirect responses and responses requiring inferences from the response recipient are classified as *non-answers*. Answers can be further divided into interjection-based answers (e.g. *yes*, *no*), marked interjection-based answers (e.g. *absolutely*) and repetition-based answers (e.g. *Are you going to the cinema tonight? - I'm going...*). The relevant part of the scheme with modifications is provided in Table B.1 of Appendix B. This annotation step specifically targeted responses to questions based on repetitions and replacements, because

6.4.2 Errors for which embedded corrections are produceable

We will argue in this section that an embedded correction is produceable in a question-answer pair if the error constituent from the question can be repeated in the answer, and if there is a replacement in it that corrects the error. We will consider the joint set $EC \cup EMB$ to find commonalities in embedded corrections and to describe them on a more abstract level.

Error categories not excluded from embedded corrections in Section 6.4.4 can be potentially implicitly corrected. We will not manage here to provide a general description of *the* error types in question that are potentially implicitly correctable, because there are different types of questions (content, polar, alternative and through-produced multi-questions) and each of these types can be further classified by, for instance, form, social action and possible response form. The question-coding scheme suggested by Stivers and Enfield (2010) and modified in this book (Appendix B) provides a good basis for further investigations of these dependencies in a separate study.

Repetition-based answers to polar questions

The set of all polar questions from the set $EC \cup EMB$, which received an answer as a response, will be referred to as $QAPA$. The size of the set is $|QAPA| = 30$ and it is composed of $|EC \cap QAPA| = 25$ and $|EMB \cap QAPA| = 5$. Examples of polar questions with different types of answers are provided in Table 6.3. The following observations were made after the analysis of the $QAPA$ set (number of examples in parentheses):

1. Confirming answers (22):
   a) based on repetitions can correct errors (4);
   b) based only on interjections (marked or unmarked) do not correct errors (14);
   c) based on replacement do not correct errors (4).
2. Disconfirming answers (7):
   a) based on repetitions do not correct errors (1);
   b) based only on interjections (marked or unmarked) do not correct errors (3);
   c) based on replacement can correct errors (3).
3. Yes and no (the infamous German *Jein* was) (1): this sort of response was found doing exposed correction of learners' errors by a disambiguation (sequence presented in Example 5.2). However, an answer version with an embedded correction is possible. Both answer variants (exposed and embedded) to this question are based on repetitions.

As explained at the beginning of this section, it was possible to find modified answers performing the same social action as the original answers, but in addition providing embedded corrections for at least one error identified in the corresponding question. All modified answers with embedded corrections and original embedded corrections are based on partial, full or modified repeats of the question. In addition, the following regularities were found in the modified answers:

1. Embedded corrections addressing spelling errors are based on repeats of the erroneous word with replacements of letters.
2. Embedded corrections addressing morpho-syntactic errors are based on repeats of the erroneous constituent with replacements of morphemes or changes in the word order.

3. Embedded corrections addressing errors in vocabulary and pragmatics are based on repeats of parts of the question with replacements of words or phrases.

To sum up, partial modified repeats and full modified repeats can implicitly correct errors.

The following examples illustrate three types of errors in learners' questions with original answers produced by native speakers and modified answers with embedded corrections. The errors and the replacements are underlined. The modified response is marked by the word *modified* and *EC* (embedded correction) on the left.

Answer form	Question-answer pair
Repetition	Q Hast du keine Artzneien zur Beruhigung deiner Nerven eingenommen ?) *Did you take no medicine [*error: spelling] to tranquilise your nerves?* A Ich habe 1000 Tabletten eingenommen ;-) *I took 1000 pills*
Interjection + repetition	Q ach, ja)so, ist das richtig:du kannst mit dem Auto fahren, d.h. du hast ein Fahrerschein. ich habe richtig verstanden? *oh yes well, is it correct: you can drive a car, this means, you have a driver licence [*errors: gender, lexical]. I understood correctly?* A ja, ich habe einen Führerschein und ich fahre selbst :-) *yes, I have a driving licence and I drive by myself*
Interjection	Q hast du etwas über deutsche Gruppe PUR gehören? *Have you heard [*error: wrong form] something about German band [*error: zero-article] PUR?* A ja, kenn ich *yes, I know [them]*
Marked interjection	Q studiertest du physik dort? *did you study [*error: wrong tense] physics there?* A genau *exactly*
Replacement	Q kennst du vielleicht irgendwelche studiumsprogramme für ausländer_ *do you maybe know some study programs [*error: composite form] for foreigners?* A hm, da muss ich mal überlegen, aber so spontan fällt mir nichts ein *hm, I need to think about it, but for now nothing comes into my mind*
Interjection + Replacement	Q ja, vielleicht ist diese Periode in Deutschland ein echtes Volksfest? *yes, maybe this period in Germany is a real carnival?* A ja, das kann man so sagen!!! Die Stimmung ist echt gut *yes, you can say that!!! The mood is really good*

Table 6.3: Forms of answer-responses to polar questions

Example 6.17 shows an instance of a morpho-syntactic error that is a wrong subject-verb congruence in person. The original answer in turn 126 is interjection-based and does not address the error. The modified response is based on a full modified repeat of the question. To correct the error, the verb-subject constituent needs to be repeated with correction in order to present the correct congruence relationship.

Example 6.17. A modified answer correcting a morpho-syntactic error: embedded correction based on a full modified repeat.

125 20:57:49 L02	Hast dir dieser Film gefallen? Have [*error: wrong person] you liked this movie? *Did you like this movie?*
126 20:58:29 N01	Ich muss ehrlich sein: Nein, nicht besonders ;-) *Frankly speaking: no, not really [smile]*
modified EC	Ich muss ehrlich sein: Nein, dieser Film hat mir nicht besonders gefallen ;-) Frankly speaking: no, I have [correction] not really liked this movie [smile] *Frankly speaking: no, I did not really like this movie*

Because it is just one additional letter, inserted into the correct form of *haben - hat* - (Engl.: *have - has*) it is also likely, that the error was just caused by quick typing, and not by lack of knowledge of German verb conjugation. However, for all similar errors (e.g. wrong congruence in number, gender or person) that need to be corrected implicitly, the verb-subject phrase needs to be repeated, and the wrong verb form needs to be replaced by the correct one.

Example 6.18. A repeat-based response correcting errors in vocabulary and spelling.

79 13:22:49 L03	)))) ja, wahrscheinlich! Sind die Grenze des Schuljahres von Urlaubssaison in Beiern abhängig? yes, maybe! Are the border [*error: wrong number] of the school year [*error: lexical] depending from the vacation time in Bavaria [*error: spelling]? *Does school vacation time depend on the vacation time in Bavaria?*
81 13:23:41 N02	ja genau! ist das bei euch auch so? *yes, exactly! is it the same in your place?*
modified EC	Ja genau! Die Ferienzeiten sind von der Urlaubssaison in Bayern abhängig. Ist das bei euch auch so? *Yes, exactly! The school vacation time depends on the vacation time in Bavaria. Is it the same in your place?*

Example 6.18 illustrates how errors in orthography and lexical choice can be corrected implicitly. In turn 79, L03 uses a non-native-like expression to refer to school vacation time. This non-native-like expression is used with a wrong number which leads to a verb-subject congruence error. In addition, she spells the German name of Bavaria wrongly, which can be interpreted as lack of knowledge and not as a typo, because it is a special case of spelling. To correct the error in the subject of the question in turn 79, two variants of correction are possible:

1. Repeat the non-native-like expression using the correct form of the noun *Grenzen* or

2. Replace the phrase with a different phrase focusing on the native-like expression and not on the form of the non-native-like expression.

We choose the native-like expression, because the majority of all corrected errors in the dataset were lexical errors, thus, errors in meaning are more important than errors in form. The congruence error is not specifically addressed in the chosen correction. To make it visible that it is a *replacement* of the subject constituent, the verb-subject constituent needs to be repeated. Therefore, a full repeat with modifications is used to produce an answer with an embedded correction. To correct the spelling error in the German name of Bavaria, it would be enough to use the correctly spelled word in the response.

The minimal correcting replacement

Here we make the first attempt to formulate abstract rules for embedded corrections in answers to polar questions. For this purpose, we introduce the concept of the *minimal correcting replacement*. Let us look again at Examples 6.17 and 6.18. *Hast* (En.: *have, II p. sg.*) is a valid German verb form, and *dieser Film* (En.: *this movie*) is a valid German noun. Only if they appear together as a verb-subject pair in a sentence, do they produce an error. On the other hand, *die Grenze des Schuljahres* (En.: *the border of the school year*) by itself may sound strange, but the congruence error cannot be detected. However, put together with the verb in plural *sind* (En.: *are*), the congruence error becomes visible. Both errors can only be corrected if the relationship between these words is corrected (*dieser Film hat, die Grenze des Schuljahres / die Ferienzeiten sind*).

The minimal correcting replacement is a repetition of a constituent containing an error with the following properties:

1. It is the smallest constituent such that the error scope is within the constituent.
2. The replacement corrects the error.

Then, if there is a question containing an error, this error is potentially implicitly correctable if there is a way to use the minimal correcting replacement in the response to this question. Specifically, an answer to a polar question will contain an embedded correction if the answer is based on a modified repeat and this repeat is a minimal correcting replacement.

6.4.3 Embedded corrections dedicated to counter questions

Some morpho-syntactic constructions used in questions cannot be repeated in direct responses to questions. However, they can be repeated in a counter question. Such morpho-syntactic constructions are pronouns and verbs in the second person (pl. and sg.), specific word order in questions, and question words (wh-words). The set $NOEC$ contains six questions where errors could be corrected in counter questions. However, the *correctability* is not determined just by the error type, but by the information that the users already exchanged, the information type requested in the question and "territories of knowledge" (Heritage, 2012). Therefore, these questions are included in the $NOEC$ set of questions.

Example 6.19. An error that can be corrected only in a counter question.

162	18:47:26	L07	im allgemeinen beenden sie Uni später als wir...wie lange denn studieren sie-? in general they [*error] finish the university later than we... how long do they [*error] study-? *in general you finish the university later than we... how long do you study-?*
163	18:48:16	N03	mein bachelor war eigentlich 3 jahre *well, my bachelor was 3 years*
164	18:48:32	N03	fuer mich aber 4 jahre weil ich ein jahr in bruessel studiert habe *but for me 4 years because I studied for one year in Brussels*
165	18:48:37	N03	und du kannst ruih *and you can feel free to [misspelling, cut off]*
166	18:48:43	N03	ruhig du sagen *[corrects and continues] feel free to say du*
167	18:48:44	N03	;-)
168	18:49:50	L07	ja ich hab verallgemeinert-... kannst du andere sprachen–? *yes, I generalised-... do you speak other languages–?*

In Example 6.19 the learner uses a wrong form of person reference: *sie* (they, III p. pl.) instead of *ihr* (you, II p. pl). However, a polite form *Sie* is also grammatically and semantically possible in this place. This error is corrected by the ative speaker in turns 165-167, explicitly showing that he interprets the original person reference as a misspelled *Sie*. *Du* (the informal form of address) is the opposite of *Sie* (the formal or polite form of address). The native speaker's correction shows that his interpretation of the learner's intention is *Sie*. She corrects his interpretation in the form of a self-correction in her turn 168: her intention was not the polite form but a generalisation. Her intended person reference should refer to people in Germany, and not only N03. To sum up, a first-person reference in the subject is required in the answer. There is no way to embed a second-person reference in the subject into answers to such questions. However, a counter question may help to correct such errors implicitly. A possible counter question after turn 164 would be *und wie lange studiert ihr normalerweise?* (En.: *and how long do you [II p. sg.] normally study?*).

Example 6.19 is interesting also from the point of view of a correction: the correct version of the learner's intended expression (*hihr beendet, ihr studiert*) is presented neither in the correction in turns 165-167, nor in the subsequent self-correction in turn 168. N03 tested in his correction one of the possible target hypotheses, and it became clear later that this target hypothesis was wrong. However, L07 started a new topic in turn 168 just after the self-correction rejecting N03's target hypothesis. N03 chose not to continue the discussion of the linguistic matters; however, it might be a possible continuation of the talk to teach L07 how a correct person reference in a generalisation can be formed. This example provides a strategy for how an artificial agent might act in situations where multiple target hypotheses are possible.

6.4.4 Errors for which embedded corrections are impossible

A common characteristic of all such error types is that the constituent in the learner's question where the error is located cannot be repeated in the response. In contrast to the examples of possible embedded corrections discussed just above, certain changes to some linguistic features are required in the answers, for instance person and negation. Therefore, if the errors are located in these parts of the question, embedded corrections are not possible. In addition, there are elements connecting two actions in conversation that cannot be repeated in the responses, as illustrated by Example 6.20. Such elements are normally not repeated even in the repetitions of the same question in repair sequences.

Example 6.20. Elements connecting two actions cannot be repeated.

26 18:12:09 L04 aber sowieso wie heißt du?
but anyhow [* error: lexical] what is your name?
but anyway, what is your name?
ZH2: Aber egal, wie heißt du?
27 18:12:13 L04))
28 18:12:26 L04 ORGANIZER hat mir nicht gesagt))
ORGANIZER did not tell me [smile]
30 18:14:06 N02 oh, nicht? ich heiße N02_FirstName
oh, no? my name is N02_FirstName

Turn 26 of Example 6.20 starts with an element which marks unit boundaries: one action is closed and another action is initiated just after *aber sowieso**. However, the adverb *sowieso* is not used as a boundary marker in German, and is probably an incorrect translation from Russian. The target hypothesis ZH2 for this utterance contains a more native-like expression *aber egal* (En.: *but anyway*), which can be used in German to mark unit boundaries. However, the unit boundary has already been marked at the beginning of turn 26, and even with the error in it, the job of this expression is done at the beginning of turn 26. A repetition of such an expression with a correct token in the response would create a *new* unit boundary in a place where it is not relevant.

Counter questions cannot be produced for every learner's question due to restrictions in pragmatics, sequential organisation or the information state (in other words, counter questions sometimes make no sense). This turns out to be a further restriction for errors that can be implicitly corrected only in the form of a counter question, as discussed in the previous part of this section. If a counter question makes no sense for such questions, then the errors of this class cannot be addressed in an embedded correction, but only in an exposed correction.

Other types of errors in questions that cannot be corrected implicitly in the responses found in the dataset:

1. Errors in negations if the answer is negative, for instance *magst du nicht spiele? - normalerweise schon* (En.: *you not like games? - normally I do*); *bleibt alles unveränderlich? - doch, es gibt änderungen* (En.: *everything stays unchangeable - no, there are changes*).

2. Word order errors in questions that cannot be answered with a counter question.
3. Errors in question words.
4. Person, case and gender errors in reflexive particles and personal pronouns that require person change in the response when a counter question does not make sense.
5. Errors in counter questions that can only be corrected in a counter question.
6. Errors which only can be corrected in a counter question if a counter question does not make sense.

In addition, the turn-taking organisation of the talk may influence the presence or absence of corrections. For instance:

1. If the question contains a request for action and an unmarked response is the required action, and not just information, for instance *Kannst du was was über sich erzählen?** (En.: *Can you tell something about yourself?*).
2. If a different action becomes more urgent than a response to the question. For instance, if the learner initiates making appointments, and the native speaker has to apologise first because of being away from the keyboard.

6.4.5 Unavoidable embedded corrections

Sometimes a reference needs to be repeated in order to focus on only a part of the previous turn. Sometimes it needs to be repeated because the turn is delayed and the context needs to be renewed. Embedded correction may be forced in such cases. Example 6.9, page 171 illustrates one such case. The learner produces a typo in turn 116 *Romana* and a counter question in turn 117. The native speaker replaces the trouble source with the correct spelling in turn 118, performing an embedded correction. Because typos are normally not corrected in chat, something else must have been more important than the need to omit the correction.

What alternatives did the native speaker have? The learner refers to two categories of literature in her utterance, but the native speaker refers to only one of them. Therefore, using *it* in the answer to the counter question posted in turn 117 would not reflect the reality because *it* would refer to *both* categories. What are the possibilities to refer to only one of the categories in the answer to such a counter question without repeating the term used by the learner with the error? Obviously, it could be a synonym or a referring expression like *the former* or *the latter*. Using such references in conceptually oral talk is uncommon. Another alternative would to omit a part of the information. The native speaker could just say what he is reading now, but not say what he used to read when he was young. However, finding similarities helps to create rapport. All of the alternatives would be either impossible or less preferred than this embedded correction of a typo, which is normally unimportant and not corrected in chat as long as it does not change the meaning.

Alternative questions and delayed responses can make embedded corrections unavoidable. This is the case if the minimal correcting replacement has to be part of the response.

6.5 Results

In this section we discuss the research results in the field of embedded corrections to answer the corresponding research question:

RQ3a. Which types of embedded corrections of linguistic errors exist in the dataset representing a chat-based Conversation-for-Learning?

To prepare an empirical basis for further computational modelling in Communicative ICALL, we focused specifically on embedded corrections of linguistic errors. In particular, we analysed sequential environments where embedded corrections of linguistic errors occur. The collection of embedded corrections found in the dataset contains two in principle different types of trouble sources:

1. L2 errors that are clear deviations from the linguistic standard;
2. Imprecisions of expression, which do not not deviate from the linguistic standard but rather do not completely correspond to the repair-speakers attitude towards particular references or actions.

The observations related to such imprecisions were summarised under categories of conceptual and stylistic embedded corrections. Stylistic embedded corrections can potentially address non-native-like expressions, too, as demonstrated by Example 6.16, page 178. Compared to replacements in Jefferson (1987)'s examples, *police→cops*, *nigger→Negro*, embedded corrections of lexical errors are closer to embedded corrections in native speakers' talk. In contrast, embedded corrections focused on form (morpho-syntactic and spelling errors) appear to be typical of native/non-native speaker interaction, while the concept of spelling errors is only relevant in medially written communication.

The present study confirms previous observations that embedded corrections may be used to modify the previous speaker's talk in order to correct linguistic errors (Section 6.2.2) but also - as in L1 talk - to deal with imprecise formulations, for example, in style and expressivity (Section 6.3).

We found embedded corrections in the following sequential positions:

1. In a second pair part if an error occurs in the first pair part.
2. In a post-expansion if an error occurs in the second pair part.

This confirms the finding by Kurhila (2006) and extends the findings by Brouwer et al. (2004). Brouwer et al. (2004) found only corrections in second pair parts. As opposed to findings described by Brouwer et al. (2004), we found embedded corrections of linguistic errors not only in the second pair parts after first pair parts with deviations, but also in counter questions and post-expansions (minimal and not-minimal) after errors occurring in second pair parts. Table 6.4 summarises the findings with regard to the sequential position of the error and the relative position and the action type of the correction.

The majority of all embedded corrections in our dataset were located in responses to questions. Therefore, question-answer pairs were chosen for modelling. This type of embedded corrections was then restricted to only embedded corrections in answers to polar questions as specified in the coding scheme by Stivers and Enfield (2010). Repetition-based answers to polar questions were found to provide opportunities for embedded corrections. Thus, a Communicative ICALL system needs to be made aware of differences between repetition-based answers and other types of responses to polar questions (answers and non-answers).

Error location	Correction location	Example
First pair part	Second pair part	Greeting - greeting Question - answer
Second pair part	Counter question	Answer - counter question
	Minimal post-expansion	Assessment Evaluation Acknowledgement
	Non-minimal post-expansion	Surprise Topicalisation realised through an information request

Table 6.4: Location of embedded corrections relative to the error location

With regard to observations by Brouwer et al. (2004) on embedded corrections in the second pair part, this research confirms that embedded corrections frequently occur in a second pair part to correct errors in the corresponding first pair part. However, as opposed to the collection analysed by Brouwer et al. (2004), the collection of embedded corrections found in our dataset contains errors in second pair parts and corrections in minimal and non-minimal post-expansions. “Sequence-closing thirds" are examples of minimal post-expansions (Schegloff, 2007). Embedded corrections with this function in the form of an evaluation, acknowledgement or assessment were described in this chapter. Non-minimal post-expansions described by Schegloff (2007) include for instance, repair initiations and topicalisation. Expressions of surprise and information requests containing embedded corrections were found in our dataset in both types of non-minimal post-expansion.

With regard to error types, embedded corrections of linguistic errors were found in corrections of lexical, morpho-syntactic and orthographic errors. To understand whether there are some restrictions by error type for embedded corrections, a collection of question-answer pairs was analysed. It was observed that there are error categories that cannot be corrected implicitly. These are errors in constituents that cannot be repeated in the relevant next action. Thus, the *correctability* is determined not by the error type, but by the error location, sequential environment, information state and availability of a target hypothesis.

Regarding dependencies between error types and correction types, this study confirms findings reported in earlier academic publications showing that types of errors produced and types of correction formats applied are not mutually dependent (Schegloff, 1987b). However, other factors in the trouble turn may influence the preference in correction formats. These factors include the availability and certainty of a target hypothesis, the sequential environment where the trouble turn occurs, and whether form or meaning is the focus of the correction. The analysis of embedded corrections shows additional restrictions. Because only repeatable units from the trouble source can be made part of an embedded correction, some errors of person, number, gender and congruence cannot be repaired implicitly.

The working mechanism of embedded corrections is described on an abstract level by the concept of the *minimal correcting replacement* introduced in Section 6.4. The minimal correcting replacement is a replacement of the smallest constituent in the trouble turn which completely contains the error by the corrected version of this constituent in the response to the trouble turn. Every constituent that contains the minimal correcting constituent will be a correction too, but it will not be minimal. Every constituent that is smaller than the minimal correcting constituent will not correct the error.

The concept of the *minimal correcting replacement* reflects findings by Schegloff (1979) where the author analysed self-correction and unit boundaries looking at what is repeated in a self-correction. Schegloff (1979) found that no repetition starts in the middle of a unit, and the whole unit is renewed (whatever the unit is). Similarly, the minimal correcting replacement repeats the smallest unit necessary to locate the error, and replaces the erroneous part of it with a correct one. A repetition of a part of such a unit would not correct the error.

Because of the complete syntactic and semantic integration of embedded and integrated corrections into the system's response *not formatted as a correction*, generation of such corrections may present a challenge for a computer system. An exact instruction needs to be given to the machine how to construct a turn with and without an embedded correction. In this work we approached this challenge by focusing only on embedded corrections in answers to polar questions. The coding scheme for classification of questions and responses introduced by Stivers and Enfield (2010) was taken as a basis to create a collection of examples of question-answer pairs. Questions produced by learners and containing "real" errors and responses to them were selected for the analysis. The focus on pairs of polar questions and answers allows us to restrict the potential search space for potentially relevant next actions. This space is termed by Schegloff (1996) the *contingency*.

Because of the contingency, polar questions (like any action) may be responded to by a number of relevant next actions, such as answers dealing with the questions as put, and responses that indirectly deal with the questions, idontknows and all other kinds of relevant next actions to a polar question. This variation is reflected in the coding scheme proposed by Stivers and Enfield (2010). From all this variety of possible responses, repetition-based answers represent the class of responses allowing corrections of linguistic errors to be embedded.

A repetition-based answer corrects an error in a polar question if some parts of the question were repeated and some other parts were replaced or changed in such a way that something wrong in the question became correct in the answer. Because embedded corrections repeat the trouble source with modifications, they can potentially correct errors in all constituents that can be repeated in the next relevant turn.

Specifically for question-answer pairs it was found that repeat-based answers to polar questions support embedded corrections. Partial or full repeats with modifications in answers to polar questions contain embedded corrections if they contain the minimal correcting replacement. In contrast, errors in word order in questions, for instance, can only be corrected if the complete question can be repeated in the next relevant turn. Counter questions (variants of *and you?*) can fulfill this task. However, counter questions are sometimes not relevant due to the information state.

Repeats of parts of the previous turn may be required in conversation without the purpose to replace a unit previously used. Such repeats may be necessary in order to update the subject of the talk in a delayed response caused by the virtual adjacency in chat. The need to restrict the scope of the question in an answer may also be a reason for a repetition. If linguistic errors occur in references to such objects or actions in the questions, such repetitions in the answers will either repeat the original reference "as is", with all errors, or they will repeat them with modifications, and thus, with embedded corrections. Such embedded corrections can be seen as unavoidable.

As in exposed corrections of linguistic errors, the problem with multiple target hypotheses exists for embedded corrections, too. Multiple errors may exist in one constituent, which can become the minimal correcting constituent for all the errors. However, as illustrated by Example 6.18, it is possible that only one of the errors can be corrected at once, and a decision has to be taken which of the errors should be corrected and which of the errors should be ignored. Computational models of embedded corrections need to be prepared to face this issue.

The analysis of assessments and acknowledgements shows that two levels of analysis are required for embedded correction. The analysis of turn pairs allows us to understand the working mechanism of the "correcting", as it was done for question-answer pairs. The analysis of the place of this turn pair within the larger turn sequence allows us to discover dependencies between sequential organisation and references to objects in conversation, including repetitions.

In order to make visible that something is implicitly corrected, one needs to keep something unchanged, and change something else. Therefore, embedded corrections are noticeable only in a direct comparison with the trouble turn. Exposed corrections, in contrast, are recognisable as corrections due to the specific correction turn formats.

In contrast to the results described by Tudini (2010) saying that "dyadic online intercultural chat favours exposed correction to deal with pedagogical repair", the present study shows that embedded corrections may occur even more frequently than exposed corrections to deal with learner errors. This confirms the result reported by Brouwer et al. (2004) and Kurhila (2001) according to which embedded corrections (corrections "in a repetition slot" (Kurhila, 2001)) are typical of native/non-native speaker interaction. However, the number of occurrences of embedded corrections varies for each pair of participants from one correction to 10 corrections for the entire duration of the interaction. The analysis of pairs of polar questions and answers in Section 6.4 showed that native speakers made use of embedded corrections only in a small number of all opportunities. From 91 answers where an embedded correction could have been provided, only 17 contained an embedded correction. An explanation for this finding may be found in an additional study.

Brouwer et al. (2004) report that they did not find any embedded correction in an answer to a polar question. In light of the analysis of question-response pairs based on the question-coding scheme (Stivers and Enfield, 2010) presented in Section 6.4, answers to polar questions can be designed in a way that supports or allows avoidance of embedded corrections. Repetition-based answers to polar questions provide opportunities to correct implicitly. Interjection-based (marked or unmarked) answers to polar questions do not embed a correction. In the collection of question-answer pairs obtained from our dataser, repetition-based answers to polar questions clearly do more than simply giving a confirmation or a disconfirmation. The same is reported by Brouwer et al. (2004). In addition, this confirms the result described by Lerner and Kitzinger (2007) showing that what is done by an embedded correction is action-specific to the trouble source.

Jefferson (1974) describes correction devices that show that current talk is a quote of directly prior talk. These devices employ a repetition of the erroneous item, which was not completely produced but could be guessed. In this regard they are very similar to acknowledgement-based embedded corrections. The difference is that there is no cut-off in the directly prior talk. The non-native speaker completely produces the erroneous item but the native speaker uses the same quotation format as a base. Due to a replacement within the quotation-based format a correction can be produced.

With regard to tracking learning progress, embedded corrections present a particular difficulty because they provide the opportunity to learners not to respond to them, as Kurhila (2006) observed. Confirming this finding, it was illustrated in Example 3.17 how a postponed uptake after an embedded correction may take place. In this example, the correction was taken up in the subsequent chat session, and not as a direct response to the correction. Postponed uptake and imitation are very difficult for human annotators to find in the data, but this might be attempted by computer-assisted qualitative data analysis (Wickham and Woods, 2005) and taken as a base for evaluation in ICALL.

Chapter Summary

This chapter focused on embedded corrections of linguistic errors in chat. Other types of corrections were also described: errors in style and conceptual errors. The sequential places supporting embedded corrections were identified. The working mechanism of embedded corrections was analysed and described. The findings were summarised and discussed.

7

Models of Learner-Error Corrections

Abstract This chapter presents a generalisation of the findings of Chapters 5 and 6 with the purpose of computational modelling of interactional practices of error correction for a Communicative ICALL application. Because proper error recognition is a crucial prerequisite for every correction, issues in the conceptual definition of an error in chat are discussed. Further, a model for automated generation of all types of exposed corrections except integrated corrections is proposed. Embedded and integrated corrections in an ICALL application are then discussed with a restriction to answers to polar questions. Results of the models are discussed in comparison with the state of the art.

7.1 Introduction

Following the need to disengage "trouble (error and nonerror) from the practices employed to deal with it" pointed out by Schegloff (1987b, p. 216), we looked at practices used by chat participants for dealing with learners' linguistic errors in Chapters 5 and 6. Because "the occurrence of repair is not prompted only by the occurrence of error," (Schegloff, 1987b, p. 216), we will separately analyse possible other reasons for occurrences of corrections in Chapter 8. For the purpose of computational modelling, it appears reasonable to distinguish models for dealing with errors from models for error recognition and models responsible for the decision whether a correction should be produced. Therefore, we will distinguish between models for practices of correction, which we will call *local models of correction*, and factors influencing whether a correction should be produced and what form it should take. This chapter focuses specifically on local models of corrections of linguistic errors.

For the purposes of computational modelling, all identified correction formats from Chapters 5 and 6 have been partitioned into two sub-classes according to their grade of integration into the next relevant projected turn. Table 7.1 shows the differences in classes with regard to the identified dimensions as well as the result of the partition.

S. Höhn, *Artificial Companion for Second Language Conversation*,
https://doi.org/10.1007/978-3-030-15504-9_7

For the remainder of this chapter, we will assume that an Error Recognition Function (ERF) detects errors in learners' utterances. ERF may incorporate techniques for error recognition discussed in Section 2.2.4. However, error recognition in learner chat language needs to deal with a huge variance in orthography in syntax, which does not count as error in chat. We will look at the issues of error annotation in learner language in Section 7.2 in order to show the necessary modifications for correction modelling. A version of Section 7.2 can be found in (Höhn et al., 2016).

Correction type \ Attribute	Explicitness	Integration	In a projected turn
On the fly	x	-	-
Simple	x	-	-
Contrasting	x	-	-
OISR-based	x	x	-
Integrated	x	x	x
Embedded	-	x	x

Table 7.1: Correction type classification and partition for computational modelling

Computational models of exposed and embedded corrections will be the subject of Sections 7.3 and 7.4, respectively. We will first see how specific exposed correction formats can be generated from a set of language-specific and medium-specific resources. Error correction formats obtained from the data build a basis for the correction types. Because of the complexity of embedded corrections, which we discussed in Chapter 6, we will restrict modelling of embedded corrections to pairs of polar questions and answers. As in the corresponding empirical part, we consider polar questions produced by a learner and containing at least one "real" error. The corrections are then incorporated into answers to these questions. The model evaluation will take the form of a technical specification in which we will analyse how the model can be implemented using available NLP tools. The specification will be described in Section 10.4. The results will be discussed in Section 7.5.

7.2 Learner-error annotation in chat

The error annotation of the questions was performed according to the annotation guidelines for FALKO Corpus of German learner language (Reznicek et al., 2012, 2013). To prepare a basis for an error annotation, two types of target hypotheses were introduced in FALKO. The minimal target hypothesis ZH1 aims at sentence normalisation and is limited to only orthography and morpho-syntax. ZH1 was constructed according to the rules of standard German grammar and orthography with the Duden dictionary as a reference. Semantics, lexical constructions and pragmatics are the subject of the extended second target hypothesis ZH2. Example 7.1 shows the two target hypotheses for a sample question.

Example 7.1. Creating target hypotheses for error correction in questions.

402 20:47:31 L08 und um wieviel Uhr gehst gewöhnlich zum Bett?
and at what time do you normally go to bed?
ZH1 Und um wie viel Uhr gehst du gewöhnlich zum Bett?
ZH2 Und um wie viel Uhr gehst du normal ins Bett?

The following issues were faced when annotating errors in chat according to the FALKO guidelines. First, special symbolic and orthographic means of expressivity used in chat must be classified as errors according to Duden and the FALKO error annotation guidelines. Second, the FALKO annotation guidelines do not provide any specific instruction for cases where errors in the verb make more than one target for the verb possible. Example 7.2 illustrates such a case. This error was corrected by the interaction partner of L09 in the dialogue and both possible targets for the erroneous question were addressed in the correction. Therefore, having in mind the application where corrections should be automatically generated in a conversation, we add both target hypotheses to the annotation.

Example 7.2. Ambiguous target hypotheses.

135 13:21:09 L09 gefiel dir das studium leicht?
Unclear target: Was the study easy for you? or Did you like your study?
ZH1a Gefiel dir das Studium?
ZH1b Fiel dir das Studium leicht?

The differences between the learner's original utterance and the two target hypotheses help to classify the errors and to generate corrections. In addition, it allows empirical analysis of what normalisation steps are really required for automated language understanding. However, chat conventions allow everything to be written with small letters only and do not consider typos to be errors that need a correction. This is why information about potential correctability of an error in chat needs to be encoded in the error annotation. Additional rules for exceptions need to be specified when deviations in orthography and punctuation are used as a means of expressivity. Therefore, the "real" error flag was introduced with the purpose to identify all errors that are *potentially addressable* in chat. The conventions that were taken into account for the "real" error flag will be discussed in detail in Section 8.2. They are all restricted to orthography and allow

1. starting an utterance, a new sentence and nouns with a small letter,
2. writing lower case or upper case or camel case,
3. using punctuation and special symbols for the purpose of expressivity,
4. omitting punctuation and using emoticons to separate turn-constructional units,
5. producing word stretches.
6. using letter combinations such as *ue* to replace German umlaut letters such as *ü*.

These rules are consciously applied by chat participants while typing. In addition, there are misspellings that are the result of a high typing pace and not lack of knowledge. They also do not qualify as errors in chat and are not considered as "real" errors. There are two exceptions that we take into account:

1. If a speaker repeats the same misspelling several times and the misspelled word sounds exactly like the correctly spelled word (e.g. Example 5.8, page 151).
2. If it is a special, difficult case where even native speakers often make mistakes, for instance *ziemlich*.

In Section 6.4.1 we introduced a method for creation of a larger set of embedded corrections by data enrichment. Every answer to a polar question containing a real error was modified by including an embedded correction in it. During this correction-authoring process, it was not always clear which ZH should be used for the embedded correction in the modified response. Example 7.3 illustrates an error in plural in a non-native-like expression. Two response versions with embedded corrections are suggested in EC1 and EC2. Each of the suggested embedded corrections corrects only one of the errors. It is hardly possible to address these two errors with a single exposed correction.

Example 7.3. Different target hypotheses correct different errors. Trouble sources are underlined. Target hypotheses and respective embedded corrections are added at the bottom.

79 13:22:49 L03	)))) ja, wahrscheinlich! Sind die Grenze des Schuljahres von Urlaubssaison in Beiern abhängig? yes, probably! Do the border of the school year [* errors: verb-subject number congruence, uncommon expression] depend on the holiday season in Beiern [* error: spelling] *yes, probably! Do the borders of the school year depend on the holiday season in Bavaria*
80 13:23:16 L03	* Bayern * Bayern [self-correction] **Bavaria*
81 13:23:41 N02	ja genau! ist das bei euch auch so? *yes, exactly! is it like this in your place, too?*
ZH1	Sind die Grenzen des Schuljahres von der Urlaubssaison in Bayern abhängig?
EC1	*Ja, die Grenzen des Schuljahres...* [corrects congruence error]
ZH2	Sind die Ferienzeiten von der Urlaubssaison in Bayern abhängig?
EC2	*Ja, die Ferienzeiten...* [corrects error in lexical choice]

Dealing with multiple target hypotheses will also be an issue for a computer program that should produce a correction. We will come back to this problem in Section 8.5.2.

7.3 Generation of exposed corrections

This section seeks to show how exposed corrections for linguistic errors can be generated. We assume that for each error in a learner utterance, the error recognition function ERF is able to recognise the error and to determine the target hypothesis. Chapters 5 and 6 showed that many correction formats are at the participants' disposal. However, it is neither feasible nor desirable to 'hard-code' a specification of each correction format for each error in a conversational system. The aim of this section is therefore to describe a generalised model for each type of exposed corrections from a given set of language-specific and medium-specific resources. A further investigation in a separate cross-linguistic study will be needed to discover what adjustments in the model are required to adapt the model to a language different from German.

Figure 7.1 shows the components needed to generate a correction of a linguistic error in a conversation with a non-native speaker. The following sections explain each of the steps in detail.

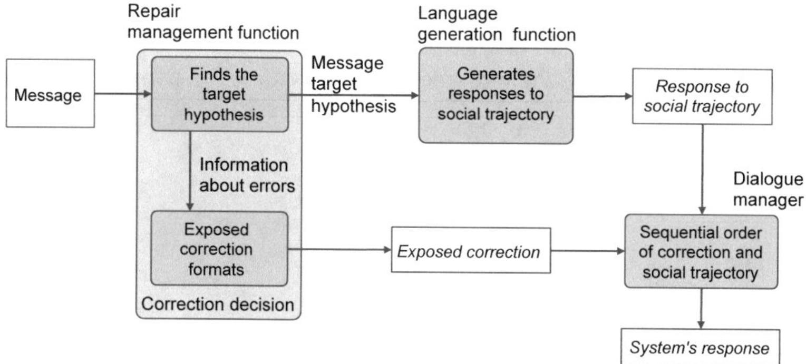

Fig. 7.1: Generation of exposed corrections

7.3.1 Turn format and turn taking

Since only one error was addressed in each correction produced by the native speakers, we assume for the purpose of this section that the user's message contains at most one error. Let the user's message contain an error $M = m_1...m_n$ and $X^* = [m_i : m_k]$, $1 \leq i \leq k \leq n$ be the deviant part of the message (the trouble source may be one or more tokens). Let X be the correct expression in the target language, or simply target, for X^*. We use A to denote the set of accountings. We will distinguish between minimal accountings A_{min} and rich accountings A_{rich}. F_l and F_r denote the sorted sets of framing means to highlight the repetitions of the trouble source and the targets, so that $f_{l,i}$ $f_{r,i}$ build a pair of framing symbols for each $f_{l,i} \in F_l$, $f_{r,i} \in F_r$ and $1 \leq i \leq |F_l|$, $|F_l| = |F_r|$. We will use the $\centerdot$ operator to denote the concatenation of the parts of the correction. Some parts of the turn formats are optional. This is taken into account in this model by the empty element ϵ included in each set where the presence of the elements of the set is optional. If the presence of an element is mandatory at a particular place, ϵ is not included. We use the letter $\mathscr{C}$ for the correction format. The specific models for each correction format are described below.

Exposed corrections on the fly

Corrections on the fly are delivered in a chunk with a subsequent turn continuing the interpersonal trajectory. Specifically, the trouble source turn is followed by the target optionally framed with highlighting symbols, immediately followed by an emoticon $e \in A_{min}$ and a response to the interpersonal trajectory R_{topic}. Then the correction on the fly $\mathscr{C}_{onf}$ will have the following format:

$$\mathscr{C}_{onf} = f_{l,i} \centerdot X \centerdot f_{r,i} \centerdot e \centerdot R_{topic} \tag{7.1}$$

The order the last two elements e and R_{topic} can be reversed, and either the framing or the position of emoticons e or even both may be empty. Either the generated correction can be broken down into three messages posted to the user one after the other with very short breaks, or they can all be posted as one message. This leads to the following two models for the turn-taking for this correction format:

1. Three separate turns, one per part:
   T1 $f_{l,i} \centerdot X \centerdot f_{r,i}$
   break
   T2 e
   break
   T3 R_{topic}
2. The correction and the response to the interpersonal trajectory are delivered in one turn: T1 $\mathscr{C}_{onf}$ as specified in Equation 7.1.

The length of the breaks can vary. Empirically grounded values can be obtained from the chat data in an additional study focused on responsiveness in instant-messaging-based communication. One attempt to get insights from our dataset into issues of responsiveness in chat was discussed in an earlier work (Danilava et al., 2013b).

Simple corrections with minimal or rich accountings

In simple corrections with minimal accountings, only a correction is presented, optionally followed by a member of the set of minimal accountings A_{min}. The correction may optionally be framed or highlighted. The correction turn $\mathscr{C}_{sma}$ then has the following form:

$$\mathscr{C}_{sma} = f_{l,i} \centerdot X \centerdot f_{r,i} \centerdot e \tag{7.2}$$

The recipient of the correction then has the choice to react to the correction or to continue on the interpersonal trajectory.

Rich accountings of different kinds are involved in corrections to express different social actions and intentions. As shown in Section 5.3, more than one element from the set of rich accountings may be placed in a chunk as part of a correction. We use a_{rich} to denote such a chunk of rich accountings composed from a non-empty subset of all possible types of rich accountings A_{rich}. If the chunk contains more than one element, they are sequentially ordered by their interactional function. A generalised format of a simple correction with rich accountings $\mathscr{C}_{sra}$ may then look as follows:

$$\mathscr{C}_{sra} = a_{rich} \centerdot e \centerdot f_{l,i} \centerdot X \centerdot f_{r,i} \centerdot e \centerdot a_{rich} \centerdot e \tag{7.3}$$

Depending on the type of rich accountings (apology, correction justification etc.) they may be correction-initial or correction-final. The correction may be presented to the user in multiple turns:

T1 $a_{rich} \centerdot e$
break
T2 $f_{l,i} \centerdot X \centerdot f_{r,i} \centerdot e$
break
T3 $a_{rich} \centerdot e$

Correction-initial accountings, such as requests for permission to correct, may be followed by a pro forma break offering the user the chance to react. However, they are not real requests for permission, and therefore, there is no need to wait for permission. Nonetheless, such requests can be used for the purpose of negotiation of conventions. In this way it can be clarified whether it is okay for the user to receive error corrections.

Specific social actions performed by each type of accountings need to be taken into account when each correction turn is generated. Therefore, the simplified model specified in Eq. 7.3 must become more specific for an implementation. We will come back to this question in Section 7.3.2 where we discuss language-specific devices and social actions performed by them.

Highlight by register change (e.g. upper case) can be used instead of or in addition to framing. In practice, however, the language resources in chat were used rather economically. Because typing pace is an issue, the participants used either framing or upper case to highlight the important parts in the correction. The model reflects this observation. We denote the register change to upper case by $upper(X)$ for the trouble source X. Then the correction format will be as follows:

$$\mathscr{C}_{sra} = a_{rich} \centerdot e \centerdot upper(X) \centerdot e \centerdot a_{rich} \centerdot e \tag{7.4}$$

A presentation of the correction in multiple turns will be similar to the variant without upper case.

This way of highlighting was never used by the native speakers for corrections on the fly or corrections with minimal accountings, probably because writing everything in upper case is interpreted as shouting in chat, and for these two correction formats the correction is equal to the entire message. As opposed to these short correction formats, upper case writing of a part of the turn helps to highlight the target in corrections with rich accountings.

Since delayed corrections require higher effort in terms of interaction management, only corrections with rich accountings (both simple and contrasting, described below) allow for delayed corrections. In addition, it is necessary to renew the context, which was done by the native speakers in the dataset by specific backlinking tokens. We use BL for the notation of the set of all backlinking tokens and *bl* for its elements, thus $bl \in BL$. Then a delayed correction with backlinks will have the following format:

$$\mathscr{C}_{sra} = bl \centerdot a_{rich} \centerdot e \centerdot f_{l,i} \centerdot X \centerdot f_{r,i} \centerdot e \centerdot a_{rich} \centerdot e \tag{7.5}$$

The variant of presentation of the correction to the learner in multiple turns will have a backlink in the first turn.

Contrasting corrections with minimal or rich accountings

Corrections formatted in such a way that both the trouble source and the target expression are presented to the learner in a direct comparison (contrast) may require minimal or rich accountings. The trouble source produced by the learner is explicitly rejected and replaced by a different unit within this correction format. The basic elements used for the contrasting correction formats are the same as for simple corrections with accountings, with one additional element: negatively marked repetition of the trouble source, which we denote by $\neg X^*$. A contrasting correction with rich accountings will then be formed as follows:

$$\mathscr{C} = a_{rich} \centerdot e \centerdot \neg(f_{l,i} \centerdot X^* \centerdot f_{r,i}) \centerdot f_{l,i} \centerdot X \centerdot f_{r,i} \centerdot e \centerdot a_{rich} \centerdot e \tag{7.6}$$

A contrasting correction with minimal accountings will differ from the correction model specified in Eq. 7.6 only in the type of accountings used:

$$\mathscr{C} = e \centerdot \neg(f_{l,i} \centerdot X^* \centerdot f_{r,i}) \centerdot f_{l,i} \centerdot X \centerdot f_{r,i} \centerdot e \tag{7.7}$$

Similarly to simple corrections with rich accountings, the highlighting of the trouble source and the target can be done with register change (upper case). A contrasting correction with rich accountings will then have the following changes:

$$\mathscr{C} = a_{rich} \centerdot e \centerdot \neg(upper(X^*)) \centerdot upper(X) \centerdot e \centerdot a_{rich} \centerdot e \tag{7.8}$$

The contrasting correction can be presented to the user in one turn or in a turn chunk, for instance the variant with rich accountings corresponding to 7.8:

T1 $a_{rich} \centerdot e$
break
T2 $\neg upper(X^*)$
T3 $upper(X) \centerdot e$
break
T4 $a_{rich} \centerdot e$

A similar chunk-wise output may be produced for 7.6. Again, the duration of the time breaks between the turns in the chunk is motivated by the responsiveness values between short turns in users' chunks. However, responsiveness values in chat need further investigation to provide a more stable, empirically grounded model for breaks between turns. Possible combinations and sequential order of rich accountings will be discussed in Section 7.3.2.

Corrections formatted as repair other-initiations

To generate repair initiations by a computer system, the reverse process of that described in Chapter 4 needs to be specified here. A recognised trouble source needs to be wrapped into a repair initiation. For this purpose, resources for signalling trouble and referencing a trouble source need to be involved in this type of correction. Two distinct formats of repair initiation as a way to correct errors were found in the dataset:

1. Repetition or recycling of the trouble source combined with marking it as unclear,
2. Presentation of one or several candidate understandings.

However, additional repair other-initiation formats cannot be excluded in general from use for the purpose of correction. Therefore, the grammar for error corrections in the form of repair other-initiation must take different possible types of trouble source into account. In contrast to the repair other-initiations produced by the learner, explicit statements of non-understanding will not fit into corrections. For instance, a repair-other-initiation-based correction "X? Nie gehört..." is either too teacher-like or too learner-like. Therefore, a different set of language-specific resources needs to be specified here. We use $CR(X)$ for all trouble signals formatted as clarification requests, and $candidate(X, Y)$ for all signals involving candidate understandings. Then a correction $\mathscr{C}$ can be defined as an element-wise product of referencing trouble source and signalling trouble:

$$\mathscr{C} = REF \times SignalFormat \tag{7.9}$$

The generation of REF and $SignalFormat$ is explained below for each type of trouble source.

A part of a longer message: specific formats based on reuse or recycling or demonstrative determiners and proterms are suitable for this type of trouble source. A part of a longer message may be, for instance, one word, a phrase consisting of several words, or a copy of a longer part of the message.

if *TIME=immediate* **then**
  $REF \in \{reuse(x),\ recycle(x),\ DD,\ DP\}$;
else
  $REF \in \{reuse(X*),\ recycle(X*)\}$;
  $SignalFormat \in \{CR(X*),\ candidate(X*, X)\}$;
end

The whole message: open-class repair initiation formats are appropriate for this case (reference by adjacent position); however, they only unambiguously reference the trouble source if used in the adjacent turn. Otherwise, formats based on recycling are preferable. In Chapter 4 we distinguished between one-word messages that became trouble sources, and longer messages that became trouble sources. They may need different approaches for repair carry-out.

if *TIME=immediate* **then**
| $REF \in \{AP,\ DP\}$;
else
| $REF \in \{reuse(X*),\ recycle(X*)\}$;
| $SignalFormat \in \{CR(X*),\ candidate(X*, X)\}$;
end

Signalling devices can be placed in the turn on the left of the reference to the trouble source or on the right, or both. Open-class repair initiators do not contain an explicit reference to the trouble source, so signalling devices are only relevant for more specific types of references (reuse, recycle, DD, DP).

A right-hand side of a signal format set contains all symbolic and lexical means that can be placed after the reference to the trouble source. Normally, they can be found in a turn-final position, on the right-hand side of the trouble source, which I denote by $CR(X*)_{right}$. For instance,

$$CR(X*)_{right} = \{\text{“?",“???",“--???", “? Wie meinst du das?", “-- unklar"}\}.$$

Repair other-initiation-based formats are functionally questions, and therefore, they are normally formatted as questions, which is done with a question mark in chat. Question marks are a very important means of expressivity in chat. They are rarely omitted by chat users, and should be used by conversational agents to ensure a better understanding of agents' intentions. Therefore, $CR(X*)_{right}$ does not contain ϵ.

In contrast, signalling means that can be placed on the left-hand side of the trouble source (normally, turn-initial) contain ϵ, because it is optional. An example of a left-hand side of a signal format set may be the following:

$$CR(X*)_{left} = \{\epsilon, \text{“wie,", “was heisst", “was bedeutet"}\}.$$

Repair other-initiation-based correction formats found in the dataset were all repeat-based: their purpose was to replace a reference that caused trouble in understanding with another reference that resolved this trouble. It was always possible for the native speakers to locate the trouble source very specifically. In cases where the meaning of an entire learner's utterance was not understandable, native speakers preferred to let-it-pass. However, sometimes native speakers initiated immediate repair with a lexicalised paralinguistic cue such as *hä?* (open class).

Repetition of the trouble turn is the usual repair carry-out type after such repair initiations in oral interaction. Learners, in contrast, delivered a *different* expression to replace the trouble source, or additional explanation to clarify their intention. It was not just a repeat in any case. Dialogue models need to decide what happens with the repaired talk and how to handle it sequentially, if the machine cannot understand the learner's utterance even after the replacement. This problem has already been addressed in the academic literature on so-called *clarification requests*, which was discussed in Section 2.4.2.

7.3.2 Language-specific and medium-specific devices

The machine needs to guess which resources for framing and highlighting the user might have used, and to recognise repair other-initiations by learners. As opposed to this, a set of resources typical for German chat needs to be given to the machine for correction generation. Scientific studies focusing on language resources in German chat may provide a more comprehensive description of medium-specific resources, for instance (Orthmann, 2004). However, technological development and the growth of the variety of device-specific and application-specific means of expression (e.g. the newest stickers, emojis and animojis) can hardly be completely mirrored in scientific articles that have been published a decade ago and tell about data that are even a few years older. Nevertheless, there are “the good old smileys", which are device independent and application independent, and are comprehensible for all chat users. We will take into account only this sort of emoticon in this section when we talk about accountings.

Resources to mark the boundaries of corrections

As discussed earlier in this section, corrections and repetitions of trouble sources are frequently highlighted by symbolic and lexical means. Symbolic resources include specific symbols to mark the boundaries of the correction (framing) and register change, such as upper case spelling. Lexical means include special words and expressions. Resources for emphasis have been taken into account in correction patterns. An example framing set may be provided to a computer system as a medium-specific resource and include the following elements:

$$F_l = \{\epsilon, [\,, \text{"}, \text{'}, (, \text{-}, \text{--}\},\ F_r = \{\epsilon,], \text{"}, \text{'},), \text{-}, \text{--}\}$$

Upper case typing was also used to highlight the error and the correct form in exposed corrections. We denoted upper case spelling as $upper(X)$ in the preceding sections.

For repair other-initiation-based correction formats, a similar set of signalling devices may be used for correction generation as provided to the machine for repair other-initiation recognition. Only native-like expressions should be used by the machine for repair other-initiation-based correction formats.

Accountings as resources for managing corrections as social actions

Minimal accountings include smileys :-) and more frequently ;-) (or their variants). These are medium-specific devices used across languages for chat communication. However, many different variants of them exist and some of them are preferred in particular cultures. For instance, Belorussian participants used only one or more parentheses “)" for smile or laugh “)))))))" while German participants preferred the version with the eyes :) or with the eyes and a nose :-). Orthmann (2004, p. 145) describes other variants of emoticons used in German youth chat, that we did not observe in our dataset. This might be explained by factors such as participants’ age, the intercultural character of the communication, changes in chat language over time and dyadic interaction instead of group chat, which was the focus of research by Orthmann (2004).

The purpose of the minimal accountings is to focus the learner's attention on correction while managing its face threatening. Therefore, minimal accountings are restricted to framing possibly combined with a single smiley. Angry or somehow negatively polarised smileys were never found in the role of accountings in my dataset. Therefore, an example set of minimal accountings may include the following elements:

$$A_{min} = \{\epsilon, \text{:-)}, \text{:)}, \text{;-)}, \text{;)}\}$$

Rich accountings may express apologising, ridiculing, accusing, instructing, forgiving, admitting ort complaining. The dataset contains only requests for permission to correct (e.g. *kurze Anmerkung zum Deutsch (wenn ich darf)* (En.: *a short note about German (if you don't mind)*) turn 237 chat N03-L07), apologising, instructing (e.g. a combination of the last two *Verzeih mir, aber es sollte heißen:...* (En.: *I apologise, but you should say:...*) Example 5.11, page 154) and justifications of corrections (e.g. *ich sage das nur weil du sonst sehr gut Deutsch sprichst/ schreibst* (En.: *I am saying this only because you speak/write German very well all the time*) turn 247 chat N03-L07). A set of phrases for each type of rich accountings may be the easiest solution. In the following example sets A_i, the index i expresses the social action performed by the set members:

A_{excuse} = {"Sorry, aber", "Verzeih mir, aber", "Entschuldigung, wenn ich dich damit nerve, aber", ϵ}

$A_{request-for-permission}$ = {"Falls ich das korrigieren darf...", "Eine kurze Anmerkung zum Deutsch (wenn ich darf)...", ϵ}

$A_{instructing}$ = {"Es sollte heißen", "Es heißt", ϵ}

$A_{instructing-neg}$ = {"So was gibt es nicht in der Form", ϵ}

$A_{intention}$ = {"Ich will dich aber nicht nerven", "Ich will ja nur helfen", ϵ}

$A_{justification}$ = {"Ich sage das nur, weil du sonst sehr gut Deutsch sprichst", ϵ}

$A_{instructing-later}$ = {"Wenn ich dich damit nicht nerve, habe ich hier noch eine Anmerkung", ϵ}

$A_{express-understanding}$ = {"Es ist sicherlich verwirrend.", "Die Deutschen blicken da selbst manchmal nicht durch.", ϵ}

$A_{encouragement}$ = {"Du machst es aber sonst recht gut.", ϵ}

$A_{emphasis}$ = {"Kein blöder Witz, das heißt wirklich", ϵ}

In a practical computer application, corrections with rich accountings can be generated using only one sort of accountings per correction or combinations of them. Both types are covered by the correction format models in Section 7.3.1. In addition, they can be accompanied by minimal accountings. In order to handle the palette of possible corrections in more detail, we discuss more specific correction models. They combine different types of social actions performed by different types of accountings. Some of the accounting types occur in correction-initial positions, and some of them were found typically in correction-final positions. If the complete correction is produced in one turn, then they are turn-initial and turn-final, respectively.

It might be a good strategy to negotiate with the user about the acceptance of error corrections, as we will see in Chapter 8. Accountings may help to do this. If the machine finds an error that should be corrected, an exposed correction with specific accountings may be produced. These specific accountings will formally ask for permission to correct and check the acceptance of error correction for the future. Hence, this specific combination of accountings is more appropriate at the beginning of the communication and at the beginning of the "correction history". We use the common notation for regular expressions to denote a set of elements from which only one has to be selected at a particular position $[a_{justification}|a_{intention}]$. Then, the first correction in the communication with a particular user may have the following structure:

$$\mathscr{C}_{init} = a_{request-for-permission} \centerdot e \centerdot F_l \centerdot X \centerdot F_r \centerdot e \centerdot [a_{justification}|a_{intention}] \centerdot e$$

As explained above in Section 7.3.1, the same correction may be split over several turns to make the messages shorter.

An exposed correction some time later or after an already produced repair may also start with an excuse followed by an instructing:

$$\mathscr{C}_{later} = [a_{excuse}|a_{excuse-later}] \centerdot a_{instructing} \centerdot e \centerdot f_{l,i} \centerdot X \centerdot f_{r,i} \centerdot e$$

$$\mathscr{C}_{later} = [a_{excuse}|a_{excuse-later}] \centerdot a_{instructing} \centerdot e \centerdot f_{l,i} \centerdot X \centerdot f_{r,i} \centerdot a_{understanding} \centerdot e$$

The contrast in contrasting corrections is achieved by opposing the trouble source and the correction with accounting types $A_{instructing-neg}$ and $A_{instructing}$. A special conjunction may help to create the contrast in the utterance, which we denote by C. In German it is done by the conjunction *nicht ... sondern*. The correction may also be prefaced by an excuse:

$$\mathscr{C} = a_{excuse} \centerdot e \centerdot a_{instructing-neg} \centerdot f_{l,i} \centerdot X^* \centerdot f_{r,i} \centerdot C \centerdot a_{instructing} \centerdot f_{l,i} \centerdot X \centerdot f_{r,i} \centerdot e$$

Specifically for the integrated corrections, it might be necessary to add an emphasis after an embedded correction in order to focus on the correction, as discussed in Section 5.4. Embedded and integrated corrections will be the subject of the next section. To cover the role of accountings in integrated corrections, we assume that an integrated correction can be produced at some point of the conversation:

T1 Trouble turn with an error X^*
T2 Integrated correction replacing X^* with X
T3 $a_{emphasis} \centerdot f_{l,i} \centerdot X \centerdot f_{r,i} \centerdot e$

The correction formats listed in this part of the current section are very specific, though they are derived from more general correction formats specified in Equations 7.6 and 7.8. However, they cover a large number of surface variants, because many other ways are possible to express the social actions of requests for permissions, instructing, excuse etc. that were not included in the example sets of respective types of accountings.

Backlinks

Backlinks help to come back to the subject of the talk in delayed exposed corrections. The machine may choose to respond first to the interpersonal trajectory prior to initiating a correction side sequence. In this case, a specific return token may be necessary. We call such tokens *backlinks*. An example set of backlink tokens is BL:

$$BL = \{\text{“PS:", “übrigens", “außerdem"}, \epsilon\}$$

Backlink tokens in our dataset were always in the turn-initial position of the correction turns in simple and contrasting corrections with rich accountings.

7.4 Generation of embedded and integrated corrections

Similarly to the conceptual definition of an error, a conceptual definition of a correction appears problematic, although most research publications rely on the intuitive understanding of this term. We restrict the definition of an embedded correction to a description of its properties, namely:

1. They obviously correct an error in the form of a replacement of a part of an erroneous utterance.
2. They are fully integrated into the syntactic and semantic structure of the correction turn.
3. They do not contain any highlighting of the correction, or accountings.

The models of exposed corrections described in the preceding section of this chapter cover the broad range of all exposed correction formats found in the reference dataset except for integrated corrections. Chapter 6 showed that there are also different sequential environments where embedded corrections can occur; however, we could not find any prototypical turn formats for embedded corrections in general. For this reason, we narrowed the focus to embedded corrections for question-answer pairs where the learner produces a question containing one or more errors and the agent is expected to produce an answer which can contain an embedded correction.

Integrated corrections differ from embedded corrections in the last property. They usually contain highlighting and may contain accountings. Both embedded and integrated corrections are semantically and syntactically integrated into the next relevant turn. Therefore, we approach the modelling task for integrated corrections with the assumption that an integrated correction can be formed from an embedded correction by adding accountings and highlighting the replacement.

A detailed analysis of errors in questions produced by the learners and embedded corrections provided by the native speakers or created by the author was given in Section 6.4. This analysis showed that there are types of learner errors that cannot be corrected implicitly. We have seen multiple cases of errors which are not implicitly correctable in Section 6.4.4. The main objective of this section is to describe a computational model of embedded corrections for implicitly correctable errors in question-answer pairs. Specifically, we focus on the set of polar questions that (a) are produced by learners, (b) received an answer as a response and (c) contain at least one “real" implicitly correctable error. The composition of this collection was explained in Section 6.4. The set received the name $QAPA$.

We use the error-annotated collection of question-answer pairs described in Section 8.2 for a systematic analysis. The target hypotheses annotated as described earlier in this Chapter in Section 7.2 were taken as the basis to create embedded corrections in this phase. As was shown in Section 6.4.3, repetition-based answers to polar questions offer opportunities for embedded corrections. The erroneous unit is replaced in the response by the assumed target unit. The concept of a *minimal correcting replacement* was introduced in Section 6.4. We will reuse this concept for the purpose of modelling of embedded corrections in answers to polar questions.

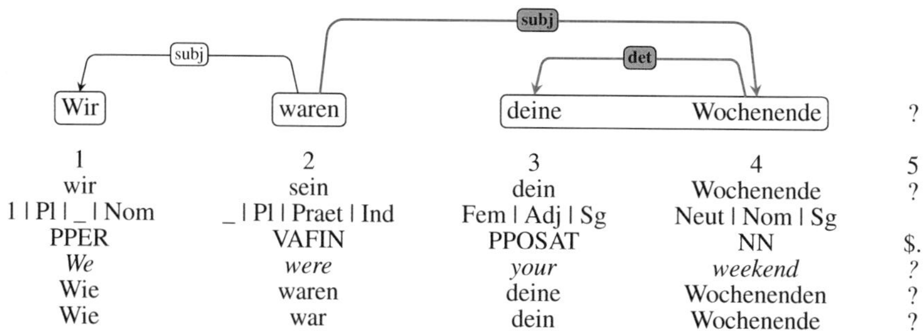

Fig. 7.2: A dependency tree for a question produced by L05 (turn 145 on 25.06.12 at 17:18:41). The last two lines correspond to ZH1 and ZH2. Red edges represent ungrammatical subtrees: noun-determiner congruence and verb-subject congruence are problematic

The maximum number of replacements equals the number of constituents in the question. Taking dependency grammar as an abstract model of syntax, the maximum number of potential embedded corrections for each utterance will be equal to the number of nodes in the syntax tree (including terminal nodes). For the example sentence illustrated in Figure 7.2, the number of potential embedded corrections will be seven: one per word, one for the subtree token 3&4, one for the subtree token 2&4 and its dependent, one for the subtree token 1&2. Two different target hypotheses can be created for the example sentence from Figure 7.2:

ZH1 Wie waren deine Wochenenden?
ZH2 Wie war dein Wochenende?

The first token *Wir* is the result of a typo; however, it is an existing word and it matches the verb in its morphology, syntax and meaning. However, in this way there are two subjects in the sentence, which is problematic. If the typo is corrected first, only one subject is left and problematic congruences can be resolved.

Both ZHs are grammatical, but only ZH2 makes sense in the interaction from the dataset, because only one weekend passed since the previous interaction of this pair of participants. A repetition of the word *deine* alone or of its grammatically correct form *dein* would not repair the congruence problem. Similarly, a repetition of the verb *sein* in its grammatically correct form would not correct the verb-subject congruence error. Instead, the whole subtrees need to be repeated with correction where incorrect forms are replaced by correct ones. This means that for each error type there must be a minimal unit that needs to be repeated with correction in order to address the error. In order *not to* address the error, the problematic unit must be referenced in a different way.

To describe the mechanism of embedded corrections, Section 6.4 compared how the problematic units are referenced in responses to questions with embedded corrections and without. The model built upon these findings is explained in the next section.

7.4.1 Embedded corrections in answers to polar questions

This section explains models of embedded corrections in question-answer pairs where learners produce polar questions containing an error and the machine is expected to produce an answer containing an embedded correction. We assume that the question contains exactly one real implicitly correctable error.

Answers to polar questions are classified in the coding scheme as confirming or disconfirming regardless to their form (Stivers and Enfield, 2010). The infamous German *jein* (En.: *yes and no*) was also contained in our dataset and needs to be mentioned as an answer variant. However, for simplicity, we can assume that only the first two possibilities exist, because the third answer type can be produced from the first two.

A sequence of operations for answer generation to a polar question will look as follows:

1. Locate the question.
2. Determine whether the answer should be confirming or disconfirming.
3. Generate responses.
4. Select an answer from the set of all generated answers: interjection-based (marked or unmarked) or repeat-based.

Repeat-based forms of answers support embedded corrections, as was shown in Section 6.4.2. Because only the last step is the focus of this section, we assume that a language generation function (LGF) generates all possible answers to an identified polar question, as specified in the first three steps.

We need to determine the minimal constituent that needs to be repeated in which a replacement needs to be performed in order to produce an embedded correction. To do this, we need an error recognition function (ERF), which finds a target hypothesis and determines the scope of the error, which we call the *minimal error constituent*.

A *minimal error constituent* (MEC) is the smallest constituent that allows identification of the error.

Thus, the desired error recognition function identifies the minimal error constituent and the corresponding target hypothesis. A larger part containing the minimal error constituent will correct the error, if repeated with a replacement in it that corrects the error. Smaller parts that do not completely contain the MEC will not correct the error, even if they are repeated or replaced. The concept of MEC helps to operationalise the term *embedded corrections* in answers to polar questions. The first property of embedded corrections can then be reformulated as follows:

1. The answer to a polar question contains a MEC for the error.
2. The replacement within the MEC corrects the error.

As was discussed in Section 6.4.4, not every unit is repeatable in an answer to a polar question. Repetition-based answers to polar questions contain only repeatable units; however, not every repetition-based answer will correct the error. The first property addresses the problem of repeatability, which in practice is already handled by the LGF. The second property covers the cases where replacements are performed in a way that leaves the error uncorrected. For instance, spelling errors can only be corrected if the same word is repeated without error. They are not corrected if the entire word with the error is replaced by a different word. A repair management function (RMF) needs to determine which of the surface variants is the best to be delivered to the user. Figure 7.3 illustrates how the three modules communicate.

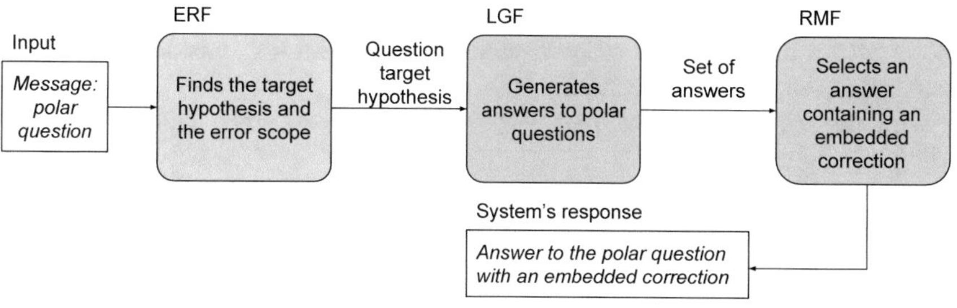

Fig. 7.3: Generation of embedded corrections

From the perspective of correction, all of the response variants that satisfy the two properties would do the correction job. However, different variants of responses with embedded corrections may have different effects on learning and social interaction. The analysis of dependencies between variants of responses with embedded corrections, learning and their interactional import can be addressed in a future study.

We can describe each format of exposed corrections with a regular expression. However, we cannot create a general regular expression for all embedded corrections as one correction format. Embedded corrections need to be made an integral part of the response, not explicitly formatted as a correction. The minimal error constituents are syntactically not always restricted to single words or neighbouring words; therefore they cannot in general be described just as simple string replacements. For the purpose of illustration of the difference between embedded and integrated corrections, a simplified format of an embedded correction as a string replacement can be described as follows.

Let $Q = q_1...q_n$ be a polar question containing a spelling error at position $i, 1 \leq i \leq n$, and $R = r_1...r_m$ a possible repeat-based answer. Let q_i be the minimal error constituent in the question. The error recognition function ERF finds the target hypothesis for the entire polar question, which includes a target hypothesis for the MEC q_i, $ERF(q_i) = c$.

Then an answer to the polar question is an **embedded correction** if the following holds:

$$R = r_1...r_m, \exists i(r_i = c), 1 \leq i \leq m \tag{7.10}$$

Thus, the corrected MEC is placed somewhere in the response turn. The position of the replacement c is determined by the syntax.

7.4.2 Integrated corrections in answers to polar questions

Exposed corrections integrated into the next relevant turn are similar to embedded corrections in that the corrections are fully syntactically and semantically integrated into the ongoing talk, and do not explicitly initiate a separate sequence, as opposed to other types of exposed corrections. However, in contrast to embedded corrections, they may contain metalinguistic information and accountings. Therefore, we will build a model for integrated corrections upon the model for embedded corrections described in the preceding section.

An **integrated correction** can be produced from an embedded correction by adding highlighting to it:

$$c_{H,j} = \begin{cases} upper(c) \ for \ j = 0 \\ f_{l,j} \cdot c \cdot f_{r,j} \ for \ 1 \leq j \leq |F_l| \end{cases} \tag{7.11}$$

$$R_j = r_1...r_m \cdot e, \ \exists i(r_i = c_{H,j}), \ 1 \leq i \leq m, \ 0 \leq j \leq |F_l| \tag{7.12}$$

where $f_{l,j}$ and $f_{r,j}$ are elements from the sets of framing resources, $upper(c)$ is the upper case spelling to highlight the correction and $e \in A_{min}$ is an element from a set of minimal accountings as defined in Section 7.3.

In implementation practice, the possibilities to generate embedded and integrated corrections are bounded by the system's capability to generate repetition-based answers to polar questions and to the used language-understanding technology in general. We will come back to this question in the next section.

7.5 Results

This chapter presented local models of all types of corrections that were described in Chapters 5 and 6. This research continued the work towards disengagement of trouble in talk and practices of dealing with it started in Conversation Analysis (Schegloff, 1987b). In particular, we distinguished between local practices of learner-error correction and the choice of error correction as one possible practice to deal with learner errors. Abstract models for the following types of corrections were presented:

Realised in a side sequence These are exposed corrections of the following types:
1. On the fly
2. Simple with minimal or rich accountings
3. Contrasting-based with minimal or rich accountings
4. Based on repair other-initiations.

Incorporated into the next relevant turn The following types are included:
1. Embedded corrections in answers to polar questions.
2. Integrated corrections in answers to polar questions.

Tudini suggests to analyse exposed and embedded corrections as different options "in the continuum of explicitness of exposed correction in online text chat" (Tudini, 2010, p. 101). Our study of corrections provides additional empirical support for this idea: simple/contrasting exposed corrections with rich accountings as one extreme and embedded corrections as another extreme, with various cases in between. In addition, further dimensions for a classification have been found in this work. The identified correction formats can be classified according to three attributes: grade of explicitness, grade of integration and grade of relevance (what is the most relevant next, the most preferred and projected type of response). Previous research on correction in CA was satisfied with the two major categories of exposed and embedded corrections. However, for the purpose of computational modelling, this classification was not sufficiently operationalised and was therefore hard to implement.

Figure 7.4 illustrates the correction space based on the three dimensions. Though Tudini (2010)'s idea to analyse corrections in the continuum of explicitness is very intuitive and supported by the sociolinguistic data, it is hardly operationalisable with respect to computational modelling of corrections. The mapping from a correction format type to the grade of explicitness is rather subjective and makes a value assignment problematic for the moment. The grade of relevance buries similar difficulties. In contrast, the grade of integration into the next relevant action may be expressed by means of syntax. Therefore, a separation of correction formats according to their syntactic integration into the next projected turn was chosen for computational modelling. OISR-based corrections were classified as not integrated into the next projected turn, because repair initiations are not projected, though they are possible after each utterance. The selection of different types of correction formats may be related to the interaction history. At the beginning of the interaction, correction formats with rich accountings may be preferred. The accountings may do the additional job of negotiating whether corrections are accepted by the user. Other types of accountings may help to make visible to the user that it is clear to the machine that corrections

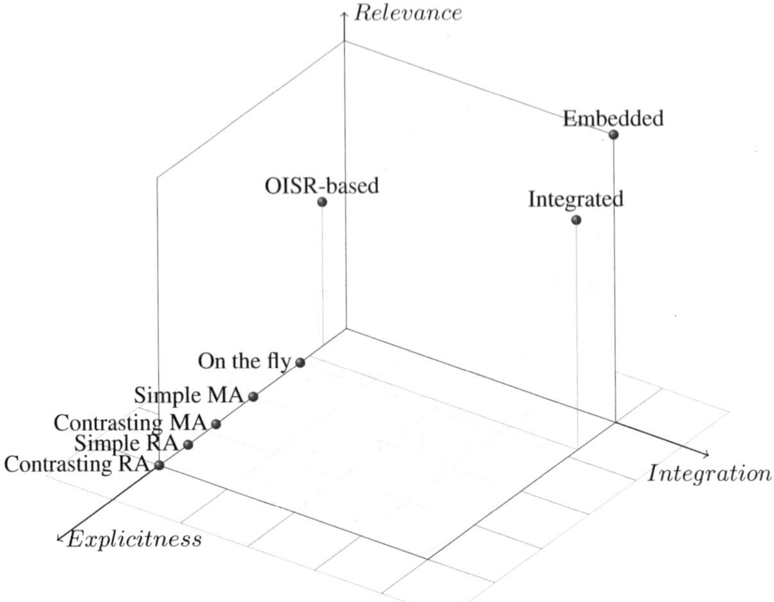

Fig. 7.4: The space determined by the explicitness, integration and relevance of correction formats; Simple MA - simple corrections with minimal accountings, Contrasting MA - contrasting corrections with minimal accountings, Simple RA - simple corrections with rich accountings, Contrasting RA - contrasting corrections with rich accountings

might be annoying. Less "intensive" types of corrections, such as simple corrections with minimal accountings, are more appropriate when the user and the machine have already established a sort of social closeness and the user perceives corrections to be helpful. Corrections on the fly and embedded corrections may be used from the beginning of the interaction because they do not make the correcting the matter of the talk. To summarise, there may be no dependency between the error and the type of exposed corrections, but there seems to be a dependency between the preferred correction formats and the state of social interaction. This will be taken into account in Chapter 8 where we will make a step towards a decision model for corrections.

7.5.1 Error recognition, error correction and learner corpus research

While multiple research projects put efforts into learner corpus annotation for conceptually and medially written learner language, only few conceptually oral learner corpora exist till now (see the overview of German learner corpora in Section 2.2.6, page 31). The corpus created for the purpose of this research may satisfy the needs of many other research endeavours and can be obtained for free from the European

Language Resource Association (Höhn, 2015b). To ensure result comparability and better evaluation, all examples discussed in this book can be found in the original corpus by using turn number and participants' codes as a reference. With the discussion of the problem with instant messaging data provided in Section 2.3.2, the corpus offers a great opportunity to perform further studies on native/non-native speaker instant messaging communication.

The corpus was published as both an untagged and an annotated version. Besides the creation of the corpus itself, this work contributes to learner corpus research in the following ways:

1. Conceptual work on learner errors in chat was performed, analysing what counts as an error and what is worth correcting.
2. Learner language annotation was done focusing on dialogue moves in other-initiated self-repair and exposed corrections; partial error annotation was completed.

Though it is still necessary to recognise as many learner errors as possible for the purpose of language understanding in ICALL, some deviations from the language standard are excluded from error corrections due to preference organisation in chat. The interplay between the variations in orthography, language standard and social closeness will be discussed more intensively in Section 8.2.2.

The majority of all other-corrections of linguistic errors in our dataset were embedded corrections. This supports the result reported by Kurhila (2001), who found embedded corrections called *corrections in a repetition slot* in the original work to be the largest class of all corrections. This shows the opposite of the findings described by Tudini (2010) as well as by Marques-Schäfer (2013), who report that the majority of all corrections in their datasets are explicit corrections. Table 7.2 summarises the number of exposed and embedded corrections found in the dataset compiled for this research. These differences in findings may be caused by differences in the speech exchange systems captured by the datasets taken for the analysis. A comparative analysis of the datasets and especially the data collection procedure may help to explain exactly why such different results were achieved. The numbers in Table 7.2 give

Learner	L01	L02	L03	L04	L05	L06	L07	L08	L09	
Type/NS	N01	N01	N02	N02	N02	N03	N03	N04	N04	Sum
Exposed	0	1	1	1	0	1	4	9	5	22
Embedded	3	7	2	3	4	3	4	10	1	37

Table 7.2: The number of all corrections of linguistic errors in the corpus: distribution over all pairs of participants labelled by the learner code: L01 - learner 01 to L09 - learner 09

an intuition how much additional data may be needed to build a collection of error corrections that is sufficient to train machine learning models. Interaction recordings of hundreds of native/non-native speaker pairs may be needed. For now, the small numbers of occurrences of error corrections was sufficient to find prototypical structures in corrections and to define rules for a dialogue system's behaviour based on these prototypes. This shows that Conversation Analysis offers a powerful tool that can be used to create computational models of rare phenomena in conversation, such as language error corrections.

With the purpose of automated learner language understanding, techniques presented in (Rei et al., 2017) for the enlargement of the training dataset and Recurrent Neural Networks for error correction introduced in (Zhou et al., 2017) can be a great way to deal with the problems in learner language. Such techniques were not available at the time this research was performed but they can be explored in a future study.

The majority of academic publications report on learner corpora with the focus on error annotation, and only a few of the projects focus on linguistic markup. This work addresses an additional dimension in learner language annotation, namely dialogue moves markup. The SLA-inspired first corpus version contains annotated dialogue moves in sequences of corrective feedback and meaning negotiation. Annotation of the interactional aspects of learner language may be of interest specifically for Communicative ICALL research, because it makes information related to sequences of repair with linguistic trouble source accessible for the machine. The corpus user's guide provides detailed information about the annotation. The relevant part of the manual can be found in Appendix A.

7.5.2 Exposed correction formats for communicative ICALL

In this section we discuss our research results in the field of exposed corrections answering the following research question:

RQ4b. How can the identified types of exposed corrections of linguistic errors be modelled in order to be implemented in a chat-based Communicative ICALL system?

How this work advances the state of the art in ICALL and NLP will be made clear by a comparison of the findings to automatic corrections and automatic feedback generation in the literature, discussed in Section 2.2.5. Implementation issues and required NLP technology will also be discussed.

The classification of corrective feedback grounded in SLA theory and discussed in Section 2.3.5 was taken up by Communicative ICALL (Petersen, 2010; Wilske, 2014). In contrast, this research proposed a different classification of error corrections grounded in CA research. A formal model for correction formats was created based on the new classification. Devices such as accountings and backlinks are part of the correction formats. This might the first model of corrections that explicitly takes them into account.

As discussed in Section 7.3, the proposed model may be implemented using simple template techniques for each of the correction types. However, automatic error recognition remains a challenging prerequisite. Various approaches have been used for automatic error recognition and these were discussed in Section 2.2. With its further development, a broader range of learner errors will be recognised automatically and potentially corrected by an artificial conversation partner. However, at present there is a tradeoff between the need to correct more errors focused on meaning and the limited ability to recognise such errors automatically.

Wilske (2014, Sec. 5.4) discusses the amount of information and the complexity of language understanding necessary to extract the required data in order to produce different types of corrections in ICALL systems. For instance, detailed error explanations require very detailed error checking while open-class (unspecific) repair initiations such as *I did not understand* only need information *that* an error occurred. As argued in Section 4.6, such types of corrective feedback correspond to open-class repair initiations. In oral native/native speaker communication, they project a repetition as a response. In chat-based native/non-native communication, such repair initiations were only found to be produced by non-native speakers to deal with trouble in comprehension. Native speakers used open-class repair initiations to initiate conversational repair, but not as a tool for error corrections. Even if such repair initiations are easy to produce automatically, their use as a format for error correction in native/non-native speaker chat is not supported by empirical data. However, they might be appropriate in a different speech exchange system or in an e-learning system with a different purpose that would focus for instance on formative feedback (Narciss, 2013).

Because the majority of error correction formats found in the dataset do not contain metalinguistic information, detailed explanations of the errors may be unnecessary for some forms of Communicative ICALL. Conversational agents that help to practice conversation and simulate a Conversation-for-Learning are one example of such forms of Communicative ICALL. The availability of at least one target hypothesis is mandatory in order to generate the correction formats from the models proposed in this research. However, different error correction formats have different import for the interaction. Correction formats identified and modelled in this work reflect the view of error corrections in talk as a social action. Accountings and metalinguistic information are included (or not included) in all of them. Therefore, the right choice of accountings (or the decision to omit them) may be a new challenge. We will come back to the problem of the correction format selection in Chapter 8, where we make a first attempt to formulate a correction decision model.

To sum up, automated generation of correction formats according to the models introduced in this work is relatively simple from the computational perspective, if the information about the target hypothesis and the decision to use a particular correction format are available. The latter two tasks are very challenging from the computational perspective.

7.5.3 Embedded and integrated corrections in ICALL

In this section we discuss research results in the field of embedded corrections and answer the corresponding research question:

RQ4a. How can the identified types of embedded corrections of linguistic errors be modelled in order to be implemented in a chat-based Communicative ICALL system?

Because ICALL research mainly builds on results reported in the SLA literature, the concept of embedded corrections was not explicitly included in ICALL until now. Implicit handling of embedded corrections was previously performed by using recasts as a form of implicit feedback in ICALL applications, such as (Morton et al., 2008; Petersen, 2010; Wilske, 2014). However, as argued earlier, recasts include embedded and exposed corrections. For instance, recasts presented by Petersen (2010) mainly correspond to corrections on the fly. This research is the first attempt to explicitly operationalise embedded corrections for Communicative ICALL.

Embedded corrections were operationalised for the computer implementation using the concepts of the *minimal error constituent* and *minimal correcting replacement*. To determine the minimal error constituent, tools for error recognition can be exploited. In Figure 7.2 an example of the recognition of morpho-syntactic errors based on dependency parsing was provided. Language-understanding capabilities of the system may vary, depending on what exactly it is, for instance a simple rule-based chatbot or a text-based dialogue system with machine learning. Different types of such systems were discussed in Section 2.2 from the perspective of learner language understanding, focusing on German as a communication language. Different levels of language understanding, however, influence the number and the types of learner errors that can be recognised. For instance, pattern-based language understanding in chatbots does not support recognition of syntactic errors (De Gasperis and Florio, 2012), as opposed to dialogue systems where parsers are used to find a mapping between the user's input with deviations and a correct form in the target language (Petersen, 2010; Amaral et al., 2011).

For spelling errors in separate words, the minimal correcting constituent will be a repetition of the word with replaced symbols. To correct errors in relationships between parts of an utterance (e.g. congruence errors), all parts of the utterance involved in the erroneous relationship need to be repeated in order to make the correct relationship visible. Sometimes, the whole utterance needs to be repeated in order to correct errors in, for instance, subject-verb congruence. All correcting replacements for an error correct this error, even if they are not minimal. This is how repetition-based answers to polar questions work: they frequently repeat the whole question content. To generate an integrated correction, an embedded correction can be produced and the unit where the error was located needs to be marked by symbolic devices (framing and highlighting); the correction may be accompanied by accountings. Therefore, integrated corrections may be seen as a sub-class of embedded corrections.

Even simple, pattern-based language-understanding techniques allow use of embedded corrections in dialogues with learners. For instance, AIML-based chatbots already implement matching of a number of surface strings to one pattern in order to cover at least the most prominent variants of spelling. This can be done either by string replacements during the preprocessing phase or by the `srai` operator. The `srai` operator allows the processing of a matched pattern to be forwarded from one category to another one in order to handle synonyms or paraphrases. Replacements allow, for instance, small variations in spelling to be recognised. Special cases of spelling errors can be targeted by such replacements. A repetition of the part of the utterance after the replacements in the machine's response would provide an embedded correction. Simple cases of integrated corrections can be based on the same embedded corrections as those handled by the AIML chatbot. In addition, they need to include information about which tokens have been changed. This can be done by highlighting the correction with upper case or framing.

Because this is the first attempt to propose a model of embedded corrections for communicative ICALL documented in the academic literature that was available at the time this research was done, pioneer work in understanding of the working mechanism of embedded corrections in talk was done for polar question-answer pairs. This was only partially successful due to the task complexity. This work produced more questions than answers in the field of computational modelling of embedded corrections. Even more pioneer work still needs to be done to cover other types of question-answer pairs and other sequential environments where embedded corrections can occur. We will discuss some of the identified questions in Chapter 11 and outline future research directions.

7.5.4 Conclusions

The following conclusions can be made with regard to the study of error corrections:

- The separation into local models of specific practices of correction and a central decision mechanism allows for independent modelling covering a large palette of various correction formats. Modelling other practices in conversation may be approached in a similar way.
- Although the majority of correction formats can be realised as utterance templates, this type of repair is still interconnected with sequential organisation and turn-taking (correction on the fly) and adjacency pairs (embedded corrections).
- Because some correction formats modify the syntax of utterances (embedded and integrated corrections), it might be reasonable to look at another direction of CA research, namely *syntax for conversation* (Schegloff, 1979) with the purpose of understanding how repair modifies the syntax of the talk.

Chapter Summary

In this chapter we formalised local models for exposed and embedded corrections. We looked at correction models separately from the question of automatic error recognition. We then presented local correction models independently of the question whether a correction of a specific format is appropriate at a particular point in the conversation. Although we analysed integrated corrections as part of exposed corrections in Chapter 5 of this book, it turned out to be more reasonable for computational modelling to group them with embedded corrections. Results in comparison with the state-of-the-art publications were discussed for each type of correction.

8

To Correct or not to Correct

Abstract This chapter presents a first empirical analysis of the factors in conversation that make a correction of a linguistic error relevant. Such factors include chat conventions, social proximity, learner's self-corrections, user model and interaction history. Further, this chapter makes the first attempt to define a computational correction decision model. The findings are discussed in comparison with the correction decision models in ICALL.

8.1 Introduction

In Chapters 6 and 5, we discussed practices deployed by native speakers in German instant messaging chat to correct learner errors. As we have seen, however, error correction is not the only possibility to deal with an error. Possible alternatives to a correction are for instance:

1. Talk off-topic: the recipient of the trouble-talk changes the subject of the talk.
2. Expressions of emotions (emoticons or lexicalised equivalents such as *hahaha*).
3. Silence.
4. Non-correcting talk on-topic:
   a) Use only discourse markers and evaluations (wow, cool, okay...);
   b) Let-it-pass strategy: continue the talk as if nothing has happened;
   c) Paraphrases;
   d) Repeat the error (this behaviour was rarely observed here but was reported also in (Marques-Schäfer, 2013).

Silence can provide an opportunity to self-correct in oral communication (Schegloff et al., 1977). However, due to the special responsiveness characteristics of an instant messaging chat, silence does not provide additional opportunities to self-correct in chat. Trouble-speakers can self-repair later than in the next turn in chat, and longer breaks between turns mostly have reasons other than giving the trouble-speaker a chance to self-correct (Danilava et al., 2013b).

S. Höhn, *Artificial Companion for Second Language Conversation*,
https://doi.org/10.1007/978-3-030-15504-9_8

If a linguistic error is produced by a participant of a conversation, the recipient of the trouble-talk can choose to address the error in the interaction using one of the available forms, or not to address it in the interaction at all. The opposite to a correction is not the absence of a correction, but a "normal talk". Many alternative ways to do a "normal talk" are potentially available for conversation participants, for instance, to stay on topic but ignore the error (let-it-pass strategy), repeat the trouble source "as is" not focusing on the error, paraphrase or reply with discourse markers. Other possible ways are off-topic talk, expressions of emotions such as laughter (Vöge, 2008) and addressing troubles with the technology (Rintel, 2015). Figure 8.1 visualises several different (but not all possible) ways of handling L2 errors in talk-in-interaction.

Not all errors are corrected in a language classroom, and not all errors can or should be corrected in a chat-based Conversation-for-Learning; see e.g. the discussion in (Marques-Schäfer, 2013, pp. 154, 163). To correct a learner error in chat, the native speaker needs first of all to recognise the error (assuming that the correction is the native speaker's job). Thus, native speakers need to have at least a basic understanding of what is correct language and what is a deviation from correct language. Then, even if a native speaker identifies some deviations in a learner's utterance, there might be reasons to omit a correction and to continue the talk using one of the alternatives listed in Figure 8.1.

An understanding of what is correct, what is acceptable and what is an error is a preliminary step for every correction. Unfortunately, there are a few problems with a conceptual definition of a linguistic error in chat. First of all, chat language is a conceptually oral language. Therefore, we should not expect to find in chat only full sentences like in an essay. Second, chat language includes symbolic means of expression such as smileys, word stretches and upper case typing, which are clear deviations from standard orthography. Moreover, quick typing often leads to misspellings and typos for both parties, learner and native speaker, but it does not mean that there is a gap in that participant's linguistic knowledge. In addition, chat participants try to increase their typing pace and omit message-initial capital letters, as well as initial capital letters for German nouns. All these deviations do not count as errors in chat, although they do not satisfy norms of grammar and orthography.

Because the actual language expertise and attention of the native speakers may vary, it is possible that they will not notice the error or will not know the corresponding grammar rule, or will not know the correct version; thus, they may have difficulties with the language similar to the learners. The following reasons may influence the presence or absence of corrections in chat (see also (Marques-Schäfer, 2013, pp. 143-145)):

1. The recipient of the trouble-talk does not notice the error because he/she is focused on the continuation of the talk or cannot recognise the error as an error due to lack of language competence or is busy with other tasks not related to chat;
2. The recipient of the trouble-talk notices the error but does not know the rule to explain the correction;

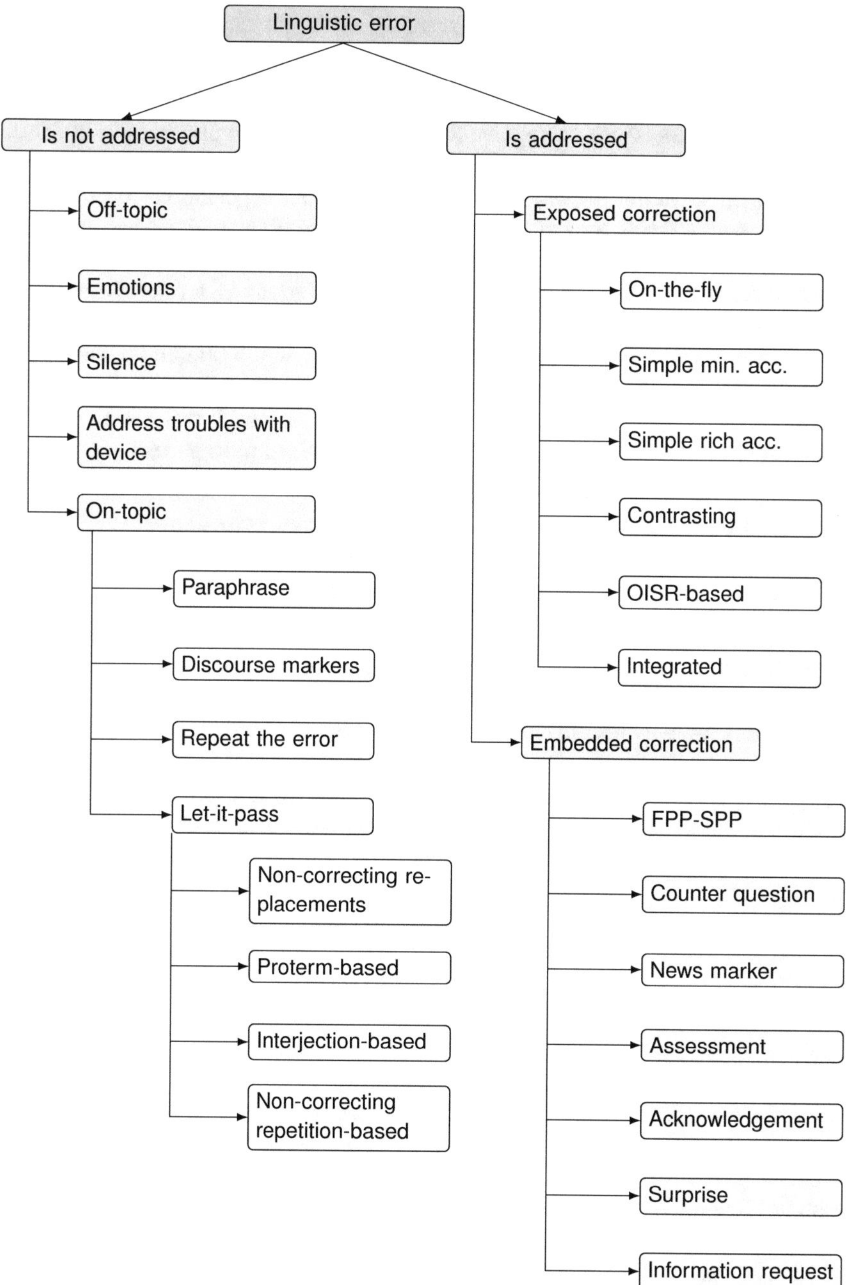

Fig. 8.1: Some options for dealing with linguistic errors in conversation

3. The recipient of the trouble-talk notices the error and knows the rules but prefers to focus on the interpersonal trajectory and keep the interaction going (fluency context).

The dataset produced for this research does not contain explicit requests for corrections, in contrast to the dataset analysed by Marques-Schäfer (2013). However, in the retrospective interviews, learners expressed their expectations to be corrected more frequently during the conversations, as opposed to the native speakers' preference to focus on the content rather than on linguistic matters. The dataset used by Marques-Schäfer (2013) for her study of learning German as a foreign language in chat contained tutored and untutored sessions. The role of the tutor was predefined by the interaction setup, he/she is allowed to correct in the tutored sessions, which made the speech exchange system more similar to a teacher-fronted classroom and represents an unequal-power speech exchange system. The tutors had to reflect on their correction behaviour in a questionnaire. The decision to correct errors in chat was taken by the tutors based on the following self-defined criteria:

1. Error frequency. A frequently occurring error needs to be corrected.
2. Relevance for comprehension.
3. Learner's wish to be corrected made relevant in conversation.

The relevance for comprehension as a reason for correction is in this sense closely related to the notion of *sequential consequences for the next relevant action* described by (Schegloff, 1987b) as a reason for repair initiation.

If a more knowledgeable chat participant decides to correct, he or she still has to make a choice among various correction formats. For each pair of participants in the dataset, for all exposed corrections of the pair, each error addressed by an exposed correction was corrected only once, even if this error was frequently produced. In contrast, embedded corrections of the same error were produced more than once per participant pair.

Embedded corrections seem to be a preferred correction format in a Conversation-for-Learning, because none of the exposed corrections repeatedly corrected the same type of error in the talk of the same learner, but there are several instances of embedded corrections repeatedly correcting the same error in a learner's talk. As Chapter 6 shows, embedded corrections are not always possible, as opposed to exposed corrections. There are dependencies between error types and turn-taking and the possibilities for embedded corrections. Incidental replacements/repetitions are not desired if the already produced embedded corrections should be taken into account for the model of future corrections. Sometimes, embedded corrections are the only way to respond if the participant does not want to repeat the error (however, this is a possible strategy, too). These dependencies will be taken into account in the decision model for corrections.

With this motivation in mind, the purpose of the present chapter is to identify an initial set of parameters relevant for a decision model determining whether an error in chat should be corrected or not. In addition to the error properties influencing opportunities for corrections discussed in Chapter 6, this chapter seeks to answer the following questions:

1. What is an error in chat?
2. Which factors may influence the presence or non-presence of a correction?
3. How can features in interaction identified in the preceding chapters as influencing corrections be operationalised for a decision model?

We will discuss the issues with the definition of a linguistic error in chat and propose a solution in Section 8.2.1. We will see in Section 8.2.2 that orthography is used by chat participants as an interactional resource. We will also look at learners' self-corrections and their role in follow-up corrections in Section 8.2.3.

Building on the empirical findings, we will create a basis for further investigations of factors relevant for the correction decision and their analysis with machine-learning-based algorithms. Because there are mutual dependencies among a large variety of features, machine learning approaches may deliver more stable and more reliable results than a hand-crafted rule-based system. We will discuss what kind of machine learning models may be the most promising and what kind of data and annotations may be needed for training.

As shown in Chapter 3 and specifically in Section 3.5.2, all the participating native speakers and all the learners were involved in conversation sequences where their linguistic identities have were made relevant. Every native speaker reacted in a very sensitive way to learners' preferences and needs, but also to learners' language proficiency and interaction management skills (independently of foreign language proficiency). Individual factors such as a native speaker's profession and education but also experience in intercultural communication and instant messengers undoubtedly played a role in decisions to correct or to engage in role-play to practice for examinations. To provide an artificial agent with such consistent behaviour, we would need to give the agent a life story and a personality, and we would need to provide the agent with *a* decision model for corrections in order to make it able to behave like *a* language expert. This would be only one individual interaction profile of a language expert from millions of possible interaction profiles (see the discussion in Section 3.5.2). However, the local models for corrections and explanations can be reused for *other* agents, and will give them *different* interaction profiles, but still one of a language expert.

We already paid much attention to conventions, agreements, error concepts, target hypotheses and sequential features in preceding chapters. The findings will be taken into account in our attempt to create a decision model for corrections, which will be presented in Section 8.6. Because much effort has already been put into error recognition (see Section 2.2.4 for references and discussion), we will assume for the purposes of this chapter that the error recognition techniques discussed in Section 2.2.4 may be employed to detect all errors which count as "real" in chat and are worth addressing to in a Conversation-for-Learning. To continue our work on the decision model for corrections, in this chapter we will first specifically focus on the role of the user model, interaction history including correction history and error properties for the final correction decision. Section 8.3 will discuss the influence of the user model and knowledge about the user. The influence of the interaction history will be discussed in Section 8.4. The role of various error properties such as error frequency, error type, number of errors and available correction formats will be explained in Section 8.5. The correction decision model will be presented in Section 8.6. Finally, we will discuss the results in Section 8.7.

8.2 Learner errors in chat and opportunities to correct

Because chat interaction is conceptually oral, and because there might be pressure to produce turns in chat as quickly as possible, the error tolerance in chat is very high. On the other hand, there is still a language standard, and there are errors that are "too serious" even for chat, because corrections were found in the dataset. Therefore, there must be at least two levels of description for learner language in chat:

1. Objective linguistic errors produced by learners compared to the language standard in terms of rules of orthography and grammar.
2. Chat conventions that make some of the identified deviations from the standard acceptable in chat as a communication medium.

In our dataset, there were no pre-assigned roles of tutors or teachers. Both native and non-native speakers already had experience of instant messaging. These experiences probably influenced their behaviour in the data collection phase. The applied chat conventions depend on the speech exchange system, the participants' chat communication expertise and their stances. Different conventions were applied by different pairs of participants in the dataset. Some of the pairs produced chat messages where all rules of the German standard were taken into account. Some of them ignored spelling rules for German nouns and used only lower case letters, started the messages with a lower case letter and did not follow the punctuation rules. However, none of the corrections of learner errors addressed such fussy deviations as errors. Consequently, native and non-native speakers must have a similar understanding of the concept of a linguistic error in chat, no matter which standard they use for their own language production.

We discuss chat conventions in Section 8.2.1 from the following perspectives:

1. Analysis of examples of explicit negotiations of language conventions that can be found in the dataset.
2. Retrospective interviews that contain native speakers' talk about their attitude towards learner errors and native speakers' own role in chat.
3. A case study of mutual dependencies within pairs of participants: how N02 and her partners make use of the chat conventions and language standard, and how N02's language is influenced by her partners' language.

From the computational perspective, for an automated error identification an error taxonomy and error models are required. There are already many projects on error-annotation for learner corpora, some of them for German. We test here the applicability of the annotation scheme created for conceptually written language (Reznicek et al., 2012). Because embedded corrections of learner errors are of particular interest, and because the majority of identified embedded corrections occur in question-answer pairs, a collection of question-answer pairs was built from the dataset. In all question-answer pairs in this collection, a learner produces a question and a native speaker answers it. In this section we will use this collection for the discussion of "real" errors in chat. We already used this collection for the analysis of embedded corrections in Chapter 6

8.2.1 Language standard, chat conventions and L2 errors

In chat data, we can see that some deviations from standard German do not count as errors. Sometimes it is even explicitly negotiated by the participants that, for instance, writing everything in lower case will be declared correct. Therefore, in addition to the objective linguistic error (difference between the produced language and the language standard) the deviations must then be seen through the lens of conventions that are valid for the specific communication medium (chat in this case) and accepted by the interaction participants. This means that it cannot be completely defined in advance for chat what will be an accepted deviation covered by conventions and what will "count" as an error that might be corrected. The following may be included:

1. *Quick typing*: everything that speeds up the typing pace does not count as errors; capital letters in sentence and noun beginning are ignored, sentence punctuation is not important.
2. *Expressivity*: word stretches, upper case, special symbols, punctuation symbols, quotes and parentheses, as well as various combinations of all of them are used to express emotions and mood and to highlight special parts of turns.
3. *Minor misspellings*: typos are not important.
4. *Oral style*: not every utterance is a full sentence, word order is similar to oral. For instance, a question has a question mark but the word order is assertion-like.

These and other conventions can be explicitly negotiated by chat participants or simply applied by them without any negotiations. We discuss these two strategies below and illustrate them with examples from the dataset and the retrospective interviews.

Explicit negotiations

Speakers in chat may choose to explicitly negotiate the applicable conventions. One such case is discussed in Example 8.1. Native speaker N03 engages in negotiation of spelling conventions in turn 10, which happens in the very beginning of the first talk. N03 argues that he needs to type everything in lower case otherwise his typing pace is too slow.

This way of addressing spelling matters in chat is uncommon in L1 chat or in chat where the linguistic identity of a non-native speaker as a language novice is not important. In turn 10, the native speaker shows that (1) it is clear to him that writing everything small violates the language standard and (2) it is relevant for this interaction to satisfy or a least to pay attention to the language standard.

Example 8.1. Alles klein (everything small).

10 15:31:05 N03 ist es ok wenn ich klein schreibe?
is it ok if I write small?
11 15:31:08 N03 geht schneller.
is quicker
12 15:31:16 N03 ich bin sonst sehr langsam...
I'm too slow otherwise
13 15:33:12 L07 =))) ich auch dann... nun erzähl etwas von sich.. wie steht es ?
then I will do the same... well tell something about yourself.. how is it going?

In Example 8.2, N04 shows that he is familiar with the German language standard, and that his language in chat does not satisfy the standard, but that it is acceptable in chat due to its conceptual orality (turn 201).

Example 8.2. Chatten ist wie schriftlich reden (chatting is like speaking in writing)

192 13:58:39 N04 streng genommen mache ich auch fehler: bei den meisten Verben in der "ich"-Form lasse ich oft das letzte "e" weg: "hab", "mach" usw.
stricktly speaking, I'm making mistakes, too: in most of the verbs in the I-form I often omit the final "e": "hab", "mach" and so on
193 13:58:53 N04 oh, und "Fehler" hab ich gerade klein geschrieben...
oh, and I've just written "Fehler" small
194 13:59:00 L09 umgangsform
way of behaving [* error: lexical choice]
colloquial form
195 13:59:04 L09 nicht?
isn't it?
196 13:59:15 N04 ja, das kommt dem gesprochenen deutsch näher
yes, it is closer to oral German
197 13:59:22 N04 süddeutsch
South German
198 13:59:26 N04 glaub ich
I think
199 13:59:27 L09 angewöhnt
a habit
200 13:59:32 L09 :)
201 13:59:54 N04 ja, chatten ist ja so ähnlich wie "schriftlich reden"
yes, chatting is something like "speaking in writing"

There is only a small number of such sequences in the dataset, but in all sequences of this type that we can identify, we can observe the following:

1. If participants engage in negotiations of spelling conventions, such negotiations are always initiated by the native speaker.
2. Production pace and conceptual orality of the interaction are the reasons for deviations addressed in chat, not a lack of knowledge.
3. Deviations from the language standard for the purpose of expressivity are not perceived as deviations by chat participants.

Insights from retrospective interviews

It is not directly observable from the data why native speakers choose to stay on-topic and to contribute to the interpersonal trajectory without addressing errors, and why they do not choose one of the alternatives (off-topic, silence...). However, it can be assumed that the participants did not want to be perceived as impolite, they wanted the talk to go on and chose to produce preferred responses (a preferred response to a question is an answer, and not silence or laughter or a news marker). N01 writes in the retrospective IM-based interview about his motivation not to correct (original orthography preserved):

> eine korrektur habe ich unterlassen, weil ich die fehler eher für unbedeutend gehalten habe (manchmal wurde das falsche tempus oder das falsche geschlecht eines wortes gewählt. es kam nie vor, dass ein satz vor fehlern nur so gestrotzt hätte) und - was noch wichtiger ist - ich wollte den inhaltlichen gesprächsfluss nicht unterbrechen. verstanden haben wir uns ja. das war mir wichtiger, als kleinliche fehler auszubessern.
> *I omitted a correction, because I considered the errors to be unimportant (sometimes a wrong verb tense or the wrong gender of a word was selected. It was never the case that a sentence teemed with errors) and - what is even more important - I did not want to interrupt the substantial flow of the talk. We understood each other. It was more important for me than correcting of petty errors.*

In contrast to N03, N01 saw himself in chat with learners as a role model with respect to orthography, such as for instance capital letters at the beginning of nouns and utterances. He explains in the retrospective interview that he tried to write according to the German standard

> weil ich gegenüber nicht-deutschen-muttersprachlern versuche, die deutsche sprache so gut wie möglich in wort und schrift zu verwenden.
> *because I am trying to use written and oral German language as well as I can in communication with non-native German speakers.*

As these two quotations show, N01 uses lower case only spelling during the interviews as opposed to the standard-compliant spelling that he chose to use during the data collection. A sample of his spelling in the dataset can be found for instance in Example 6.9, page 171. Consequently, the orthography that N01 uses in chat with different partners is *recipient-designed*.

8.2.2 Orthography and social closeness

The presence of a high number of deviations from the language standard in text chat has been explained by pressure to type quickly and demand for a high production pace in CALL studies (Loewen and Reissner, 2009). However, language learners report that they had (or took) the time to use additional resources (such as dictionaries) for dealing with trouble in comprehension and production. Hence, the production overhead necessary for a standard-conforming language in chat might have a particular interactional import and may have an impact on participants' understanding of their social roles and be used for the regulation of social closeness.

Example 8.3 presents the very beginning of the talk between L03 and N02. Because the participants have never met before, L03 does not know who is on the other side of the connection. She comes too late to her first appointment and formulates her first message (turn 1) to her chat partner in a very polite way using a polite German form of address *Sie* (III p, pl., no English equivalent). In addition, she produces an email-style turn - conceptually closer to written than to oral language - according to the German spelling standard and closes if with a "best regards + signature" non-typical for instant messaging.

Example 8.3. Mutual dependencies between orthography and social closeness.

1 19:57:31 L03 Hallo! Entschuldigung, Ich weiß nicht, wie heißen Sie. Ich bitte um Verzeihung, ich habe total über heutige Unterhaltung vergessen. Ich schäme mich, wirklich, aber ich war beschäftigt, und musste dringend einige Probleme lösen, deshalb habe ich total über den Chat vergessen- ich bitte noch ein Mal um Entschuldigung, und verspreche, dass es nie wiederholen wird. Ich hoffe, dass unser Chat wird uns Spaß machen. mit freundlichem Gruß, L03_FirstName L03_LastName!
Hello! I am sorry, I don't know your [III p. pl.] name. Please forgive me, I totally forgot about [error: wrong preposition] today's conversation. I feel ashamed, really, but I was busy, and had to solve several problems urgently, this is why I totally forgot about [* error: wrong preposition] the chat - please forgive me again, I promise that it will never happen again. I hope that our chat will be pleasant. best regards, L03_FirstName L03_LastName!*

2 19:59:57 N02 Hallo L03_FirstName, das ist überhaupt kein Problem! Ich hoffe, alle Probleme sind gelöst und wir können ein bisschen chatten.
Hello L03_FirstName, it is absolutely no problem! I hope all the problems are solved and we can chat a little bit.

3 20:01:58 L03 Ja, natürlich! wie heißt du?
Yes, of course! what is your [II p. sg.] name?

4 20:02:21 N02 oh Entschuldigung, ich heiße N02_FirstName, bin 27 Jahre alt und wohne in München.
oh, I'm sorry, my name is N02_FirstName, I am 27 and live in Munich.

5 20:03:45 L03 sehr angenehm! und ich bin 21 und wohne in Vitebsk, Belarus!
nice to meet you! and I am 21 and live in Vitebsk, Belarus

6 20:04:37 N02 oh, ich bin schon alt ;)
oh, I am already old

7 20:04:54 N02 warst du schon mal in Deutschland? Ich war noch nie in Belarus
have you already been to Germany! I have never been to Belarus

8 20:05:11 L03 ja, aber ich bin schon verheiretet)))
yes, but I am already married

9 20:05:22 N02 oh echt?? wow! seit wann denn, wenn ich fragen darf?
oh really?? wow! may I ask you, how long?

L03 produces multiple morpho-syntactic and semantic errors; however, her phrases start with a capital letter (except for the closing expression), and she is doing her best to position herself as a competent German speaker. N02 answers with a "no problem", and her message satisfies the German language standard, too. L03 switches from *Sie* to *du* (you, II p. sg.) in turn 3. In addition, she changes the spelling in the second phrase, starting with a small letter instead of a capital. N02 responds with the changed standard in turn 4, writing only nouns with an initial capital letter.

The participants continue with the rule "write only nouns with a capital letter". Shorter time intervals between turns 5-9 in Example 8.3 show how higher engagement leads to higher talk pace and therefore higher production pace. Deviations from the language standard are the price for the typing pace, but in addition, they express a higher grade of engagement and social closeness.

There are mutual dependencies between participants. A closer look at N02 and her partners L03, L04 and L05 helps us to understand how participants deal with spelling and punctuation conventions, and how they influence each other. N02 behaves differently with her different partners:

L03 Both participants start with the standard-compliant spelling and shift then to a version where they move between standard-compliant spelling and "write-only-nouns-with-a-capital". L03 starts with "Sie" but switches to "du" in turn 3.

L04 starts with a "relaxed" version of spelling: only nouns are written with a capital, a very oral style. N02 starts with a norm-compliant version but adapts to the non-native speaker's spelling version after 10 turns. Later on, both participants even use lower case for all words. L04 starts with "du". Overall the chat of this pair can be characterised as very oral: short phrases, quick, many short turns.

L05 starts with a norm-compliant orthography and "Sie". L05 makes lexical errors in her first turn. N03 replies with "Sie" but she decides to write the first word in each sentence small. Later on, L03 changes between a norm-compliant spelling and the relaxed "first-letter-small" version. L05 adopts this way of spelling from time to time. In the second chat, L03 start with "du" (first turn in this meeting) using proper spelling, but switches later to the relaxed "first-letter-small" version. It remains an open question whether N03 noticed that L05 is not that much of an independent language user (compared to the others) and shows her how to do "chat-in-German".

The other native speakers in the dataset prefer to keep the same orthography style with all their partners: N01 presents himself as a role model, N03 prefers to optimise the spelling to increase the typing pace and types everything in lower case, and N04 normally types all nouns with an initial capital, but starts all new sentences with a small initial letter.

8.2.3 The role of learners' self-corrections

Even if an error is potentially correctable in chat, meaning that it is a "real" error and corrections are welcome etc., learners may notice the deviations in their production and correct themselves. Normally, no second correction is produced after a self-correction. This does not mean that a correction is missing after a self-correction. It is not present, but not missing.

Example 8.4. No correction after a self-correction (prev. Ex. 6.18).

79 13:22:49 L03	)))) ja, wahrscheinlich! Sind die Grenze des Schuljahres von Urlaubssaison in Beiern abhängig? yes, maybe! Are the border [*error: wrong number] of the school year [*error: lexical] depending from the vacation time in Bavaria [*error: spelling]? *Does school vacation time depend on the vacation time in Bavaria?*
80 13:23:16 L03	* Bayern * Bayern [self-correction] *Bavaria*
81 13:23:41 N02	ja genau! ist das bei euch auch so? *Yes, exactly! Is it the same in your place?*

Example 8.4 illustrates a typical case of a non-present other-correction after a self-correction, even if there are other, non-self-corrected errors that might be corrected by the native speaker. Learner L03 produces several errors in turn 79 and self-corrects one of them in turn 80. The native speaker N02 does not correct the remaining uncorrected errors and provides an interjection-based response.

Example 8.5, as opposed to all other cases of self-correction, illustrates how an embedded correction may appear after a self-correction. L08 produces a grammatically correct utterance in turn 310. However, she finds the verb tense that she uses in this utterance wrong and makes a first attempt to correct it in turn 311: she replaces a present with a past form, this time with a grammatical error. In addition, German imperfect (past simple) is a marked verb tense (not neutral).

Example 8.5. Delayed embedded correction after multiple self-correction attempts. Replaced units are underlined.

310 17:48:08 L08	ok)siehst du "Eurovision"? see [present tense] you "Eurovision"? *do you see Eurovision*
311 17:48:36 L08	richtiger "sah" more correct "saw" [*error: wrong tense and person - self-corrected tense] *more correct "saw"*
312 17:49:05 L08	o nein)"sahst" o no [smile] "saw" [*error: wrong tense - self-corrected person] *oh no, "saw"*
... ...	[Elided: three turns belonging to a different sequence are hidden]
316 17:50:39 N04	ja, den Eurovision hab ich gesehen, die russischen Omas mit den Plätzchen waren toll :-) yes, I have seen [correction: change to unmarked verb form] the Eurovision, the Russian grannies with cookies were great [smile] *yes, I watched the Eurovision, the Russian grannies with cookies were great*

The learner's second self-correction attempt in turn 312 is successful in producing a grammatically correct verb form; however, an unmarked verb tense is more appropriate. Finally, in turn 316, two replacements are performed by N04: *Eurovision* $\rightarrow$ *den Eurovision* (determiner added) and *sahst* $\rightarrow$ *habe gesehen* (verb tense changed from marked to unmarked).

Because three turns belonging to a different dialogue thread (a different topic) are placed between the question in turn 310 and the answer in turn 316, a repetition-based answer to the polar question is needed. The repetition has first of all the purpose to update the subject of the talk, and the correction is secondary business. However, because of the replacements that have been made, an embedded correction is produced in an answer to a question despite the presence of the self-correction. Subject update may have priority over a preference not to other-correct after a self-correction.

r	ctl	ttl	ttl_{av}	Trouble source	Correction type
1-4	1-3	10-66	33	typo: question mark	One symbol
5-11	2-31	14-56	29	typo, case, missing subject, word order	One word
14-20	3-22	27-176	103	typo, spelling, missing or wrong words	One word, two-word phrases, *ich meine*+correction
23-30	6-15	15-188	90	verb forms, gender, spelling, typos	rejection token+verb
34-58	7-55	55-481	222	gender in DET+ADJ, case, wrong word, missing *zu*	repeat utterance, repeat verb + object, one word

Table 8.1: Responsiveness values: responsiveness r in seconds, correction turn length ctl, trouble turn length ttl, average trouble turn length ttl_{av} in symbols

The influence of self-correction on the semantic response was the subject of academic publications discussed in Chapter 2. Previous research focused mainly on self-corrections in speech recognition applications. Same-turn self-corrections were the major concern for such applications. As opposed to spoken interaction, such self-corrections are normally produced in chat *before* a message is posted. Nonetheless, transition-space self-corrections remain for the analysis in chat protocols. Due to specific characteristics of responsiveness in chat, the time slot where a self-correction can be expected depends on many factors, such as type of trouble source, length of the correction turn and length of the trouble turn. For the machine, an estimate is needed of how long is it reasonable to wait for the user's self-correction. The dependencies in responsiveness values in the dataset are presented in Table 8.1.

The majority of all self-corrections occur in the first 30 seconds after the trouble turn (85%). The longest responsiveness values (15%, between 34 and 58 seconds) appeared if the learner chose to repeat the whole turn or the error was hard to find because the trouble turn was very long, longer than 300 symbols. However, long responsiveness was also found in two cases where the trouble turn was relatively short and the produced self-correction consisted of only one token. In these two cases the errors were morpho-syntactic (wrong case of a noun and wrong form of the auxiliary verb “sein"). In both cases it was only one missing letter that led to the erroneous form, which probably was the result of a typo. It may have been unlucky for the learners that they made these errors, but it seems to be unlikely that they made these errors due to a lack of knowledge. While longer responsiveness values can be predicted after longer turns, the length of a learner’s self-correction cannot be predicted from the small number of examples. However, the probability to receive a learner’s self-correction after 30 seconds is quite low.

8.2.4 Preliminary findings and discussion

We started this chapter with a bird’s eye view of various possibilities to do non-correcting talk and the place of corrections. Some reasons for non-present corrections were already discussed in Chapters 5 and 6. We decided to go deeper into understanding of all possible reasons for a preference to correct at a specific point in talk. In this way we found that the following factors play a role in the decision to correct or not to correct:

1. Speech exchange system:
   a) Conversation-for-Learning combines properties of classroom talk and free conversation; however, there is variation within this space.
   b) Focus on fluency normally has higher priority than focus on form and accuracy.
2. Communication medium:
   a) Both deviations from the language standard and meeting all language standards can be used as interactional resources.
   b) The communication pace may cause more deviations during productions, conscious and unconscious.
3. Participant’s linguistic expertise:
   a) Is the recipient of the trouble-talk able to recognise the errors?
   b) Does the recipient of the trouble-talk see the errors as severe enough to be corrected?
   c) Is the recipient of the trouble-talk able to produce a correction? Is there a clear target hypothesis?
4. Participants’ negotiations and agreements:
   a) Learners may explicitly ask their more knowledgeable conversation partners to correct.
   b) Participants may agree not to count some deviations as errors.
5. Participants’ engagement:
   a) Other, more interesting things may prevent the recipient of the trouble-talk from noticing the errors.
   b) Moving the conversation forward has a higher priority than focusing on errors.

6. Sequential organisation of chat:
   a) Delayed responses may lead to corrections where they are normally dispreferred, e.g. after self-corrections or after typos.
   b) Relevance for comprehension: a correction (e.g. a clarification request) may be the only possible next relevant action.
7. Error properties:
   a) Is there a clear deviation from standard language?
   b) Is this deviation covered by chat conventions?
   c) How frequently does this error occur?
   d) Which types of correction formats can be produced to correct this specific type of error?
8. Correction history:
   a) Has this error already been explicitly corrected?
   b) Has this error already been implicitly corrected?
   c) Has this error already been self-corrected?

As demonstrated in Section 8.2.1, there is no such thing as *the* chat conventions. There is rather a range, or a step-wise relaxation of the standard. This shows that many acceptable spelling versions exist at the same time. In addition it shows that standard-conforming spelling is not important, because there is no consistency in use of the convention rules. Conventions can be negotiated or assumed, they can change, be accepted or rejected by the participants. However, mostly deviations in orthography related to capital letters (including upper and camel case), incidental misspellings due to typing pace, and deviations in punctuation are covered by the category “chat conventions". Other oral features such as omission of the grammatical subject in turns are also allowed. In general, it is expected by chat participants that the chat language is morpho-syntactically and semantically and pragmatically “correct".

We rarely observed that participants wrote everything with lower case; however, this is a common practice in L1 German chat or in native/non-native speaker German chat where language learning is not relevant for the interaction. The most common range of acceptable orthography in the dataset is between the standard and the version where at least nouns are written with an initial capital letter.

As demonstrated in Section 8.2.2, participants of an instant messaging chat use deviations from the language standard as the interactional resource to regulate social closeness and to present themselves as members of specific categories, such as a native speaker who positions herself as a role model, or a competent non-native speaker who is a competent instant messaging user.

Each of the features in each of the groups may be more or less important for the final decision whether or not to correct, however, more examples are required to generate a reliable machine learning model and to estimate the importance (weight) of each of them. The final decision of the model should not be just yes or no, but a specific correction format that will then be presented to the user. However, responsiveness in chat needs to be considered before the output is presented to the user, because the user may produce a self-correction. Hence, a human-like responsiveness in chat may be an advantage. Danilava et al. (2013b) made an attempt to find patterns in responsiveness in chat. However, there are many unobservable and uncontrollable elements influencing responsiveness values, such as parallel activities of the users and network connection values. A different, more detailed recording of the chat production process is required in order to come to reliable conclusions about the patterns in responsiveness.

The dataset used for this work was created with participants for whom language learning has a high professional relevance: they all were students of German as a foreign language and were going to work as teachers and translators. All findings and conclusions made in this work are first of all applicable to similar groups of potential users, which is okay, because every product and every application has its own, specific user group. Further datasets are required to cover different groups of language learners, such as people who learn additional foreign languages just as a leisure activity without any professional interest, and people who want to go on vacation to a foreign country and need conversational skills in the language of the country.

An additional study focused on operationalisation of the social closeness in interaction may help to find parameters that would allow the grade of the social closeness to be measured, and may be included in the decision model for corrections. Because every correction is a social action, this model may be crucial for the correction decision. However, the data collection used for this work was not designed to contain this kind of information; therefore, participants' perception of the social closeness is not explicitly reflected in the questionnaires or in the retrospective interviews, and cannot be connected to the chat protocols. An additional data collection and a study based on it may help to close this gap.

Error properties reported as important for the correction decision by the tutors in the study by Marques-Schäfer (2013), such as error frequency, can hardly be operationalised for the computational model of corrections without further investigations. An important question is how many errors the learners actually made and how frequently these errors were actually corrected in that dataset. If an error occurs too frequently, it is often ignored. Even the first occurrences of errors have been corrected in our dataset. Other datasets do not contain such examples, see (Tudini, 2010; Marques-Schäfer, 2013). In contrast, other error properties such as error type, number of errors in the turn and sequential consequences seem to be more important for the correction decision. For instance, spelling errors are normally not addressed in chat because of the high probability of mis-typing due to high typing pace and conscious deviations in orthography, as discussed earlier in Section 8.2.2. However, if it is likely that a deviation in typing is caused by lack of knowledge, even spelling errors may be addressed in a chat-based Conversation-for-Learning.

A stronger connection between the chat protocols and a native speaker's motivation to correct may be achieved by explicitly focusing on error corrections in retrospective interviews, as was done in other studies for which the relation between the dialogue data and participants' perception was of interest, for instance (Mitchell et al., 2012). Because error corrections were not the specific focus of our work in the beginning, only a few observations can be made about this issue based on the existing dataset. Focusing on corrections in questionnaires, however, is not desirable because questions about them during the data collection might influence the behaviour of the chat participants.

8.3 Correction decision and user model

Because every correction is a contribution to a social interaction with the user, and because corrections are dispreferred social actions, a model for prediction of a user's acceptance of a correction may be helpful. The user may explicitly let the machine know that corrections are expected and perceived as helpful. It may be done in the form of a request for correction or in the form of an expression of thanks after a correction.

The machine can gather knowledge about the user focusing on the relevance of the target language for the user's life, profession or study. If language learning is somehow important, then it is likely that the user will benefit from corrections and will accept corrections in chat with the machine. Several user models can be provided to the system at the beginning, for instance, stereotype-based (Rich, 1979) covering potential user groups. The models can also be designed for potential users of the artificial agent using, for instance a user-centred approach (Petrelli et al., 1999) or personas (Casas et al., 2008).

It cannot be predicted who will be the final concrete user, therefore the machine will be initialised with a number of user models for potential user categories. Because there are mutual dependencies between the actual user behaviour and the interaction history including the interaction process and the machine's behaviour, individual-based user models (Pavel et al., 2015) may help to incrementally adjust initial models and adapt to the user's needs.

8.3.1 Professional relevance of the second language

Language students are used to being corrected by teachers in language classes. They also perceive corrections as helpful to improve, and sometimes the only way to learn. Probably therefore they do not perceive corrections to be as face threatening as in, for instance, an online-dating situation. On the other hand, if the second language knowledge is relevant for the user's profession or study, every chance to improve language skills may be perceived as useful. Because the traditional school approach to language teaching is very much determined by SLA theory, which emphasises the importance of corrective feedback for learning, the learners may be motivated to get corrected more frequently in order to improve. Information about the user's preference regarding corrections and professional relevance of the second language can be obtained by the Communicative ICALL system from the user in the first dialogue, in a similarly to the way the participants of the study gathered information about their conversation partners.

Dialogue scripts and templates targeting information about the professional relevance of the second language can be prepared even for a very simple language-understanding technology such as chatbots. The gathered knowledge might trigger the activation of one of the user models.

Because language learning was professionally relevant for all learners in the dataset, we cannot make any observations about any other category of users. The same problem with the data appears in the majority of all publications in SLA and ICALL, because their subjects are usually language students from universities. All other kinds of language learners need to be taken into account in the user-modelling phase, for instance people who learn a foreign language just for fun or for family reasons. We cannot make any conclusions about their behaviour or motivation based on the dataset collected for this research. We can observe only features for individual user models for learners who seek to become a foreign language professional. Nonetheless, other user categories may also choose similar strategies to signalise a preference for correction. Additional studies with other categories of participants will help to adjust the models to other user groups and may potentially lead to discovery of new relevant features for the correction decision model.

The fact that only one user group is covered by the dataset does not make this research less valuable, because the size of the potential user group is quite large: the Goethe Institute[1] reports 14,668,346 learners of German as a foreign language in the world in 2015.

8.3.2 Learner's requests to correct and uptake

Marques-Schäfer (2013) reports that learners' explicit requests to correct their errors were important for the native speakers in the tutored sessions in their decision to correct. The dataset chosen for this work does not contain any instance of such requests. This may be explained by the absence of any interaction participant who had a pre-assigned teacher-like role, like the tutors in Marques-Schäfer (2013)'s study. However, such requests may potentially appear in conversations between language learners and artificial conversation partners, and should be properly handled.

Explicit requests to correct

In our dataset, learners' positive feedback after corrections of linguistic errors encouraged native speakers to continue with corrections (recall Example 3.18, page 96 with non-native speaker's turn *es ist gut für mich, dass du meine Fehler korrigierst*, En.: *it is good for me that you correct my errors*). Learners' turns in close sequential positions after the correction may contain information about learners' perception of corrections. A positive attitude towards corrections may be expressed, for instance, in words of thanks, explicit requests to correct more and evaluations of the correction activity (*es ist gut für mich...*). To summarise, learners can produce statements equivalent to explicit requests to correct in two places relative to the (potential) correction position:

1. Before the agent starts to correct.
2. Soon after a correction.

[1] https://www.goethe.de/de/spr/eng/dlz.html

Though the dataset does not contain any example of a negatively coloured post-correction evaluation, it cannot be completely excluded in conversations with an artificial agent. The agent may need to recognise whether there is a kind of post-correction interaction management in turns directly after a correction. If so, their polarity towards the correction will help to adapt the correction decision model for the individual user. Polarity recognition in short messages like Amazon comments and Twitter posts is an area where much research effort has been put in; see for instance (Thelwall et al., 2010; Davidov et al., 2010; Becker et al., 2013) for English and (Evert et al., 2014) for German. Sentiment analysis tools preferably taking into account a user's individual style of expressing sentiments would be helpful for this task. Examples of such personalised sentiment analysis approaches are described in (Chen et al., 2016; Guo et al., 2018).

Implicit signalling and agent's initiative

Other forms of learners' orientation to their linguistic identity may be *handled* by the artificial agent as an implicit request to correct. For instance, apology-based face-work may be responded to by encouragement, a positive assessment *or* by a suggestion to correct errors. Such a reaction would show the learner that this apology-based social action was interpreted as a request for help.

Uptake signalises the learner's acceptance of the correction. Learners' uptake has been intensively studied from the SLA perspective because it is seen as a measurement for learning progress (Smith, 2005; Panova and Lyster, 2002). Learners' uptake in long-term chat-based dyadic interaction needs to be studied separately from a different perspective in order to find patterns related to correction decision models. The study can be performed based on our dataset and other similar corpora, if they become available.

The non-native speakers who participated in the data collection reported in the retrospective interviews that they desired and expected to receive corrections of their errors more frequently. In order to proactively anticipate this expectation the agent may ask users whether their linguistic errors should be corrected in conversation. This information can be gathered in a similar way as other kinds of knowledge about the user required for user model initialisation, for instance, based on dialogue templates.

8.4 Interaction process, interaction history and correction decision

As we discussed in Section 3.5.2, both the artificial conversation partner and the user have only a limited influence on their interaction profiles, and the existence of the linguistic identity of a language expert (or a more knowledgeable participant) implies the co-existence of a language novice (or a less knowledgeable participant). Hence, there are mutual dependencies between the user and the agent in their co-construction of the interaction (however, the term co-construction cannot be applied in human-machine interaction in the same way as it is applied in human-human interaction). Every participant of the data collection had her or his own story, and each new user will have a new story. However, several features from past interactions and past turns of the ongoing interaction look relevant for the correction decision. We discuss each of the identified features below.

8.4.1 Initialisation of system's beliefs about the user

At some point of every conversation in our dataset, it came to the first, initial construction of linguistic identities of the participants, in the form of face work, definition work or other activities described in Chapter 3. Previous research showed that in an equal-power speech exchange system like Conversation-for-Learning, construction of a less powerful linguistic identity of a language novice is normally initiated by the owner of this identity. As a consequence, the construction of a more powerful linguistic identity of a language expert is initiated later, usually as a response to the construction of the novice identity. However, we can observe a different result in our dataset: native speakers initiated the construction of their own identity as a language expert earlier than learners displayed a demand for it. After N04 learned from interactions with one of the learners that error corrections are not only acceptable, but even desirable and helpful, he inferred that this might be valid for the other learner, too. N04 initiated construction of linguistic identities, including his own as a language expert, although this "first step" is normally reserved for the learner.

This observation makes it reasonable to have two mutually exclusive alternatives in the correction decision model:

1. The machine is allowed to initiate construction of linguistic identities with the initial assumption that the learner will find it at least acceptable.
2. The machine has to wait for the learner's initiation of the construction of linguistic identities, whatever form they may take. If the learner positions herself as a language novice, then the learner is likely to accept the machine as a language expert.

This decision for the initiation is one of the key criteria for the system's initialisation and, thus, for the production of the first exposed correction. Embedded corrections do not make correcting the interactional business. There is no explicit orientation to participants' linguistic identities in embedded corrections. However, the dataset provides evidence for participants' *noticing* of implicitly corrected errors (Example 3.17) and, thus, noticing of differential language expertise without any explicit orientation to it.

8.4.2 The role of preceding forms of orientation to linguistic identities

Preceding types of participants' orientation to their linguistic identities in talk may influence the correction decision positively or negatively. The dataset provides the evidence that other-corrections immediately follow a learner's requests for explanations. Learners demonstrate in the form of repair other-initiation that they prefer the native speaker as an information source about linguistic matters over a dictionary or a machine translation system.

In contrast, other-corrections of linguistic errors never immediately follow excuses for deficiencies in linguistic knowledge. If a learner produces negative self-assessments or emphasises his/her own linguistic incompetence in a different way, immediately following error corrections would confirm this negative self-assessment, and make positive evaluations and encouragement unbelievable. Post-correction face work may help to deal with these issues if a correction is absolutely necessary after excuses and negative self-assessments.

Normally no correction was provided by native speakers after learners' self-corrections (self-initiated self-repair). It was not important whether the self-correction targeted the errors that might be addressed by an other-correction. Therefore, the machine needs to deal with self-corrections, too. Even if a correction was successfully generated before it is presented to the user, the machine needs to check the user's input again. If a self-correction is posted by the user, the machine should cancel the correction and continue the talk on the interpersonal trajectory. The self-correction must then be taken into account for the production of the semantic response.

Machine learning approaches based on further similar datasets would help to find further mutual dependencies among various forms of orientation to linguistic identities in conversation. We will discuss this and other questions related to long-term dependencies in dialogue modelling in Section 8.4.3.

8.4.3 Correction history and format selection

Every exposed correction for each pair of participants corrected each error only once. In addition, the dataset does not contain any sequence of two corrections where the same exposed correction format was applied. However, there are pairs of participants and pairs of embedded corrections for them that correct the same error in the same way more than once. Nevertheless, we can see that the better the participants knew each other, the lower restraints were between them in conversation, the less interactional work native speakers devoted to exposed corrections. Time passed since the last correction, however, seems not to play a big role. We can find cases in the dataset where two exposed corrections were produced one close after the other for a pair where in total only a few corrections were found.

To gather this kind of information for each user, all corrections of all errors and all applied correction formats need to be tracked. Because corrections do not occur frequently, this data structure is not expected to grow quickly. Information about a learner's uptake might also be stored in the same data structure and used for the individual user model, as already noted earlier in Section 8.3.2.

Two distinct cases of correction format selection can be observed in the dataset:

1. *Sensitive to interaction history*: formats that gave the learner less chance to focus on corrections were preferred for the first correction (embedded or on the fly).

If it was necessary to make the correction to the interactional business, formats with rich accountings were selected (requests for permission to correct, justifications of correction).

2. *Insensitive to interaction history*: one native speaker started to correct in the first meeting without any learner's orientation to her own linguistic identity in the form of an exposed correction of a morpho-syntactic error that occurred for the first time. In this case, the native speaker selected a simple delayed correction with rich accountings (request for permission and instructing) and back-links ("PS:"). Thus, more interactional work was required to deal with the face-threatening effect of the correction. Making the correction delayed makes the error less severe; however, it is not possible if the error has sequential consequences (e.g. the meaning is not clear).

These two cases may be taken as a model for the system's initialisation according to the initial state of the system's beliefs about the user's needs, as explained in Section 8.4.1. A preference scale for initial correction may be needed, for instance:

1. Embedded correction should be preferred over exposed.
2. On-the-fly correction should be preferred over exposed with rich accountings if there is an uncertainty that corrections are welcome.
3. Repair-initiation-based correction formats should be preferred for correction of lexical errors that have sequential consequences.

In the continuation of the talk, corrections with fewer accountings may be more appropriate if there is some evidence for increase of social closeness between the user and the machine.

Because of many features with multiple mutual dependencies, it is easy for a human system designer to lose his/her overview over all the rules and their interdependencies. If new features are detected, all interdependencies have to be checked for consistency in a hand-crafted rule-based system. Machine learning approaches may deliver a more consistent model.

8.5 Error properties and correction decision

In this section we need to decide, which error properties of all those previously mentioned need to be included in the correction decision model. We discuss in the following two subsections the applicability of features such as frequency of a specific error, error number in the non-native speaker's utterance, sequential consequences of an error and the availability of different correction formats. Because the correction decision model will prefer embedded corrections over exposed, as we discussed in the preceding section, we will specifically check this condition.

8.5.1 Error number, error frequency and error types

As discussed in Chapter 6, native speakers see error frequency as a criterion for correction (Marques-Schäfer, 2013). However, there are two problems with this criterion as a feature for an implementation. First, there is a difference between what people say they do and what they actually do. We can observe in our dataset that native speakers did not wait until an error started to occur repeatedly. Mostly, they even corrected the first occurrence of a specific error; thus there is a contradiction. Second, native speakers' intuition with regard to error frequency may be very subjective and needs to be cross-checked with the chat log files in order to see what is perceived as frequent. For these reasons, it needs to be specified more precisely how frequent is frequent. Furthermore, if an error occurs too frequently, a different strategy of dealing with it was preferred in native/non-native speaker communication, such as *let-it-pass*.

With this motivation, error frequency may be included in a correction decision model as a weak feature, and it needs to be made more concrete. To track error frequency, a special data structure or a database is required, where all automatically detectable learner errors need to be stored. It needs to be mentioned that native speakers do not have the same chances to track and to catalogue all the errors as an artificial chat partner. A human would have more chance of recognising all errors but will probably not remember all of them, at least in an informal conversation. A machine will be able to store the information about all identified errors, but very likely will not identify all error instances and types correctly.

Different error type-number relations are handled differently in a Conversation-for-Learning. We found the following regularities:

- Typos were sometimes classified as spelling errors and were corrected either if several cases of the same error occurred in a small window and the reading of the word was the same as with the correct spelling *or* if several cases of the same error occurred and it was a "hard" case where native speakers make mistakes, too. "Hard" cases can be part of the knowledge base. A phonetic index such as Kölner Phonetik (Postel, 1969; von Reth and Schek, 1977) for German or Soundex for English (Russell and Odell, 1918), can be used to find the other cases.
- Morpho-syntactic errors were corrected even after their first occurrence, however, errors occurring constantly were not addressed. Dependencies between the frequency of morpho-syntactic errors and their corrections may exist.
- Lexical errors were corrected even after their first occurrence, because wrong lexical choice and lexical creations cause misunderstandings or even make comprehension impossible, and thus have sequential consequences.

Hence, error type and error frequency are not two independent features for a correction decision model, but need to be seen as a complex feature.

With regard to the number of different errors in an utterance, we have the following situation. Every correction in the dataset addressed only one error. If too many errors were located in a learner's turn, it was difficult for the native speaker to provide a correction, and therefore a different strategy was selected. Hence, the number of errors in the learner's turn will be taken as a feature in the correction decision model.

8.5.2 Dealing with multiple target hypotheses

All types of errors (orthography, morpho-syntax and lexicon) may imply multiple target hypotheses. However, only one target hypothesis was normally selected by native speakers in corrections. The machine's certainty in its target hypothesis selection may be included as a feature in the correction decision model. There is no need to produce as many corrections as possible, but if a correction is produced, it has to be accurate. Otherwise, the machine will not be accepted as a language expert. The user will not believe the machines opinion if "mis-corrections" are produced.

Three strategies for dealing with multiple target hypotheses were identified in the dataset. We will therefore restrict the discussion in this section to the following three cases:

1. Test one of the hypotheses in the form of an exposed correction.
2. Reduce the number of target hypotheses by reasoning involving for instance information state and knowledge about the user.
3. Demonstrate uncertainty by accountings.

The qualitative analysis of embedded corrections in answers to polar questions described in Chapter 6 showed that embedded corrections appear most of all if there are sequential consequences, a possible difference in understanding of an answer without a correction. If many readings of the learners utterance are possible (independently of linguistic errors), an embedded correction helps to channel further development of the dialogue. Thus, an embedded correction is also a strategy for *target hypothesis testing*.

Petersen (2010) chose *uncertainty demonstration* as a preferred strategy. Every misspelled lexeme triggers a repair initiation and every unsuccessful parsing triggers a repair initiation. However, chat conventions allow many variations in orthography and do not allow too much focusing on these variations; thus, Petersen (2010)'s strategy cannot be adopted. Other types of errors, such as a missing verb, may lead to problems with parsing. Example 8.6 illustrates one such case: the answer of N01 in turn 280 becomes an embedded correction because of the verb insertion.

Example 8.6. L01 omits a verb in her question, N01 inserts a verb in his answer.

277 21:08:00 L01	Wie deine Arbeit?	
	How [error: missing verb] your work?*	
280 21:09:57 N01	Meine Arbeit war ganz ok. [elided]	
	My work was totally ok.	

Other verbs or verb forms might potentially be placed instead of *war* (En.: *was*) in the learner's question, for instance *ist* (En.: *is*), *läuft* (En.: *runs*), *verkauft sich* (En.: *is being sold*) and *endete* (En.: *ended*). Each of them leads to a different meaning of the question, and therefore, to a different space for potential responses. The embedded correction in the response in turn 280 clearly documents, which of the possible verbs N01 actually took for the interpretation of the question. Hence, corrections are a device to deal with sequential consequences of an error by *reducing the number of target hypotheses*. If the machine can detect similar cases and can produce a correction, it should be done.

As already discussed in Section 6.4 and illustrated by Example 6.19, page 187, conversation partners of language learners have the same problems with interpretation of erroneous learner utterances as annotators who have to error-annotate learner corpora. Both have to guess which target hypothesis most likely corresponds to the learner's intention. Example 6.19 showed that hypothesis testing can be also done by repair initiations. In this case, if the first hypothesis tested turns out to be wrong, the next one can be tested, or the topic can be changed.

However, there are strategies to narrow down the number of potential target hypotheses for a correction. For instance, only one target hypothesis is correct in Example 6.6 of Section 6.2.1 and in Figure 7.2, because the interlocutors know that only one weekend passed between the previous and the current conversation. In practice, this might be not feasible because it might be difficult or even impossible to determine in advance what kind of knowledge is relevant for each case.

8.5.3 Error properties for the decision model

To summarise, the following error properties need to be taken into account in a correction decision model:

1. Correctability of the error by an embedded correction;
2. The number of target hypotheses;
3. Error frequency (weak feature);
4. The number and the types of errors in the learner's turn.
5. Sequential consequences.

Error-tracking data (e.g. number and types) may then be taken into account for the individual user model. If errors occur only rarely, a strategy for increasing the language complexity may be needed to make the conversation more challenging for the learner and maybe trigger repair other-initiations, as was observed in conversations with N01. There are also mutual dependencies with the correction history. Every corrected error by a learner was never corrected again explicitly, but embedded corrections were observed several times for the same error produced by the same learner.

8.6 Correction decision model

From what has been discussed in the preceding sections of this chapter, the following factors need to be taken into account in a correction decision model:

User model the system may be initialised with for instance a number of stereotypes or personas, and needs to be incrementally adapted to the user to form an individual user model for each user. The initial selection of the user model may be done according to the relevant knowledge about the user:

1. Knowledge about the user: purpose of language learning, experience with language classroom or self-directed learning etc.
2. The learner's requests to correct (explicit and implicit) and the learner's uptake.

Because the individual user model needs to be incrementally updated according to what happened in the interaction, there are mutual dependencies between the interaction history and the user model.

Interaction process and interaction history A set of rules for the beginning of the interaction and for the continuation of the interaction is required.

1. Initial state of beliefs. Who is allowed to initiate orienting to linguistic identities, only the user or both the user and the machine?
2. Dependencies on preceding forms of orientation to linguistic identities. Some of them negatively influence the occurrence of corrections, some of them provide opportunities for correction.
3. Correction history plays a role in correction format selection. Repetitiveness should be avoided: do not explicitly correct the same error twice, use different formats for subsequent corrections. Embedded corrections of the same error are allowed.
4. A data-driven model for social closeness may be helpful but needs to be developed first. Relationship models can be taken as a start.
5. The learner's self-correction leads to correction cancellation even if the correction decision model decides to generate a correction.

All the important features need to be documented and will be used to update the user model (e.g. detected errors and corrected errors).

Error properties are relevant for the correction decision:

1. Frequency may be a factor but needs to be specified more exactly or learned from the data.
2. Number: many errors in a turn make it too difficult to correct.
3. Type: different rules for different error types.
4. Sequential consequences.

Information about the recognised errors may be useful for the user model and will influence the interaction process indirectly.

A set of features can be defined and observed for each discussed factor. Taking into account the current situation with the data from this specific speech exchange system and the given language, only a rule-based implementation of the proposed decision model is feasible.

Having a dataset of a sufficiently large size, a machine learning model for each of the feature sets may help to find proper weights for each of the factors and to calculate dependencies. Each of the parts may generate its own decision based on internal factors using, for instance, a decision tree generation method, such as C4.5 (Quinlan, 2014). The results of the separate decisions may be composed into a feature vector. Another machine learning model will be needed to generate a (pre-)final decision from this vector.

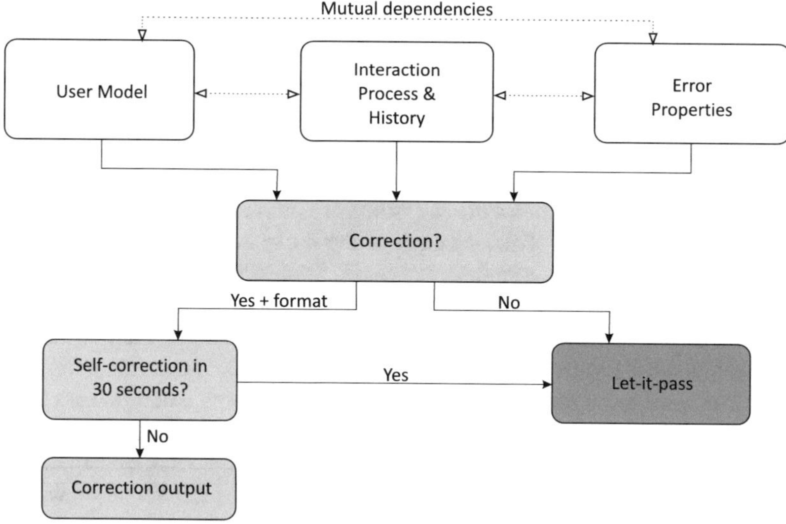

Fig. 8.2: Schema of the correction decision model. White blocks represent the feature sets. Black arrows represent the information flow in the decision model, dotted arrows show mutual dependencies

Each of the values in the vector may have its own weight, which, in turn, needs to be estimated from training data. Mutual dependencies between the features must be covered by the machine learning model. Finally, if the user still does not produce a self-correction, the machine may correct the learner's linguistic error using a specific correction format, which needs to be selected as part of the decision model. Figure 8.2 illustrates the feature sets and their interdependencies on a high level.

8.7 Results on correction decision

In this section we discuss our research results with regard to a correction decision model addressing the following research questions:

RQ5 Which factors besides an occurrence of an error are relevant for an occurrence of a correction of a linguistic error in native/non-native speaker chat-based Conversation-for-Learning?

RQ6 How can these factors be modelled for an implementation in a chat-based Communicative ICALL system?

Because this question was not on the research radar at the time of the data collection, only partial information about participants' decisions to correct or not to correct is available. Nonetheless, all the local correction formats and their model are useless for a Communicative ICALL system if it cannot decide when they are applicable. Therefore, this research faced this challenge.

As noted by Schegloff (1993), "... in examining large amounts of data, we are studying *multiples or aggregates of single instances*". From the relatively small number of correction examples in the dataset (22 exposed and 37 embedded corrections contained in 4,548 messages), it was possible to identify important features for correction decisions and to propose a correction decision model. Participants in the chats decided to correct not based on any statistical metrics, but when it was relevant. We made here an attempt to express the relevance of a correction of a linguistic error as a set of features. The importance of each of them can be expressed as weights that need to be estimated from more data or specified manually for the small number of examples.

Several issues need to be solved for a practical implementation of the model. First of all, a quantification of mutual dependencies and calculation of weights of each feature need to be attempted. Because still not enough examples are available for machine learning, manual calculations may be performed by creating linguistic variables and assigning fuzzy numbers to them (Zadeh, 1983). A quantitative study of dependencies among the identified features and, maybe, discovery of new features, would not reduce the results of this qualitative study, but rather help researchers to deal with complexity and to preserve consistency within a complex system of rules and mutual dependencies.

8.7.1 Interactional relevance of a correction

Studies of native/non-native speaker and non-native/non-native speaker chat interaction show different and sometimes contradictory results with regard to frequencies of exposed corrections. The conclusions of the studies mostly connect the presence or non-presence of correction to participants' linguistic identities or the communication medium. For instance, Tudini (2007) explains that native/non-native speaker chat does not support corrections as much as non-native/non-native speaker chat does. Tudini (2010) concludes that intercultural chat does not support embedded corrections. Having the results of this research at hand, we can see such conclusions as insufficient, because they do not address reasons for non-present or present corrections in conversation in terms of discourse type, sequential consequences and interactional import of the corrections and their alternatives. Other studies discussed in Section 2.3 describe efforts made towards an explanation of the presence or non-presence of correction, for instance (Kurhila, 2001, 2004; Hosoda, 2006; Kasper, 2004). Differences between language classroom interaction and less formal types of native/non-native speaker interaction need to be taken into account in terms of decisions to correct or not to correct and which form of correction should be preferred.

As analysed by Schegloff (Schegloff, 1987b) and observed in the present work, an error does not immediately trigger a correction. In other words, a correction is not the only way to deal with learner errors. As was shown in multiple CA-driven SLA studies, interactional import of specific correction formats is relevant for a speaker's decision to correct and a speaker's selection of a specific correction form. As Kurhila (2006) summarises the main features of error corrections in non-pedgagogic native/non-native speaker conversation:

> first, (grammatical) deficiencies are subject to outright repair but not to repair initiations and, second, (linguistic) correction is done so as to diminish the interactional prominence of the activity. Kurhila (2006, p. 43)

As is reflected in the number of corrections in Table 7.2, page 215, there is a huge variation in the number of both exposed and embedded corrections over different native speaker-learner pairs. A detailed analysis of all corrections was helpful to understand which factors may be relevant for a decision to correct or not to correct. The let-it-pass strategy was preferred by some of the pairs while other pairs frequently engaged in discussions of linguistic matters.

The presence or non-presence of a correction is determined not only by the statuses of the participants and the medium of the communication. It is also determined by other integral parts of the conversation such as

- conventions and agreements,
- turn properties (e.g. length and present or non-present narrative character),
- error complexity and availability of a target hypothesis allowing or not allowing for a quick and clear correction,
- engagement with the topic and
- sequential consequences of error.

In this sense, this study continues work on the reasons for corrections started by (Kurhila, 2001, 2004; Hosoda, 2006; Kasper, 2004). Mutual dependencies among these factors make both empirical analysis and computational modelling a very challenging research endeavour.

Tudini (2010, p.19) notes that the Italian native speakers in her dataset tend to "tone down" chat jargon in conversations with language learners and use mainly informal colloquial Italian. From this observation it can be concluded that native speakers modify their chat language and design their turns to make them understandable for not yet fully proficient language users. However, changes in the chat language discussed in Section 8.2.2 show that making utterances comprehensible for non-native speakers is only one aspect in the selection of the interactional resources. There is at least one more function performed through deviations from linguistic standard, which is regulation of social proximity.

While this finding may play a less important role for conceptually written learner language corpora, the interactional function of deviations from the standard is important for conceptually oral learner corpora. Specifically, the difference between "real" or potentially correctable linguistic errors and those that do not count as errors in chat is important. In addition, further conceptual work on error annotation in chat data is required.

8.7.2 Correction decision model for Communicative ICALL

Because earlier Communicative ICALL applications usually built upon existing SLA theories, the selection of a correction format (or type of corrective feedback) was mostly driven by the supposed effectiveness of particular correction types to promote or facilitate learning. In contrast, this work presented the first attempt to define a feature-based correction decision model in a Conversation-for-Learning. Until now, two main factors have been considered in Communicative ICALL as relevant for correction decision: first, the occurrence of a recognisable error, and second, the ability of the machine to provide meaningful and accurate feedback; see for instance the discussion in (Wilske, 2014, Sec. 5.4). Other factors identified in the empirical part of the present book as relevant have not yet been taken into account. These factors are related to the interaction history going beyond corrections in the past, and to the user model including but not limited to linguistic features and error properties.

The disengagement between errors, corrections and decisions to correct was realised in a separation of local models for correction and a correction decision model. Local models for corrections are responsible for the generation of a particular correction format. The correction decision model determines whether a correction should be produced at a particular given point of the interaction. As a whole it can be represented as a product of two regulatory formalisms, of which one is responsible for the activation of a particular type from the other one. Figure 8.3 visualises the interaction of the two regulatory mechanisms in the correction framework. ICALL research

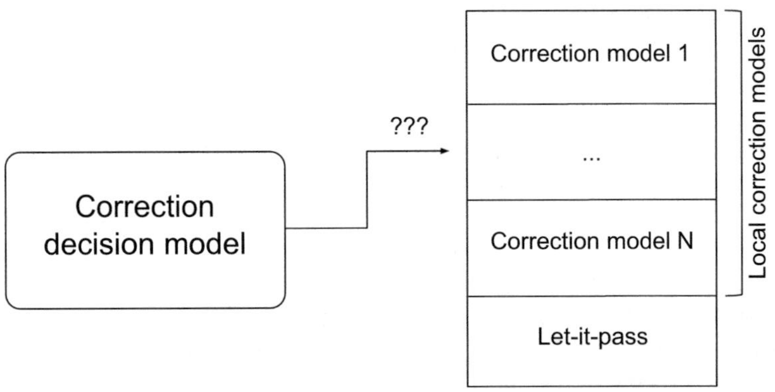

Fig. 8.3: Local and global regulation in the correction model

addressed the issue of correction decisions from a different perspective. Factors such as the number of errors, error types in the user's language and activity types were considered. For instance, Amaral et al. (2011) describe the following priority for feedback messages:

> Feedback messages for reading, listening and description activities should prioritise meaning over form. [...] If multiple errors are diagnosed, meaning-based errors will be displayed first for these types of activities. Feedback messages for rephrasing activities, on the other hand, can focus on syntactic errors at the sentence level." (p. 8).

Such activities are not specified explicitly in a Conversation-for-Learning, however they may be introduced by participants in the course of social interaction and made *part of* the interpersonal trajectory, for instance, in sub-dialogues of collaborative learning. Because focus on learning is emphasised in such sub-dialogues, context-sensitive modifications in correction decisions may be required and can be addressed in a future study. However, activities listed by Amaral et al. (2011) such as reading and writing are involved in chat throughout the entire conversation.

Social interaction with the user influenced the decision to correct in the work by Petersen (2010) in the way that the social trajectory was followed immediately after corrections, forming every time the same type of correction. However, empirically grounded research in this and other studies shows that correction formats and correction focus change over time (Dings, 2012). Choosing different types of correction formats over time will also help to deal with the machine's repetitiveness which has been seen as problematic in conversations with artificial agents (Bickmore and Picard, 2005).

Because every correction in talk is also a social action, observable features of social interaction were included in the correction decision model, such as interaction history and user model. Amaral et al. (2011) integrate information from the activity model and the user model (e.g. which errors the learner typically makes) to improve learner language understanding. Several academic publications discussed in Section 2.2.5 take information from the user model and interaction context into account for providing corrective feedback (Heift, 2003; Amaral and Meurers, 2008, 2011). However, the decisions that Non-Communicative ICALL applications have to take and the features that need to be observed are different. While context understanding for a Non-Communicative ICALL system may include information about the activity and the task, interactional history needs to be tracked in addition to the actual activity understanding. The actual activity in a Conversation-for-Learning may range from teacher-student simulation (collaborative learning) to chit-chat about the work day to telling jokes and stories. The sub-dialogues of collaborative learning make corrections less dispreferred. In addition, preceding forms of participants' orientations to their linguistic identities influence the decision to correct. Specifically, preceding learners' negative self-assessments make a correction less preferred as opposed to learner-initiated explanations (other-initiated self-repair). In contrast, focus on meaning in immediately preceding explanation sequences initiated by language learners (other-initiated self-repair) supports subsequent focus on form, as discussed in Section 4.2.1.

Figure 8.4 shows the place of the decision mechanism in the repair manager. In the suggested architecture, the dialogue manager receives several inputs such as a possible response to the social trajectory, and possibly a correction format for an error or a repair proper (but not necessarily all at once). The dialogue manager needs to decide the sequential order of these messages. For messages that belong to a side sequence (explanations or special types of exposed corrections), the dialogue manager needs to remember the dialogue state for the social trajectory and to come back to it after the side sequence is closed. A suitable implementation for this would be an

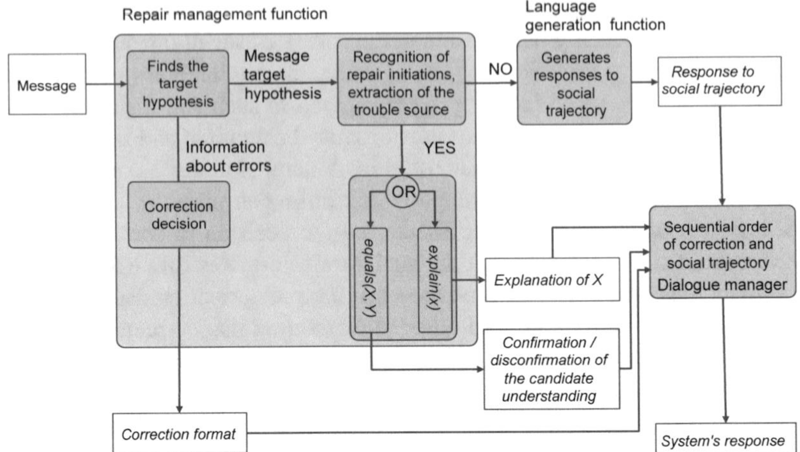

Fig. 8.4: The repair manager and the place of the correction decision mechanism

information-state architecture where all components have access to a shared memory that stores the current dialogue state (Lison and Kennington, 2015, 2016).

Issues such as dealing with multiple target hypotheses and selection of one surface string from many possible once are already known from previous ICALL publications. In addition, in Communicative ICALL applications where corrections need to be provided within the ongoing dialogue, the interactional import of the correction *besides the error correction by itself* needs to be taken into account. This interactional import is accomplished by various types of rich or minimal accountings, backlinks, giving the learner the opportunity to respond to the correction or "keeping the floor" (correction on the fly) as well as the primary decision to make the correction into interactional business or not (exposed vs. embedded correction). Previous academic publications in Communicative ICALL did not focus on this issue.

Though this research made a clear contribution to Communicative ICALL, it has several limitations with regard to the correction decision model. Motivation to perform the learning task is listed by human tutors as an important factor for a correction (Amaral et al., 2011). The concept of *motivation* was operationalised as *professional relevance* in this work. All of the learners participating in the study were students from the same university and studied German as a second language to become teachers and translators. Therefore, the dependencies between the motivation and the learning behaviour are only partially analysable from the given dataset. Although this user group is very large, further adjustments based on more observations are required to cover other user groups than students of foreign languages at the university level.

Even though the group of learners in the corpus was homogeneous in terms of their affiliation, variations in motivation and consequent changes in interaction were observed. Specifically, exam preparation was made relevant in several chat sessions, because the data collection took place as the learners had their exam time at the university. In this time, the learners were more motivated to engage in pedagogical activities (e.g. exam preparation) and even to communicate with native speakers in general (see Section 3.3, Example 3.7, page 84).

Features such as the degree of social closeness may be relevant for the correction decision model, specifically for the selection of the correction format and accountings. Unfortunately, at the time when this research was performed, no such model operationalisable for a computer implementation was available that would allow us to "measure" the grade of social closeness. However, a few articles made a step towards this problem, for instance through the concepts of the *language of the closeness, language of the distance* (Koch and Oesterreicher, 1985; Thaler, 2007; Birkner and Meer, 2011; Dürscheid, 2016). As has been reported in various studies, social closeness and intimacy is an interactional achievement (see for instance (Rintel, 2015) and references therein). In particular, the absence of ceremonials and invitations typically index intimacy (Sacks, 1995). A similar tendency could be identified in this research. First, the native speakers changed their correction formats over time from more complex to less complex (e.g. from exposed with rich accountings to exposed with minimal accountings). Second, the participants changed the form of address and used more informal orthography over time (Danilava et al., 2013a). Existing models for relationships might be used for an implementation, for instance the relationship model for relational agents (Bickmore, 2003) and the concept of verbal convergence (Mitchell et al., 2012).

Because of multiple mutual dependencies among the factors, machine learning approaches may be more useful for finding priorities over different factors and calculating the importance of each of them. Due to the small number of examples in the dataset the creation of a machine learning model was left for a future study. Several ideas for solving the data issue are discussed in Section 11.5.2.

It is important to keep in mind that the dataset in focus represents an equal-power speech exchange system called a Conversation-for-Learning. A *different* decision model may be needed for a different speech exchange system, such as teacher-student communication in a language classroom (non-equal power). A new comparative study involving data from the two mentioned speech exchange systems may show whether the set of features identified in this work is applicable for some non-equal-power speech exchange systems.

8.7.3 Conclusions

The study of interactional factors relevant for a correction decision and their computational modelling led to the following conclusions:

- Microanalytic methods of CA can be effectively used in order to identify and describe complex mutual dependencies in speakers' selection of a particular practice to deal with a particular input in interaction. This shows in general that the problem of *contingency* (Schegloff, 1996) in interaction "to serve computational interests" can be effectively tackled by such methods.

- Because the action of correction has a pedagogical and a social import in interaction, both need to be studied. From the analysis of factors it became clear that the social import of corrections is more important in a Conversation-for-Learning than their pedagogical import. Therefore the correction decision is mainly determined by social factors. This may change in a different speech exchange system.

Chapter Summary

In this chapter we made the first attempt to formulate a computational decision model for corrections. The features relevant for this decision which we identified in preceding chapters were analysed from the perspective of the decision modelling. We discussed the role of each of the features and listed several mutual dependencies among them. The presence of an error does not necessarily trigger a correction. Other factors such as user professional interests, user's explicit requests to correct, the grade of social closeness, preceding corrections, other forms of orientation to linguistic identities, possible learner's self-corrections and different error properties may be crucial for this decision. Each of these factors can be formulated as a feature for a feature-based decision model. We discussed which components the model would need and how they would interact based on the identified set of features. Finally, we discussed the contribution of this research compared to the state-of-the-art publications.

9 Method Evaluation

Abstract The methodological novelty of this research is mainly determined by the inclusion of Conversation Analysis in the multidisciplinary research paradigm of Communicative ICALL. This chapter evaluates the presented research and its implications for Communicative ICALL with respect to the SWOT model (Strengths, Weaknesses, Opportunities and Threats). Theoretical implications of the research and recommendation for the future Communicative ICALL will be formulated.

9.1 Introduction

As motivated in Chapter 1, this research aimed at exploring how participants of native/non-native speaker dyadic chat orient to their linguistic identities with the purpose of computational modelling of conversational agents for Communicative ICALL in roles other than teachers or tutors.

Driven by the initial idea of creating a machine for practising conversation in chat, the study had the following objectives:

I Find and describe interactional practices in native/non-native speaker chat-based Conversation-for-Learning where chat participants orient to their linguistic identities of language experts and language novices.

II Create computational models of those practices and analyse technical requirements and limitations to implement the resulting models in a Communicative ICALL application.

This work shows that methods of Conversation Analysis (CA) can be successfully applied when facing such open research objectives in computational modelling. Specifically, it shows that CA methods can be applied to find typical structures in longitudinal dyadic chat-based Conversations-for-Learning, using recordings of chats between German native speakers and advanced learners of German as a foreign language as an example. Further, the study shows that the identified structures can be used as a basis to build data-driven computational models for conversational agents

S. Höhn, *Artificial Companion for Second Language Conversation*,
https://doi.org/10.1007/978-3-030-15504-9_9

in roles other than teachers or tutors communicating with users who are foreign language learners.

Based on the intensive discussions in this part of the book, Section 9.2 summarises the theoretical implications following from this research for the related research disciplines. Further, Section 9.3 makes use of the SWOT model (Strengths, Weaknesses, Opportunities and Threats) to formulate systematic recommendations for the future Communicative ICALL. Section 9.4 presents a bird-eye perspective on the research described in this book.

9.2 Theoretical implications

From all the research questions and issues discussed so far, we can infer the following theoretical implications for Communicative ICALL from this research:

- Including Conversation Analysis in the circle of disciplines related to Communicative ICALL has several practical advantages, which are reported in this work. However, it also has the disadvantage that a rethinking of the mainstream theoretical paradigm may be needed.
- Because orientation to linguistic identities in a chat-based Conversation-for-Learning is mainly initiated by the non-native speaker, the primary focus in computational modelling of such sequences of talk needs to be put on recognition of non-native speakers' orientations to linguistic identities and appropriate reactions to them. Active positioning as a language expert by an artificial conversation partner is only rarely appropriate, but also needs attention.
- There are places in conversation where non-native speakers' orientations to their linguistic identities are more likely, that is at the beginning of the first talk and after sequences of repair with linguistic trouble source. This locational information may be made part of the recognition model.
- A model to capture social proximity in conversation is urgently needed. Incremental changes of the social proximity need to be covered by the model since there are dependencies between social proximity and error corrections.
- Because only a small number of errors are corrected in a Conversation-for-Learning, the current state of the art in error recognition may provide sufficient information for automatic correction generation in Communicative ICALL. However, there is a mismatch between the current state of the art in automatic recognition of lexical errors and errors in pragmatics and the empirical evidence that the majority of corrected errors in a Conversation-for-Learning are focused on meaning.
- There is a gap between the need to produce more embedded than exposed corrections and the current dialogue systems' capabilities to do this. This gap is caused by the lack of models for embedded corrections covering the entire range of those, as described in this research. Embedded corrections are more frequent and more preferred but they are harder to operationalise for an implementation in a dialogue system. Regular expressions are sufficient to describe exposed corrections while embedded corrections require syntax-based modelling (with a few

exceptions). Therefore, there is a need to further investigate embedded corrections from both empirical and computational perspectives in order to better transfer the findings from empirical data into dialogue systems.

Though language learning was not the primary focus of this research, we can see the following theoretical and methodological implications of this research for Second Language Acquisition (SLA):

- This research supports findings reported in multiple academic publications in CA-for-SLA such as (Markee, 2000; Kasper, 2004, 2006; Markee, 2008; Vandergriff, 2013) stating that the existing conceptual definition of learning and the experimental approach as the only research instrument are not sufficient to analyse naturally occurring opportunities for language acquisition. Specifically, occurrence of deviations from the language standard, error corrections and their interactional import have no place in traditional SLA and require a cardinal rethinking of the underlying concepts of errors and corrections.
- Orthography, vocabulary and syntax are interactional resources used to regulate social closeness and update participants' identities, and not merely a display of language proficiency or typing pace. A closer interdisciplinary collaboration between CA and SLA may help to explain *why* some deviations from a language standard occur in chat. Simply to register *that* deviations are present and conclude that they are caused by lack of knowledge is not sufficient.
- Uptake after embedded corrections is documented by sociolinguistic data, therefore, embedded corrections and their effect on learning should be put under the loupe of SLA research.
- Postponed uptake documented in this research may make it difficult to provide empirical evidence of learning. Automated tracking of learning objects may offer additional value for both SLA and CA-for-SLA.

Finally, it is important to bear in mind that reacting to a repair initiation with a repair proper is the preferred response, but not the only possible one. Similarly, reacting to an error with a correction is one, but not the only acceptable way to continue the interaction. This study did not aim at simplification of the complexity of the talk, but it tried to break down the complexity into manageable pieces. Therefore, we can see the following theoretical implications for NLP, specifically dialogue research:

- Natural Language Understanding in dialogue implies understanding of the social action encoded in an utterance. Speech acts are *the* model used in NLP to manage this issue (Schiffrin, 2005). However, CA researchers found that there are social actions not covered by the speech act classifications, such as pre-offers, pre-tellings and other pre-sequences (Schegloff, 1996). However, an operationalisation of the new concepts the computational purposes with CA methods is costly in terms of data from specific speech exchange systems and researcher time required.
- Disengagement of specific triggers in talk and practices for dealing with these triggers can be handled in a similar way as has been done for errors and corrections in this work. This disengagement helps to manage the complexity in

the form of concise descriptions of *practices*, that is potentially eligible ways of producing specific actions. Another mechanism can then decide when each of them can be activated.

As announced in the Introduction chapter of the book, this research also has implications for learner language and learner corpus research:

- Learner corpus research needs to go beyond error and linguistic annotation, especially for conceptually oral corpora. Social actions and interaction practices employed by language learners to perform such actions are also of interest.
- Learner corpus research needs to distinguish between objective deviations from the written language norm and conventions applicable for a specific speech exchange system and communication medium.
- Taking the radically emic perspective in error annotation in conceptually oral corpora will allow us to deal with potentially multiple target hypotheses.
- Because data of good quality, that is, replicating the speech exchange system of interest, are crucial for CA-informed modelling, the methodology of data collection is always important and should be described in detail in data-informed publications.

9.3 Recommendations for future communicative ICALL

In this section we will evaluate the advantages and disadvantages of the method applied for this research. We will analyse opportunities and risks of the method for future studies in Communicative ICALL. We will make use of a structured planning method known as SWOT (Strengths, Weaknesses, Opportunities and Threats (Mintzberg, 1994)) to identify strategic implications of this research for Communicative ICALL. In Section 9.3.1 we will analyse internal and external positive and negative factors. In Section 9.3.2 we will make inferences on strategic implications following from the analysis.

9.3.1 Strengths, weaknesses, opportunities and threats

Table 9.1 presents the SWOT canvas to evaluate the applicability of the used method for Communicative ICALL research and to identify strategies for future development of Communicative ICALL based on this study. The evaluation is determined by a detailed analysis of internal and external factors. Internal factors include strengths and weaknesses of the research method itself. External factors include opportunities and risks due to the environment.

The top half of the SWOT canvas in Table 9.1 describes the situation with regard to advantages and limitations of the method used in the research described in this book. The bottom half lists advantageous and disadvantageous factors determined by the state of the art, language complexity, factors related to potential users, existing machine learning models and efforts required to obtain a larger number of examples for machine learning.

Strengths	**Weaknesses**
• Hypothesis formation with regard to new user and system models. • Structures and prototypes from naturally occurring data. • Takes special characteristics of the speech exchange system into account. • Microanalysis allows detection of new features and dependencies. • Separation in local and global models allows both to be easily extended. • Long-term changes can be observed.	• Voluntary participants from only one population group. • Only one language and medium. • Microanalysis is time-expensive and exhausting. • Sparse information about the correction decision and social import of corrections due to study design. • The very small number of examples may be problematic for modelling. • Manual creation of rules of mutual dependencies is tricky. • Comparability to other methods, quantitative validation is tricky.
Opportunities	**Threats**
• Contingency. • Dealing with complexity in the form of role play. • Current NLP tools allow us to make good models and applications for well-defined short tasks. • Integration in an ICALL system as an additional service. • Big data, deep learning. • More data for various other populations may be found in current ICALL applications.	• Contingency. • Interaction with a machine may work completely differently. • Learners may not accept the machine as a language expert. • More data does not imply more examples. • Mismatch between automatically detectable error types and most frequently corrected error types.

Table 9.1: SWOT analysis

We already discussed all these factors throughout the preceding chapters of the book. Table 9.1 provides a concise summary of them in order to make further decisions easier.

Most of the factors occur only once in the table, except *contingency*. We can interpret the *contingency* (Schegloff, 1996) as both risk and opportunity for dialogue systems in general, and specifically Communicative ICALL. Contingency is the reason why such primitive conversation machines as retrieval-based chatbots work. Contingency is also a reason why user experience in unrestricted conversations with chatbots is frequently unsatisfactory. There are many contexts where one utterance is appropriate, and this is one of the reasons why users perceive chatbots as repetitive. This is why maybe the most important strategic implication is the need to handle contingency in order to make it manageable.

9.3.2 Strategic implications and recommendations

The SWOT canvas is rather a static representation of the situation and does not include any recommendations for actions. However, different strategies for future development can be elaborated based on the description of the situation. The *matching strategy* builds on the combination of strengths and opportunities and searches for new chances. The *transformation strategy* combines weaknesses and opportunities in order to transform weaknesses into new strengths. The *neutralisation strategy* combines strengths and threats with the purpose of risk prevention. Finally, the *defense strategy* combines weaknesses and threats to prevent identified weaknesses from becoming a target for the risks. We identify the strategies and make recommendations for future research in the remainder of this section.

The strategies should always be developed towards a concrete goal. The goal in this case is to create new and to improve existing Communicative ICALL systems equipped with CA-informed computational modelling. We will formulate the strategies in the form of DOs and DON'Ts below.

Matching strategy

To find a strategy for identification of new chances for development, strengths and opportunities are combined.

DO Integrate well-defined short dialogue models to practice specific situations (e.g. those mentioned in Section 11.5.1) into existing workbook-like ICALL systems.
DO Develop short role-play-based situations for specific speech exchange systems where participants' identities (not only linguistic identities) are relevant, for instance a job interview in the language to be learned.
DO Develop methods for long-term tracking of learning objects and learning behaviour.
DO Create partnerships with data holders from which Communicative ICALL can learn.
DO Use qualitative approaches to evaluating learners' performance.
DO Develop CA-informed machine learning approaches to dialogue modelling.

Transformation strategy

The *transformation strategy* combines weaknesses and opportunities in order to transform weaknesses into new strengths.

DO Create collaborations to obtain sufficient data to cover user groups and languages not covered in this study.

DO Look even at very rare phenomena, because a small number of examples helps to identify at least the phenomenon in focus and to understand its role and structure. Then try to find more examples in other datasets, where such phenomena are more likely to be found, in order to build larger collections of examples.

DO Identify the most suitable machine learning approaches for dependency identification and weight estimation.

Neutralisation strategy

The *neutralisation strategy* combines strengths and threats with the purpose of risk prevention.

DO Apply qualitative evaluation methods to dialogue assessment.

DO Setup a Wizard-of-Oz study as a proof of concept of the chatbot that helps to practice conversation in a foreign language. Provide the Wizard with instructions identified in this research with regard to language novice and language expert identities.

DO Identify the most frequent errors with focus on meaning and concentrate on them in automated recognition and corrections.

DON'T Work with artificially created examples.

Although we suggest here not to work with artificially created examples, it might sometimes be unavoidable because of the need to have large training corpora to train machine learning systems. As we already discussed in Section 2.2.3, automated error generation is one of the cases where artificially generated data may be a good alternative to naturally occurring examples (Rei et al., 2017).

Defense strategy

The combinations of weaknesses and threats allows us to prevent identified weaknesses from becoming a target for the risks.

DO Apply contingency to deal with contingency. Develop “back doors" to deal with inputs that the system does not cover explicitly on the necessary level of detail. Rely on similar strategies observed in naturally occurring data.

DO Use existing findings on structures of interest to set up new data collections (specifically design of interviews and questionnaires) in order to get sufficient information from the data.

DO Set up a new study targeting the correction decision from different perspectives.

DO Take the speech exchange system into account starting with the data collection or data selection.

DO Approach modelling “free conversation" by practicing specific actions, for instance, variants of possible reactions to news telling.

DON'T Promise practicing free conversation at the current state of research.

Thus, after many decades of dialogue systems research including this study, we will be on the safe side if we do not promise practicing free conversation with an artificial conversation partner.

9.4 Conclusions

This work continues the research efforts bringing Artificial Intelligence and Conversation Analysis closer together, which is intensively applied in Human-Robot Interaction but has not received enough attention in Communicative ICALL. In this way, innovative software to improve users' experience can be created. Models of specific interactional practices and their pragmatic function will provide the agents with the ability to react appropriately to specific social actions. The same can be performed for various speech exchange systems and interaction modalities in the same or a similar way as was shown in this book. Conversational agents for specific purposes in specific interactional roles such as personal assistant, fitness coach or housekeeper can get closer to users' expectations.

Although the study shows that specific phenomena in interaction may be discovered, described and modelled for computational purposes with CA-informed methods, it should not be understood as an antidote to the complexity of the interaction. To emphasise this point, we will close the theoretical part of this work with a quotation that is applicable to this research as much as it is an integral part of the original article:

> The several themes to which I have called attention all involve a major challenge to computational interests in discourse. [...] The challenge is *contingency*. Although the organisation of talk-in-interaction is orderly [...], it is characterised by contingency at virtually every point. [...]
>
> One underlying "burning" issue for computational interests in discourse analysis is how to come to terms with the full range of contingency which talk-in-interaction allows and channels. [...]
>
> The problem of contingency [...] poses truly formidable obstacles to computational approaches. But if some useful interchange between these modalities of work is to be realised, it is most likely to come not from transforming the object from which you would like to learn, but from taking it seriously in its own terms. In the end, it will be the computationalists who will have to figure out how to do this. (Schegloff, 1996, pp. 21-22, 29)

Thus, we can see CA-informed modelling as a sustainable approach to deal with *contingency*. This research was not an attempt to simplify the object of study, namely conversation, but an attempt to break down the complexity into manageable pieces. We took the object of our studies seriously, and approached contingency by distinguishing between local models of corrections and a decision mechanism that is able to select correction as one of the options in the space of contingency. We showed how this approach can work on the example of chat conversations with language learners. In this way, this research advances the state of the art in ICALL research described in Section 2.2 and strengthens multidisciplinary connections to related disciplines, such as Conversation Analysis and NLP.

Chapter Summary

This chapter evaluated the proposed method of CA-informed dialogue modelling in the context of Communicative ICALL according to the SWOT model. Theoretical implications of the method for the fields of Communicative ICALL, SLA, dialogue and learner corpus research have been discussed. Recommendations for future Communicative ICALL have been formulated.

Part III

Model Validation and Future Directions

10

Implementation of an Artificial Conversation Companion

Abstract This chapter describes an implementation case study for the data-driven models introduced in Part II of this book. Besides the explanations and error corrections, many other practical design decisions need to be made, which are discussed in this chapter. The possibility of implementing the proposed models using chatbot technology is tested. The issues with the evaluation of such a system are discussed.

10.1 Introduction

The primary purpose of this chapter is to provide a practical applicability test of the abstract models of other-initiated self-repair and error corrections described in Part II of this book. Because we started this research with the idea of creating a machine that behaves like a language expert, we will discuss in this chapter which other questions need to be solved in order to create an artificial conversation partner that interacts with a language learner for a prolonged period of time. Some of these issues were already discussed in earlier publications and include learner language understanding, emotion understanding, the ability to adapt to the user in terms of social proximity and cognitive abilities such as using interaction history to extract facts about the user and use of this information in future dialogues (Danilava et al., 2012, 2013a). Here we will focus on the problems of the chatbot's individual interaction style, frequently called *personality*, and the input restriction.

Because language understanding and generation capabilities of different conversational systems determine the possibilities for implementation of the proposed models, we need to decide which technology to use. For simplicity, we will call the artificial conversation partner that we plan to build simply a *chatbot*. The following criteria are important for the selection of the chatbot technology:

1. Robustness: it needs to be robust enough to deal with learner language;
2. Extendability of the language-understanding capabilities and the possibility to enrich the input with new language resources;
3. Extendability of the language generation capabilities; additional linguistic resources must be made accessible for the language generation;

S. Höhn, *Artificial Companion for Second Language Conversation*,
https://doi.org/10.1007/978-3-030-15504-9_10

4. Access to dialogue context: the system needs to access information from past turns.
5. Availability for German: the technology needs to cover German, and the available dialogue scripts/data need to be in German.

At the time this work was performed (2011-2015), recent intent-based NLU systems such as Microsoft LUIS, Watson Conversation, RASA, wit.ai and Dialogflow (formerly api.ai) were not available. We can see all possible types of social actions in conversation as special types of intents, such as greetings, pre-offers, pre-requests, offers, sequence closings etc. However, as discussed in Section 4.6.2, the concept of intents in the form in which it is implemented in current NLU services is not suitable for the recognition of, for instance, repair initiations. In this case we would need each training example to consist of at least two turns (the trouble source turn and the repair initiation). This does not conform with the expected data format for these systems. In addition, as discussed earlier, nothing in the talk is a trouble source by itself, but anything can become a trouble source during a conversation; therefore, it can be recognised only after a repair initiation was produced, but is always located in one of the preceding turns. The same concerns other repeat-based actions, such as some reactions of surprise, some jokes and repair other-initiation-based error corrections.

Various challenges of automated learner language understanding were discussed in Section 2.2.3. In chat conversations between the artificial conversation partner and language learners, the challenges will be even bigger due to the dialogue setting. Short utterances that are not formed as grammatically full sentences dominate instant messaging. In addition, it is not clear in the beginning how many errors the non-native speakers would make in conversations with the chatbot, pattern-based language understanding or keyword spotting may be the most robust technology for learner-language understanding, despite the limitations of these techniques for error recognition. An additional component can be used for the recognition of learner errors in order to provide corrections.

Several open-source chatbots based on the Artificial Intelligence Markup Language (AIML) are available for many languages and meet the selection criteria. One of them was taken as a baseline for this implementation case study: the AIML interpreter called *Program D* (Bush, 2006) and the free German AIML set (Droßmann, 2005). The baseline chatbot will be extended by a component responsible for the two types of repair that we focused on in Part II of this book, namely other-initiated self-repair initiated by non-native speakers and other-corrections of non-native speakers' linguistic errors. We call this component a *repair manager*.

General design issues that need to be solved to implement an artificial conversation partner will be discussed in Section 10.2. The part of the repair manager responsible for the generation of explanations following users' repair initiations will be the subject of Section 10.3. The implementation of the correction of linguistic errors using the AIML-based technology as a part of the repair manager will be addressed in Section 10.4. The results will be discussed in Section 10.5.

10.2 General design issues

In this section we discuss the design questions that need to be solved in addition to those discussed in Part II of this book and in earlier publications (Danilava et al., 2012, 2013a). We will examine the design questions from three perspectives:

1. findings about specific issues mainly based on Conversation Analysis (CA) research,
2. practical chatbot designers' advice formulated by experienced chatbot designers and
3. the technical potential of the technology chosen for the implementation, namely the AIML-based chatbot.

We will make practical suggestions about how to bridge the identified gaps and to improve existing chatbot technology having findings from CA at hand.

The main AIML unit used for language understanding and generation is called a *category* and has two mandatory elements: a *pattern description* needed for language understanding and a *template* responsible for the retrieval of the response. An example of an AIML `category` is shown below. If the chatbot finds an input that matches WIE GEHTS, the utterance stored in the `template` tag will be delivered to the user as a response.

```
<category>
   <pattern>WIE GEHTS</pattern>
   <template>Gut, und selbst? Alles paletti?</template>
</category>
```

To make the responses less repetitive, the AIML language allows the use of lists of possible responses and the possibility to retrieve a random response from a list or using conditions. For more detailed references on AIML see (Wallace, 2003; MacTear et al., 2016).

The AIML interpreter Program D is based on so-called processors. Each processor is responsible for the processing of a specific AIML tag. There is the possibility to introduce new AIML tags and to extend Program D with the corresponding new processors.

Though the participants of the conversations from the dataset used in Part II of this book were asked to simply chat and do just whatever they wanted, we cannot do the same with the artificial conversation partner. Maintaining a free, close-to-natural conversation with a chatbot is a very complex task. This task cannot be solved with the currently available conversational technology with the required quality. Attempts to use AIML chatbots for practicing a free, unrestricted conversation are described in several academic publications, for instance (Jia, 2009). However, the user engagement was quite low and the most users did not continue talking with the bot after the first dialogue, as reported by the author. AIML allows a huge range of potential user's utterances to be covered, but the price for this is that the bot's responses are very generic, impersonal and repetitive. Therefore, for a practical but still CA-informed implementation we will need to place restrictions on conversations with the chatbot. One very popular possibility to set such restrictions is to limit the conversations by domain or topic. However, as Schegloff (1990) puts it "*'topic' as an analytic tool is vulnerable to a number of problems*", and probably the biggest problem for such a restriction is, that it is a recurring challenge to determine exactly what topic is. Other types of restrictions may come from the speech exchange system that we are going to simulate and concern user and bot identities and, thus, the interactional resources that can be used. We will discuss these restrictions and opportunities in the remainder of this section.

10.2.1 User experience and the chatbot's individual interaction type

Shevat (2017) emphasises the influence of the chatbot's individual interaction type on the user experience and suggests investing a sufficient amount of time into the design of a consistent bot's behaviour in terms of the personal, distinguishable style of the bot's language. Such individual chatbot characteristics are frequently called *personality*. Shevat (2017) suggests approaching the design of the bot's personality depending on the bot's main user audience, which is consistent with the recipient design principle discussed in the preceding parts of this book. A conversation designer needs to bridge the gap between the research results about conversation and the practical purpose of a special chatbot representing a particular service or a product. A top-down approach is sometimes chosen when a UX designer needs to decide how a chatbot should talk to represent a particular business or product. A data-driven perspective on the creation of a chatbot's personality is reported by Callejas-Rodríguez et al. (2016), who created a chatbot that behaves like a teenager based on a corpus of youth chats.

As we argued in Chapter 3, each chat participant showed different behaviour in terms of interaction resources used with different co-participants. In addition, participants' individual shape in a conversation depends not only on their own actions but on the actions of all co-participants and the interaction process. Thus, many *different* interaction profiles can be identified in the chat data, depending on *with whom* the same person talks and what happened earlier in the interaction. Hence, we argued that the artificial conversation partner needs to be flexible and react to users' behaviour.

Experienced chatbot designers describe such practices as *randomisation* and *decoration* with the purpose to make the interaction with the chatbot more personal, less boring and less repetitive (Shevat, 2017). By randomisation Shevat (2017) means that the chatbot should not use the same expression every time to accomplish a specific action. For example, the bot should not say every time *I understood*, but randomly choose a synonym from a set of utterances with the same meaning, such as *I see* and *Got it*. The main argument is that unexpectedness is the feature that makes interaction with the bot less predictable and therefore more pleasant.

From the CA perspective, every utterance performs first a social action and projects a set of possible nexts, thus social actions that can potentially follow the utterance. For instance, after a question, an answer is expected, and a sequence closing may follow the answer. *I understood*, *I see* and *Got it* are examples of such "sequence closing thirds" (Schegloff, 2007). However, which closing format a speaker chooses is not random but depends on the speech exchange system and is recipient designed. Even though each speaker may have their own style of speaking, the role of the speech exchange system, the preference system in it and the recipient design is huge, as we saw in the analysis of the orthography of the native speaker N01 in Section 8.2.2.

By decoration Shevat (2017) means that the bot should use not only text but also emoticons, GIFs and other resources that make the interaction less boring. However, emoticons, pictures, sounds and hyperlinks to other resources do not simply decorate the chat interaction but have a specific, pragmatic interactional function. In addition, each emoticon may have several different pragmatic functions depending on the context where it is used; see for instance (Vandergriff, 2014).

How does it help us here to make design decisions for the Artificial Conversation Companion using AIML technology? As argued earlier in Chapter 3, we can describe local practices for different types of social actions similarly to how we did it for local practices of error corrections and explanations. AIML categories are a good start to describe such utterance pairs. A more sophisticated model would be needed to connect these local practices in a sequence in a fluent way, deciding what is the next relevant action. The following steps can be suggested for a CA-informed design and implementation of the Artificial Conversation Companion using AIML technology and the dataset that we used for the analysis of participants' orientations to their linguistic identities:

1. Find and analyse multiple examples of similar actions for at least two different speakers: sequence closings, topic change, greetings etc. Are the actions of different speakers (say, A and B) performed in different ways? If yes, can we find a formal description for these differences or find a pattern? Are there individual features for each speaker that make speaker A different from Speaker B? If yes, what are these? If not, try to find an explanation.
2. Identify typical preceding turns after which follow the turns that you analysed in the first step. How can we describe or approximate them by AIML patterns?
3. Create at least two different individual chatbots' responses so that one chatbot replies more similarly to A and the other chatbot replies more similarly to B.
4. Analyse the pragmatic function of emoticons and other non-textual interactional resources in the selected utterances. Are there differences in use of emoticons by speakers A and B?
5. Add emoticons to the responses of the two chatbots.
6. Formulate the just created utterance pairs into AIML categories.

Having a dataset at our disposal where one native speaker interacts with several non-native speakers may help us to understand the influence of different co-participants on the selection of interactional resources. However, it may be very difficult to find examples of the same actions for different pairs of participants, because the dialogues are all different.

We can add the new AIML categories to a free AIML set. The number of all categories in the set is quite large, and we need to make sure that exactly these categories will be activated in a free conversation, if we plan to test them with users. However, it is difficult to predict which specific AIML categories will be activated, because it depends on the user. Although all AIML categories can be represented as a deterministic finite state machine, we cannot predict which states of this machine will be used or unused, because we do not know the input words. This makes an empirical evaluation of such chatbots with users quite challenging.

10.2.2 Topic management in conversation with chatbots

Shevat (2017) distinguishes between a topic-led and a task-led conversation for chatbots. Having the use case of a chatbot that helps to practice conversation in a foreign language in mind, we can see that the task of such a conversation is the conversation itself. Thus, we may be closer to a topic-led conversation (assumed we manage to define what a topic is). Shevat (2017) provides examples of chatbots that are designed for a topic-led conversation, for instance a bot designed for chatting about Star Wars movie. Artificial agents' ability to maintain topical talk has been investigated in multiple academic publications, for instance (Breuing and Wachsmuth, 2012; Zhu et al., 2016).

We need to keep in mind that participants of a conversation use the language (talk-in-interaction) in order to accomplish social actions, position themselves as members of special social categories, maintain the social self and regulate the grade of social proximity by their choice of interactional resources. Hence, from the perspective of Conversation Analysis, which we took as the reference science for this research, we need to talk about a topic management.

The following practical issues need to be solved if we plan to make use of the tools provided by Conversation Analysis for a naturalistic experience with the new chatbot. First, we need a formal description of the sequential organisation of the structure in conversation that we intuitively call a topic. The following places may be of special interest:

1. interaction management required to start a topic and to recognise that the other started a topic;
2. interaction management required to end a topic;
3. interaction management required to change a topic;
4. sequential organisation of the piece of talk that we intuitively call a topic (pre-expansions, insert-expansions, adjacency pairs and similar);
5. sequential organisation within a special type of post-expansions called *topicalisation*.

A topic can start with a first pair part such as a question, greeting, pre-offer, pre-invitation or similar. To make the interaction with the new chatbot a pleasant and consistent experience, it can be useful to look at the parts of our dataset outside of repair sequences again through the lens of Conversation Analysis in order to identify interactional practices typical for the given speech exchange system.

Interactional practices for topic change and topic termination include laughter, figurative and idiomatic expressions, evaluations and discourse markers. A large number of publications in CA analyse interactional practices and the function of each of them; see for instance (Holt and Drew, 2001, 2005; Holt, 2010; Gilmartin et al., 2013; Barron and Black, 2015).

The AIML tag `<topic>` is responsible for channeling the conversation to a specific topic that allows different responses to the same user's utterance to b retrieved in a more controlled way depending on the topic, and not simply using the random operator. An example of topic switch in AIML is shown below. In this case, the user will initiate an explicit negotiation about the selection of the next topic and the chatbot will randomly suggest one topic from the predefined list of topics and set the topic variable of the conversation to the corresponding value.

```
<category>
  <pattern>WORÜBER WOLLEN WIR REDEN</pattern>
    <template>
      <random>
       <li>Wir können über das Wetter anfangen.
          Wie ist das <set name="topic">Wetter</set>
          bei dir heute?</li>
       <li>Interessierst du dich für
             <set name="topic">Fußball</set>?</li>
       </random>
    </template>
</category>
```

To make it work in the continuation of the talk, we need to specify also the topics for the AIML categories that we use:

```
<topic name="WETTER">
  <category>
      [... put your WETTER categories here]
 </topic>

 <topic name="FUSSBALL">
  <category>
      [... put your FUSSBALL categories here]
 </topic>
```

This way to select a topic for the conversation is based on an explicit negotiation, as was observed in the dataset used for this work. However, other, more implicit practices for topic selection and topic change need to be mapped to AIML, too. Further analysis of the dataset will be helpful to find other patterns for topic management, which can be then used for the chatbot. Nevertheless, the topic management in AIML is rather rudimentary, and needs to be improved by adding new components, for instance, a dialogue manager that will also be responsible for topic management.

10.3 Implementation of other-initiated self-repair

In this section, we discuss how an AIML-based implementation of the model for other-initiated self-repair (OISR) discussed in Chapter 4 can be added to the baseline chatbot as a part of the repair manager. The repair manager will need to deal with all types of repair initiations discussed in the empirical part, from open-class repair initiations to more specific repeat-based repair initiations.

To handle OISR sequences, the work of the repair manager will be organised in two steps determined by the model:

1. Recognition of repair other-initiation and trouble source extraction,
2. Self-repair carry-out.

Based on the rules for repair initiation, as described in Chapter 4, we can develop patterns for the recognition of repair initiations. From these patterns, we need to create specific AIML categories for the two main classes of signalling:

1. $unclear(x)$. Every user input that requires an explanation of a single entity (word, idiom) will be redirected to the category that implements this function. We introduce a new AIML tag `<explain>`, which helps us to handle this type of repair initiation. We will need an additional processor that we call `explanation processor` to generate a response.
2. $equals(x, y)$. Every user input that corresponds to an inquiry "does x mean y?" will be redirected to the AIML category implementing meaning checks. An additional tag `<meaningcheck>` will help to handle this type of repair initiation in AIML. To handle this tag properly, we add a `meaning check processor` to the Program D in order to carry out the repair of this type.

Because we cannot predict which repair initiations will be posted by the users and which parts of the chatbot's utterances will become trouble sources, we cannot prepare AIML categories with predefined repairs for each trouble source. Instead, we need to make the chatbot capable of generating repairs at runtime from a database containing required information, such as definitions, synonyms and similar. Nevertheless, we can prepare AIML templates that will be filled with this knowledge if a repair should be produced. The following two sections describe the language-specific resources and knowledge bases used by the repair manager for the recognition of repair other-initiations and the generation of self-repairs.

Example 10.1 illustrates how a chatbot can benefit from patterns extracted from the dataset to come closer to the behaviour of a language expert.

Example 10.1. A sub-dialogue with the chatbot: other-initiated self-repair where the chatbot is the trouble-speaker.

1 `User` wie gehts?
how are you?
2 `Bot` Gut, und selbst? Alles paletti?
I'm fine, and you? Everything okay?
3 `User` paletti?
4 `Bot` umgangssprachlich alles gut, alles in Ordnung, alles okay.
colloquial everything good, everything fine, everything okay.

The bot uses a colloquial expression in turn 2 that is not clear to the user. The user initiates the repair in turn 3 using a specific repair initiation format: repetition of a part of the trouble source combined with a question mark. The bot recognises turn

3 as a repair initiation and extracts the trouble source: the repeated word *paletti* and the corresponding idiomatic expression *alles paletti*. The bot's response in turn 4 is a repair carry-out generated from a linguistic database, which we call *ExplanationDB*.

The ExplanationDB was created from Wiktionary[1] and contains information about German nouns, verbs, adverbs, adjectives, abbreviations, idioms and proverbs. To make the search faster and more efficient, a Wiktionary dump was preprocessed and only information in German and about German words was extracted that was related to linguistic features such as synonyms, meanings, examples and notes about use. Every explanation will be automatically generated from these fields according to AIML templates.

10.3.1 Recognition of $unclear(x)$ and repair generation

The repair manager searches in every user input for symptoms of a non-understanding that could be used for a repair initiation, such as multiple question marks, lexical and non-lexical expressions of non-understanding, demonstrative determiners and pronouns. If an immediate repeat-based repair other-initiation is identified, the trouble source is extracted from the repair initiation immediately. However, users may repeat only a part of an idiomatic expression in the repair initiation, and the complete expression needs to be extracted for a proper explanation, as was illustrated in Example 10.1. Therefore, other turns are taken into account for the trouble source extraction as follows:

1. If the type of signal found is typical for an immediate repair other-initiation, and the reference is not repeat-based, the program tries to locate the trouble source in the last utterance of the chatbot.
2. If the type of signal found is typical for a delayed repair other-initiation, the program searches the last three utterances of the chatbot for a trouble source.

The heuristic starts the identification of a repair initiation with symbolic, medium-specific resources for signalling trouble such as for instance ---, --, -, *?*, *??*, *???*, and lexical, language-specific recourses, such as *Ich verstehe nicht*, *unklar* or *was bedeutet?*. Then, if it is likely that the utterance in focus is a repair initiation, the repair manager searches for the trouble source. Upper case writing or quotation marks may be used to highlight the trouble source, but also emoticons, to display dissatisfaction with the trouble. To deal with learner language in repair other-initiations produced by language learners, Levenshtein distance of 20% of the average length of the word pair is set to recognise recycled words (e.g. retyped by the learner with errors).

Difficulties can occur in locating a trouble source that is longer than one word. This case arises when the user does not understand an idiom (collocation, proverb) or the meaning of an entire utterance or a longer part of an utterance. We can assume that idiomatic expressions are more difficult to learn and require a higher level of language proficiency than single words. However, it can happen that, as shown in Example 10.1, the user repeats only a part of an idiom. In this case we can make

[1] https://www.wiktionary.org/

use of the fact that everything that the chatbot can say, except the repair, is known in advance. Specifically, all idiomatic expressions are known in advance. We can create a file containing all idiomatic expressions used by the chatbot and link them with their explanations in the ExplanationDB and a keyword list. The chatbot searches for keywords in the user's repair initiation and checks whether they could be part of an idiom that the bot possibly used in one of the last three utterances. If so, the program generates an explanation from the corresponding entry in the ExplanationDB.

Entire native speaker utterances or their longer parts can become sources of non-understanding if they contain unknown words or all words are familiar to the non-native speaker but the meaning of the utterance is not clear. A satisfying explanation can be a full or partial paraphrase of the utterance or a word-by-word explanation of potentially problematic tokens (we called this strategy *split-reuse* in the empirical part of the work).

The dataset collected for this work contains only a small number of instances of OISR where paraphrasing or split-reuse is used for explanations. The majority of all repair-initiations produced by non-native speakers address single words. Paraphrase generation and recognition, also referred to as textual entailment, is a research direction in which many authors have invested lots of effort (Wubben et al., 2014; Oh et al., 2015; Brad and Rebedea, 2017; Gupta et al., 2017). Because of the complexity of the paraphrase generation, we implement only a simplified version of this type of repair carry-out. Paraphrasing as a repair carry-out strategy is useful for chatbot utterances that contain collocations. For those utterances we can create a set of corresponding paraphrases and simply retrieve them if needed. Paraphrasing is also another possible way to explain idiomatic expressions instead of obtaining definitions from the ExplanationDB.

A word-by-word explanation only makes sense for words that might be difficult for the learner. To filter the difficult words, we can use the following heuristics. We create a list of the 100 and 1,000 most frequently used German words[2] and assume that these words are not difficult for the non-native speakers. The chatbot ignores words that are supposed to be well known to everybody and will not generate any explanations for them. We first apply the filter of 1,000 most frequent words by hiding them in the chatbot utterance that became a trouble source. If all words were hidden after this step, the second filter of the 100 most frequent words is tested on the original chatbot utterance. If the remaining set of words contains more than one word, they will be explained separately using the ExplanationDB. If the list of potentially difficult words is empty even after the shorter filter is applied, a paraphrase may be a better strategy, if available.

The information from the ExplanationDB is rendered into chatbot responses in special AIML categories. An example of such categories is shown below. The `<think>` tag allows processing of an input without any immediate output. The explanation processor searches for the trouble source in the linguistic database. If the trouble source cannot be found in the linguistic database, the explanation processor returns `NOENTITY` and the pre-stored *Response-1* is sent to the user. If the trouble

[2] http://wortschatz.uni-leipzig.de/html/wliste.html

source is found but its meaning is not stored in the database, the explanation processor returns ENTITY NOMEANING. A predefined *Response-2* is then sent to the user. Finally, if the explanation processor finds the trouble source in the database and at least one meaning of it is described, an explanation will be rendered. Five additional categories not shown here are responsible for rendering of the explanation and process meanings, examples and notes.

```
<template>
 <think>
  <set name="explanation-tmp">
   <explanation><star/></explanation>
  </set>
 </think>
 <condition name="explanation-tmp">
  <li value="NOENTITY">Response-1</li>
  <li value="ENTITY NOMEANING">
     Response-2</li>
  <li><srai>GETFIRSTMEANING
   <get name="explanation-tmp"/></srai>
  </li>
 </condition>
</template>
```

10.3.2 Recognition of $equals(x, y)$ and repair carry-out

The repair manager searches every user input for sequences that match the pattern $x = y?$. This pattern is a generalisation of multiple practices used by non-native speakers in chat to present a candidate understanding, which we also call a meaning check. The meaning check processor helps to identify meaning checks and to extract x (the expression used by the system) and y (the user's understanding of this expression). Once extracted, x and y will be redirected to the main AIML category responsible for the response generation.

The heuristic starts with the search for the middle part, which may be realised by symbolic, medium-specific means such as --, -, = or lexicalised, language-specific means, for instance *heißt, bedeutet*. The left-hand part and right-hand part are checked in addition for any framing or highlighting, such as for instance quotation marks or upper case writing. Moreover, the left-hand side must be a repeat-based reference to the trouble source. Only if all these conditions are satisfied, the utterance is classified as an other-initiation of repair requiring a confirmation/disconfirmation as a response (otherwise, utterances such as *Wie heißt du?* (EN.: *What's your name?*) might be recognised as repair initiations).

To generate a response, the chatbot needs to answer the polar question *Does x mean the same as y?* This is again an instance of paraphrase detection. We can reuse for that the simplified implementation of the paraphrases from the explanation generation. If x is a single word, an idiom, a collocation or a proverb, the system can check the list of the synonyms of the corresponding entry in the ExplanationDB.

Then the repair manager will do the same for y. If x and y are listed as synonyms in the ExplanationDB, a positive answer will be generated (yes, x=y). Otherwise, the system will explain the meaning of x using the $explain(x)$ method described in Section 10.3.1.

10.4 Implementation of local models for error corrections

In this section we analyse the practical applicability of the models for exposed and embedded corrections introduced in Chapter 7. To make them work in practice, we first need a component that allows linguistic errors in non-native speaker's utterances to be recognised. For instance, the LanguageTool[3] can be used for several languages including German.

Leacock et al. (2010) describe a range of error detection technologies for learner English. Because there is no dependency between the type of error and the correction practice (except the limitations on embedded correction discussed earlier), we can use the local correction models for correction of all error types that we can detect automatically using the available error detection tools. Error recognition in the baseline chatbot Program D is limited to a predefined list of substitutions, which are applied to the input string in the pre-processing phase (normalisation) in order to reduce the number of potential inputs.

Equipped with the chatbot technology for the implementation introduced in Section 10.3, the repair manager can be further extended with a correction function. New AIML-categories need to be introduced for each type of correction format. For each variant of the surface, a separate output variant must be specified in the AIML file (specific accountings types, specific smileys). These templates then need only to be filled in with the correct expression. We discuss several possible templates for exposed corrections on one example of an error in Section 10.4.1. For embedded and integrated corrections, in contrast, the ability of the system to find repetition-based answers to polar questions is crucial. We will discuss the prospecta and the limitations of AIML-based language understanding with regard to embedded corrections in Section 10.4.2.

10.4.1 Templates for exposed corrections

Different exposed correction formats can be applied to correct each error. In the original correction, the native speaker chose a correction on the fly to address the error shown in Example 10.2. Although a correction on the fly was the selected form of correction in this example, other correction formats can be generated to address *the same error*. We will see below how other types of corrections can be generated using the correction templates obtained from the correction models as specified in Section 7.3.

[3] https://www.languagetool.org

Example 10.2. A sample error and a correction from the corpus.

242 19:19:10 L08	hast du etwas über deutsche Gruppe PUR gehören? have you something about [*error: zero-article] German band PUR heard [*error: wrong form of the participle] *have you heard anything about the German band PUR?*
243 19:19:21 N04	gehört ;-) *heard [*correction]*
244 19:19:24 N04	ja, kenn ich *yes, I know them*

For simplicity we assume that at most one error is contained in each user utterance and each detected error is corrected.

Corrections on-the-fly

To generate a correction on the fly as it was done by the native speaker in Example 10.2, the chatbot will need to concatenate two responses to the same utterance. One of these responses will contain only the error correction, and the other will contain only the response to the social trajectory, but it will respond to the utterance without the error. Therefore, the chatbot will need to perform the following steps to produce a correction on the fly:

1. For a user utterance with an error $U*$ find the equivalent without errors U, and locate the error $u*$ in $U*$ and its equivalent u in U;
2. Retrieve the response using the AIML correction category "on the fly" for u;
3. Retrieve the standard response for U;

The AIML category responsible for the correction on the fly will simply repeat u as shown below:

```
<category>
  <pattern>ON-THE-FLY *</pattern>
  <template><star/></template>
</category>
```

The first step in this sequence is mandatory for each correction: we need to extract the trouble source and to find the target hypothesis.

Simple and contrasting corrections with minimal accountings

Templates for simple corrections with minimal accountings of the error from Example 10.2 will not differ much from the correction on the fly chosen by the native speaker in the dataset. However, the machine will not post a message responding to the interpersonal trajectory immediately after the correction. The chatbot will give the user a chance to react to the correction.

Example 10.3. A simple correction with minimal accountings.

i `User` hast du etwas über deutsche Gruppe PUR gehören?
i+1 `Bot` gehört :-)
i+2 User's turn

The place of the emoticon in the correction may be occupied by one of the emoticons from the set A_{min}. Other versions of the correction in turn i+1 may be, for instance:

- "gehört" :-)
- *gehört* :-)
- -- gehört -- :-)

The corresponding AIML template for the simple correction with minimal accountings will look as follows:

```
<category>
  <pattern>SIMPLE-MINIMAL *</pattern>
  <template>
    <random>
       <li>"<star/>" :-)</li>
       <li>*<star/>* ;-)</li>
       <li>--<star/>-- B-)</li>
     </random>
  </template>
</category>
```

A repetition of the error and a negation added to this will form a contrasting correction with minimal accountings:

Example 10.4. Contrasting correction with minimal accountings.

i `User` hast du etwas über deutsche Gruppe PUR gehören?
i+1 `Bot` gehört, nicht gehören ;-)
i+2 User's turn

The following AIML category will take care of the generation of this type of correction:

```
<category>
  <pattern>CONTRASTING-MINIMAL FROM * TO *</pattern>
  <template><star index=1/>, nicht <star index=2/> :-)
  </template>
</category>
```

Even if only this simple correction format is used, a few variants are available to the machine in order to avoid repetitiveness, which is perceived by users as demotivating and disturbing the interaction (Bickmore and Picard, 2005). In both simple and contrasting corrections, the chatbot gives the user a chance to respond to the correction. However, if the chatbot notices that too much time has passed after the correction and the user does not say anything, the chatbot may take the initiative.

Simple and contrasting corrections with rich accountings

Simple corrections with rich accountings at the beginning of the interaction with a conversational agent may have the following form:

- Falls ich das korrigieren darf: “gehört" :-) Ich sage das nur, weil du sonst sehr gut Deutsch sprichst :-)

An exposed correction following a different sequence of repair with linguistic trouble source may be obtained from templates and have the following form:

- Wenn ich dich damit nicht nerve, habe ich noch eine Anmerkung: es sollte heißen “gehört" ;-).
- Sorry, aber es heißt “gehört" :-)

Each of these surface variants can be stored as a template in a special AIML category and retrieved in a similar way as for simple corrections with minimal accountings. An example of such an AIML category is shown below:

```
<category>
  <pattern>SIMPLE-RICH *</pattern>
  <template>
    <random>
       <li>Falls ich das korrigieren darf: "<star/>"
       Ich sage das nur, weil du sonst sehr gut Deutsch
       sprichst :-)</li>
       <li>Sorry, aber es heißt "<star/>" ;-)</li>
       <li>Wenn ich dich damit nicht nerve, habe
       ich noch eine Anmerkung: es sollte heißen
       "<star/>" :-)</li>
     </random>
  </template>
</category>
```

A template for a contrasting correction may deliver the following correction form:

- Entschuldigung wenn ich dich damit nerve, aber so was gibt es nicht in der Form “gehören" sondern es sollte heißen “gehört" :-)

The corresponding AIML category will look as follows:

```
<category>
  <pattern>CONTRASTING-RICH FROM * TO *</pattern>
  <template>Entschuldigung wenn ich dich damit nerve,
    aber so was gibt es nicht in der Form "<star index=1/>"
    sondern es sollte heißen "<star index=2/>" :-)
  </template>
</category>
```

Each of the correction templates needs to be specified separately and to contain a placeholder for the correct word and the repetition of the trouble source. In addition, they may be split over several turns to make the messages shorter. Other variants can be created with the sets of accountings specified in Section 7.3. The accounting sets may be extended with other expressions, and new sets of accountings may be introduced. This will make the number of potential correction surfaces for each of the formats even larger. However, at most one of the surface variants should be presented to the user. A strategy for this selection is needed. A random selection as is common in AIML is one way for the implementation to go, but not the only one possible.

Repair other-initiation-based corrections

Various templates for corrections based on repair other-initiation may be created based on the corresponding formal model:

- Was heißt das, gehören. Meinst du “gehört"? :-).
- Gehören --??? Meinst du ’gehört’? :-)

However, in the dataset this type of correction was used only to correct lexical errors. Native speakers use this type of correction to correct lexical errors when learners used a word not existing in German or an existing word in a wrong context. Although errors of form can potentially be corrected by repair other-initiation-based formats, such corrections may be misplaced in a Conversation-for-Learning but appropriate in a language classroom.

10.4.2 Generation of embedded and integrated corrections

The chatbot technology used in the implementation case study foresees a very simple mechanism for finding a response to any user question, namely, select an answer from a predefined list of possible answers. To cover as many potential inputs as possible, a lot of generic responses to questions are part of the AIML-based brain of the chatbot. A typical example of this behaviour is shown below: for every polar question starting with something matching to GEHST DU *, the same response will be delivered to the user:

```
<category>
  <pattern>GEHST DU *</pattern>
  <template>
     Nur wenn mich jemand auf seinem Laptop mitnimmt.
   </template>
</category>
```

This simple question-answering mechanism does not require response generation in real time. Therefore, the choice between interjection-based and repetition-based answers to deal with an error needs to be determined in advance. ELIZA-like responses may be used to create repetition-based answers. An additional AIML processor can be introduced to retrieve the information about the error.

In the example below we call such a processor `<contained-error>`. The processor in the example returns either NOERROR, in which case the first response variant will be delivered to the user, or it returns ERROR, and the second variant of the response with a correction will be delivered to the user. In this case, the response to the user's utterance matching GEHST DU * may be produced by the following template:

```
<category>
  <pattern>GEHST DU *</pattern>
  <template>
    <think>
      <set name="contained-error-tmp">
        <contained-error><star/></contained-error></set>
    </think>
    <condition name="contained-error-tmp">
      <li value="NOERROR">
      Nur wenn mich jemand auf seinem Laptop mitnimmt.</li>
      <li value="ERROR">
      Ich gehe <star/>, aber nur wenn mich jemand auf
      seinem Laptop mitnimmt.</li>
    </condition>
  </template>
</category>
```

The star symbol is used in the patterns to match any input that follows GEHST DU. Every input is first normalised in order to cover at least a part of the variance in spelling and frequent typos. Therefore, the pattern GEHST DU * will match the normalised input, which is in the best case without error. The same part of the input is then repeated in the answer, if the answer template contains the `<star/>` tag. For the error check, however, the original user input needs to be stored by the chatbot. An embedded correction should repeat the *corrected* version of the input matched by the star symbol.

With regard to error coverage, standard AIML interpreters make use of simple replacements for input normalisation to make pattern recognition more stable. This is in general not sufficient for dealing with the variety of learner errors, but can be used to recognise special cases of spelling errors. String replacements are defined in a separate file and performed prior to matching the input to the most likely pattern. The AIML interpreter knows all recognisable errors in advance and can reuse this information later in the various correction formats. Spell checkers can be used to recognise a large number of errors. In this case, the information about performed changes in the input string needs to be stored and made available for the `<contained-error>` processor.

Integrated corrections usually contain emphasis of the corrected error. In this case, simple ELIZA-like repetitions are in general not sufficient if the exact error location is not known. The information about the replaced strings can be used to highlight the replacement only on the string level. Additional NLP tools such as a spellchecker and a parser need to be involved to deal with learner language, perform error recognition and highlight the corrected error.

10.5 Discussion and conclusions

In order to determine what is required from the computational perspective to simulate sequences of OISR, an implementation case study was set up. It was tested in the course of the case study what kind of metalinguistic information might be required, what kind of NLP tools might be necessary, and where the limitations are. With a very simple conversational technology such as an AIML-based chatbot, it is already possible to make recognition of repair other-initiations part of the system using the model presented in this chapter.

The implementation case study covered only a simplified version of all possible repair carry-outs. Repairs were generated from a pre-processed Wiktionary dump called ExplanationDB. The database contained synonyms, meaning explanations, examples and notes on pragmatics. If multiple meanings of a trouble source were found in the database, the machine generated an explanation for each of the meanings based on a response template. If examples were available, each meaning was accompanied by an example. More sophisticated language technology than a simple AIML-based chatbot is required to cover the broad range of repair carry-out formats found in the empirical data.

Any of the formats for exposed corrections realised in a side sequence in a dialogue can be used to correct any of the errors. Template-based responses can be formed according to the models of exposed corrections. The slots in the templates need to be filled by the corrected version of the trouble source. Even with a technology as simple as chatbots, this may be sufficient to implement these correction formats.

Embedded and integrated corrections, however, need to repeat the constituent with the corrected error in the answer within the interpersonal trajectory, without a separate correction side sequence. Simple ELIZA-like mechanisms like those used in chatbots may be exploited to generate repetition-based answers (Weizenbaum, 1966). However, error recognition tools need to reliably find the correct target hypothesis.

To set up a live chatbot test, many adjustments need to be performed in the chatbot besides those related to OISR: learner-language understanding, dealing with errors in repair initiations, what to talk about and how to deal with a user's frustration because of the limited conversational capabilities. The local models of OISR can be evaluated by standard quantitative methods using precision/recall metrics with the accuracy of the repair initiation recognition and trouble source extraction as evaluation criteria. However, even human conversation participants may have difficulties in recognition of an other-initiation of repair due to a learner's limited linguistic knowledge of the target language. We discussed this issue in Section 4.2.2. Therefore, we should not expect 100% accuracy in the recognition of repair initiations in conversation with non-native speakers.

The evaluation of the local models for error corrections comes along with the following challenges. First, we need to decide what is a "good" correction. Second, we need to find an appropriate measurement scale for the error corrections. A good correction can be a correction that finds the best target hypothesis. Then the evaluation of corrections would be equivalent to the evaluation of the error recognition component. This was, however, not the subject of this research. Instead, a good correction may be seen as a correction that is positively perceived by the user of the chatbot. This means that the correction decision component chose the most appropriate place and form of the correction. In this case, we would evaluate the correction decision model, but not so much the local correction models. Given that the local correction templates formulated as AIML categories already use the correctly extracted trouble source and the repair, and simply need to insert one of them or both into a template prepared by a human author, we can see that there is not much work left for the machine to generate the final correction. Therefore, in this implementation, we can assume that at least the local correction practices will be of high quality.

Moreover, a non-present repair or correction does not mean that it is missing. Other things may be done instead of a repair initiation, and other strategies may be chosen by conversation participants to deal with trouble in understanding. The learners ask native speakers to explain something unclear because they assume that the native speakers are able to do it, because it is native speakers' "territory of knowledge" (Heritage, 2012). However, in the tests with the machine, the users may choose to look up the dictionary instead of a repair initiations, if they do not trust the machine's language understanding and language generation capabilities. Therefore, the most reasonable way to evaluate these dialogue models is qualitative analysis of chat protocols combined with other methods of qualitative social research, such as interviews and questionnaires.

The question of the evaluation of the models presented in this book correlates with the more general question of the evaluation of dialogue systems. As (Kaleem et al., 2016) put it, "The evaluation of conversational agents is an area that has not seen much progress since the initial developments during the early 90's". Multiple quantitative metrics common in the machine translation domain have been applied to the evaluation of dialogue systems, for instance (Galley et al., 2015; Li et al., 2016). These approaches have been criticised for their insufficiency in the dialogue domain, because they mainly rely on word overlaps in speakers' turns, which is not supported by dialogue data (Liu et al., 2016).

Other metrics that rely on measuring task success (Walker et al., 1997) are more suitable for task-centred conversation, but less applicable to application cases where the conversation itself is the task. Moller et al. (2009) formulated a taxonomy that takes the quality of services and the quality of experience into account. However, as the authors note in their conclusions, there are issues with the applicability of the metrics, e.g. standardised questionnaires are needed to assess the dialogue systems, and there are issues with the interpretation of the results. In a system like an Artificial Conversation Companion, the difference between the quality of services and the quality of experience is blurred (see also (Varela et al., 2014) for a discussion of the same problem).

MacTear et al. (2016, Chapter 17) provide a comparison of different approaches to the evaluation of conversational interfaces. They argue that performance metrics do not disclose any information about the quality of the dialogue system. Quality assessment can be only reasonably done when it involves the users of the system.

With this background, the applicability of the quality assessment measures to the implementation described in this chapter is rather limited. A conversation between an artificial conversation partner and its potential users needs to go far beyond sequences of repair and error corrections. Therefore, any evaluation of the system in its current state will not say much about the value of the proposed models.

Chapter Summary

In this chapter, we discussed a practical implementation of the models introduced in Part II of the book. In addition to the repair models which were the focus of the research, this chapter discussed other design issues such as input restriction and a chatbot's individual interaction style. An implementation of the proposed model using the chatbot technology based on the Artificial Intelligence Mark-up Language was discussed.

11

Future Research Directions

Abstract The preceding chapters of this book raised more questions than they answered. In this chapter we outline potential research directions that would build on the results of this study or continue the research initiated in this work.

11.1 Introduction

We discussed various types of participant orientations to their linguistic identities in Chapter 3. All of them are important for computational modelling of corresponding types of sub-dialogues for conversational agents in Communicative ICALL. However, only a small part of them could be made the focus of this book. Each of the remaining types of positioning described in Chapter 3 is a potential research challenge and can be approached by methods used for data analysis and modelling in this book. The types of positioning handled only sparingly in the present work include:

1. Face work and evaluation
2. Meta-talk about learning and collaborative learning
3. Repair types other than exposed error corrections and embedded corrections in answers to polar questions, as well as other-initiated self-repair initiated by the learner.

In addition, the repair types that became the main subject of this work triggered other, follow-up questions. In this chapter, we outline future research directions for which we made a start and identified in this book. Some of the problems may be approached by further analysis of the dataset that was created in order to make this kind of research possible. More or different types of data might be required for the others. In this case we will make suggestions about how the necessary data can be obtained.

S. Höhn, *Artificial Companion for Second Language Conversation*,
https://doi.org/10.1007/978-3-030-15504-9_11

11.2 Further work on repair for Communicative ICALL

Section 3.4 described various types of repair with linguistic trouble source that make participants' linguistic identities relevant in conversation. Although this work is dedicated to models of repair to a great extent, several repair types are left for future studies, namely:

1. Other-initiated self-repair when the learner is the trouble-speaker, which goes beyond error corrections formatted as repair initiations.
2. Self-initiated other-repair when the learner is the trouble-speaker, such as word searches.
3. Embedded corrections in places other than answers to polar questions, for instance other types of second pair parts and post-expansions (nexts to the second pair parts).

Moreover, only a preliminary, initial decision model for corrections in a Conversation-for-Learning was specified in this work. The idea of an intensity-based correction format classification introduced by Tudini (2010) and extended here is definitely worth further attention and may be promising for Communicative ICALL research. In the remainder of this section we discuss some open problems and suggest how they can be addressed.

11.2.1 Other-initiated non-native speaker's self-repair

We discussed the relevance of other-initiated self-repair when the learner is the trouble-speaker for Communicative ICALL in Section 3.4.2. With regard to SLA theory it falls under the concept of *meaning negotiation*, which is seen as important for language learning (Varonis and Gass, 1985). Although it was partially handled as a type of error correction (repair initiation-based correction formats), a systematic analysis and modelling of all such repair sequences remains for a future study. In particular, a description of differences between repair with linguistic trouble source and all other kinds of trouble may be needed to formulate models for Communicative ICALL.

This type of repair initiation caught HCI researchers' attention, as discussed in Section 2.4.1. Because different formats of repair initiation are designed to signal troubles of different levels in terms of the Austin/Clark action ladder (Austin, 1962; Clark, 1996), a model systematically taking these differences into account may help to generate more natural repair initiations in order to deal with problems in speech recognition and language understanding.

11.2.2 Learner's self-initiated other-repair

In Section 3.4.3 I illustrated by a number of examples how word searches may be composed. Similar requirements for computational modelling are valid for word searches as for OISR. The machine will need to recognise that the learner initiated a word search and to extract the trouble source. However, the trouble in this case is the inability to find the proper word or expression. Therefore, a different way will be selected by the user to describe what she is looking for. To find abstract models for word searches might be a great challenge. This research question is related to such hard NLP problems as paraphrase recognition and generation (Regneri and Wang, 2012; Marton, 2013) and word sense disambiguation (Martin and Jurafsky, 2009, Ch. 20).

11.2.3 Embedded corrections located elsewhere

Only a small part of all turn types where embedded corrections were identified could be expressed in models for Communicative ICALL in this work. Many questions remained unsolved because of the problem complexity. Specifically, the following research questions and objectives may be addressed in future studies of embedded corrections:

1. Comparative analysis of embedded corrections in L1 and L2 talk: are there differences in environments where the corrections occur and their function?
2. Computational modelling of embedded corrections in non-answers to polar questions and in responses to non-polar questions are worth research efforts to complete the work that was started in this book. As a preliminary step, it might be necessary to complete the question-coding scheme initiated by Stivers and Enfield (2010). Responses to content questions and non-answers to polar question need to be classified first in order to complete the scheme. Systematic analysis of necessary modifications of the coding scheme to code text chat data may be needed.
3. A separate study focusing on responses with and without corrections may help to discover further reasons for non-present embedded corrections besides the error location and error types described in Section 6.4.4. This will allow us to make the correction decision model more stable.
4. Embedded corrections are based on repetitions; however, we need to keep in mind that repetitions have a function in talk. Repeating a reference to an object or an action in an answer to a question needs to be analysed through the lens of research on references in conversation (Schegloff, 1972; Enfield, 2007; Enfield et al., 2013) and referring-expression generation (Janarthanam and Lemon, 2009, 2010).
5. Further analysis and modelling of embedded corrections in post-expansions and sequence closings after errors in second pair parts would extend the current understanding of their role in interaction. This is a necessary step to prepare computational models for such embedded corrections, not only for ICALL. Task-oriented dialogue systems and chatbots that constantly need confirmations that they fulfil tasks correctly can benefit from embedded corrections instead of explicit confirmations, making the interaction closer to natural.

11.2.4 Exposed corrections of language form

Correction of language form in a Conversation-for-Learning is very rare, as our dataset shows and as has already been reported in the academic literature, for instance (Hauser, 2010). The majority of all linguistic errors corrected in my dataset were focused on meaning (both exposed and embedded). As Hauser (2010) shows in his analysis of other-corrections of language form in a Conversation-for-Learning, language learners may focus on form after an error occurs so that a repair sequence is placed between the error and the correction. In such cases the corrections are exposed and the errors are usually repeated in order to renew the context. The difference between focus on form and focus on meaning may be important for the correction decision; however, their sequential position plays a role, too. Further analysis of error corrections with the focus on form as opposed to those focused on meaning is required in order to understand participants' decisions and the influence of the interaction process, and with the purpose to make better distinctions for correction decision models in Communicative ICALL.

11.2.5 A more stable correction decision model

A formal decision model for correction based on the preliminary model proposed in Chapter 8 needs further investigations. The following steps may be helpful on the way to a formal definition of a correction decision model. As explained in Chapter 8, finding a correction decision model was not the focus of the work in the early stages when the data were collected. Therefore, little information is available about participants' motivation to correct and learners' correction perception. Direct connections between participant's feelings about corrections and the data logs cannot be completely reconstructed from our dataset. A different study focusing on this problem may be designed in a way that allows us to grasp further important factors in conversation that make a correction relevant. A more stable and accurate model may follow from such a study.

Simmons-Mackie and Damico (2008) examined the use of exposed and embedded corrections in individual and group aphasia therapy sessions. They found that exposed corrections occur more frequently in sessions focusing on repairing deficits, as opposed to embedded corrections, which dominated in sessions focusing on natural communication events. It will be interesting to see, whether similar regularities can be found in Conversations-for-Learning. Because there is a variation within this speech exchange system with regard to distributions of social and pedagogical talk, a comparative analysis of different types of "sessions" may help us to find more features to define a more accurate correction decision model.

A decision to correct is not only a binary yes/no answer, but a selection of a specific correction format. For instance, as argued in Chapter 8, there is a preference for embedded corrections, but they are not always produceable. The correction decision model introduced in Chapter 8 suggests a correction format should be selected according to the state of social interaction among other factors. As already noticed by Tudini (2010) and supported by this study, all error corrections are intuitively perceived as more intensive or less intensive. An intensity-based model for error corrections might have the advantage of an intuitive mapping from the state of social interaction to a correction format selection. This idea is closely related to the vision of conversational systems and virtual personal assistants as our long-term companions. Section 11.4 will outline a few ideas regarding modelling long-term interaction and social closeness with inspiration from Conversation Analysis.

11.3 Dialogue Processing and Affective Computing

In this work we focused specifically on text chat interaction with non-native speakers. The same methodology (CA-informed data-driven design and modelling) may be used to tackle open problems in Dialogue Processing and Affective Computing, such as creation of individual user models, topic detection and tracking, and emotion recognition and generation. As argued in Section 2.4.1, the relationships between CA and NLP (Computer Linguistics) was difficult from the beginning. However, optimistic voices have predicted a happy common future for these two disciplines. One of the objectives of this work was to strengthen the multidisciplinary connections between the two disciplines. This section suggests further topics for collaborative investigation.

11.3.1 Dialogue topics

Different definitions of "topic" can be found in the conversational agent literature, linguistics, discoure analysis and social sciences. The academic literature frequently appeals to an intuitive understanding of "topic" when attempts at automatic detection of what people talk or write about are made, for instance (Dong et al., 2006).

Building on conversational maxims by Grice (1975), Brown and Yule (1983, p. 84) use the notion of *speaking topically*, which means "making your contribution relevant in terms of the existing topic framework". The mechanism of *speaking topically* may be noticed in conversations where participants pick up elements from others' contributions and incorporate them into their own contributions (Brown and Yule, 1983, p. 84). A similar conceptual understanding of topic is frequently used in the academic literature on conversational agents. For instance, Breuing et al. (2011) define a topic as *an independent, self-selected category superordinate to a co-constructed sequence of dialog contributions*.

While conversational agent research is mainly concerned with topic detection, classification and selection (don't talk about dispreferred topics!), conversation analysis investigates how to talk on-topic or to change a topic, thus how a talk on-topic is sequentially organised and managed. Schegloff (2007) describes two in principle different organisations for talk on-topic, which are both sequentially post-expansions:

1. Preferred responses are relevant for sequence closing and dispreferred responses are relevant for post-expansions.
2. Preferred responses lead to expansions and dispreferred responses imply sequence closing.

With regard to *speaking topically* (Brown and Yule, 1983), the contributions are relevant in both response versions for each of the cases; however, the interactional, sequential consequences are different in each case.

To improve the abilities of conversational agents to *speak topically*, both understanding of what the talk is about and the ability to perform a relevant next action with regard to topical talk (e.g. sequence closing) are important for conversational agent research. Methods and data used in this book may be applied to create data-driven models of sequence openings and closings as well as topic-proffering utterances.

Action recognition (what the user is doing with a particular utterance) is as important as recognition of what the user wants to talk about. For instance, the adjacency pairs in apology-based face work sequences described in Chapter 3 (learners apologise for their errors) should not be understood by the agent as a user's wish to talk about language errors. The preferred responses in the corresponding examples were sequence closures in the form of encouragement (e.g. Examples 3.1 and 3.2 in Section 3.2, pages 79 and 80). Such adjacency pairs can be taken as templates for conversational agents communicating with language learners. Other typical adjacency pairs may be found, too.

11.3.2 Emotions in text chat

Symbolic and lexicalised representations of emotions are available in chat to express participants' emotional state. Various attempts have been made to describe and to classify representations of emotions in chat, for instance for German (Orthmann, 2004). However, display of affective states is not the only function of emotions in text chat.

We saw in this work how emoticons may be used as accountings in error correction turns. Vandergriff (2014) analysed pragmatic functions of emoticons in chat between native and non-native speakers of English. The identified functions of emotions are markers of affective stance (joy, happiness or relief), but also as keying markers or contextualisation cues. Two functions of the latter were identified by Vandergriff (2014):

1. orientation to a dispreferred action and mitigation of the face-threatening potential of requests, and
2. cueing conversational humour, irony and contextual inappropriateness.

A similar study may be performed on the corpus used for this work to continue work on pragmatic functions of emotions in native/non-native speaker chat and to detect possible differences in use of emoticons by language learners who are native speakers of different languages. A comparative analysis of multiple existing corpora will be an advantage (e.g. Russian native speakers who learn German (Höhn, 2015b), Swedish native speakers who learn English (Sauro, 2009) and Australian English native speakers who learn Italian (Tudini, 2003)). Differences in speech exchange systems need to be considered.

Such qualitative studies have the potential to provide empirically grounded classifications and data-driven models for automatic emotion recognition and sentiment understanding for different types of applications, such as sentiment analysis of short text messages (for example product evaluations, Twitter news and Facebook comments), artificial companions for daily care (Wilks et al., 2015; Ren et al., 2014) and artificial coaches (Yasavur et al., 2014).

Vandergriff (2014) outlined possible connections between non-native speakers' use of emoticons and language proficiency. If there are differences in use of emoticons by native and non-native speakers, they may be part of interactional competence in computer-mediated communication, and need to be acquired as part of the foreign language. Communicative ICALL applications may help to address this learning goal.

11.3.3 Improving conversational agents with Conversation Analysis

Various problems have been investigated in statistical NLP and CA separately, such as references in conversation, temporal and spatial expressions, paraphrases and formulaic expressions. From this perspective, only insufficient multidisciplinary collaboration can be observed between the two disciplines. However, NLP and Computer Linguistics may greatly benefit from CA results and methods, specifically in dialogue-focused research.

In this work, we only covered a small part of the variety of structures in chat conversations, namely two types of repair with linguistic trouble source. However, in order to implement the findings in a real-life application more effort needs to be put into the opposite of them, thus "normal talk". In this research we mentioned such problems as references in conversation for the purpose of trouble source recognition and correction format generation. A lot of work has been done on references in conversation outside repair sequences. Research results from CA on references in conversation may help to improve existing reference resolution techniques, for instance by more specific models for references to places and persons (Enfield, 2007; Enfield et al., 2013; Schegloff, 1972) and expert-novice talk (Isaacs and Clark, 1987).

As was discussed in the example of emoticons in chat in Section 11.3.2, classifications and models for recognition of pragmatic functions of specific structures in conversation might help to improve language understanding models. We can suggest several areas where we might see a potential knowledge transfer from CA:

1. Work on epistemic stances and states (Heritage, 2012).
2. Questions and answers (Stivers and Enfield, 2010; Heritage, 2012; Schegloff, 1988).
3. The role and pragmatic function of repeats (Perrin et al., 2003; Stivers, 2005).
4. The role of figurative idiomatic expressions in topical changes (Holt and Drew, 2001, 2005).

11.3.4 Using NLUaaS and chatbots for Communicative ICALL

Though we suggested in Section 4.6.2 that current intent-based NLU services are not completely suitable as a back end for an Artificial Conversation Companion, they may have several advantages. First, the intent-based approach to conversation may be promising at least in sub-dialogues where specific tasks need to be completed. For instance, the participants of each conversation in the dataset that we used for this research made appointments for the subsequent chat session at the end of each of the first seven conversations. The turn types typically occurring in such sequences can be mapped to intents such as availability requests and date/time suggestions. Second, some non-task-related sequences in conversation could be better classified and open new opportunities for, for instance, topic management. More specifically, first pair parts that initiate a topic are potential candidates for an intent-like classification. Finally, an NLU service can potentially be extended by a repair component similarly to the AIML-based baseline chatbot.

As discussed in Section 2.5, NLU services are usually involved in the implementation of conversational interfaces and chatbots. Although early chatbots have been criticised for their limited capabilities in language understanding (Klüwer, 2011), several attempts have been made to adapt chatbots for the purpose of language learning, for instance (Jia, 2009; Zakos and Capper, 2008). We discussed in Chapter 10 which types of repair can be implemented even with simple chatbot technology. This investigation can be continued with regard to other structures in conversation, such as sequence initiations and closings, making appointments and topicalisation, as suggested in Chapter 10.

Specific application scenarios may benefit from employing chatbots for language learning, for instance, acquisition of the recent orthography standard for native and non-native speakers. German orthography has changed several times, and language users have difficulties deciding what the current standard is (e.g. *am Mittwoch Nachmittag* vs. *am Mittwochnachmittag*). Chatbot technology might be useful to retrieve and learn the recent orthography standard. Similarly, information about specific structures in the native language of the user may be provided to the chatbot (*ogo!* as a news marker and surprise token in the dataset) and the chatbot might help the learner to acquire the corresponding structures in the foreign language.

11.3.5 Deep learning

Recent developments in machine learning for Natural Language Processing report remarkable results achieved in using various architectures of neural networks for dialogue state prediction, machine translation, natural language generation and speech recognition (Henderson et al., 2013; Serban et al., 2016; Li et al., 2016; Gupta et al., 2017; Yin et al., 2017). Each of the approaches to language-processing tasks relies on some assumptions about the language itself: sequence of phones, sequence of words, sequence of dialogue acts etc.

Conversation Analysis has documented in a huge number of publications that conversation is organised sequentially. However, conversation is seen in CA rather as a sequence of social actions than as a sequence of words. A very interesting research question may be what a CA-informed approach to using neural networks for dialogue systems might look like. What kind of annotated data would we need for training the model? How can the networks learn long-term dependencies, such as remembering relevant information and reusing it in future dialogues with the same person many conversations later?

A more specific but not much easier question is, can neural networks help to deal with contingency in, for instance, disambiguation tasks for repetition-based repair other-initiations and other social actions that have a similar format?

So far, the use of neural networks for language processing is grounded in other theories. It would be interesting to see whether CA-informed deep-learning techniques bring further advantages or improvements.

11.4 Long-term human-machine interaction

Artificial companions (Wilks, 2005), relational agents (Bickmore and Picard, 2005) and companion technologies (Wendemuth and Biundo, 2012) are the focus of multidisciplinary research projects related, for instance, to health, sports and fitness (Ståhl et al., 2009), ambient assisted living (Dorr et al., 2015; Caire and van der Torre, 2009), coaching and stress relief (Pulman et al., 2010; Wilks et al., 2015) and second language acquisition (Danilava et al., 2013a). The interpretation of the term *companionship* is slightly different for each of them, but they all have in common the expectation that the companion interacts with the user for a prolonged period of time and adapts its behaviour to the user's needs. (Danilava et al., 2012) argued that analysis and modelling of long-term interaction may be a promising approach to companionship. The authors outlined how the challenge of modelling long-term interaction may be addressed using methods of Conversation Analysis in the attempt to transfer the concept of *interaction profiles* into the field of Artificial Intelligence (Höhn et al., 2015).

From the classical computer science perspective, interaction profiles are defined by a static set of attributes to which values from a specified interval or set of classes can be assigned. For instance (de Alencar et al., 2014) specify a user's interaction profile as a set of attribute-value pairs where the attributes are input and output method (e.g. keyboard), physical and cognitive characteristics of the person (e.g. visual impairment and attention deficit), interests, literacy level and age. The interaction profile of each interaction participant as defined by Spranz-Fogasy (2002) emerges during the interaction and is influenced by all interaction participants and the interaction process. In this way, interaction profiles as understood by Spranz-Fogasy (2002) may be a useful concept for long-term human-machine interaction design. In particular, interactional practices of dealing with specific events in interaction can be modelled in a similar way to our formulation of local models of correction and explanations. Another model (or maybe a number of models) decides under which circumstances which of the local models may be activated. In this way, a different interaction profile emerges during the interaction with the user. We illustrated this perspective on the example of different profiles of "language experts" in Section 3.5.2. Conversational agents for roles other than a more knowledgeable language user in an equal-power speech exchange system may be designed in a similar way.

We started the discussion on the role of variations in orthography for the regulation of social closeness in Section 8.2.2. Further work on medium-specific variations in orthography and its relationship to social closeness on one hand and the language standard on the other hand needs to be done. We argued in Section 8.4 that a model for social closeness derived from CA results could be helpful for different applications where long-term human-machine interaction is desired, including Communicative ICALL. However, operationalisation efforts are needed to translate "Language of the closeness, language of the distance" (Koch and Oesterreicher, 1985) into data-driven computational models of social closeness in interaction. Because social closeness and intimacy are found to be interactional achievements (Rintel, 2015; Sacks, 1995), features indexing them can be translated into formal models by methods used in this book.

11.5 Effects on learning and learner corpus research

This work did not focus directly on the effect on language learning, however, it prepared a computational basis to implement the longitudinal language-learning methodology initiated and elaborated in CA-for-SLA (Kasper, 2004; Markee, 2008). With the findings of this work, recommendations for further directions in learner corpus research can be made. Because the non-presence of data is a huge problem for this kind of research, we make suggestions about how to overcome this limitation. Finally, we outline how a changed perspective on computer-assisted language learning may change the learning experience and, consequently, the learning effect.

11.5.1 Evidence of language learning

ICALL and Communicative ICALL research has been criticised for not paying enough attention to the aspects of learning and its lack of evaluation of a learning effect (Petersen, 2010; Wilske, 2014). The evaluation of learning effect by ICALL systems has been addressed using methods grounded in SLA theory, such as experimental comparison of specific types of corrective feedback provided by human tutors vs. those of ICALL systems (Petersen, 2010; Wilske, 2014). Such experimental methods are not feasible when evaluating a Conversation-for-Learning, because specific moments of learning such as error correction and repair initiations should not be elicited in a free conversation, as opposed to experiments in laboratory conditions. In addition, other, not so easily observable moments of learning may be present, such as learning by imitation. CA-for-SLA suggests a different method to track the effects on learning by tracking learning objects (specific expressions or words) and learning behaviour (specific interactional practices) in longitudinal studies (Markee, 2008). This research takes the perspective that this approach is more suitable for evaluation of effects on learning in Communicative ICALL applications.

We can suggest two specific directions in learning-behaviour and learning-object tracking that may be tracked automatically by an ICALL application:

- An analysis of postponed uptake after embedded corrections would help to get insights into noticing issues. Because embedded corrections do not make correcting the interactional business, there is no direct evidence of noticing of the correction by the learner.
- Immediate uptake after an exposed correction but postponed error repetition will help to track the stability of interlanguage modifications. Usually, this issue is approached by a comparison of results of immediate and delayed post-tests (Wen and Mota, 2015).

Learners' interactional competence may be measured in addition by metrics focused on their ability to perform specific social actions, such as formulating questions, initiating repair or providing appropriate responses to compliments. The last of these are very difficult even for proficient speakers (Hauser, 2010) citing (Golato, 2002, 2005). Classifications and typologies of repair other-initiations obtained from native-speaker talk offer a valuable base for comparison, for instance those described in (Drew, 1997; Dingemanse et al., 2014; Benjamin, 2013; Egbert, 2009; Enfield et al., 2013). This work provides the necessary computational models to track such development and to detect differences automatically in an ICALL application or in a traditional language classroom involving computer-mediated communication.

The *imitation hypothesis* formulated by Aguado Padilla (2002) suggests that second language learning may happen by imitation, similarly to first language acquisition. On the other hand, conversation participants adapt their language to the language of the co-participants. This phenomenon is referred to as *convergence* (Mitchell et al., 2012). It may be an interesting research question how these two concepts correlate in communication with language learners.

11.5.2 The data issue

As motivated in Section 2.3.2, data of high quality is an essential part of any data-driven research. Because several datasets of chat Conversations-for-Learning exist, studies requiring additional datasets might potentially be started without waiting for more data. However, the majority of the datasets of interest are not publicly available (Fredriksson, 2012; Tudini, 2010; Marques-Schäfer, 2013). An *open-data initiative* for CALL may be beneficial for all CALL and ICALL researchers, but also for learner corpus research and Natural Language Technology.

Given that such an open-data initiative is far from being a reality for now, it would be interesting to get more examples, for instance, of error corrections, with fewer data. We made a comparison between types of corrective feedback in classroom and chat-based Conversation-for-Learning. More examples of correction types present in both chat corpus and classroom data may be obtained from classroom datasets to improve local models of corrections.

Current language-learning platforms and social networks supporting instant messaging between language learners and native speakers have large quantities of data of desired types. For instance, Busuu[1] and Wespeke[2] targeted tandem language learners from the beginning, and their community of tandem learners is growing. Text chat is one of the communication options for the learners of different languages who benefit mutually from each other's native language skills. Collaboration with such platforms may be beneficial for data-driven research. Facebook is a place, too, where language-learning communities meet. New language-learning groups may be created with the purpose of data generation.

Wizard-of-Oz methodology is a popular solution to do research about technology that does not yet exist or is not mature enough for tests with users. Wizards normally receive instructions how to behave like a machine, and the users interact with a machine operated by the Wizard. At the beginning of this study we could not know what instructions a Wizard should receive to "behave like a language expert" in an informal chat. As a result of the present research it can be specified how to "do being a language expert". Some of the ways to "behave like a language expert" can even be implemented. However, we still have limitations given by language technology with regard to talk on topic, error recognition, emotion recognition and generation and so on. This is a state where a wizarded data collection might reasonably be attempted in order to test the models, to collect more data and to see if a machine might be accepted as a language expert by language learners.

With regard to repair annotation, addressed in Section 7.5.1, a new version of the corpus is being prepared where all repair types discussed in this book will be annotated. A new annotation scheme needs to be worked out that takes turn-taking, virtual adjacency, repair structure and repair formats into account in order to encode all the information found during this work. This will be a step towards preparing a repair-annotated corpus, which can be useful in many ways.

11.5.3 Rethinking language learning

Markee (2008) proposed a longitudinal methodology in CA-for-SLA to capture learning called learning-behaviour tracking. This methodology includes learning-process tracking and learning-object tracking. What Markee (2008) suggests is quite cumbersome for teachers; however, ICALL and other computer-assisted learning tools (not only for languages) may be good teaching assistants in tracking.

Our thinking about how learning happens is very much influenced by the ways in which we have been taught in traditional schools. This traditional approach to language learning is reflected in multiple ICALL applications where a language learner needs (or is forced) to learn vocabulary and grammar, and do different kind of workbook-style exercises in order to accomplish levels. And after all the levels, the person still cannot speak and use all the memorised words in a real-world communication. The radically emic perspective taken by CA-for-SLA may be a game changer in the understanding of learning, if applied systematically. The detailed analysis of conversations with non-native speakers from different speech exchange systems may be

[1] https://www.busuu.com/

[2] http://en-us.wespeke.com/index.html

a rich source of evidence of how learning *really* happens. This in turn may help to restructure ICALL applications and language classrooms in a way that optimises the natural way of learning, which may be very different from correction of linguistic errors.

Chapter Summary

In this final chapter, several future research directions have been outlined. They include a detailed analysis of the remaining repair types listed in Chapter 3 of this book that did not receive the same amount of attention as explanations and corrections. Further, potential research directions in dialogue processing, affective computing, long-term human-machine interaction and language learning have been proposed.

Part IV

Supplements

A

Data

Abstract This supplement chapter describes the process and the results of the data collection. In an attempt to resolve the problems that exist in investigating chat conversations, this appendix presents the data-capturing approach that was chosen to overcome the limitations of instant messaging dialogue datasets.

A.1 Data collection

This section documents the study design process, the decisions that had to be taken and the issues. Prior to setting up the data collection experiment, the data collection tools and three interaction scenarios were tested in a pilot study. Two candidates for the data collection method were considered:

Wizard-of-Oz experiment: human operators simulate technology; usually performed when the research is focused on users' behaviour while the desired technology does not exist (WOE).
Qualitative experiment: natural interaction modified in a controlled way (QE).

Based on the results of the pilot study, it was decided which of these methods should be used in the longitudinal study. Both methods are used for data collection where human behaviour in a near-to-natural environment is in focus, however the former is more frequently used in the HCI domain (Gould et al., 1983; Bradley et al., 2009), and the later is more commonly used in social science (Lamnek, 2010).

A.1.1 Study preparation

During the pilot study the following scenarios were tested:

$S1$ Interaction flow for the WOE setting where a German native speaker plays the role of an artificial conversation partner, i. e. pretends to be a chatbot.
$S2$ Interaction flow for the QE setting without any additional instructions.

S. Höhn, *Artificial Companion for Second Language Conversation*,
https://doi.org/10.1007/978-3-030-15504-9_12

$S3$ Interaction flow for the QE setting with an additional instruction for the native speaker of German to correct language mistakes of the learner.

These scenarios were tested on five pairs of voluntary participants. The Wizard participant in setting $S1$ was told to behave like a computer program without further instructions. The participants in settings $S2$ and $S3$ had to communicate over a forwarding chatbot system. They had an appointment for the chat made by the researcher, and the length of the chat was given. In a natural chat conversation, these restrictions usually do not exist. After each interaction, the researcher had a semi-structured phone interview with each of the interaction parties. The goal of the interviews was to find out how the participants felt while talking with a person whom they have never met before, and what was perceived as pleasant, what was disturbing or annoying. The interviewer made notes for questions and answers. The interviews have not been recorded. All interviews were based of the following frame questions:

1. Was there something difficult, unpleasant or annoying?
2. Was there something outstandingly pleasant?
3. Was it difficult to find a topic to talk about?
4. If the other party were a chatbot, would you like to chat with such a chatbot? (Only for $S2$ and $S3$.)

To parametrise a "pleasant" interaction, the researcher performed a set of chat-interviews combined with a questionnaire survey with two questions:

$Q1$ What is for you a pleasant interaction or a pleasant dialogue?
$Q2$ How would you describe an unpleasant interaction or an unpleasant dialogue?

The non-native speaker (NNS) participants were all Russian native speakers. They were allowed to give their answers either in German or in Russian; they could select the language in which they could better express themselves. German native speakers (NS) gave their answers in German.

Results of the Pilot Study

The interaction became unnatural if one of the parties thought that she/he talked to a computer program, as in $S1$. For example, the participants tended to test the conversational abilities of the machine in order to find out what the machine did not understand. They also tried to hide some personal information or used grammatical forms that they thought would be better understood by the machine. In addition, it was unclear to the researcher which specific instructions might be necessary for the Wizard. It was clear as a result of this part of the pilot study that an answer to the open question "What exactly is *doing being a language expert* in text chat?" is important in order to be able to formulate a functional specification for the computer program.

For setting $S3$, it was difficult for the participants to do error correction, because they did not want to be impolite or annoying. For setting $S2$, the participants reported that they had a nice conversation, but the situation itself ("let's chat") was unnatural; they did not know what to say at the beginning.

We selected the $S2$ setting for the final study, but we were aware of this risk. Furthermore, other risks for the data collection were identified and are described in the next section.

In order to create the connection between the data and participants' personal perception of the interaction, the researcher created a questionnaire based on the interview and survey outcome that needed to be filled in after each interaction by each of the participants of the longitudinal study. The questionnaire contained three open questions concerning a general description of the chat and pleasant and unpleasant moments of it, and two quantitative questions where the participants were asked to to quantify their feeling about the interaction (how pleasant was it in general, did the participant feel well understood by the partner, were there interesting topics etc.).

The risks for data collection

There are several risks for data collection and data quality that had to be taken into account for the longitudinal study. The major risk for data collection in this free chat interaction scenario was that study participants might not chat at all. We discuss here other risks that have to be kept in mind when targeting longitudinal data.

Topics: it is not so easy to find topics for communication with persons whom one has never seen or talked to before. Therefore, it was not granted that the participants can "just chat" for the period of time long enough for the analysis. It was possible that the participants would lose their interest or would not know what to say. In this case, the researcher planned to suggest some topics for the parties.

Motivation and relationship: the participants might lose their motivation if the interaction was unpleasant or boring, if they could not understand their partner or if they did not match at the interpersonal level. In this case the researcher planned to change the partners.

Language: despite the instruction to use the target language for communication, it was not guaranteed that the participants would not interact in a different language. This risk can be reduced by choosing a population which is not multilingual. In my data collection, both native speakers and non-native speakers of German spoke other languages and thus, this risk could not be avoided.

Learner language: although all learners were already at an advanced DaF level, it was still a foreign language for them. It was likely that they would use the lexical resources correctly. Misinterpretations of native speakers' utterances (e.g. social signals) are always possible. However, it is another important aspect for user modelling in ICALL applications.

A.1.2 The longitudinal instant messaging dialogues

CMC studies show that unlike face-to-face conversation where participants can spontaneously speak to each other, chat interaction presents difficulties related to the non-natural aspect of electronic devices (Loewen and Reissner, 2009). In order to make the IM data as natural as possible, the freedom of the participants was emphasised during their selection and throughout the experiment. Hence, all participants were volunteers to the experiment and the only instruction they received was "just chat!" As noted in the preceding section, the principal risk of this method is that participants might not chat at all. The communication was set up as explained below.

Participants, instructions and software

The participants were four native speakers of German (G1) and nine advanced learners of German as a foreign language (G2). NS were all from my private circle and learners were contacted through their university in the Republic of Belarus where they studied German as a foreign language in order to become German teachers. The communication started in May and ended in August 2012. Prior to starting the communication, participants had to sign an agreement that their IM talk would be recorded, and that an anonymised version of it would be used later on in a publicly available corpus.

Participants needed only a Jabber or a Google account on their electronic devices, and they could use any IM client of their preference or chat via the Google Talk web site. Participants were allowed to chat using any device (PC, laptop, smartphone or tablet) and they could switch these devices at their convenience. There were no time constraints and participants were also free to chat whenever they wanted during the weeks of data collection. There was no other instruction given to participants than "just chat!"

Participant	Age	Gender	Native language	Other languages	Occupation	Experience with IM
L01	22	F	ru	de, en, be	Student	No
L02	22	F	ru	de, en, be	Student	No
L03	22	F	ru	de, en, be	Student	Yes
L04	23	F	ru	de, en, be, it	Student	Yes
L05	20	F	ru	de, en, be	Student	Yes
L06	22	F	ru	de, en, be	Student	Yes
L07	22	F	ru	de, en, be	Student	Yes
L08	22	F	ru	de, en, be	Student	Yes
L09	22	F	ru	de, en, be	Student	Yes
N01	27	M	de	en, la	Student	Yes
N02	27	F	de	en, es	Teacher	Yes
N03	22	M	de	en, fr, lb	PhD student	No
N04	22	M	de	en, fr, es	Physicist	Yes

Table A.1: Participants' demographics in the longitudinal study; language abbreviations: ru (Russian), de (German), en (English), be (Belorussian), it (Italian), fr (French), es (Spanish), la (Latin), lb (Luxembourgish)

Connection between participants occurred through the chatbot because participants did not have the direct private address of their partners, rather the address alias registered by the chatbot. Figure A.1 illustrates how the users were connected, how the communication was designed, and what the role of the researcher was. If the NS sent a message to the NNS, technically, the message arrived at the NNS alias address of the forwarding chatbot, and the original message was immediately forwarded to the addressee. A copy of the message was automatically saved in the database. The forwarding chatbot was not visible to the participants, who could chat as if they were connected directly. However, the participants were informed that there was a special system connecting them with their partners. The forwarding chatbot was implemented using Google Web Toolkit and hosted on Google App Engine. These computer tools are offered by Google for free and are easy to use.

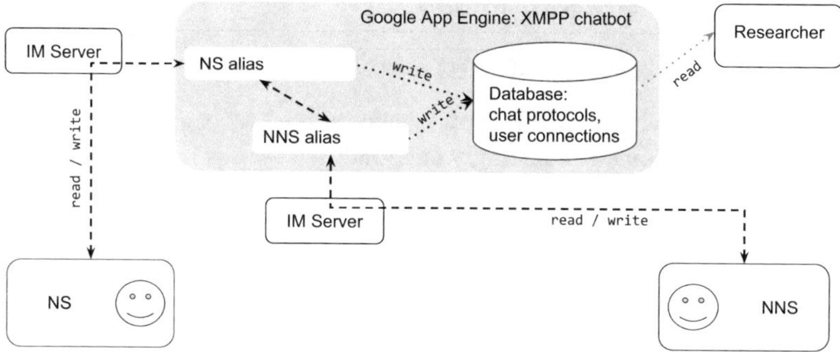

Fig. A.1: Connections between participants using the forwarding chatbot

Design of the study

Connections between the participants did not overlap: each participant from G1 communicated with exactly one participant from G2, whereas each participant from G2 communicated with two or three participants from G1. The communication was established over the forwarding chatbot described in the previous section. Though difficulties occurred in connecting the parties, participants could communicate with the same partner for the complete duration of the experiment. Since the participants communicated voluntarily in their leisure time, the total amount of time that they could invest in the experiment was subject to personal agreement with the researcher. Nevertheless, the lowest bound of time per connection was set to two sessions per week, each 30 minutes. The experiment was planned for four weeks, which corresponds to at least eight sessions of chat per pair.

For the first chat, the researcher coordinated the interaction between the parties. The pairs were chosen only according to participants' availability for the first interaction since the parties did not know anything about their partners at the beginning.

After each chat session, each of the parties had to fill in the questionnaire (online feedback form) described in Section A.1.4. The participants were allowed to answer the open questions in German or in Russian. This bilingual mode of filling in the questionnaire was more convenient for the Belorussian participants because sometimes they could better express themselves in their native language.

After eight sessions were completed, the researcher interviewed each participant separately via IM. Considering the advantages and disadvantages of IM interviews (Voida et al., 2004), learners' motivation to communicate and to engage and native speakers' motivation for "doing being a teacher" were studied, e.g. in providing error corrections and explanations of linguistic matters. All interviews were semi-structured, based on a set of frame questions provided in Section A.1.3 for completeness.

A.1.3 Questions for retrospective interviews

Frame questions for the retrospective IM interviews:

1. Was there something difficult, unpleasant or annoying?
2. Was there something outstandingly pleasant?
3. Was it difficult to find a topic to talk about?
4. If the other party were a chatbot, would you like to chat with such a chatbot?

Other questions were included in the interviews when they were relevant, for instance "Why did you decide not to correct errors?" to the NS and "Did you feel like the chat helps you with the language?" to the NNS.

A.1.4 Questionnaires

1. Wie angenehm war das heutige Chatgespräch insgesamt? (Scale)
2. Gib an, inwieweit die folgenden Aussagen für den heutigen Chat zutreffen:
   a) Wir haben interessante Themen / ein interessantes Thema besprochen.
   b) Das Thema des Gesprächs war mir unangenehm.
   c) Wir haben Spaß miteinander gehabt.
   d) Es war schwer, ein Gesprächsthema zu finden.
   e) Ich habe mit meinem Chatpartner nur gesprochen, weil man das von mir erwartet hat. Eigentlich habe ich besseres zu tun.
   f) Ich verstehe meinen Chatpartner gut.
   g) Mein Chatpartner versteht mich gut.
   h) Wir reden oft aneinander vorbei.
   i) Wir sind auf derselben Wellenlänge.
   j) Ich war erleichtert, als die 30 Minuten um waren.
3. Gab es etwas im heutigen Chatgespräch, was Dir unangenehm aufgefallen ist oder Dich gestört hat?
4. Was fandest Du bei dem heutigen Chatgespräch besonders angenehm?
5. Wie würdest Du den heutigen Chat beschreiben?

A.1.5 Technical issues

Technical support was provided by the researcher conducting the study and participants were invited to contact her in case of any difficulty. The following issues were identified during the experiment:

1. Connection: geographical moves during a chat created problems with the Internet connection and interrupted conversations. In order to minimise these problems, participants informed their partners about their moves and specific locational circumstances (e.g. entering a tunnel while travelling by train).
2. Awareness of presence: unlike classical IM clients, which offer the possibility to send an automatic status update to all contacts as an interactional resource (is somebody online or offline?), the forwarding chatbot always occurs online and participants cannot see each other directly. However, participants quickly learned to deal with this inconvenience by sending a presence request like "Are you there?", for instance.
3. IM service reliability: when IM provider services were not available, the connection was disrupted. This might lead to misunderstanding between the participants who did not know that the problem was due to the technical system rather than to their partners.
4. Connection between users in the database. One of the NS specified for the connection his private account at a free Jabber server. However, problems with IM service availability and reliability of this provider caused an account change. It was necessary to change the connection between this NS and all his partners in the DB. An additional unforeseeable issue was faced as Google offered all German users the choice to change from the *googlemail* to the *gmail* domain. One of the NS made use of this offer and did not think about the relevance of this change for her connection with her partners. The researcher had to clarify why the message exchange with this participant was disturbed.

A.1.6 Participant-related issues

- Missing appointments: this refers to situations where participants could not come to their appointments for chat and did not inform their partners.
- Time investment: participants might underestimate the time that they needed to invest in the experiment and not be able to fulfil their commitments. Their partner reported that they felt uncomfortable.
- Offline messages: the majority of participants were familiar with instant messaging in Skype and Facebook, but new to Jabber and Google Talk. Hence, they could not find messages that they had received while offline and would ask for help although they were provided with a help document at the beginning of the experiment. Problems related to offline messages required technical support that was very time-consuming for the researcher due to the wide variety of web browsers and IM clients and hardware.

- Duration: the experiment took longer than the planned four weeks. Some sessions were longer than 30 minutes (up to 90 minutes) and this might be an issue for specific research questions that might be addressed based on the presented corpus.
- Code-switching: the instruction to the participants was to chat in German as the target language in the study. Nevertheless, code-switching occurs into English and Russian within the dialogues in German. NNS used English translation as an interactional resource to explain the meaning of unknown German words to the NNS. One NS used Russian in greetings, farewells and repair sequences. In addition, NNSs used Russian words for greetings and farewell in order to teach their partners a bit of Russian.
- Responsiveness: this refers to uncontrolled elements that led to longer time intervals between messages, and that influenced the interaction. For instance, participants might be busy while chatting or network delays might slow down the delivery of messages. In addition, typing in a different language using the same devices as usually may be slower.

A.1.7 Ethical issues

At the beginning of the experiment, participants were informed about the purpose of the study, the recordings and the use of the produced chat protocols for research endeavours. Only those people who signed an agreement could participate in the experiment. Participants' privacy was protected and all email addresses and other identification possibilities were replaced after the data collection. Researchers only have access to the anonymised copy of the chat protocols. The demographic information about the participants was encoded in the corpus as provided in Table A.1.

A.2 Corpus creation

The attributes of each message stored in the database are timestamp, sender ID, receiver ID and message body (UTF-8 encoding). The log files for each pair of participants consist of eight dialogic sessions and some single messages that were not answered (non-dialogic). The corpus consists of 72 dialogues (eight dialogues by each of six pairs, nine dialogues by each of two other pairs, and seven dialogues by the nineth pair), which correspond to ca. 2500 minutes of instant messaging interaction, 4,548 messages with ca. 52,000 tokens in total, and ca. 6,100 single tokens both calculated with wordpunkt_tokenizer of Python Natural Language Toolkit (NLTK) (Bird et al., 2009). Three aspects are particulary important for longitudinal CMC studies for SLA:

1. Data quality: the chatbot-in-the-middle approach allows for the instant capture of messaging dialogues and at the same time preserves the natural way of IM communication already adopted by the users, i.e. the freedom of participants to chose IM client software and hardware, time and location for communication

is not disturbed. Moreover, participants deal quite competently with the limiting effects of technology-mediated communication such as network delays and connection interruptions.
2. SLA aspects: the chatbot-in-the-middle approach allows for the analysis of learning during instant messaging between NS and NNS of German. Hence, corrective feedback (Lyster et al., 2013), meaning negotiations (Varonis and Gass, 1985) and embedded corrections (Jefferson, 1987) were analysed as described in detail in this book. Following the imitation hypothesis (Aguado Padilla, 2002), it could be observed that learning takes place in chat also by imitation.
3. Long-term interaction: having a nice conversation and curiosity is the most important motivation for long-term interaction. "Being taught" by the NS is only a secondary aspect for the NNS. However, it was perceived as helpful by NNS if the NS and NNS engaged in talk about linguistic matters. According to Loewen and Reissner (2009), participants may have difficulties in CMC scenarios. Our analysis of CMC with the chatbot-in-the-middle shows, however, that instant messaging participants may deploy different intelligent strategies in order to deal with technology-mediated communication.

The dataset was initially annotated in the following way:

1. Dialogue moves in sequences of corrective feedback and meaning negotiation.
2. Partial error annotation.

Two versions of the corpus were published, with and without annotations (Höhn, 2015b). A new repair-annotated corpus version is planed for publication.

The annotation was performed by two independent annotators in the time from August to September 2013. The first annotator was a non-native German speaker with near-native fluency in German and Russian as native language, with a strong professional background in linguistics, natural language processing and language teaching. The second annotator was a native German speaker with no professional background in linguistics but with strong knowledge of the German language. In August 2014 and in February 2015, the annotation was rechecked by the first annotator; several annotation errors and ambiguous cases were corrected.

A.2.1 TEI-P5 modules and customisation

The TEI-P5 standard already contains several customisations for spoken interaction data, poetry, linguistic corpora and drama. Chat or instant messaging data have similar features with some of these, but none of the existing customisations could be used without modification and with the appropriate semantics of the tags. Therefore, the decision was taken to create a new customised annotation scheme using the existing TEI customisation for linguistic corpora as a basis. This allows for continuous extension of the annotation of linguistic phenomena in the dataset.

For the purpose of the related PhD project only annotation of repair sequences in chat has been performed, and the TEI schema was customised according to the annotation requirements (see Section A.2.4 below).

The corpus is provided as a set of 10 files: one root file containing the description of the corpus and information about participants (TEI header), and nine files with chat logs produced by nine pairs of participants, one file per pair. Each file containing chat logs includes all dialogues produced by one pair of participants. The root file contains links to each of those files.

A.2.2 Text replacements

In general, the original spelling and textual symbols used are kept as produced by the users. However, there are a few exceptions made for the purpose of storing the data in XML format and data analysis. All the replacements are summarised in Table **??**.

Original	Replaced by
&	&
All posted hyperlinks	HYPERLINK
Facebook ID	FACEBOOK_ID_{LXX,NXX}
Email address	EMAIL

Table A.2: Text replacements

A.2.3 Chat structure in TEI-P5 XML

The goal of this annotation was to provide an encoding for chat data conforming with TEI-P5. Two new tags were introduced:

- `<message>` contains the text of one instant message produced by a chat participant OR more than one non-empty message line (`<ml>` tag). Message lines were introduced for cases where chat participants inserted line breaks in their messages. Different lines may relate to different previous messages of the partners, and need to be linked separately. Important attributes of a message are sender, timestamp and id. The sender is specified by the standard TEI attribute `who` and is linked to a chat participant listed in the root file. The `timestamp` attribute specifies the server time when the message arrived at the server (time zone GMT+0, which needs to be recalculated to determine the actual time in the time zones of the chat participants - Germany and Belarus).
- `<ml>` contains a message line if and only if the sender of the message inserted breaklines in the message.

The corresponding schema is contained in the file `tei_corpus_chat.rng`, which is provided with the corpus.

A.2.4 Chat log annotation

For the purposes of the PhD project, the data have been annotated according to two classifications:

1. Corrective Feedback (CF) as explained by Lyster et al. (2013). The sequences containing CF usually consist of three types of interactional moves described in classroom research literature: error, correction, uptake.
2. Meaning Negotiation (MN) as introduced by Varonis and Gass (1985). According to this model, a MN sequence is composed of 4 moves: trouble source, indicator, response, reaction to response. The messages were labelled according to these types of moves.

All moves in these sequences may consist of several turns (messages). The TEI `note` tag is used for explanations of some complicated cases of annotation (ambiguities, complex sequences).

All of these sequences are repair sequences from the point of view of Conversation Analysis. However, at the beginning of the related PhD project the data analysis was influenced by the language classroom research and Second Language Acquisition theory.

Corrective Feedback

Types of Corrective Feedback (CF) adopted for this work are:

- conversational recast,
- repetition,
- clarification request,
- explicit correction,
- explicit with metalinguistic explanation (MLE),
- didactic recast,
- metalinguistic clue,
- elicitation,
- paralinguistic signal.

The types of the corrections are explained in the article by Lyster et al. (2013). Not all of them occur in the dataset because of the text-based nature of the chat and due to the informality of the conversation in contrast with a teacher-fronted classroom from which the original classification was obtained. Metalinguistic clues, elicitations, repetitions and paralinguistic signals were not found in CF-sequences in this dataset.

An example of an annotated CF-sequence is provided below:

```
<im:message xml:id="L06N0320120710-281"
who="deL1L2IM-root.xml#L06"
timestamp="2012-07-10T08:44:09">
man kann versuchen </im:message>
<im:message xml:id="L06N0320120710-282"
who="deL1L2IM-root.xml#N03"
```

```
timestamp="2012-07-10T08:44:29">
[[wir koennen es versuchen]] </im:message>
<im:message xml:id="L06N0320120710-283"
who="deL1L2IM-root.xml#N03"
timestamp="2012-07-10T08:44:32"> :-) </im:message>
<im:cfseq>
<im:cfturn turntype="ts" corresp="L06N0320120710-281"/>
<im:cfturn turntype="cf" corresp="L06N0320120710-282"
cftype="explicit_correction"/>
</im:cfseq>
```


No uptake was produced in this sequence.

Partial error annotation

The error annotation was performed in place (the error is tagged where it occurs). If an item is missing (missing main verb or missing prefix), the content of the tag is empty. The following error types were annotated in the corpus (all occurrences of them, not only the corrected ones).

1. Morpho-syntactic errors:
   a) Missing main verb in Futur 1 (future simple): missing_main_verb_futur1
   b) Wrong word order in a sentence. Only the following types have been annotated:
      - Wrong position of the main verb in the main or subordinate close, or missing main verb.
        Possible types:
        missing_finite_verb_main_clause
        missing_finite_verb_subordinate_clause
        position_finite_verb_main_clause
        position_finite_verb_subordinate_clause
      - Wrong position of or missing separable prefix in the verb.
        Possible types:
        missing_verb_prefix_main_clause
        missing_verb_prefix_subordinate_clause
        position_verb_prefix_main_clause
        position_verb_prefix_subordinate_clause.
2. Lexical erros: only lexical errors in collocations. Definition, classification and types for locations: s. Paper "Towards a Motivated Annotation Schema of Collocation Errors in Learner Corpora". Examples of collocations: *frei haben* (En: *have free time), leicht fallen* (En: *be easy for someone*), *Fliege machen* (En: *to leave*, colloquial).
   Possible types:
   substitution | creation | synthesis | analysis | different_sense
   Possible locations:
   base | collocate | collocation

```
<im:error
errtype="position\_finite\_verb\_subordinate\_clause"
target="man kann darüber recherchieren" corrected="NO">
man darüber rescherschieren kann</im:error>.
```

NOTE: The error annotated above can be analysed and corrected in a different way (multiple target hypotheses). An alternative annotation of the same error is shown below.

```
<im:message xml:id="L07N0320120716-602"
who="deL1L2IM-root.xml#L07"
 timestamp="2012-07-16T19:29:15">
 [content hidden for the example]
 und das wichtigste ich müsse so spät wie möglich heiraten,
<altGrp>
 <alt>
  <im:error errtype="substitution" location="collocate"
   target="sonst geht alles kaputt" corrected="NO"/>
  </alt>
 <alt>
  <im:error errtype="missing_main_verb_futur1"
   target="sonst wird alles kaputt gehen" corrected="NO"/>
 </alt>
sonst wird alles kaputt
</altGrp>
 ...)))))) xD </im:message>
```

Meaning Negotiation

According to the model of a Meaning Negotiation (MN) sequence suggested by Varonis and Gass (1985), the classification of the dialogue moves includes the following classes:

- Trouble source: the problematic item that is not clear and needs a clarification;
- An indicator that something previously said is not clear;
- A response to the indicator (normally a clarification or an explanation);
- A reaction to a response (for example an acceptance or a rejection of a term).

This model is very simple but MN sequences can be very complex. The indicator for example can also be a trouble source and trigger a nested MN sequence or a cascade of MN sequences. To tag such sequences this basic model has been used; each nested or cascading sequence has been handled as a part of a large sequence.

- `mnseq`: Contains a Meaning Negotiation sequence.
- `mnturn`: Contains a reference to a turn that is part of a specific `mnseq`. Turn types must be specified in the attribute `turntype`, which contains the type of the turn that is part of this MN sequence. Typical turn types are trouble source

(ts), indicator (ind), response (resp) and reaction to response (rr). Types are not predefined in the schema because different types not fitting the basic classification are possible. Cascading and nested MN sequences can also be part of `mnseq` (see turns from L08N0420120531-226 to L08N0420120531-237 of the corpus and their annotation).

Example of a Meaning Negotiation sequence:

```
<im:message xml:id="L01N0120120618-268"
who="deL1L2IM-root.xml#N01"
   timestamp="2012-06-18T21:02:44">
   Das schaffst du mit links :-)
</im:message>
<im:message xml:id="L01N0120120618-269"
who="deL1L2IM-root.xml#N01"
   timestamp="2012-06-18T21:02:55">
   (Verstehst du die Bedeutung?)
</im:message>
<im:message xml:id="L01N0120120618-270"
who="deL1L2IM-root.xml#L01"
   timestamp="2012-06-18T21:03:42">
   Und was bedeutet das?
</im:message>
<im:message xml:id="L01N0120120618-271"
who="deL1L2IM-root.xml#N01"
   timestamp="2012-06-18T21:04:37">
   mit links schaffen/erledigen/
   erreichen = ohne Probleme schaffen/erledigen/erreichen
</im:message>
<im:message xml:id="L01N0120120618-272"
who="deL1L2IM-root.xml#L01"
   timestamp="2012-06-18T21:05:46">
    Vielen Dank für Erklärung :)
</im:message>
<im:message xml:id="L01N0120120618-273"
who="deL1L2IM-root.xml#N01"
   timestamp="2012-06-18T21:06:36"> Kein Problem :-)
</im:message>

<im:mnseq>
  <im:mnturn turntype="ts" corresp="L01N0120120618-268"/>
  <im:mnturn turntype="ind" corresp="L01N0120120618-269"/>
  <im:mnturn turntype="ind" corresp="L01N0120120618-270"/>
  <im:mnturn turntype="resp" corresp="L01N0120120618-271"/>
  <im:mnturn turntype="rr" corresp="L01N0120120618-272"/>
</im:mnseq>
```

B

Coding Scheme for Polar Questions

Stivers and Enfield (2010) suggest a data-driven coding scheme for questions. Their study was performed for questions collected from naturally occurring dyadic and multiparty conversations in ten languages: Akhoe Haillom (Namibia), Danish, Dutch, English (US), Italian, Japanese, Korean, Lao, Tzeltal (Mexico) and Yélî Dnye (Papua New Guinea).

The coding scheme proposed by Stivers and Enfield (2010) was used for the analysis of question-answer pairs. Because this coding scheme is relevant for the description of embedded corrections and for the formulation of the computational model of embedded corrections, a detailed description of the relevant part of the coding scheme is provided here showing which polar questions and responses to polar questions are handled. Because neither German nor text chat language were part of the study presented by Stivers and Enfield (2010), it was necessary to modify the scheme according to the question properties found in the dataset. All modifications are explicitly declared.

What utterances qualify as questions needs to be determined first. The basic set of criteria as suggested by (Stivers and Enfield, 2010, p. 2621) was used but with adjustments for chat:

1. A question had to be either (or both) a formal question (i.e. it had to rely on lexico-morpho-syntactic or prosodic interrogative marking) or a functional question (i.e. it had to effectively seek to elicit information, confirmation or agreement whether or not it made use of an interrogative sentence type).
2. News markers such as *wirklich?* (En.: *really?*) were coded as functional questions. Under the categorisation of questions suggested by Stivers and Enfield (2010), news markers qualify because they are routinely treated as seeking confirmation.

Stivers and Enfield (2010) note that "it was difficult to attain validity or reliability in the coding of some aspects of sequential position" (p. 2620). As a result, information about sequential position was not included in the coding scheme. For the purposes of this research and in general for the analysis of chat data, it is necessary to add at least

S. Höhn, *Artificial Companion for Second Language Conversation*,
https://doi.org/10.1007/978-3-030-15504-9_13

the following inclusion criterion for questions with regard to sequential organisation of chat:

3. One question may be delivered in one turn (message) or in multiple turns (messages).

Following the question coding scheme by Stivers and Enfield (2010), all questions were classified as polar, content, alternative or through-produced multi-questions (two or more questions produced as a chunk). Questions delivered in multiple turns are not necessarily through-produced multi-questions. Because only polar questions and responses to polar questions were the focus of this work, the further explanation of the coding scheme will be restricted to polar questions. Readers interested in the remaining question types are invited to see the original publication by Stivers and Enfield (2010).

According to the coding scheme, responses to polar questions can be classified as *answers* (deal directly with the question "as put") and *non-answers* (all the I-don't-knows, maybes and indirect responses). Answers can be further classified by polarity (confirming or disconfirming) and by the form they take. A confirmation for a negative answer in German could be done by a *nein* (no). Sometimes it is not possible to clearly say yes or no; the infamous German *jein* (En.: *yes and no*) might be an additional class in the coding of polar questions, which is a modification of the scheme. With regard to the form of the answers to polar questions, Stivers and Enfield classify the answers as repetitional answers (include full, partial or modified repeats of the question), interjection answers (*ja* or *nein* and their variations) and marked interjection answers (*absolut*, *total* and similar).

Form and aspects of polar questions

Questions can be formed as a declarative question, as an assertion followed by a confirmation request, or as a full question with interrogative word order. The following forms of polar questions were found in the dataset:

1. Declarative word order. Example:
   8 17:13:19 L08 wir müssen heute um 21-00(belorussischer Zeit) chaten, oder wir können jetz anfangen?)
2. Declarative word order with turn-final element. Example:
   15 18:44:44 L07 einen bechlor bekkommt mat nach der Absolvierung der Uni.... stimmt das–?
3. Interrogative word order. Example:
   154 20:35:28 L02 Habt ihr zusammen mit Freunden etwas Tolles untergenommen?

Polar questions can be marked negatively and dubitatively. Stivers and Enfield (2010) suggest to use these characteristics as binary features (yes/no). For simplicity, I used the following coding:

0 Unmarked polar questions.
1 Negatively marked polar questions (*nicht*, *keine*, *un-...*).
2 Dubitatively marked polar questions (*vielleicht*, *wahrscheinlich*).

If both negative and dubitative marking was present, the question received both codes in this field.

Responses to polar questions

Stivers and Enfield (2010) suggest the following classification of responses to polar questions:

0 No response.
1 Answer, a response dealing directly with the question "as put".
2 Non-answer, a response dealing indirectly with the question, all clarifications, I-dont-knows etc.

Only answers were considered for further analysis in this thesis, therefore the part of the coding scheme for answer responses is explained below. Moreover, non-answers were not further coded in the original coding scheme by Stivers and Enfield (2010). A consistent classification of types of non-answer responses to polar questions remains an open question for a future study.

Answers

The coding scheme by Stivers and Enfield (2010) distinguishes between confirming and disconfirming answers with regard to answer polarity and regardless of form. Several examples were found where responses to polar questions deal with the question as put and should be classified as "answers", but neither confirm nor disconfirm. Such answers contain partial confirmations (*nur teils*) or both confirmation and disconfirmation that may count as partial confirmation or partial disconfirmation (*jein*), and disambiguations in order to deal with learner errors (*leicht fallen* vs. *gefallen* as discussed in Example 7.2). Therefore, the following extension of the classification of answers to polar questions may be useful:

1. Confirming answer.
2. Disconfirming answer.
3. Partial confirmation (e.g. *jein* or *nur teils*). This category has been added to the coding scheme because it deals with the question directly as put, but is neither confirming nor disconfirming.
4. Disambiguation (corrective feedback). This category has been introduced for responses dealing with the question as put where native speakers were not able to directly confirm or disconfirm due to the learner's linguistic errors. It may contain both confirmation and disconfirmation.

With regard to answer form, Stivers and Enfield (2010) distinguish among interjection-based answers, marked interjection-based answers and repetition-based answers. Repetitions with replacements (embedded corrections) were covered by this category.

Summary question-coding scheme

Modifications were necessary due to the communication medium (text chat, multi-turn questions) and learner language (linguistic errors in the question made disambiguation in the answer necessary). Partial confirmation may be needed in other languages, too, not only in German. Table B.1 summarises the scheme with modifications (bold).

Unit	Features	
Question	Form	Declarative word order with a question mark (including questions without verb)
		Declarative word order followed by turn-final element (e.g. *ok?*, *stimmt das? ist es so?*)
		Interrogative word order
	Marked:	Negatively (e.g. *nicht*, *keine*)
		dubitatively (e.g. *vielleicht*, *wahrscheinlich*)
	Location	**Delivered in one turn or multiple turns**
Answer	Form	Repeat-based
		Interjection-based
		Marked interjection-based
	Polarity	Confirming
		Disconfirming
		Partially confirming
		Disambuguation

Table B.1: Coding scheme for question-answer pairs with polar questions with modifications (bold)

C

Examples

This supplement contains a longer excerpt of the chat partially shown in Examples 3.7, page 84 and 3.8, page 85.

Example C.1. Role play.

101	18:11:08	L07	leider muss ich meinem Lektor über EU, Menschenrechte oder Globalisierung erzählen... *unfortunately I have to tell my lecturer about EU, human rights or globalisation...*
102	18:11:20	L07	:'(
103	18:12:09	N03	das sind doch aber spannende themen! *but those are exiting topics!*
104	18:12:26	N03	was denkst du denn ueber die EU und ihre derzeitige situation? *what do you think about the EU and its current situation?*
105	18:13:45	L07	insbesondere EU-Gremien und so viele Daten aufeinmal viel zu viel für ein Mädchen :) especially EU-committees and so many data [* error: lexical choice] at once [* error: missing space] to much for a girl *especially EU-committees and so much information at once to much for a girl*
106	18:14:12	N03	hahaha
107	18:14:20	N03	was heisst denn hier fuer ein maedchen *what does it mean here for a girl*
108	18:14:31	N03	viele maedchen koennen besser lernen als jungen *many girls can learn better than boys*
109	18:15:21	N03	erzaehle mal (ohne nachschauen), welche EU gremien gibt es denn? *tell me (without searching) which EU institutions are there?*

S. Höhn, *Artificial Companion for Second Language Conversation*,
https://doi.org/10.1007/978-3-030-15504-9_14

110 18:17:23 L07 ja, aber solche Themen sind für Mädchen nicht besonders interessant! im forigen Jahr stidierten wir u Stellung von Männer und Frauen in der Gesellschft oder CharrireaussichenKarrireaussichten-.... so gab es viele Auseinandersetzungen dabei-...=)))))
yes, but such topics are not really interesting for a girl! last year we studied positions of men and women in society or career opportunities... there were many discussions

111 18:20:03 N03 wARTE EINEN AUGENBLICK, BIN GLEICH WIEDER DA!
wait one moment I will be back immediately!

112 18:21:01 L07 :)

113 18:30:12 N03 bin wieder da
am here again

114 18:30:54 L07 das freut mich!
I am glad!

115 18:31:00 N03 mich auch
me too

116 18:31:03 N03 ;-)

117 18:31:07 L07 =)))))

118 18:31:24 N03 aber ich verstehe dich nicht
I don't understand you

119 18:31:46 N03 es gibt doch eigentlich nichts das per definition fuer frauen oder maenner nicht interessant ist
there are no such things that are by definition not interesting for women or men

120 18:31:57 L07 ich lächele...=)
I'm smiling

121 18:31:58 N03 manche frauen interessieren sich fuer fussball
some women are interested in football

122 18:32:06 N03 manche maenner fuer hautcremes
some men in skin creams

123 18:32:12 N03 oder?
or?

124 18:32:43 L07 ja unsere verrückte Welt...))) alles jetzt umgekehrt
yes, our crazy world... everything is now reversed

125 18:32:52 N03 nicht alles
not everything

126 18:32:56 N03 aber manches
but some things

127 18:33:04 N03 und manches ist auch gut so
and some things are exactly the right way

128 18:33:22 N03 vor 100 jahren haettest du wahrscheinlich nicht studieren koennen
100 years ago you probably could not have studied

129 18:33:26 N03 oder?
or?

130 18:34:01 L07 jeder versteht verschieden, was gut ist..was schlecht!
people have different understanding, what is good... what is bad!

131 18:35:12 N03 das stimmt
this is true

132 18:35:26 N03 was findest du denn gut an unserer verrueckten welt
what do you consider good in our crazy world?
133 18:35:31 N03 und was schlecht
and what is bad?
134 18:36:37 L07 meinst du...reicht es hier Platz...alles das zu schreiben—Leben ist überhaupt gut...!
you think... here enough space... to write all these things — life is good in general...!
135 18:37:35 N03 das stimmt
this is true
136 18:37:44 N03 aber was ist nicht gut?
but what is not good?
137 18:37:50 N03 in der EU?
in the EU?
138 18:37:58 N03 an der globalisierung?
with globalisation?
139 18:38:00 N03 ...
140 18:38:02 N03 ;-)
141 18:39:24 L07 hahaha........ Arbeitaplatzverlagerung, Ausbeutung im Süden, Überflutung von Informationen usw....!!! :) :) :)
workplace relocation [* error: typo], exploitation in the South, information flood etc....!!!
hahaha workplace relocation, exploitation in the South, information flood etc....!!!
142 18:40:33 N03 ok
143 18:40:40 N03 usw klingt gut
etc sounds good
144 18:40:43 N03 ;-)
145 18:42:24 L07 willst du jetzt meine Prüfung mal repetieren..? :)
want you now my exam repeat [* error: lexical choice]..? [smile]
do you want to rehearse my exam now?
146 18:42:42 N03 ja
yes
147 18:42:51 N03 also ich dachte das koennte nuetzlich sein
well I thought this could be useful
148 18:43:02 L07 :)
149 18:43:04 N03 ich habe einen bachelor in politikwissenschaft
I have a bachelors in Political Science
150 18:43:07 N03 :-)
151 18:43:14 N03 aber ich will dich auch nicht nerven
but I don't want to annoy you

References

Abel, A., Glaznieks, A., Nicolas, L., and Stemle, E. (2014). KoKo: an L1 Learner Corpus for German. In *Proceedings of the 9th International Conference on Language Resources and Evaluation (LREC 2014)*, pages 2414–2421.

Abrams, Z. I. (2003). The effect of synchronous and asynchronous CMC on oral performance in German. *Modern Language Journal*, pages 157–167.

Aguado Padilla, K. (2002). *Imitation als Erwerbsstrategie. Interaktive und kognitive Dimensionen des Fremdsprachenerwerbs*. Habilitationsschrift, Universität Bielefeld.

Ai, R., Krause, S., Kasper, W., Xu, F., and Uszkoreit, H. (2015). Semi-automatic generation of multiple-choice tests from mentions of semantic relations. In *2nd Workshop on Natural Language Processing Techniques for Educational Applications (NLP-TEA-2) at ACL-IJCNLP 2015*. ACL.

Ai, R. and Xu, F. (2015). A system demonstration of a framework for computer assisted pronunciation training. *ACL-IJCNLP 2015*, page 1.

Al-Zubaide, H., Issa, A., et al. (2011). Ontbot: Ontology based chatbot. In *Innovation in Information & Communication Technology (ISIICT), 2011 Fourth International Symposium on*, pages 7–12. IEEE.

Alemi, M., Meghdari, A., Basiri, N. M., and Taheri, A. (2015). The effect of applying humanoid robots as teacher assistants to help Iranian autistic pupils learn English as a foreign language. In *Social Robotics*, pages 1–10. Springer.

Allen, J. F. and Small, S. L. (1982). Discourse understanding at the University of Rochester. *SIGART Bull.*, pages 83–85.

Allwood, J. (1995). An activity based approach to pragmatics. *Gothenburg papers in theoretical linguistics*, (76):1–38.

Amaral, L. and Meurers, D. (2007). Conceptualizing student models for ICALL. In *User Modeling 2007*, pages 340–344. Springer.

Amaral, L. and Meurers, D. (2008). From recording linguistic competence to supporting inferences about language acquisition in context. *CALL*, 21(4):323–338.

Amaral, L., Meurers, D., and Ziai, R. (2011). Analyzing learner language: towards a flexible natural language processing architecture for intelligent language tutors. *Computer Assisted Language Learning*, 24(1):1–16.

S. Höhn, *Artificial Companion for Second Language Conversation*,
https://doi.org/10.1007/978-3-030-15504-9

Amaral, L. A. (2011). Revisiting current paradigms in computer assisted language learning research and development. *Ilha do Desterro: A Journal of English Language, Literatures in English and Cultural Studies*, (60):365–390.

Amaral, L. A. and Meurers, D. (2011). On using intelligent computer-assisted language learning in real-life foreign language teaching and learning. *ReCALL*, 23(01):4–24.

Amaral, L. A. and Meurers, W. D. (2009). Little things with big effects: On the identification and interpretation of tokens for error diagnosis in ICALL. *CALICO Journal*, 26(3):580–591.

Amoia, M., Brétaudiere, T., Denis, A., Gardent, C., and Perez-Beltrachini, L. (2012). A serious game for second language acquisition in a virtual environment. *Journal on Systemics, Cybernetics and Informatics (JSCI)*, 10(1):24–34.

Anderson, J. N., Davidson, N., Morton, H., and Jack, M. A. (2008). Language learning with interactive virtual agent scenarios and speech recognition: Lessons learned. *Computer Animation and Virtual Worlds*, 19(5):605–619.

Auer, P. (1999). *Sprachliche Interaktion - Eine Einführung anhand von 22 Klassikern*. Tübingen: Niemeyer.

Austin, J. L. (1962). *How to do things with words*. Oxford: Clarendon Press.

Avramidis, E., Popovic, M., and Burchardt, A. (2015). DFKI's experimental hybrid MT system for WMT 2015. In *Proceedings of the 10th Workshop on Statistical Machine Translation*, pages 66–73. ACL.

Barron, A. and Black, E. (2015). Constructing small talk in learner-native speaker voice-based telecollaboration: A focus on topic management and backchanneling. *System*, 48:112–128.

Bartz, T., Beißwenger, M., and Storrer, A. (2014). Optimierung des Stuttgart-Tübingen-Tagset für die linguistische Annotation von Korpora zur internetbasierten Kommunikation: Phänomene, Herausforderungen, Erweiterungsvorschläge. *Zeitschrift für germanistische Linguistik*, 28(1):157–198.

Becker, L., Erhart, G., Skiba, D., and Matula, V. (2013). Avaya: Sentiment analysis on twitter with self-training and polarity lexicon expansion. In *Second Joint Conference on Lexical and Computational Semantics (* SEM)*, volume 2, pages 333–340.

Becker, M., Bredenkamp, A., Crysmann, B., and Klein, J. (2003). Annotation of error types for German Newsgroup Corpus. In *Treebanks*, pages 89–100. Springer.

Beißwenger, M. (2002). Getippte "Gespräche" und ihre trägermediale Bedingtheit. In Schröder, I. W. and Voell, S., editors, *Moderne Oralität.*, CURUPIRA. Philipps-Universität Marburg.

Bender, E. M., Flickinger, D., Oepen, S., Walsh, A., and Baldwin, T. (2004). Arboretum: Using a precision grammar for grammar checking in CALL. In *InSTIL/ICALL Symposium*.

Benjamin, T. (2013). *Signaling trouble. On the linguistic design of other-initiation of repair in English conversation*. PhD, University of Groningen.

Bickmore, T. and Picard, R. (2005). Establishing and maintaining long-term human-computer relationships. *ACM Transactions on Computer Human Interaction*, 12:293–327.

Bickmore, T. W. (2003). *Relational Agents: Effecting Change through Human-Computer Relationships*. PhD thesis, MIT.

Bird, S., Klein, E., and Loper, E. (2009). *Natural Language Processing with Python*. O'Reilly Media.

Birkner, K. and Meer, D. (2011). Institutionalisierter Alltag: Mündlichkeit und Schriftlichkeit in unterschiedlichen Praxisfeldern. *Mannheim: Verlag für Gesprächsforschung*.

Blake, R. (2008). *Brave new digital classroom*. Washington, DC: Georgetown University Press.

Blake, R. and Delforge, A. M. (2004). Language learning at a distance: Spanish without walls. In *Selected papers from the 2004 NFLRC Symposium*.

Bolden, G. B. (2009). Beyond answering: Repeat-prefaced responses in conversation. *Communication Monographs*, 76(2):121–143.

Bonneau, A. and Colotte, V. (2011). Automatic feedback for L2 prosody learning. In *Speech and Language Technologies*, pages 55–70. Intech.

Bono, M., Ogata, H., Takanashi, K., and Joh, A. (2014). The practice of showing 'who i am': A multimodal analysis of encounters between science communicator and visitors at science museum. In *Universal Access in Human-Computer Interaction. Universal Access to Information and Knowledge*, pages 650–661. Springer.

Boyd, A. (2010). EAGLE: an Error-Annotated Corpus of Beginning Learner German. In *Proc. of LREC*. ELRA.

Brad, F. and Rebedea, T. (2017). Neural paraphrase generation using transfer learning. In *Proceedings of the 10th International Conference on Natural Language Generation*, pages 257–261.

Bradley, J., Mival, O., and Benyon, D. (2009). Wizard of Oz Experiments for Companions. In *Proc. of the 23rd British HCI Group Annual Conf. on People and Computers: Celebrating People and Technology*, pages 313–317. British Computer Society.

Brandt, A. (2011). *The Maintenance of Mutual Understanding in Online Second Language Talk*. PhD thesis, Newcastle University, School of Education, Communication and Language Sciences.

Braun, D., Hernandez-Mendez, A., Matthes, F., and Langen, M. (2017). Evaluating natural language understanding services for conversational question answering systems. In *Proceedings of the 18th Annual SIGDial Meeting on Discourse and Dialogue*, pages 174–185. ACL.

Breckle, M. and Zinsmeister, H. (2010). Zur lernersprachlichen Generierung referierender Ausdrücke in argumentativen Texten. *Textmuster: schulisch-universitär-kulturkontrastiv.*, pages 79–101.

Breuing, A. and Wachsmuth, I. (2012). Let's talk topically with artificial agents! providing agents with humanlike topic awareness in everyday dialog situations. In *Proceedings of the ICAART'12*, pages 62–71.

Breuing, A., Waltinger, U., and Wachsmuth, I. (2011). Harvesting Wikipedia knowledge to identify topics in ongoing natural language dialogs. In *Proc. of the 2011 IEEE/WIC/ACM Int. Conf. on Web Intelligence and Intelligent Agent Technology*, pages 445–450. IEEE Computer Society.

Brouwer, C. E., Rasmussen, G., and Wagner, J. (2004). Embedded corrections in second language talk. In Gardner, R. and Wagner, J., editors, *Second Language Conversations: Studies of Communication in Everyday Settings*, pages 86–103. A&C Black - Verlag.

Brown, G. and Yule, G. (1983). *Discourse analysis*. Cambridge University Press.

Bunt, H. (2011). The semantics of dialogue acts. In *Proceedings of the Ninth International Conference on Computational Semantics*, pages 1–13. Association for Computational Linguistics.

Burchardt, A., Lommel, A. R., Rehm, G., Sasaki, F., van Genabith, J., and Uszkoreit, H. (2014). Language technology drives quality translation. *MultiLingual*, 143:33–39.

Bush, N. (2006). Program D. http://www.aitools.org/Program_D.

Buß, O. and Schlangen, D. (2011). DIUM – An Incremental Dialogue Manager that Can Produce Self-Corrections. In *Proceedings of Proceedings of the 15th Workshop on the Semantics and Pragmatics of Dialogue (SemDial)*, pages 47–54.

Cahill, A. (2015). Parsing learner text: to shoehorn or not to shoehorn. In *The 9th Linguistic Annotation Workshop held in conjuncion with NAACL 2015*, page 144.

Caire, P. and van der Torre, L. (2009). Convivial ambient technologies: Requirements, ontology and design. *The Computer Journal*, 52.

Callejas-Rodríguez, Á., Villatoro-Tello, E., Meza, I., and Ramírez-de-la Rosa, G. (2016). From dialogue corpora to dialogue systems: Generating a chatbot with teenager personality for preventing cyber-pedophilia. In *International Conference on Text, Speech, and Dialogue*, pages 531–539. Springer.

Canale, M. and Swain, M. (1980). Theoretical bases of communicative approaches to second language teaching and testing. *Applied linguistics*, 1(1):1–47.

Casas, R., Marín, R. B., Robinet, A., Delgado, A. R., Yarza, A. R., McGinn, J., Picking, R., and Grout, V. (2008). User modelling in ambient intelligence for elderly and disabled people. In *11th International Conference on Computers Helping People with Special Needs*, ICCHP 2008, pages 114–122. Springer.

Chang, C.-W., Lee, J.-H., Chao, P.-Y., Wang, C.-Y., and Chen, G.-D. (2010). Exploring the possibility of using humanoid robots as instructional tools for teaching a second language in primary school. *Journal of Educational Technology & Society*, 13(2):13–24.

Chee, B. T. T., Wong, A. H. Y., Limbu, D. K., Tay, A. H. J., Tan, Y. K., and Park, T. (2010). Understanding communication patterns for designing robot receptionist. In *Social Robotics*, pages 345–354. Springer.

Chen, T., Xu, R., He, Y., Xia, Y., and Wang, X. (2016). Learning user and product distributed representations using a sequence model for sentiment analysis. *IEEE Computational Intelligence Magazine*, 11(3):34–44.

Chrysafiadi, K. and Virvou, M. (2013). Student modeling approaches: A literature review for the last decade. *Expert Systems with Applications*, 40(11):4715–4729.

Clark, H. H. (1996). *Using language*. Cambridge University Press.

Dahan, D., Tanenhaus, M. K., and Chambers, C. G. (2002). Accent and reference resolution in spoken-language comprehension. *Journal of Memory and Language*, 47(2):292–314.

Danilava, S., Busemann, S., and Schommer, C. (2012). Artificial Conversational Companion: a Requirement Analysis. In *Proc. of ICAART'12*, pages 282–289.

Danilava, S., Busemann, S., Schommer, C., and Ziegler, G. (2013a). Towards Computational Models for a Long-term Interaction with an Artificial Conversational Companion. In *Proc. of ICAART'13*.

Danilava, S., Busemann, S., Schommer, C., and Ziegler, G. (2013b). Why are you silent? Towards responsiveness in chatbots. In *Avec le Temps! Time, Tempo, and Turns in Human-Computer Interaction. Workshop at CHI 2013, Paris, France*.

Darhower, M. A. (2008). The role of linguistic affordances in telecollaborative chat. *Calico Journal*, 26(1):48–69.

Davidov, D., Tsur, O., and Rappoport, A. (2010). Semi-supervised recognition of sarcastic sentences in Twitter and Amazon. In *Proceedings of the Fourteenth Conference on Computational Natural Language Learning*, pages 107–116. Association for Computational Linguistics.

de Alencar, T. S., Machado, L. R., de Oliveira Neris, L., and de Almeida Neris, V. P. (2014). Addressing the users' diversity in ubiquitous environments through a low cost architecture. In *Universal Access in Human-Computer Interaction. Aging and Assistive Environments*, pages 439–450. Springer.

De Gasperis, G., Chiari, I., and Florio, N. (2013). AIML knowledge base construction from text corpora. *Artificial intelligence, evolutionary computing and metaheuristics*, 427:287–318.

De Gasperis, G. and Florio, N. (2012). Learning to read/type a second language in a chatbot enhanced environment. In *International Workshop on Evidence-Based Technology Enhanced Learning*, pages 47–56. Springer.

De Marco, A. and Leone, P. (2012). Computer-mediated conversation for mutual learning: acknowledgement and agreement/assessment signals in Italian as L2. In *Proceedings of the EUROCALL Conference*, pages 70–75.

Delmonte, R. (2003). Linguistic knowledge and reasoning for error diagnosis and feedback generation. *Calico Journal*, 20(3):513–532.

DeSmedt, W. H. (1995). Herr Kommissar: An ICALL conversation simulator for intermediate german. In Holland, V. M., Sams, M. R., and Kaplan, J. D., editors, *Intelligent language tutors: Theory shaping technology*. Routledge.

Díaz-Negrillo, A. and Domínguez, J. F. (2006). Error tagging systems for learner corpora. *Revista española de lingüística aplicada*, 19:83–102.

Díaz-Negrillo, A., Meurers, D., Valera, S., and Wunsch, H. (2010). Towards interlanguage POS annotation for effective learner corpora in SLA and FLT. In *Language Forum*, volume 36, pages 139–154.

Dickinson, M. and Ragheb, M. (2015). On grammaticality in the syntactic annotation of learner language. In *The 9th Linguistic Annotation Workshop held in conjuncion with NAACL 2015*, page 158.

Dingemanse, M., Blythe, J., and Dirksmeyer, T. (2014). Formats for other-initiation of repair across languages: An exercise in pragmatic typology. *Studies in Languag*, 3(81):5–43.

Dingemanse, M., Roberts, S. G., Baranova, J., Blythe, J., Drew, P., Floyd, S., Gisladottir, R. S., Kendrick, K. H., Levinson, S. C., Manrique, E., et al. (2015).

Universal principles in the repair of communication problems. *PloS One*, 10(9):e0136100.

Dings, A. (2012). Native speaker/nonnative speaker interaction and orientation to novice/expert identity. *Journal of Pragmatics*, 44(11):1503–1518.

Dodigovic, M. (2005). *Artificial intelligence in second language learning: Raising error awareness*, volume 13. Multilingual Matters.

Dong, H., Cheung Hui, S., and He, Y. (2006). Structural analysis of chat messages for topic detection. *Online Information Review*, 30(5):496–516.

Dorr, B., Galescu, L., Golob, E., Venable, K. B., and Wilks, Y. (2015). Companion-based ambient robust intelligence (CARING). In *Workshops at the Twenty-Ninth AAAI Conference on Artificial Intelligence*.

Drew, P. (1997). Open class repair initiations in response to sequential sources of troubles in conversation. *Journal of Pragmatics*, 28:69–101.

Droßmann, C. (2005). German AIML set. http://www.drossmann.de/wordpress/alicebot/.

Duquette, J.-P. (2008). Chatbot Mike representing Cypris Chat in Second Life. http://maps.secondlife.com/secondlife/Wellston/167/88/23, http://cyprischat.org.

Dürscheid, C. (2016). Nähe, Distanz und neue Medien. *Zur Karriere von Nähe und Distanz. Rezeption und Diskussion des Koch-Oesterreicher-Modells*, 306:357–385.

Dzikovska, M. O., Callaway, C. B., Farrow, E., Moore, J. D., Steinhauser, N., and Campbell, G. (2009). Dealing with interpretation errors in tutorial dialogue. In *Proceedings of the SIGDIAL 2009 Conference: The 10th annual meeting of the special interest group on discourse and dialogue*, pages 38–45. Association for Computational Linguistics.

Edlund, J., Heldner, M., and Gustafson, J. (2005). Utterance segmentation and turn-taking in spoken dialogue systems. *Sprachtechnologie, mobile Kommunikation und linguistische Ressourcen*, pages 576–587.

Egbert, M. (2009). *Der Reparatur-Mechanismus in deutschen Gesprächen*. Verlag für Gesprächsforschung, Mannheim.

Enfield, N. J. (2007). Meanings of the unmarked: How 'default' person reference does more than just refer. In *Person reference in interaction: Linguistic, cultural, and social perspectives*, pages 97–120. Cambridge University Press.

Enfield, N. J., Dingemanse, M., Baranova, J., Blythe, J., Brown, P., Dirksmeyer, T., Drew, P., Floyd, S., Gipper, S., Gisladottir, R. S., Hoymann, G., Kendrick, K. H., Levinson, S. C., Magyari, L., Manrique, E., Rossi, G., Roque, L. S., and Torreira, F. (2013). Huh? What? - a first survey in twenty-one languages. In Hayashi, M., Raymond, G., and Sidnell, J., editors, *Conversational Repair and Human Understanding*, chapter 12. Cambridge University Press.

Evert, S., Proisl, T., Greiner, P., and Kabashi, B. (2014). Sentiklue: Updating a polarity classifier in 48 hours. In *Proceedings of SemEval 2014*, page 551.

Fellbaum, C. (2010). Princeton university: About WordNet. http://wordnet.princeton.edu. WordNet.

Firth, A. and Wagner, J. (1997). On discourse, communication, and (some) fundamental concepts in SLA research. *The Modern Language Journal*, 81(3):285–300.

Fredriksson, C. (2012). About collaboration, interaction, and the negotiation of meaning in synchronous written chats in L2-German. In Bradley, L. and Thouësny, S., editors, *CALL: Using, Learning, Knowing, EUROCALL Conference, Gothenburg, Sweden, 22-25 August 2012, Proceedings*, pages 88–92. Research-publishing.net.

Fredriksson, C. (2013). Learning German by chatting–a study of social interaction and language production in an academic German online course. In *ICT for Language Learning, Florence, Italy 14-15 November 2013*, pages 218–222. Pixel.

Fryer, L. and Carpenter, R. (2006). Emerging technologies - bots as language learning tools. *Language Learning & Technology*, 3(10):8 – 14.

Gabsdil, M. (2003). Clarification in Spoken Dialogue Systems. In *AAAI Technical Report*. AAAI.

Galley, M., Brockett, C., Sordoni, A., Ji, Y., Auli, M., Quirk, C., Mitchell, M., Gao, J., and Dolan, B. (2015). deltaBLEU: A discriminative metric for generation tasks with intrinsically diverse targets. In *Proceedings of the 53rd Annual Meeting of the Association for Computational Linguistics and the 7th International Joint Conference on Natural Language Processing*, pages 445–450, Beijing, China. ACL.

Gardent, C., Lorenzo, A., Perez-Beltrachini, L., and Rojas-Barahona, L. (2013). Weakly and strongly constrained dialogues for language learning. In *the 14th annual SIGdial Meeting on Discourse and Dialogue SIGDIAL 2013*, pages 357–359.

Gehle, R., Pitsch, K., and Wrede, S. (2014). Signaling trouble in robot-to-group interaction. emerging visitor dynamics with a museum guide robot. In *Proceedings of the second international conference on Human-agent interaction*, pages 361–368. ACM.

Georgeff, M., Pell, B., Pollack, M., Tambe, M., and Wooldridge, M. (1999). The belief-desire-intention model of agency. In *Intelligent Agents V: Agents Theories, Architectures, and Languages*, pages 1–10. Springer.

Gilmartin, E., Bonin, F., Vogel, C., and Campbell, N. (2013). Laughter and topic transition in multiparty conversation. In *Proceedings of SIGDIAL 2013 Conference*, pages 304–308.

Ginzburg, J. (2012). *The interactive stance*. Oxford University Press.

Ginzburg, J., Fernández, R., and Schlangen, D. (2007). Unifying self- and other-repair. In *Proceeding of DECALOG, the 11th International Workshop on the Semantics and Pragmatics of Dialogue (SemDial07)*.

Godfrey, J. J., Holliman, E. C., and McDaniel, J. (1992). Switchboard: Telephone speech corpus for research and development. In *Acoustics, Speech, and Signal Processing, 1992. ICASSP-92., 1992 IEEE International Conference on*, volume 1, pages 517–520. IEEE.

Golato, A. (2002). German compliment responses. *Journal of pragmatics*, 34(5):547–571.

Golato, A. (2005). *Compliments and compliment responses: Grammatical structure and sequential organization*, volume 15. John Benjamins Publishing.

González-Lloret, M. (2011). Conversation analysis of computer-mediated communication. *Calico Journal*, 28(2):308–325.

Gould, J. D., Conti, J., and Hovanyecz, T. (1983). Composing letters with a simulated listening typewriter. *Commun. ACM*, 26(4):295–308.

Gray, E. F. (1992). Interactive language learning: "a la rencontre de Philippe". *The French Review*, 65(3):499–507.

Greene, C. E., Keogh, K., Koller, T., Wagner, J., Ward, M., and Van Genabith, J. (2004). Using NLP technology in CALL. In *InSTIL/ICALL 2004 Symposium on Computer Assisted Learning*. International Speech Communication Association.

Grice, H. P. (1975). Logic and conversation. *Syntax and semantics*, 3, Speech Acts:41–58.

Grote, B., Hagen, E., Stein, A., and Teich, E. (1997). Speech Production in Human-Machine Dialogue: A Natural Language Generation Perspective. In Meier, E., Mast, M., and Luperfoy, S., editors, *Dialogue Processing in Spoken Language Systems*, volume 1236 of *Lecture Notes in Computer Science*, pages 70–85. Springer.

Guo, S., Höhn, S., Xu, F., and Schommer, C. (2018). PERSEUS: A personalization framework for sentiment categorization with recurrent neural network. In *Proceedings of ICAART 2018*.

Gupta, A., Agarwal, A., Singh, P., and Rai, P. (2017). A deep generative framework for paraphrase generation. *arXiv preprint arXiv:1709.05074*.

Gut, U. (2009). *Non-native speech: A corpus-based analysis of phonological and phonetic properties of L2 English and German*, volume 9 of *English Corpus Linguistics*. Peter Lang.

Hallili, A. (2014). Toward an ontology-based chatbot endowed with natural language processing and generation. In *26th European Summer School in Logic, Language & Information*.

Hamp, B., Feldweg, H., et al. (1997). GermaNet - a lexical-semantic net for German. In *Proceedings of ACL workshop Automatic Information Extraction and Building of Lexical Semantic Resources for NLP Applications*, pages 9–15. ACL.

Han, J. (2012). Emerging technologies: Robot-assisted language learning. *Language and Learning Technology*, 16(3):1–9.

Hasan, S., Heger, C., and Mansour, S. (2015). Spelling correction of user search queries through statistical machine translation. In *EMNLP*, pages 451–460.

Hauser, E. (2010). Other-correction of language form following a repair sequence. *Pragmatics and Language Learning*, 12:277–296.

Hayes, P. and Reddy, R. (1979). Graceful interaction in man-machine communication. In *Proceedings of the 6th International Joint Conference on Artificial Intelligence - Volume 1*, IJCAI'79, pages 372–374. Morgan Kaufmann Publishers Inc.

Heift, T. (2002). Learner control and error correction in ICALL: Browsers, peekers, and adamants. *Calico Journal*, 19(2):295–313.

Heift, T. (2003). Multiple learner errors and meaningful feedback: A challenge for icall systems. *CALICO journal*, 20(3):533–548.

Heift, T. (2007). Learner personas in CALL. *CALICO Journal*, 25(1):1–10.

Heift, T. (2015). Web delivery of adaptive and interactive language tutoring: Revisited. *International Journal of Artificial Intelligence in Education*, pages 1–15.

Heift, T. and Schulze, M. (2007). *Errors and intelligence in computer-assisted language learning: Parsers and pedagogues*. Routledge.

Heine, L., Witte, M., and Holl, T. (2007). Babbel! https://www.babbel.com/.

Henderson, M., Thomson, B., and Young, S. (2013). Deep neural network approach for the dialog state tracking challenge. In *Proceedings of the SIGDIAL 2013 Conference*, pages 467–471.

Heritage, J. (2012). The epistemic engine: Sequence organization and territories of knowledge. *Research on Language & Social Interaction*, 45(1):30–52.

Heritage, J. and Goodwin, C. (1990). Conversation analysis. *Annual review of anthropology*, 19:283–307.

Hirst, G. (1991). Does conversation analysis have a role in computational linguistics? *Computational Linguistics*, 17(2):211–227.

Hjalmarsson, A., Wik, P., and Brusk, J. (2007). Dealing with deal: a dialogue system for conversation training. In *Proceedings of SIGDIAL*, pages 132–135.

Höhn, S. (2015a). Dealing with trouble: A data-driven model of a repair type for a conversational agent. In *Proceedings of the twenty-ninth AAAI conference on Artificial Intelligence*. AAAI.

Höhn, S. (2015b). deL1L2IM: Corpus of long-term instant messaging NS-NNS conversations. ELRA http://islrn.org/resources/339-799-085-669-8/.

Höhn, S. (2017). A data-driven model of explanations for a chatbot that helps to practice conversation in a foreign language. In *Proceedings of SIGDIAL 2017 Conference*. ACM.

Höhn, S., Busemann, S., Max, C., Schommer, C., and Ziegler, G. (2015). Interaction profiles for an artificial conversational companion. In *Proceedings of the first International Symposium on Companion Technology*, ISTC, pages 73–78.

Höhn, S., Pfeiffer, A., and Ras, E. (2016). Challenges of error annotation in native/non-native speaker chat. In *Proceedings of the 13th Conference on Natural Language Processing (KONVENS)*. Bochumer Linguistische Arbeitsberichte.

Holt, E. (2010). The last laugh: Shared laughter and topic termination. *Journal of Pragmatics*, 42(6):1513–1525.

Holt, E. and Drew, P. (2001). Idiomatic expressions as topical pivots. In *Proceedings of Interdisciplinary Workshop on Corpus-Based & Processing Approaches to Figurative Language (part of Corpus Linguistics Conference 2001)*. Lancaster University.

Holt, E. and Drew, P. (2005). Figurative pivots: The use of figurative expressions in pivotal topic transitions. *Research on Language and Social Interaction*, 38(1):35–61.

Hosoda, Y. (2006). Repair and relevance of differential language expertise in second language conversations. *Applied Linguistics*, 27(1):25–50.

Hutchby, I. (1995). Aspects of recipient design in expert advice-giving on call-in radio. *Discourse processes*, 19(2):219–238.

Hymes, D. (1972). On communicative competence. In Pride, J. and Holmes, J., editors, *Sociolinguistics*, pages 269–293. Harmondsworth: Penguin.

Hynninen, N. (2012). Icl at the micro level: L2 speakers taking on the role of language experts. *AILA Review*, 25:13–29.

Hynninen, N. (2013). *Language Regulation in English as a Lingua Franca: Exploring language-regulatory practices in academic spoken discourse*. PhD thesis, University of Helsinki.

Iida, R., Kobayashi, S., and Tokunaga, T. (2010). Incorporating extra-linguistic information into reference resolution in collaborative task dialogue. In *Proceedings of the 48th Annual Meeting of the Association for Computational Linguistics*, pages 1259–1267. Association for Computational Linguistics.

Isaacs, E. A. and Clark, H. H. (1987). References in conversation between experts and novices. *Journal of Experimental Psychology: General*, 116(1):26–37.

Ivanov, A. V., Ramanarayanan, V., Suendermann-Oeft, D., Lopez, M., Evanini, K., and Tao, J. (2015). Automated speech recognition technology for dialogue interaction with non-native interlocutors. In *16th Annual Meeting of the Special Interest Group on Discourse and Dialogue*, page 134.

Janarthanam, S. and Lemon, O. (2009). A Wizard-of-Oz environment to study referring expression generation in a situated spoken dialogue task. In *Proceedings of the 12th European Workshop on Natural Language Generation*, pages 94–97. Association for Computational Linguistics.

Janarthanam, S. and Lemon, O. (2010). Learning to adapt to unknown users: referring expression generation in spoken dialogue systems. In *Proceedings of the 48th Annual Meeting of the Association for Computational Linguistics*, pages 69–78. Association for Computational Linguistics.

Jefferson, G. (1974). Error correction as an interactional resource. *Language in society*, 3(02):181–199.

Jefferson, G. (1987). On exposed and embedded correction in conversation. In Button, G. and Lee, J., editors, *Talk and social organization*, volume 14, pages 86–100. Clevedon, UK: Multilingual Matters.

Jia, J. (2004). The Study of the Application of a Web-based Chatbot System on the Teaching of Foreign Languages. *Proc. of Society for Inf. Tech. and Teacher Education Int. Conf.*, pages 1201–1207.

Jia, J. (2009). CSIEC: A Computer Assisted English Learning Chatbot Based on Textual Knowledge and Reasoning. *Know.-Based Syst.*, 22(4):249–255.

Jian, C., Zhekova, D., Shi, H., and Bateman, J. (2010). Deep Reasoning in Clarification Dialogues with Mobile Robots. In *Proceedings of the 19th European Conference on Artificial Intelligence*, pages 177–182. IOS Press.

Jin, L. (2013). Language development and scaffolding in a Sino-American telecollaborative project. *Language Learning & Technology*, 17(2):193–219.

Johansson, M. and Skantze, G. (2015). Opportunities and obligations to take turns in collaborative multi-party human-robot interaction. In *SIGDIAL Conference*, pages 305–314.

Kaleem, M., Alobadi, O., O'Shea, J., and Crockett, K. (2016). Framework for the formulation of metrics for conversational agent evaluation. In *RE-WOCHAT: Workshop on Collecting and Generating Resources for Chatbots and Conversational Agents-Development and Evaluation Workshop Programme (May 28 th, 2016)*, page 20.

Kasper, G. (1985). Repair in foreign language teaching. *Studies in Second Language Acquisition*, 7:200–215.

Kasper, G. (2004). Participant Orientations in German Conversation-for-Learning. *The Modern Language Journal*, 88:551–567.

Kasper, G. (2006). Beyond repair: Conversation analysis as an approach to SLA. *AILA Review*, 19(1):83–99.

Katagiri, Y., Bono, M., and Suzuki, N. (2004). Capturing conversational participation in a ubiquitous sensor environment. In *Pervasive 2004 Workshop on Memory and Sharing of Experiences*, pages 101–106.

Kaur, J. (2011). Doing being a language expert: The case of the ELF speaker. In *Latest trends in ELF research*, pages 53–75. Cambridge Scholars Publishing.

Kim, J. (2003). A study on negotiation of meaning in NNS-NNS interactions - Focusing on synchronous CMC. In *Proceedings of the 8th Conference of Pan-Pacific Association of Applied Linguistics*, pages 190–210. PPAL.

Kitade, K. (2000). L2 learners' discourse and SLA theories in CMC: Collaborative interaction in internet chat. *Computer assisted language learning*, 13(2):143–166.

Klüwer, T. (2009). RMRSBot – using linguistic information to enrich a chatbot. In *IVA*, pages 515–516. Springer.

Klüwer, T. (2011). From chatbots to dialogue systems. In Perez-Marton, D. and Pascual-Nieto, I., editors, *Conversational Agents and Natural Language Interaction: Techniques and Effective Practices*, pages 1–22. IGI Global Publishing Group.

Koch, P. (1994). Schriftlichkeit und Sprache. In *Schrift und Schriftlichkeit. Ein interdisziplinäres Handbuch internationaler Forschung*, pages 587–604. Walter de Gruyter.

Koch, P. and Oesterreicher, W. (1985). Sprache der Nähe – Sprache der Distanz. Mündlichkeit und Schriftlichkeit im Spannungsfeld von Sprachtheorie und Sprachgeschichte. In *Romanistisches Jahrbuch*, volume 36. Walter de Gruyter.

Koehn, P., Hoang, H., Birch, A., Callison-Burch, C., Federico, M., Bertoldi, N., Cowan, B., Shen, W., Moran, C., Zens, R., et al. (2007). Moses: Open source toolkit for statistical machine translation. In *Proceedings of the 45th annual meeting of the ACL on interactive poster and demonstration sessions*, pages 177–180. Association for Computational Linguistics.

Kost, C. R. (2004). *An investigation of the effects of synchronous computer-mediated communication (CMC) on interlanguage development in beginning learners of German: Accuracy, proficiency, and communication strategies*. PhD thesis, The University of Arizona.

Kramer, M., Yaghoubzadeh, R., Kopp, S., and Pitsch, K. (2013). A conversational virtual human as autonomous assistant for elderly and cognitively impaired users? Social acceptability and design considerations. *Lecture Notes in Informatics (LNI)*.

Krashen, S. (1981). *Second Language Acquisition and Second Language Learning*. Oxford: Pergamon.

Kruijff, G.-J. M., Brenner, M., and Hawes, N. (2008). Continual planning for cross-modal situated clarification in human-robot interaction. In *The 17th IEEE In-*

ternational Symposium on Robot and Human Interactive Communication, pages 592–597. IEEE.

Kruijff, G.-J. M., Zender, H., Jensfelt, P., and Christensen, H. I. (2006). Clarification dialogues in human-augmented mapping. In *Proceedings of the 1st ACM SIGCHI/SIGART conference on Human-robot interaction*, pages 282–289. ACM.

Krummes, C. and Ensslin, A. (2014). What's Hard in German? WHiG: a British learner corpus of German. *Corpora*, 9(2):191–205.

Kurhila, S. (2001). Correction in talk between native and non-native speaker. *Journal of Pragmatics*, 33(7):1083–1110.

Kurhila, S. (2004). Clients or language learners–being a second language speaker in institutional interaction. *Second language conversations*, pages 58–74.

Kurhila, S. (2006). *Second language interaction*, volume 145. John Benjamins Publishing.

Kwok, V. H. (2015). Robot vs. human teacher: Instruction in the digital age for ESL learners. *English Language Teaching*, 8(7):p157.

Lamnek, S. (2010). *Qualitative Sozialforschung*. BELTZ.

Lavolette, E., Polio, C., and Kahng, J. (2015). The accuracy of computer-assisted feedback and students' responses to it. *Language Learning and Technology*, 19(2):50–68.

Leacock, C., Chodorow, M., Gamon, M., and Tetreault, J. (2010). Automated grammatical error detection for language learners. *Synthesis lectures on human language technologies*, 3(1):1–134.

Lee, C. K. (2007). Text-making practices beyond the classroom context: Private instant messaging in Hong Kong. *Computers and Composition*, 24(3):285–301.

Lee, M. K., Kiesler, S., and Forlizzi, J. (2010). Receptionist or information kiosk: How do people talk with a robot? In *Proceedings of the 2010 ACM Conference on Computer Supported Cooperative Work*, CSCW '10, pages 31–40, New York, NY, USA. ACM.

Lee, M. K. and Makatchev, M. (2009). How do people talk with a robot?: an analysis of human-robot dialogues in the real world. In *CHI'09 Extended Abstracts on Human Factors in Computing Systems*, pages 3769–3774. ACM.

Lerner, G. H. and Kitzinger, C. (2007). Extraction and aggregation in the repair of individual and collective self-reference. *Discourse Studies*, 9(4):526–557.

Levelt, W. J. M. (1993). *Speaking: From intention to articulation*. MIT Press.

L'Haire, S. (2011). *Traitement automatique des langues et apprentissage des langues assisté par ordinateur: bilan, résultats et perspectives*. PhD thesis, University of Geneva.

Li, J., Galley, M., Brockett, C., Spithourakis, G. P., Gao, J., and Dolan, B. (2016). A persona-based neural conversation model. *arXiv preprint arXiv:1603.06155*.

Liddicoat, A. J. (2011). *An Introduction to Conversation Analysis*. Continuum.

Lipowsky, F. (2015). Unterricht. In *Päd. Psychologie*, pages 69–105. Springer.

Lison, P. (2014). *Structured probabilistic modelling for dialogue management*. PhD thesis, University of Oslo.

Lison, P. and Kennington, C. (2015). Developing spoken dialogue systems with the opendial toolkit. *SEMDIAL 2015 goDIAL*, page 194.

Lison, P. and Kennington, C. (2016). Opendial: A toolkit for developing spoken dialogue systems with probabilistic rules. *ACL 2016*, page 67.

Liu, C.-W., Lowe, R., Serban, I. V., Noseworthy, M., Charlin, L., and Pineau, J. (2016). How not to evaluate your dialogue system: An empirical study of unsupervised evaluation metrics for dialogue response generation. *arXiv preprint arXiv:1603.08023*.

Loewen, S. and Erlam, R. (2006). Corrective feedback in the chatroom: An experimental study. *Computer Assisted Language Learning*, 19(1):1–14.

Loewen, S. and Reissner, S. (2009). A comparison of incidental focus on form in the second language classroom and chatroom. *Computer Assisted Language Learning*, 22(2):101–114.

Long, M. H. (1996). The role of the linguistic environment in second language acquisition. *Handbook of second language acquisition*, 2(2):413–468.

Lüdeling, A., Briskina, E., Hantschel, J., Krüger, J., Sigrist, S., and Spieler, U. (2010). *LeKo Lernerkorpus Handbuch*. Humboldt-Universität zu Berlin, Institut für Deutsche Sprache und Linguistik, Philosophische Fakultät II.

Lüdeling, A., Walter, M., Kroymann, E., and Adolphs, P. (2005). Multi-level error annotation in learner corpora. *Proceedings of corpus linguistics 2005*, pages 15–17.

Luff, P., Frohlich, D., and Gilbert, N., editors (1990). *Computers and Conversation*. London: Academic Press.

Lyster, R. and Ranta, L. (1997). Corrective feedback and learner uptake. *Studies in second language acquisition*, 19(01):37–66.

Lyster, R., Saito, K., and Sato, M. (2013). Oral corrective feedback in second language classrooms. *Language Teaching*, 46.

Mackey, A. (2006). Feedback, noticing and instructed second language learning. *Applied linguistics*, 27(3):405–430.

MacTear, M., Callejas, Z., and Griol, D. (2016). *The Conversational Interface: Talking to Smart Devices*. Springer.

Maier, E. (1997). Clarification Dialogues in VERBMOBIL. In *ACL/EACL Workshop on Interactive Spoken Dialog Systems: Bringing Speech and NLP Together in Real Applications*. ACL.

Makkonen, J., Ahonen-Myka, H., and Salmenkivi, M. (2004). Simple semantics in topic detection and tracking. *Information Retrieval*, 7(3-4):347–368.

Markee, N. (2000). *Conversation Analysis*. Mahwah, N.J.: Lawrence Erlbaum.

Markee, N. (2008). Toward a learning behavior tracking methodology for CA-for-SLA. *Applied Linguistics*, 29(3):404–427.

Marques-Schäfer, G. (2013). *Deutsch lernen online. Eine Analyse interkultureller Aktionen im Chat*. Gunter Narr Verlag.

Martin, J. H. and Jurafsky, D. (2009). *Speech and language processing: an introduction to natural language processing, computational linguistics and speech resognition*. Pearson International Edition, second edition.

Martinez, M. (2013). Adapting for a personalized learning experience. In Huang, R., Kinshuk, and Spector, J., editors, *Reshaping Learning*, New Frontiers of Educational Research, pages 139–174. Springer Berlin Heidelberg.

Marton, Y. (2013). Distributional phrasal paraphrase generation for statistical machine translation. *ACM Transactions on Intelligent Systems and Technology (TIST)*, 4(3):39.

Matthews, C. (1993). Grammar frameworks in intelligent call. *CALICO Journal*, 11(1):5–27.

McGinn, J. J. and Kotamraju, N. (2008). Data-driven persona development. In *Proceedings of the SIGCHI Conference on Human Factors in Computing Systems*, pages 1521–1524. ACM.

Meena, R., Skantze, J. L. G., and Gustafson, J. (2015). Automatic detection of miscommunication in spoken dialogue systems. In *16th Annual Meeting of the Special Interest Group on Discourse and Dialogue*, pages 354 – 363.

Metzler, D., Hovy, E., and Zhang, C. (2011). An empirical evaluation of data-driven paraphrase generation techniques. In *Proceedings of the 49th Annual Meeting of the Association for Computational Linguistics: Human Language Technologies: short papers-Volume 2*, pages 546–551. Association for Computational Linguistics.

Meurers, D. (2009). On the automatic analysis of learner language: Introduction to the special issue. *CALICO Journal*, 26(3):469–473.

Meurers, D. (2012). Natural language processing and language learning. *The Encyclopedia of Applied Linguistics.*

Mintzberg, H. (1994). The fall and rise of strategic planning. *Harvard Business Review*, 72(1):107–114.

Mitchell, C. M., Boyer, K. E., and Lester, J. C. (2012). From strangers to partners: Examining convergence within a longitudinal study of task-oriented dialogue. In *Proceedings of SIGDIAL 2012 Conference*, pages 94–98. ACL.

Moller, S., Engelbrecht, K.-P., Kuhnel, C., Wechsung, I., and Weiss, B. (2009). A taxonomy of quality of service and quality of experience of multimodal human-machine interaction. In *Quality of Multimedia Experience, 2009. QoMEx 2009. International Workshop on*, pages 7–12. IEEE.

Morton, H., Davidson, N., and Jack, M. (2008). Evaluation of a speech interactive CALL system. In *Handbook of research on computer-enhanced language acquisition and learning*, page 13. IGI Global.

Mubin, O., Shahid, S., and Bartneck, C. (2013). Robot assisted language learning through games: A comparison of two case studies. *Australian Journal of Intelligent Information Processing Systems*, 13(3):9–14.

Nagata, N. (2009). Robo-sensei's NLP-based error detection and feedback generation. *CALICO*, 26(3):562–579.

Narciss, S. (2013). Designing and evaluating tutoring feedback strategies for digital learning. *Digital Education Review*, (23):7–26.

Oh, K.-J., Choi, H.-J., Gweon, G., Heo, J., and Ryu, P.-M. (2015). Paraphrase generation based on lexical knowledge and features for a natural language question answering system. In *Big Data and Smart Computing (BigComp), 2015 International Conference on*, pages 35–38. IEEE.

Orthmann, C. (2004). *Strukturen der Chat-Kommunikation: konversationsanalytische Untersuchung eines Kinder- und Jugendchats*. PhD thesis, Freie Universität Berlin.

Oxford, R. L. (1993). Intelligent computers for learning languages: The view for language acquisition and instructional methodology. *Computer Assisted Language Learning*, 6(2):173–188.

Panova, I. and Lyster, R. (2002). Patterns of corrective feedback and uptake in an adult ESL classroom. *TESOL Quarterly*, 36(4):573–595.

Pavel, M., Jimison, H. B., Korhonen, I., Gordon, C. M., and Saranummi, N. (2015). Behavioral informatics and computational modeling in support of proactive health management and care. *IEEE Trans. on Biomedical Engineering*, 62(12):2763–2775.

Peres, F. and Meira, L. (2003). Educational software evaluation centered on dialogue: Interface, collaboration and scientific concepts. In *Proceedings of the Latin American Conference on Human-computer Interaction*, CLIHC '03, pages 97–106, New York, NY, USA. ACM.

Perrin, L., Deshaies, D., and Paradis, C. (2003). Pragmatic functions of local diaphonic repetitions in conversation. *Journal of pragmatics*, 35(12):1843–1860.

Petersen, K. A. (2010). *Implicit Corrective Feedback in Computer-Guided Interaction: Does Mode Matter?* PhD thesis, Georgetown University.

Petrelli, D., De Angeli, A., and Convertino, G. (1999). A user-centered approach to user modeling. In *Proceedings of the 7th International Conference on User Modeling*, UM99, pages 255–264. Springer.

Pikkarainen, M. (2015). *Finnish and Russian as lingua francas. Joint activity in conversations*. PhD thesis, University of Helsinki, Faculty of Arts, Department of Modern Languages, Russian language and literature.

Pillet-Shore, D. (2012). Greeting: Displaying stance through prosodic recipient design. *Research on Language & Social Interaction*, 45(4):375–398.

Pitsch, K., Gehle, R., and Wrede, S. (2013a). Addressing multiple participants: A museum robot's gaze shapes visitor participation. In Hermann, G., editor, *Proceedings of ICSR*, volume 8239 of *LNAI*, pages 587–588.

Pitsch, K., Gehle, R., and Wrede, S. (2013b). A museum guide robot: Dealing with multiple participants in the real-world. In *Workshop "Robots in public spaces. Towards multi-party, short-term, dynamic human-robot interaction" at ICSR 2013*.

Pitsch, K., Kuzuoka, H., Suzuki, Y., Süssenbach, L., Luff, P., and Heath, C. (2009). 'The first five seconds': Contingent stepwise entry into an interaction as a means to secure sustained engagement in HRI. In *Robot and Human Interactive Communication, 2009. RO-MAN 2009. The 18th IEEE International Symposium on*, pages 985–991. IEEE.

Pitsch, K., Neumann, A., Schnier, C., and Hermann, T. (2013c). Augmented reality as a tool for linguistic research: Intercepting and manipulating multimodal interaction. In *Multimodal corpora: Beyond audio and video (IVA 2013 workshop)*.

Pitsch, K. and Wrede, S. (2014). When a robot orients visitors to an exhibit. Referential practices and interactional dynamics in real world HRI. In *The 23rd IEEE*

International Symposium on Robot and Human Interactive Communication, 2014 RO-MAN, pages 36–42.

Plurkowski, L., Chu, M., and Vinkhuyzen, E. (2011). The implications of interactional “repair" for human-robot interaction design. In *Web Intelligence and Intelligent Agent Technology (WI-IAT), 2011 IEEE/WIC/ACM International Conference on*, volume 3, pages 61–65. IEEE.

Postel, H. J. (1969). Die Kölner Phonetik–Ein Verfahren zur Identifizierung von Personennamen auf der Grundlage der Gestaltanalyse. *IBM-Nachrichten*, 19:925–931.

Pulman, S. G., Boye, J., Cavazza, M., Smith, C., and de la Cámara, R. S. (2010). “How was your day?”. In *Proc. of the 2010 Workshop on CDS*, pages 37–42. ACL.

Purver, M. (2004). *The theory and use of clarification requests in dialogue*. PhD thesis, King’s College, University of London.

Purver, M. (2006). CLARIE: Handling clarification requests in a dialogue system. *Research on Language and Computation*, 4(2-3):259–288.

Purver, M. and Hough, J. (2014). Strongly Incremental Repair Detection. In *Empirical Methods in Natural Language Processing (EMNLP)*, pages 78–89.

Quinlan, J. R. (2014). *C4. 5: programs for machine learning*. Elsevier.

Quintano, L. and Rodrigues, I. P. (2008). Question / Answering Clarification Dialogues. In *MICAI2008*, pages 155–164. Springer.

Ragheb, M. and Dickinson, M. (2013). Inter-annotator agreement for dependency annotation of learner language. *NAACL/HLT 2013*, page 169.

Raux, A. and Eskenazi, M. (2004a). Non-native users in the let’s go!! spoken dialogue system: Dealing with linguistic mismatch. In *HLT-NAACL*, pages 217–224. Citeseer.

Raux, A. and Eskenazi, M. (2004b). Using task-oriented spoken dialogue systems for language learning: potential, practical applications and challenges. In *In-STIL/ICALL Symposium 2004*.

Read, T. and Bárcena, E. (2014). Modelling user linguistic communicative competences for individual and collaborative learning. In *From Animals to Robots and Back: Reflections on Hard Problems in the Study of Cognition*, pages 205–218. Springer.

Regneri, M. and Wang, R. (2012). Using discourse information for paraphrase extraction. In *Proceedings of the 2012 Joint Conference on Empirical Methods in Natural Language Processing and Computational Natural Language Learning*, pages 916–927. Association for Computational Linguistics.

Rei, M., Felice, M., Yuan, Z., and Briscoe, T. (2017). Artificial error generation with machine translation and syntactic patterns. In *Proceedings of the 12th Workshop on Innovative Use of NLP for Building Educational Applications*, pages 287–292.

Ren, J., Schulman, D., Jack, B., and Bickmore, T. (2014). Supporting longitudinal change in many health behaviors. In *Proceedings of the ACM SIGCHI Conference on Human Factors in Computing Systems (CHI)*, pages 17:1–17:7. CHI.

Reznicek, M., Lüdeling, A., and Hirschmann, H. (2013). Competing target hypotheses in the Falko corpus: A flexible multi-layer corpus architecture. In Díaz-

Negrillo, Ana, N. B. and Thompson, P., editors, *Automatic Treatment and Analysis of Learner Corpus Data*, pages 101–123. Amsterdam: John Benjamins.

Reznicek, M., Lüdeling, A., Krummes, C., Schwantuschke, F., Walter, M., Schmidt, K., Hirschmann, H., and Andreas, T. (2012). *Das Falko-Handbuch. Korpusaufbau und Annotationen.* Humboldt Universität zu Berlin, 2.01 edition.

Rich, C., Ponsleur, B., Holroyd, A., and Sidner, C. L. (2010). Recognizing engagement in human-robot interaction. In *Proceedings of the 5th ACM/IEEE International Conference on Human-robot Interaction*, HRI '10, pages 375–382, Piscataway, NJ, USA. IEEE Press.

Rich, E. (1979). User modeling via stereotypes. *Cognitive science*, 3(4):329–354.

Rieger, C. L. (2003). Repetitions as self-repair strategies in English and German conversations. *Journal of Pragmatics*, 35(1):47–69.

Rintel, S. (2015). Omnirelevance in technologised interaction. In Fitzgerald, R. and Housley, W., editors, *Advances in Membership Categorisation Analysis*. SAGE.

Robins, B., Dickerson, P., Stribling, P., and Dautenhahn, K. (2004). Robot-mediated joint attention in children with autism: A case study in robot-human interaction. *Interaction studies*, 5(2):161–198.

Rodríguez, K. J. and Schlangen, D. (2004). Form, intonation and function of clarification requests in german task-oriented spoken dialogues. In *Proceedings of Catalog (the 8th workshop on the semantics and pragmatics of dialogue; SemDial04)*, pages 101–108.

Rubio, A. (2017). The new busuu bot for Microsoft Teams. https://tech.busuu.com/the-new-busuu-bot-for-microsoft-teams-597147d6c29a.

Russell, R. and Odell, M. (1918). Soundex. US Patent.

Sabelli, A. M., Kanda, T., and Hagita, N. (2011). A conversational robot in an elderly care center: an ethnographic study. In *Human-Robot Interaction (HRI), 2011 6th ACM/IEEE International Conference on*, pages 37–44. ACM.

Sacks, H. (1995). *Lectures on Conversation*, volume 1 and 2. Wiley Online Library.

Sacks, H., Schegloff, E. A., and Jefferson, G. (1974). A simplest systematics for the organization of turn-taking for conversation. *language*, pages 696–735.

Sagae, A., Johnson, W. L., and Valente, A. (2011). *Conversational Agents in Language and Culture Training*, pages 358–377. IGI Global.

Sauro, S. (2009). Computer-mediated corrective feedback and the development of L2 grammar. *Language Learning and Technology*, 13(1):96–120.

Savenkov, K. (2017). Intent detection benchmark. https://www.slideshare.net/KonstantinSavenkov/nlu-intent-detection-benchmark-by-intento-august-2017.

Sawchuk, P. H. (2003). Informal learning as a speech-exchange system: Implications for knowledge production, power and social transformation. *Discourse & Society*, 14(3):291–307.

Schäfer, U. (2008). Shallow, deep and hybrid processing with UIMA and Heart of Gold. In *Proc. of the LREC-2008 Workshop Towards Enhanced Interoperability for Large HLT Systems: UIMA for NLP, 6th Int. Conf. on Language Resources and Evaluation*, pages 43–50.

Schegloff, E. (1997). Practices and actions: Boundary cases of other-initiated repair. *Discourse Processes*, 23(3):499–545.

Schegloff, E. A. (1972). Notes on a conversational practice: Formulating place. *Studies in social interaction*, 75:75–119.

Schegloff, E. A. (1979). The relevance of repair to syntax-for-conversation in discourse and syntax. *Syntax and Semantics Ann Arbor, Mich.*, 12:261–286.

Schegloff, E. A. (1987a). Recycled turn beginnings: A precise repair mechanism in conversation's turn-taking organization. *Talk and social organization*, pages 70–85.

Schegloff, E. A. (1987b). Some sources of misunderstanding in talk-in-interaction. *Linguistics*, 25(1):201–218.

Schegloff, E. A. (1988). Presequences and indirection: Applying speech act theory to ordinary conversation. *Journal of Pragmatics*, 12(1):55–62.

Schegloff, E. A. (1990). On the organization of sequences as a source of "coherence" in talk in interaction. *Conversational Organisation and its Development*, 38:51–77.

Schegloff, E. A. (1992). Repair after next turn: The last structurally provided defense of intersubjectivity in conversation. *American Journal of Sociology*, 97(5):pp. 1295–1345.

Schegloff, E. A. (1993). Reflections on quantification in the study of conversaiton. *Research on Language and Social Interaciton*, 26(1):99–128.

Schegloff, E. A. (1996). Issues of relevance for discourse analysis: Contingency in action, interaction and co-participant context. In *Computational and conversational discourse: Burning Issues – An Interdisciplinary Account*, pages 3–35. Springer-Verlag Berlin Heidelberg.

Schegloff, E. A. (2000). When 'others' initiate repair. *Applied Linguistic*, 21(2):205–243.

Schegloff, E. A. (2007). *Sequence Organization in Interaction: Volume 1: A Primer in Conversation Analysis*. Cambridge University Press, 1 edition.

Schegloff, E. A., Jefferson, G., and Sacks, H. (1977). PreferenceSelfCorrectSm.pdf. *Language*, 53(2):361–382.

Schiffrin, A. (2005). *Modelling Speech Acts in Conversational Discourse*. PhD thesis, The University of Leeds.

Schlangen, D. (2004). Causes and Strategies for Requesting Clarification in Dialogue. In *5th Workshop of the ACL SIG on Discourse and Dialogue*.

Schlobinski, P. (1997). *Syntax des gesprochenen Deutsch*. Westdeutscher Verlag.

Schmidt, R. W. (1990). The role of consciousness in second language learning. *Applied linguistics*, 11(2):129–158.

Schnier, C., Pitsch, K., Dierker, A., and Hermann, T. (2011). Adaptability of communicative resources in AR-based cooperation. In *Proceedings of the 2nd Workshop on Gesture and Speech in Interaction (GESPIN 2011)*.

Schulze, M. (2008). AI in CALL–artificially inflated or almost imminent? *Calico Journal*, 25(3):510–527.

Searle, J. R. (1969a). Speech act theory. *Cambridge: Cambridge University Press*.

Searle, J. R. (1969b). *Speech acts: An essay in the philosophy of language*, volume 626. Cambridge University Press.

Serban, I. V., Sordoni, A., Bengio, Y., Courville, A. C., and Pineau, J. (2016). Building end-to-end dialogue systems using generative hierarchical neural network models. In *AAAI*, pages 3776–3784.

Shevat, A. (2017). *Designing Bots: Creating Conversational Experiences*. O'Reilly Media.

Shriberg, E. E. (1994). *Preliminaries to a Theory of Speech Disfluencies*. PhD thesis, University of California at Berkeley.

Shute, V. J. (2008). Focus on formative feedback. *Review of educational research*, 78(1):153–189.

Simmons-Mackie, N. and Damico, J. S. (2008). Exposed and embedded corrections in aphasia therapy: issues of voice and identity. *International Journal of Language & Communication Disorders*, 43(sup1):5–17.

Skantze, G. and Hjalmarsson, A. (2010). Towards Incremental Speech Generation in Dialogue Systems. In *SIGDIAL*, pages 1–8.

Small, S., Cottrell, G., and Tanenhaus, M. (1987). *Lexical ambiguity resolution*. Morgan Kaufmann Publishers, Inc., Los Altos, CA.

Smith, B. (2005). The relationship between negotiated interaction, learner uptake, and lexical acquisition in task-based computer-mediated communication. *Tesol Quarterly*, 39(1):33–58.

Smith, B. (2008). Methodological hurdles in capturing CMC data: The case of the missing self-repair. *Language Learning and Technology*, 12(1):85–103.

Spranz-Fogasy, T. (2002). *Interaktionsprofile: Die Herausbildung individueller Handlungstypik in Gesprächen*. Radolfzell: Verlag für Gesprächsforschung.

Ståhl, O., Gambäck, B., Turunen, M., and Hakulinen, J. (2009). A mobile health and fitness companion demonstrator. In *EACL '09*, pages 65–68.

Stewart, I. A. D. and File, P. (2007). Let's chat: A conversational dialogue system for second language practice. *Computer Assisted Language Learning*, 20(2):97–116.

Stivers, T. (2005). Modified repeats: One method for asserting primary rights from second position. *Research on Language and Social Interaction*, 38(2):131–158.

Stivers, T. and Enfield, N. J. (2010). A coding scheme for question–response sequences in conversation. *Journal of Pragmatics*, 42(10):2620–2626.

Stoyanchev, S., Liu, A., and Hirschberg, J. (2013). Modelling human clarification strategies. In *Procedings of the SIGDIAL 2013 Conference*, pages 137–141.

Suchman, L. A. (1985). *Plans and situated actions: the problem of human-machine communication*. XEROX.

Sussenbach, L., Riether, N., Schneider, S., Berger, I., Kummert, F., Lutkebohle, I., and Pitsch, K. (2014). A robot as fitness companion: towards an interactive action-based motivation model. In *Robot and Human Interactive Communication, 2014 RO-MAN: The 23rd IEEE International Symposium on*, pages 286–293. IEEE.

Tannen, D. (1987). Repetition in conversation: Toward a poetics of talk. *Language*, pages 574–605.

ten Have, P. (2007). *Doing Conversation Analysis*. SAGE Publications, 2 edition.

Tetreault, J. R. and Chodorow, M. (2008). Native judgments of non-native usage: Experiments in preposition error detection. In *Proceedings of the Workshop on Human Judgements in Computational Linguistics*, pages 24–32. Association for Computational Linguistics.

Thaler, V. (2007). Mündlichkeit, Schriftlichkeit, Synchronizität. Eine Analyse alter und neuer Konzepte zur Klassifizierung neuer Kommunikationsformen. *Zeitschrift für germanistische Linguistik*, 35(1-2):146–181.

Thelwall, M., Buckley, K., Paltoglou, G., Cai, D., and Kappas, A. (2010). Sentiment strength detection in short informal text. *Journal of the American Society for Information Science and Technology*, 61(12):2544–2558.

Thórisson, K. R. (2002). Natural turn-taking needs no manual: Computational theory and model, from perception to action. In *Multimodality in language and speech systems*, pages 173–207. Springer.

Timpe-Laughlin, V., Evanini, K., Green, A., Blood, I., Dombi, J., and Ramanaranayan, V. (2017). Designing interactive, automated dialogues for l2 pragmatics learning. In *Proceedings of SEMDIAL 2017*, page 143.

Tudini, V. (2003). Using native speakers in chat. *Language Learning and Technology*, 7(3):141–159.

Tudini, V. (2007). Negotiation and intercultural learning in Italian native speaker chat rooms. *The Modern Language Journal*, 91(4):577–601.

Tudini, V. (2010). *Online Second Language Acquisition: Conversation Analysis of Online Chat*. Continuum.

Vandergriff, I. (2013). "My major is English, belive it or not:)"-Participant orientations in nonnative/native text chat. *CALICO Journal*, 30(3):393.

Vandergriff, I. (2014). A pragmatic investigation of emoticon use in nonnative/native speaker text chat. *Language@Internet*, 11(4).

Vandewaetere, M. and Clarebout, G. (2014). Advanced technologies for personalized learning, instruction, and performance. In *Handbook of Research on Educational Communications and Technology*, pages 425–437. Springer.

Varela, M., Skorin-Kapov, L., and Ebrahimi, T. (2014). Quality of service versus quality of experience. In *Quality of experience*, pages 85–96. Springer.

Varonis, E. M. and Gass, S. (1985). Non-native/non-native conversations: A model for negotiation of meaning. *Applied Linguistics*, 6(1):71–90.

Vicente-Rasoamalala, L. (2009). *Teachers' reactions to foreign language learner output*. PhD thesis, Universitat de Barcelona.

Vickers, C. H. (2010). Language competence and the construction of expert–novice in NS–NNS interaction. *Journal of Pragmatics*, 42(1):116 – 138.

Vöge, M. (2008). *All You Need is Laugh*. PhD thesis, Syddansk Universitet.

Voida, A., Mynatt, E. D., Erickson, T., and Kellogg, W. A. (2004). Interviewing over instant messaging. In *CHI'04 extended abstracts on Human factors in computing systems*, pages 1344–1347.

von Ahn, L. and Hacker, S. (2012). Duolingo. https://de.duolingo.com/.

von Reth, H. and Schek, H. (1977). *Eine Zugriffsmethode für die phonetische Ähnlichkeitssuche*. Heidelberg Scientific Center Technical reports. Wiss. Zentrum.

Wagner, J. and Gardner, R. (2004). Introduction. In Gardner, R. and Wagner, J., editors, *Second Language Conversations*, pages 1–17. Continuum, New York.

Wahlster, W. and Kobsa, A. (1986). Dialogue-based user models. *Proceedings of the IEEE*, 74(7):948–960.

Walker, M. A., Litman, D. J., Kamm, C. A., and Abella, A. (1997). Paradise: A framework for evaluating spoken dialogue agents. In *Proceedings of the eighth conference on European chapter of the Association for Computational Linguistics*, pages 271–280. Association for Computational Linguistics.

Wallace, R. S. (2003). *The Elements of AIML Style*. Alice A.I. Foundation, Inc.

Waterworth, J. (1986). Conversational analysis and human-computer dialog design. *ACM SIGCHI Bulletin*, 18(2):54–55.

Weizenbaum, J. (1966). ELIZA - a computer program for the study of natural language communication between man and machine. *Commun. ACM*, 9:36 – 45.

Wen, Z. E. and Mota, M. B. (2015). *Working Memory in Second Language Acquisition and Processing*, volume 87. Multilingual Matters.

Wendemuth, A. and Biundo, S. (2012). A companion technology for cognitive technical systems. In *Cognitive Behavioural Systems*, pages 89–103. Springer.

Wickham, M. and Woods, M. (2005). Reflecting on the strategic use of CAQDAS to manage and report on the qualitative research process. *The qualitative report*, 10(4):687–702.

Wik, P. and Hjalmarsson, A. (2009). Embodied conversational agents in computer assisted language learning. *Speech communication*, 51(10):1024–1037.

Wik, P., Hjalmarsson, A., and Brusk, J. (2007). Computer assisted conversation training for second language learners. In *Fonetik 2007, 30 maj-1 juni 2007, Stockholm*, volume 50, pages 57–60.

Wilkinson, S. and Kitzinger, C. (2006). Surprise as an interactional achievement: Reaction tokens in conversation. *Social psychology quarterly*, 69(2):150–182.

Wilks, Y. (2005). Artificial Companions. *Interdisc. Science Rev.*, 30(2):145–152.

Wilks, Y., Jasiewicz, J., Catizone, R., Galescu, L., Martinez, K., and Rugs, D. (2015). CALONIS: An artificial companion within a smart home for the care of cognitively impaired patients. In Bodine, C., Helal, S., Gu, T., and Mokhtari, M., editors, *Smart Homes and Health Telematics*, volume 8456 of *Lecture Notes in Computer Science*, pages 255–260. Springer International Publishing.

Wilske, S. (2014). *Form and Meaning in Dialog-Based Computer-Assisted Language Learning*. PhD thesis, University of Saarland.

Wubben, S., van den Bosch, A., and Krahmer, E. (2014). Creating and using large monolingual parallel corpora for sentential paraphrase generation. In *Proceedings of LREC2014*. European Language Resources Association (ELRA).

Yaghoubzadeh, R., Kramer, M., Pitsch, K., and Kopp, S. (2013). Virtual agents as daily assistants for elderly or cognitively impaired people. In *Intelligent Virtual Agents*, pages 79–91. Springer.

Yamazaki, A., Yamazaki, K., Kuno, Y., Burdelski, M., Kawashima, M., and Kuzuoka, H. (2008). Precision timing in human-robot interaction: Coordination of head movement and utterance. In *Proceedings of the SIGCHI Conference on*

Human Factors in Computing Systems, CHI '08, pages 131–140, New York, NY, USA. ACM.

Yang, H.-C. and Zapata-Rivera, D. (2010). Interlanguage pragmatics with a pedagogical agent: the request game. *Computer Assisted Language Learning*, 23(5):395–412.

Yasavur, U., Lisetti, C., and Rishe, N. (2014). Let's talk! speaking virtual counselor offers you a brief intervention. *Journal on Multimodal User Interfaces*, 8(4):381–398.

Yin, Z., Chang, K.-H., and Zhang, R. (2017). Deepprobe: Information directed sequence understanding and chatbot design via recurrent neural networks. In *Proceedings of KDD'17*, pages 1–9. ACM.

Zadeh, L. A. (1983). A computational approach to fuzzy quantifiers in natural languages. *Computers & Mathematics with applications*, 9(1):149–184.

Zakos, J. and Capper, L. (2008). CLIVE - an artificially intelligent chat robot for conversational language practice. In *Proceedings of the 5th Hellenic conference on Artificial Intelligence: Theories, Models and Applications*, pages 437 – 442. Springer-Verlag.

Zhou, Y., Porwal, U., and Konow, R. (2017). Spelling correction as a foreign language. *arXiv preprint arXiv:1705.07371*.

Zhu, W., Chowanda, A., and Valstar, M. (2016). Topic switch models for dialogue management in virtual humans. In *International Conference on Intelligent Virtual Agents*, pages 407–411. Springer.

Zinsmeister, H. and Breckle, M. (2012). The ALeSKo learner corpus: design–annotation–quantitative analyses. *Multilingual Corpora and Multilingual Corpus Analysis. Amsterdam: John Benjamins*, pages 71–96.

Zock, M. (1996). Computational linguistics and its use in real world: the case of computer assisted-language learning. In *Proceedings of the 16th conference on Computational linguistics-Volume 2*, pages 1002–1004. Association for Computational Linguistics.

Zourou, K. (2011). Towards a typology of corrective feedback moves in an asynchronous distance language learning environment. In *Media in Foreign Language Teaching and Learning*, chapter 10, pages 217–242. Walter de Gruyter.

Zwarts, S., Johnson, M., and Dale, R. (2010). Detecting Speech Repairs Incrementally Using a Noisy Channel Approach. In *Proceedings of the 23rd International Conference on Computational Linguistics (Coling 2010)*, number August, pages 1371–1378.

Printed in the United States
By Bookmasters